Colombia's Nar
Nightmare

Colombia (Santino Ambrogio/Thinkstock)

Colombia's Narcotics Nightmare

How the Drug Trade Destroyed Peace

James D. Henderson

McFarland & Company, Inc., Publishers
Jefferson, North Carolina

Originally published in Spanish as *Víctima de la Globalización: La historia de cómo el narcotráfico destruyó la paz en Colombia.* Bogotá: Siglo del Hombre Editores, 2012.

LIBRARY OF CONGRESS CATALOGUING-IN-PUBLICATION DATA

Henderson, James D., 1942–
Colombia's narcotics nightmare : how the drug trade destroyed peace / James D. Henderson.
p.   cm.
Includes bibliographical references and index.

ISBN 978-0-7864-7917-7 (softcover : acid free paper) ∞
ISBN 978-1-4766-1884-5 (ebook)

1. Drug traffic—Colombia—History.   2. Drug control—Colombia—History.
3. Narco-terrorism—Colombia—History.   4. Insurgency—Colombia—History.
5. Colombia—History—1974–   6. Colombia—Politics and government—1974–   I. Title.

HV5840.C7H46 2015   364.1'336509861—dc23   2014047494

BRITISH LIBRARY CATALOGUING DATA ARE AVAILABLE

Cover image: *Soldier Rodríguez and Yellow Butterflies* (on the banks of the Caguán River, Caquetá department, southeastern Colombia, during the Colombian military's year of the offensive against the FARC) © 2004 León Darío Peláez / *Revista Semana*

Printed in the United States of America

McFarland & Company, Inc., Publishers
Box 611, Jefferson, North Carolina 28640
www.mcfarlandpub.com

To Linda—and to Tom

Acknowledgments

The person who has helped me most with this book is my wife Linda Roddy Henderson, whose counsel and proofreading of the manuscript were of great value. I thank Bonnie Senser, Administrative Specialist of the Department of Politics and Geography of Coastal Carolina University, for her patient and ever cheerful help in the multiple tasks of manuscript preparation. I thank too my colleagues in the department of Politics and Geography, Ken Rogers, Richard Collin, and Pam Martin, for their support and encouragement over my six years' work on this book. Thanks too are owed Coastal Carolina University which awarded me sabbatical leave, an additional semester of leave from duties, and additional financial support to complete this study. Stu Lippe, Senior Advisor, Western Hemisphere Affairs/Office of Andean Affairs, U.S. Department of State, was generous with his help and advice, especially that concerning Plan Colombia. I thank many friends and colleagues in Colombia, especially Gustavo Duncan for his critical reading of the manuscript. I also thank Alfredo Rangel, Diana Patricia Restrepo, Father Antonio José Sarmiento, Carlos Muñoz, and Eduardo Rueda. Special recognition is owed Jorge A. Restrepo, Director of the Conflict Analysis Research Center, CERAC (*Centro de Recursos para el Análisis de Conflicto*), and Andres Corredor of CERAC. To all of you, and to many other colleagues in the United States and Colombia, I offer my sincere thanks for your help and advice over the past six years.

Table of Contents

Acknowledgments   vi

Introduction: The Left and Right of Violence and Illegal Drugs in Colombia   1

Song of Love (Between My Country and Me) by Luz Marina Posada   10

1. Colombia's Decade of Peace, 1965–1975
   Dynamism of the 1965–1975 Period   11
   Colombia's Iron Triangle of Violence   16
   Rise of the Drug Culture in the United States   18
   Initial U.S. and Colombian Responses to Illegal Drugs, 1965–1975   23

2. The Illegal Drug Hydra, 1970–1983
   Colombia Gold   26
   Cocaine Comes to Colombia   33
   Drugs, Violence, Impunity   41
   The Cartels' Golden Moment, 1978–1983   47

3. The Cartels' War Against the State, 1984–1994
   The Extraditables   53
   The New Violence   65
   Democratic Responses to the Violence   75
   Moment of Hope   81

4. The Guerrillas' War Against the State
   Introduction: Guerrillas and Drugs   89
   The Guerrillas During Colombia's Decade of Peace, 1965–1975   92
   Guerrilla Advance During the Illegal Drug Boom, 1975–1993   97
   The Guerrilla Offensive of 1994–2002   112

5. The Paramilitary Offensive
   Introduction: Civil Defense and Impunity   121
   Paramilitary Growth During the 1970s and 1980s   124

the 1980's cocaine boom → msol'dito ns Central American whmof oppression/ political violence

The Narco-Paramilitary 134
The Paramilitary Offensive of 1994–2002 139

6. Colombia Gets Tough, 2002–2013
The Uribe Phenomenon 154
Plan Colombia 165
Slogging Toward Peace 173

Conclusion
Victim of Globalization 185
Illegal Drugs and Colombia's New Violence 186
Post-Conflict Colombia 187

Glossary 193
Chapter Notes 197
Bibliography 216
Index 223

Introduction:
The Left and Right of Violence
and Illegal Drugs in Colombia

The Good Colombia

"It is a country of many qualities."
—*The Economist*, April 21, 2001

This book is a history of Colombia's illegal drug industry, and its focus is the impact of the international drug trade on the country and its people. Colombia is portrayed here as a victim of the global trade in illegal drugs. Prior to the 1960s the country had no history of large-scale drug export, becoming a major player in the trade only when smugglers from the United States arrived there during the decade paying top dollar for Colombian-produced marijuana. Marijuana, and then cocaine, brought the country a tsunami of illegal dollars that fed every variety of crime. Levels of crime and violence rose steadily and by the end of the twentieth century Colombians wondered whether national institutions could withstand the multi-faceted disorder financed by massive and seemingly endless flows of illegal drug money. By the time Colombians at last began effectively addressing the crisis in 2002, more than 300,000 lay dead. They were victims of violence finding its source in the Pandora's box of evils that drug money unleashed.[1]

Colombia's rise as supplier of cocaine to the United States and the wider world was in keeping with the historic commercial role prescribed for it under international capitalist theory. For half a millennium, through its long colonial period and later as an independent republic, the Andean country had obligingly supplied minerals, medicines, and foodstuffs desired by the rich and powerful nations of the world. In earliest times it was gold, emeralds, and quinine. Later it was coffee. Most recently it has been recreational drugs and cut flowers, coal, nickel, and petroleum. Seen from this perspective Colombia has ever been a good and compliant member of the international trading system. Only in the case of illegal drugs did the business acumen of Colombians lead them astray.

Present-day Colombia's bad reputation is a far cry from that of earlier times. At the end of World War II its people were known throughout Latin America for their sobriety and industry, their staunch Roman Catholicism and their Spanish, bell-like in clarity and said to be the

1

best in the world. They had played a significant role in the recent war, helping guard approaches to the Panama Canal and supplying strategic raw materials and manufactured goods to the Allied powers. And in a region known for military coups and a proclivity for strongman rule, Colombia's democratic tradition shone as a splendid anomaly. An exceedingly beautiful country crowded with verdant mountains and abundant tropical flora and fauna, it had long since gained fame for the excellence of its mild, shade-grown coffee. As the halfway-point of the mid–twentieth century approached Colombia was developing significant industrialization in and around its principal cities, especially its second largest city, Medellín, thanks to its booming textile-manufacturing sector. At that moment Colombia was continuing its pell-mell rush into modernization. Already a nation of cities, it would become more urban than rural by the 1960s.

Nor was there anything in Colombia's earlier history that marked it as a place destined to become the Western World's illegal drug emporium. Its historical process had been much like that of the rest of Spanish America. For three hundred years its people were loyal subjects of the Spanish crown. Throwing off Spanish rule early in the 1800s, they proclaimed themselves an independent republic in 1819. Turbulent decades followed during which details of national life were worked out, frequently through brief civil wars centering largely if not exclusively on determining the Church's place in politics and society. By the twentieth century that process was largely complete. Colombians were generally in agreement that their nation was a constitutional liberal democracy where church and state were separate. Its political system was a presidential one whose chief executive was elected at four-year intervals with no right of immediate re-election. It possessed a two-house popularly elected congress, and a Supreme Court charged with interpreting the constitution and seeing that it was upheld.

Colombia's relationship with the United States was harmonious. Save for early twentieth-century anger over U.S. connivance in the separation of Panama, Colombians were well-disposed toward the North American power. The countries' close economic link was confirmed when, following World War I, the U.S. supplanted Europe as chief purchaser of Colombian coffee and as its principal supplier of manufactured goods. During the 1920s the U.S. paid Colombia a large and sorely needed cash indemnity for its involvement in the Panamanian secession. When World War II broke out Colombia was a strong supporter of both the United States and the Allied Powers, hence assuring its place as a member in good standing of the inter–American system. It went on to become a signatory of the Bretton Woods accord of 1944, and a charter member of the United Nations one year later. One of its former national presidents served as the first Secretary General of the Organization of American States in 1948. Suffice it to say that when Alberto Lleras Camargo was named chief presiding officer of the newly created inter–American body, Colombia's prestige was unrivalled in the hemisphere.

From Paragon to Pariah

"Colombians are the most sophisticated criminals in the world."
—Journalist Robert Sabbag, *Loaded,* 2002[2]

The besmirching of Colombia's national reputation began with a self-inflicted wound known as the *Violencia,* a prolonged low-level civil war claiming nearly 200,000 lives over eighteen years' time, 1947 to 1965. Rooted in Liberal-Conservative partisanship reaching back a hundred years, and nourished by the irresponsible leadership of party elites, the *Violencia* brought a spell of authoritarian rule during the 1950s.[3]

Chastened by their failings, Liberal and Conservative party leaders returned the country to democratic rule in 1958. They did so by implementing a sixteen-year power-sharing pact called the National Front. Political passions cooled and the *Violencia* ended by 1965. Levels of violence fell, reaching the average of Latin America as a whole over the ten years that followed. Modernization continued at a rapid pace and economic growth was, as ever, continuous.

When Fidel Castro's success in Cuba stirred fears of communist revolution in Latin America, the United States launched a much-heralded aid program known as the Alliance for Progress. Friend and ally Colombia became the showcase for Alliance programs, a fact underlined by the 1961 state visit of U.S. president John F. Kennedy and his wife. By the mid–1960s Colombia stood as the world's second-most-popular destination for idealistic young Americans enlisted as volunteers in Kennedy's Peace Corps.

But early in the 1970s the benign image of post–*Violencia* Colombia quickly disappeared and was replaced by an entirely negative one. Early in the decade U.S. drug smugglers discovered the country to be a seemingly inexhaustible source of high-quality marijuana. And by the early 1980s Colombia had become a prodigious supplier of vastly more profitable cocaine. Soon Colombians were being portrayed in U.S. film and television programs as the most cold-blooded and violent of all drug smugglers, killers who enjoyed using chain saws to execute those who crossed them.

Meanwhile, the trade in illegal drugs eroded and corrupted Colombia's national institutions, and financed every form of illegal activity. Cocaine production increased in step with the weakening of national institutions. By the mid–1990s it was apparent to all that illegal drug dollars were massively present in politics. Between 1994 and 1998 the United States punished Colombia for allowing drug money to corrupt its politicians, a policy that only strengthened criminal and anti–State actors. Violence levels surged. Colombia became infamous as both the world's most violent nation as the global leader in kidnappings. By 2000 the country's communist guerrillas were defeating units of the national army in the field and attacking towns on the outskirts of the national capital. At that time the guerrillas were major drug dealers in their own right, using their earnings to buy weaponry rivaling and surpassing that of the national army and police. In the countryside, citizens caught in the crossfire died in growing numbers. Human rights violations increased exponentially during the 1990s as paramilitary militias battled the guerrillas for preeminence in drug-producing regions. The world grew alarmed. Was Colombia becoming a failed state run by drug traffickers? Would it become a haven for terrorists and criminal elements? Would its lawlessness spread to neighboring Ecuador and Peru, and perhaps into Central America as well? The U.S. government warned its citizens not to visit the violent and dangerous nation.

Democratic Security

"For the first time in years Colombians can drive between most of the country's cities without risk of kidnapping or hold-up."
—*The Economist,* March 24, 2007

Colombians answered questions about their country's future in a prosaic way: through an election. In mid–2002 they installed a new president, Álvaro Uribe Vélez, who promised to make them safe again by vigorously attacking the forces of disorder. His task was made easier by outgoing president Andrés Pastrana, who had begun modernizing the armed forces and had invited the United States to join in a wide-ranging program aimed at combating the drug trade and strengthening national institutions, especially the military. Called Plan Colombia, it channeled $5.4 billion in aid to Colombia between 2001 and 2007, most of it paying for coca and opium poppy fumigation and for military training, equipment, and technology.

Álvaro Uribe took full advantage of Plan Colombia. Acting as commander-in-chief of the armed forces he pursued what he named his "Democratic Security" policy, the chief component of which was an offensive against the country's largest guerrilla group and destruction of the coca plantations and cocaine laboratories that were its principal source of revenue. Plan Colombia aid became fully available just as Alvaro Uribe entered office and he used it to good advantage. Thanks to his vigorous action against the guerrillas, the drug mafia, paramilitary forces, and common criminals, violence levels fell sharply throughout Uribe's first term in office. Grateful Colombians overwhelmingly elected him to a second term in 2006, having amended their national constitution to do so.

Human rights abuses also decreased significantly during Uribe's first term. This was owed to the fact that he and his government convinced some 30,000 paramilitary troops to demobilize and their leaders to submit to detention. Meanwhile massive extradition of drug traffickers to stand trial in the United States drove the illegal drug industry underground, thereby lessening its damage to society.

The Uribe presidency did not end Colombia's problems. But it did turn the tide against the country's violence and lawlessness. For the first time in thirty years Colombia and its people were not on the defensive before violent and criminal elements enjoying virtually unchecked use of illegal drug monies. Colombians could at last focus on the task of strengthening national institutions, rather than attempting to defend them. And they could do so with the satisfaction that they had done these things not only by their own volition but by democratic means.

States versus Markets

"Globalization is nothing more than the reemergence of markets that States temporarily suppressed in the aftermath of the Great Depression and World War II."
—Political economist Herman Schwartz[4]

This book is also about international relations, especially about binational relations between Colombia and the United States. As such it sends contradictory messages about the two countries' effort to stem the illegal drug trade. It finds the Colombo-U.S. anti-drug effort to have been successful in helping Colombia halt its spiral of drug-related violence. On the other it finds that the billions of dollars invested in the U.S. anti-drug campaign have failed to reduce either the quantity or quality of psychoactive drugs reaching U.S. consumers. Illegal drugs are presently cheaper, more readily available, and of greater purity in the United States today than at any other time in history.[5] Meanwhile intensified enforcement of U.S. drug laws merely serves to increase the competence of dealers in illegal drugs and to drive less efficient merchandisers from the field.[6] The only meaningful domestic result of U.S. anti-drug efforts has been to bring unpopular ethnic minorities—particularly young men of color—to heel through their massive incarceration on drug-related charges, while enhancing the political careers of anti-drug crusaders and making incarceration a new and non-exportable national industry.

So the recent history of the War on Drugs is an ambiguous one. In an era of global market integration U.S. attempts to harshly proscribe a popular albeit illegal consumer good have been largely self-defeating. The prohibition of a range of popular psychoactive consumer goods has placed the United States in an unwinnable war against market forces. At the same time the Colombian case shows that the illegal drug trade cannot be allowed to run unchecked, precisely because it is a business in the hands of criminals.

Another persistent theme in this volume is that of state-strengthening, and the role foreign aid can play in the process. Below it is shown both that Colombia's painful experience with illegal drugs eventually led to the strengthening of national institutions, and that U.S. foreign aid provided through Plan Colombia has played a meaningful role in the process. It also makes clear that when there is poor understanding of one country by another, as in the case of the United States and Colombia over most of the period analyzed here, the weaker of the two will suffer. Until the formulation of Plan Colombia in the late 1990s, U.S. policy makers had a poor understanding of the harm that drug-related violence and criminality had done to its Andean ally. Nor did they acknowledge the extent that their own failure to control illegal drug consumption at home contributed to Colombia's problems. Hence officials in the United States made demands of Colombia that the country could not satisfy and that in fact hastened the country's descent into violence.

The history told in the pages below is not bereft of positive elements. Slowly over twenty-five arduous years the United States came to perceive the baleful effect of the illegal drug trade on Colombia, and both countries came to understand that they must act jointly and vigorously to attack the socially destructive commerce. In the process Colombia and its people came to look at themselves more analytically than before, going on to undertake long-needed structural reforms. And U.S. policy makers recognized that their country had a moral obligation to help resolve the ghastly constellation of Colombian problems that were in large part made in the U.S.A.

* * *

This study of Colombia's rise as an illegal drug exporter begins with consideration of the decade of relative peace that the country enjoyed following the end of the *Violencia* in 1965. Figuring prominently in its first chapter is a discussion of the country's "iron triangle of violence," a term employed here to explain the set of conditions making Colombia especially susceptible to law-breaking and violence. Chapter 1 ends by describing the rise of the "drug culture" in the United States during the 1960s and early 1970s, and initial U.S. and Colombian responses to illegal drug consumption and production.

Chapter 2 describes how Colombia became the chief supplier of illegal drugs to the United States during the 1970s and early 1980s. It goes on to describe the shocking violence attending the drug trade both in Colombia and the U.S., and how that infant industry stimulated every sort of criminality and anti–State activity.

The book's third chapter recounts the bloody decade-long attempt of Colombia's Medellín and Cali cartels to bend the State to their will. The battle was joined in the mid–1980s, continued through the early 1990s, and was attended by appalling violence, and injury to national institutions. Yet through it all Colombians made strides in political reform, a long-standing demand of many citizens. The chapter ends at the moment of optimism attending the rewriting of the national constitution, the demobilization of several guerrilla groups, and the destruction of the Medellín and Cali cartels.

Chapter 4 traces the expansion of Colombia's communist FARC and ELN guerrillas, a process aided and accelerated by the national government's preoccupation with defeating the drug cartels. It describes the guerrilla's growing involvement with illegal drugs and details their complex interaction with the drug traffickers themselves. The chapter ends by telling the history of the guerrilla offensive against the Colombian state that began in 1994 and ended in 2002.

The fifth chapter treats the origin and rise of Colombia's paramilitary groups. Attention is paid to their relationship with the illegal drug mafia and to the way guerrilla expansion during the 1980s and '90s hastened their growth. It examines the paramilitary antiguerrilla offensive begun in 1994, which reached its most intense phase during the first two years of the twenty-first century. The chapter ends by recounting of the paramilitary demobilization begun during 2003–4.

Chapter 6 details Álvaro Uribe's Democratic Security initiative through which the Colombian State struck effectively against the FARC and ELN guerrillas, and against those connected with the illegal drug industry. Important to that discussion is assessment of the role of U.S. aid administered through Plan Colombia. The chapter ends with discussion of the anti-violence and anti-illegal drug measures taken during by Alvaro Uribe during his second term (2006–2010). It also contains a brief conclusion.

The Left and the Right of Violence Scholarship in Colombia

> "Colombia is today the least studied of the major Latin American countries, and probably the least understood."
> —Historian David Bushnell, *The Making of Modern Colombia*, 1993[7]

Modern historical writing was born in Colombia during the 1950s and 1960s, when the first of the country's brightest scholars began returning from European and North American universities, advanced academic degrees in hand. Many of them were of middle-class origin and represented the first graduates of the country's rapidly-expanding system of public universities. They brought contemporary and cutting-edge theory to the craft of historical and social science writing, driving the non-professionally-trained from the field, sometimes with considerable brutality.[8] Up to that time historical writing had been the purview of lawyers, retired politicians, journalists, and other non-academically-trained scholars.

By the 1970s and 1980s a substantial and highly influential body of work had emerged from this impressive new scholarly writing that would orient the thinking of Colombians well into the twenty-first century. While drawing on all social science disciplines the new scholarship came to be known collectively as the New History of Colombia.[9] It is important to touch on the New History because of the way it has presented Colombia's recent past, and especially the country's violence, to the country and the world.

The New History was born at a time of turmoil in Colombia. The *Violencia* was ending and the same Liberal and Conservative party leaders in power when it started had re-assumed national leadership under the sixteen-year power-sharing National Front agreement. It was an arrangement in effect freezing Colombia's outmoded political system in place at a moment when the country desperately needed a more open and representative democratic structure. Defects of the National Front became all the more apparent within months of its inception in August 1958, just months before Fidel Castro's seizure of power in Cuba. Castro moved quickly to implement wide-ranging programs highlighted by land reform and moves to restrict foreign, particularly U.S., economic interests. The Cuban Revolution and its attending reforms were alluring to many young Colombians, including most members of the new generation of academically trained scholars. Not all writers of the New History were Marxists, but a significant number of them were. And virtually all of them shared Castro's nationalism and anti-imperialism. They were especially critical of the United States, a country they saw as in league with Colombia's ruling class. Both were perceived as bent on exploiting Colombia and its people for their own narrow economic interests.

Generational conflict further intensified the critique of those standing at the center of the country's new scholarly discourse. Colombia was a place where change came at a snail's pace and where the older generation yielded power to the younger with excruciating slowness. The National Front power-sharing regime was a perfect target of the left-leaning scholars of the New History. They portrayed it as a metaphor of their country's political backwardness and its domination by corrupt elites who blocked progress at home in order to promote their own interests and those of the imperialist masters they served. It's no wonder that the vision of Colombia emerging from their scholarship was an exceptionally critical one. The country depicted in much early New History scholarship was a place shot through with inequality and where an oppressed proletariat stood poised to take power, violently if necessary.

When Colombia entered its new time of violence in the 1970s most members of the scholarly community viewed the upset as flowing from internal, rather than from external causes. For many of them that violence was seen as representing the first stages of a long-anticipated proletariat revolution. As the violence intensified during the 1980s, a group of academics emerged who were dedicated to its analysis. Known as the "violentologists" (*violentólogos*), they counted the brightest lights of New History scholars among their number. When in 1987 they were asked by the government to analyze the country's worsening violence they found it rooted in Colombia's notorious social inequality. Make the country a more just and democratic place, they concluded, and violence will lose its motive force. The illegal drug trade and its attending violence received only passing reference in their report.[10]

A positive consequence of the violentologists' critique of national institutions was that it kept the idea of political reform constantly in the minds of the Colombian public and the nation's leaders. The reform movement gained momentum after 1974 when the National Front officially ended, and culminated in 1991 with the rewriting of the national constitution. Yet there were negative consequences of the New History's unremitting critique of national flaws. As violence intensified during the 1980s and '90s some writers began asserting that the bloodshed was rooted in flaws in the national character and in the nature of Colombian society itself. On one hand this led to ambivalence regarding the flourishing communist guerrilla. If Colombia was irredeemably corrupt and unjust, then the guerrilla presence was justified and their depredations a necessary price paid to achieving a positive revolutionary end. Hence the guerrillas would logically and necessarily remain in the field until their egalitarian vision was realized. Essayists also mused that Colombian society was so flawed as to have damaged the character of Colombians themselves. Their self-deprecating arguments gained momentum as levels of violence and disorder rose throughout the 1990s. Such assessments became the norm in the public expressions of national opinion-makers. By the twenty-first century harsh self-criticism dominated the op-ed sections of national newspapers and the pages of journals of political opinion. Such pieces had the quality of anti-chauvinistic mantras describing their fellow citizens and their national institutions in the worst possible light.[11]

It's no wonder that foreigners, from those only casually interested in Colombia to those specialized in Latin American studies, have found the country difficult to understand. How, they wonder, can a country shown as manifestly defective in the analysis of its own scholarly community have many good qualities apparent through even the most passing association with the country and its people? The answer is found at least in part in the gloomy image of the nation found in New History scholarship. It represents an intellectual movement so dominant in Colombia over so long a time, and having long since driven competing visions of the country from the field, as to stand unchallenged as the gold standard for understanding the nation and its people. Founded in splendid scholarship produced by the country's best historians and social scientists, its class-analysis paradigm necessarily focused on national flaws—on the bad Colombia. But in misreading the country's new violence, by attributing it to internal rather than external causes, it fundamentally misinformed Colombians. It failed to properly link the country's ongoing crime and violence to the international trade in illegal drugs, whose negative effects started becoming apparent during the 1970s.

Violence scholarship in Colombia at last began to change during the late 1990s, when studies appeared showing close correspondence between the growth of crime and violence from the mid–1970s, and Colombia's entrance into the international trade in illegal drugs. Those responsible for this new interpretation were mostly scholars from the fields of economics and criminology, the latter a relatively new academic discipline in Colombia. Their statistical analyses revealed no link between economic deprivation and violence, and a powerful connection between rates of crime and violence and the advance of the illegal drug industry.[12]

Colombians have welcomed this fresh analysis of their nation's troubles. It not only dispels the notion that they are violent and corrupt by nature, but holds out the promise of peace in the near term. If the country's past thirty years of crime and violence are principally a function of the illegal drug trade, then an effective attack on that industry will severely weaken support for most illegal and anti–State activity. Immediate relief can be had through enhanced law enforcement and improved legal institutions. Contemporary events in Colombia prove this to be the case.

Thinking about Colombia is far from static today. A new critical spirit is at large in the country and it promises to revise the class-based analysis informing the New History. Recent revisionist scholarship on Colombia by Colombians is rooted in an older tradition emphasizing positive features of the national experience, such as the country's republican tradition and its people's shared sense of nationality.[13] It's the stuff of the old civics courses that were banished from public school curricula during the left political offensive of the 1960s and 1970s. As had been the case with the New History, the recent search for positive and unifying features of national life is the product of events unfolding over the past few years. If the New History was informed by the ghastly *Violencia,* the oligarchic National Front, and the heady vision of reform through revolution, the recent search for positive values of nationhood springs in part from the new understanding that Colombia's recent crime and violence spring from an identifiable cause and not from ingrained defects of national character and society. Implicit in that new spirit is the understanding that when the country returns to peace it will be able to address its real and pressing social problems more or less as other countries do. That is, deliberately and within a climate of personal security.

The present writer is convinced that Colombia will again be a country at peace. Having first lived there in 1966, he remembers the relief and optimism of a people who had recently put the *Violencia* behind them. Something of that same spirit is present in Colombia today, at the end of three decades and more of struggle to combat the effects of the country's illegal drug industry. At last the magnitude of the problem is fully understood both within Colombia and abroad. So too is the means of addressing it. Colombia may well never end its illegal drug industry, certainly not as long as users in foreign countries are willing to pay handsomely for Colombian-produced cocaine. But by mounting an effective assault on the bloody trade and attending evils Colombians have paved the way for dealing with social problems that have gone unattended from the time that foreign drug users started putting limitless wealth into the wrong hands.

Canción de amor (entre mi patria y yo)
LUZ MARINA POSADA

Es mi suelo y mi sol, heredad y promisión
Y en su fértil verdor se empecina la vida
Yo conozco su olor, su lamento, su canción
No hay nada que ocultar entre mi patria y yo

La podría abrazar desde la selva hasta el mar
Si con mi abrazo se sanaran sus heridas
Y a pesar del dolor sigue partiendo color,
Prodiga sus dulzuras, alienta mi voz

Y es verdad cuando dicen que estos días
No han sido buenos días para mi patria y yo
Se nos anda escondiendo la alegría
Pero no es fácil acallar el ansia de una nueva luz
Que tenemos mi patria y yo...

Más no sé que ofrecer por no verla padecer
Aunque ella oculte su tristeza entre mil flores
Si con sólo cantar la pudiera confortar
Sin duda cantaría hasta perder la voz
Una canción de amor entre mi patria y yo

Song of Love (Between My Country and Me)
(translation James D. Henderson)

She's my soil and my sun, my inheritance and promise
In her fertile greenness life persists
I know her smell, her lament, her song
There's nothing to hide between my country and me

I could embrace her from the jungle to the sea
If my embrace would heal her wounds
Despite the pain she offers color,
Lavish sweetness lifts my voice

They truly say that these days
Have not been good days for my country and me
Happiness goes fleeing
Yet it's hard to still our longing for a new day
For my country and me

I don't know what more to offer, to see her not suffer so
Though she hides her sadness in a thousand flowers
If I could comfort her with my song
I would doubtless sing until my voice was stilled
A song of love between my country and me

CHAPTER 1

Colombia's Decade of Peace, 1965–1975

Dynamism of the 1965–1975 Period

"By 1965 it was hard to find 500 *violentos* in all of national territory."
—Historian Russell Ramsey[1]

Colombia was an exciting place in the decade following the *Violencia*'s end. It was a country at peace, if not exactly peaceful. Deaths from *Violencia*-related causes were fewer than a thousand, down from more than 50,000 in 1950, the worst year of the civil war. Meanwhile most of the infamous bandit chiefs had fallen in army and police operations. They were men with names like "Black Blood," "Revenge," and "Sparks," who had continued their depredations after the conflict was defused through the signing of the Liberal-Conservative power-sharing National Front pact. The last of them, a Conservative bandit named Efraín González, died in June of 1965. Cornered by an army detachment in a house in south Bogotá, he was killed only after a tank was brought in that reduced his hideout to rubble.

National modernization continued at breakneck speed during those ten years. Color television and computers made their appearance, the country's major cities Bogotá, Medellín, Cali, and Barranquilla all passed a million in population, while the flood of citizens abandoning the countryside in favor of urban areas continued to accelerate. Gabriel García Márquez published his blockbuster novel *One Hundred Years of Solitude* in 1967, helping consecrate the boom in Latin American literature and make Magical Realism common literary currency throughout the region and world.

It was a country of young, strident, and mostly youthful voices united in the cause of breaking cultural icons and waging war on bourgeois society. Colombia had its own counterculture, marijuana-smoking bohemians who called themselves *Nadaístas* (nothingists), and its hippies, who didn't write poetry but who did smoke marijuana and who engaged in a range of activities that scandalized society at large. The birth control pill contributed to sharply falling birth rates and to exponential increases in casual sex. Teenagers in towns and cities danced the nights away at clubs with evocative names like The Golden Pill. A great many high school and college students threw themselves into political activity. They demanded reform of an antiquated political system made even more immutable and unresponsive by the sixteen-year power-

11

sharing National Front accord. Not a few of them became outright revolutionaries, traveling to the mountains and joining guerrilla groups—and in many cases promptly getting themselves killed. All in all it was a heady and romantic time in the nation's history.

The country was in touch with the world as never before. Air travel had long since freed Colombians to soar above their mountains. But now air travel was helping the world discover the country and embrace it. Foreign direct investment poured in once democracy returned in 1958. Colombia became the World Bank's darling in Latin America, with the country rising to fourth place among all borrowers, receiving loans for the building of new highways, ports, dams, and a host of other infrastructure projects.

Colombia's links with the United States grew ever stronger. It was the height of the Cold War and the Americans were keenly interested in the country's several communist guerrilla groups. Colombian officers trained at the U.S. Army School of the Americas in Panama had put what they had learned to use in 1964 when they attacked communist settlements in several rural areas, driving inhabitants into inaccessible mountains and jungles in the far southeastern part of the country. Meanwhile thousands of young Americans arrived to serve two-year stints with the Peace Corps, returning home to tell family and friends about the country of orchids, emeralds, coffee, and friendly people. Many more foreigners came to do business. The return of political peace only enhanced Colombia's reputation as the Latin American nation famous for prudent macroeconomic management and solid economic growth that continued even through the *Violencia* years.[2]

Economic conditions improved steadily during Colombia's decade of peace. Coffee prices rose steadily, reaching bonanza proportions by the mid–1970s. Meanwhile national leaders began promoting export diversification and liberalized trade policies as import substitution reached its limit, with local manufactures supplying the country's relatively small market. Steps were taken to exploit the vast deposits of coal located near the country's northern Caribbean coast, and contracts were let for petroleum and natural gas exploration in the Eastern Llanos, a plains area several hundred kilometers south of Venezuela's Lake Maracaibo oil fields. Within a few years significant oil and gas deposits would be found there. Meanwhile the first greenhouses had started appearing on the highland savanna surrounding Bogotá. They served notice that a cut flower industry would soon spring up capable of supplying U.S. and European markets from the 1980s onward.

During the latter 1960s a new and controversial non-traditional export started making news. Around 1965 Colombians living in and around the Sierra Nevada de Santa Marta, a towering range of mountains along the northern Caribbean coast, learned there was demand for locally grown marijuana in the United States. People in the region had always helped supply that illegal drug to the small domestic market, but they had never grown cannabis for export, certainly not for large-scale export. Yet insistent young American smugglers bearing badly needed dollars started appearing on the Caribbean coast during the mid–'60s. Colombians were happy to collaborate with the gringos. Soon they were shipping the local product northward to Miami, New Orleans, and Houston, hidden in shipments of bananas departing the Gulf of Urabá on United Fruit Company ships. The new export was a godsend to the impoverished region, no stranger to the contraband trade. But never before had the people of northeastern Colombia smuggled so lucrative a commodity.

One area not doing well in Colombia during the latter 1960s and early 1970s was politics, specifically the government of the National Front, which grew more unpopular with each passing year. That had not been the case in 1958, when the pact was put into effect. At that moment Liberal-Conservative power-sharing was seen by nearly everyone in the country as the only route to peace. Faith in the agreement was not misplaced, for the National Front brilliantly achieved its objective of ending the *Violencia*. The civil conflict running from the mid 1940s to the mid 1960s was rooted in Liberal and Conservative party allegiances that had long divided and polarized Colombians of all social classes. For a hundred years much in life had depended on whether or not one's party was in control in Bogotá. Partisan affiliation determined whether Colombians could get a government job, what their children were taught in school, and even how they were treated in courts of law and by the police. A great deal rode on elections. Every time there was a shift in power at the national level it sent tremors throughout society. That was the case in 1946, when a divided Liberal party lost to the minority Conservatives. Irate Liberals refused to give up political posts in towns and cities across the country, and the Conservatives, who were now in control, responded vigorously. Blood began flowing and in 1947 nearly 14,000 Colombians lost their lives, most of them humble citizens living in rural areas. New president Mariano Ospina Pérez tried to quell the disorder but it was beyond his control.[3]

What eventually came to be known as the *Violencia* was rooted in self-interest, fueled by a century of animosity and given peculiar intensity by ideological differences founded in profound religious differences. Liberals believed in church-state separation and secularism, while Conservatives were fervent Roman Catholics who viewed liberalism as immoral. Political leaders whipped up enthusiasm among supporters by appealing to traditional party values consecrated by the blood of family members fallen in previous partisan contests.

The conflict was vastly accelerated in 1948 when Liberal party leader Jorge Eliécer Gaitán was assassinated in downtown Bogotá. In the riot that followed 2,000 people died in Bogotá alone, where the city's center was reduced to rubble. By year's end more than 43,000 Colombians had died, most of them ordinary people residing in rural areas.[4]

The *Violencia* reached its peak in 1950 when right-wing Conservative Laureano Gómez was elected president amidst Liberal party abstention. That year alone 50,253 died, driving the country's mortality rate to 446 per 100,000. And that figure did not include deaths from other than *Violencia*-related causes.

Nothing short of rigid Liberal-Conservative power-sharing was capable of halting the civil war, and that is what the National Front achieved. Only 2,370 Colombians died during the last year of its first presidential term, that of Liberal Alberto Lleras Camargo, 1958–1962. And at the agreement's halfway point, in 1966, the conflict was effectively over. In 1966, the year Conservative Guillermo León Valencia left office, only 496 Colombians died from *Violencia*-related causes.[5]

Colombians have the ability to put civil violence behind them quickly, and this is what they did with the *Violencia*. Each day that it faded from memory, deficiencies in the power-sharing agreement became more glaring. Colombia's political system suffered many defects, and the National Front only worsened them. Clientage that had traditionally fed on the country's iron-clad party identification only grew more intense. Candidacies and public jobs were doled out to family members, political retainers, and party hacks. That guaranteed inferior public administration and heightened the tendency to corruption and venality. These flaws were all the more critical because Colombia also suffered serious structural flaws, chief among them high rates of poverty and inequality, aggravated by the failure of government to extend basic services to Colombians living in rural areas. In these ways the National Front further weakened an already rachitic political system. Worse still, the country was required to endure the arrangement for sixteen years. During that seemingly interminable period Liberals and Conservatives divided all political posts equally between them, swapped the presidency at four-year intervals, and denied other political parties a place in politics.

Unhappiness with the National Front came to a head as the 1970 election approached. The last National Front president was to be a Conservative, and the man selected was Misael Pastrana, an unexciting technocrat. Pastrana was not only uninspiring, but his party represented less than one-third of the electorate. Pastrana's candidacy was all the more galling because it was being forced on Colombians through a political deal originally crafted by the man most of them blamed for the *Violencia,* the fire-breathing right-winger Laureano Gómez. Thus in 1970 the Colombian electorate was in a surly mood and the atmosphere politically charged.

It was the unenviable task of the third National Front president, Carlos Lleras Restrepo, to preside over the constitutionally mandated presidential transition in 1970.[6] Vastly complicating his task was the appearance of a spoiler in the person of retired army commander Gustavo Rojas Pinilla. Rojas was the man who overthrew President Laureano Gómez in 1953, helped to do so by a faction of Gómez's own Conservative party. Once in power Rojas had established himself as a sort of Colombian Juan Perón, ruling the country with populist élan that won the hearts of the country's urban poor and leftist dissidents.[7] Several years after his own overthrow in 1957 Rojas had formed the populist ANAPO party and led it against the National Front.[8] As the 1970 election approached ANAPO and its candidate Gustavo Rojas Pinilla presented a strong challenge to Misael Pastrana and his supporters. By early evening of April 19, the day of the election, it appeared that Rojas was on his way to victory. But as the vote mounted in his favor and Rojas surged ahead, Carlos Lleras silenced all news of the count. The next day Colombians learned that Pastrana had won by a small margin. Most believed the election was stolen. Amidst widespread protest, Rojas Pinilla was placed under house arrest.

In succeeding years the ANAPO movement faded, its demise hastened by the death of Rojas Pinilla in 1976. Many Colombians were relieved that the populist threat had been thwarted. A substantial number of them feared populist rule because of the redistribution of wealth it would doubtless bring. Meanwhile, those who had supported Rojas accepted their defeat with bitterness. For some the episode confirmed their belief that in Colombia political power could only be won through the barrel of a gun.

Misael Pastrana went on to serve out an uneventful term. With his departure from the presidency in 1974 the National Front came to an end. When normal politics resumed in 1974 a progressive Liberal won, one who had been an outspoken critic of the power-sharing deal. Alfonso López Michelsen had even formed his own party in 1960, the MRL, or Revolutionary Liberal Movement (*Movimiento Revolucionario Liberal*), thereby briefly becoming the darling of the anti–National Front left. He spoke highly of Fidel Castro's reforms in Cuba, and liked to repeat one of his campaign slogans: "Will passengers for the revolution please board."

But in 1974 Alfonso López Michelsen was not the leftist firebrand of fifteen years earlier. He was the wealthy son of a former president, after all, and by then leader of the Liberal party. While he won the presidency promising social reform, it was not reform of the radical variety. His first year in office was marked by a series of rather conventional initiatives aimed at narrowing the gap between rich and poor, especially between better-off Colombians living in the cities and poorer ones residing in rural areas. To that end he engineered a modest increase in taxes to fund a variety of social programs.

One problem faced by López Michelsen was created by a sudden influx of foreign exchange that while positive threatened to drive up inflation. Although most of the inflow was generated by exceptionally high coffee prices, a significant portion of it came from illegal drug sales, especially from marijuana exports. During the first year of his term López and most Colombians were only mildly concerned by the flow of illegal drug money. For them illegal drug consumption was a rich-country problem, especially a U.S. problem. López had little love for the United States. Like many other Latin Americans he viewed that powerful nation as an imperialist bully which professed good neighborliness toward the region while at the same time shamelessly exploiting it.

López' ambivalence toward the marijuana trade was illustrated by the way he attempted to neutralize the economic impact of illegal drug money. He encouraged the country's central bank to open a window in its basement where such monies could be exchanged, no questions asked. Referred to as *ventanilla siniestra* (the little window on the left), it raised eyebrows both at home and abroad.[9] As a liberal, López Michelsen was not of a proscriptive turn of mind when it came to what many Colombians considered an innocuous weed. He believed, as did many of his fellow citizens, that if the smoking of Colombian-grown cannabis caused trouble for the gringos, then so much the better.

As López Michelsen ended his first year in office there seemed to be no critical problems looming on the political horizon. Aside from the seemingly minor problem of illegal marijuana cultivation, there was the nagging issue of several small insurgent groups active in outlying regions. Along with the communist FARC and the ELN, founded in the mid–1960s, there was the Maoist EPL, or Popular Liberation Army (*Ejército Popular de Liberación*). And there was a brand new urban guerrilla group as well, a non-communist group calling itself the M-19. The M-19 was founded in 1972 when it became clear to radical members of the ANAPO party that the establishment would never allow Gustavo Rojas Pinilla to come to power by electoral means. Populist in character, the M-19 was dedicated to helping the poor and to reforms of a social democratic nature. It had announced its presence in January 1974, when its members stole Simón Bolívar's sword from a museum, leaving a note explaining their goal of restoring Bolivarian values to the country.

Still, as of 1975 the presence of these groups was not excessively troubling to the Colombian government. Their members were few in number and, save for the M-19, lived in remote jungle areas. One of them, the ELN, had been nearly wiped out in a 1973 army operation carried out in northern Antioquia. The few surviving members of what until that moment had been the country's second-largest communist insurgent group limped away into the fastness of the Eastern Cordillera.

But the ELN did not pass out of existence. It was revived with the help of a defrocked Spanish priest named Manuel Pérez, emerging during the 1980s with renewed vigor. That the guerrilla group could do so points to an important fact about Colombia during most of its first 200 years as a nation: it was easy to be violent there. During that span of time if an anti-state actor was sufficiently dedicated to his cause he was more likely to die of natural causes than in a firefight with government forces.[10] Such ability to defy the state with impunity, and the citizenry's belief that it was their right to do so if sufficiently provoked, was one of the things setting Colombia apart from other Latin American nations.

Colombia's Iron Triangle of Violence

"Colombia is a country of singular things.
Civilians wage war and the military brings peace."
("*Colombia es un país de cosas singulares.*
Dan guerra los civiles y paz los militares.")
—Couplet from the early 20th century

Prior to reform of Colombia's armed forces and judiciary early in the twenty-first century it was easy to break the law, to be violent there. Three things explain why this was the case. First was the country's intractable geography, second its weak government, and third the small minority of the country's population inclined to break the law because they knew they could do so with a considerable degree of impunity. These three sources of Colombia's easy law-breaking and violence prior to the present day are best perceived as a triangle, an iron triangle of violence and impunity.

A place of forested mountains and jungles, Colombia has the third most broken terrain among the world's nations.[11] This means that its mountains and valleys, its lightly populated Eastern Llanos and Amazonian watershed, offered *violentos* convenient hiding places. Because of this, and standing as the second reason for the country's easy violence, was the state's historic difficulty in enforcing its laws across the breadth of national territory. As a relatively poor country having low rates of tax collection and consequently a chronically under-funded military and police, the Colombian state was never, until recent times, up to the task of efficient law enforcement. This led to the third source of the country's notorious violence, its citizens' understanding of their government's geographically intensified structural weakness, and knowledge that they could break the law and likely not be prosecuted for their crimes.

Despite its name this triangle of national violence and impunity has not been immutable. This has proven to be the case with the legs representing state and citizenry. When Colombians view the state as legitimate they are inclined to support it and its laws. When that is the case law enforcement improves and violence declines, a condition that further improves the image of the government among the citizenry. Even the leg of the iron triangle representing the country's rugged geography is mutable. As the country's remote regions become physically accessible, especially through improved means of transportation, Colombians living in such places experience a greater presence of the state and its services while becoming more integrated into the national economy. Thus they have a better chance for an improved and legal livelihood. As this process takes place the country's topography loses some of its ability to shelter law-breakers.

The iron triangle notwithstanding, no armed movement has ever succeeded in overthrowing a Colombian national government. Nor is armed revolution ever likely to triumph there. The reason for this is simple. Most Colombians respect the rule of law and reject violence as a means of achieving power. The country was established as a republic, and elections have always served as the accepted route to establishing political control. In fact, when the National Front ended in 1974 levels of violence were low despite the best efforts of armed groups like the FARC and ELN to enlist Colombians in their revolutionary project. The election of that year was won handily by a popular Liberal party candidate who went on to institute a plan of action highly acceptable to most citizens.

Violence levels began rising around 1975 and over ensuing decades placed Colombia's civil institutions under mounting pressure. It is the argument of this book that the powerful external force of illegal drug money fueled disorder that by the early twenty-first century made the Colombian state unable to adequately enforce its laws or defend its people. Drug money funded bribery of public officials and outright attacks on the state by leaders of the infamous cartels. It provided full employment to thousands of criminally-inclined citizens who placed themselves at the service of the illegal industry. And it paid for the arming of revolutionary groups dedicated to violent overthrow of the state and of pro-state paramilitary organizations dedicated to exterminating the leftist rebels. Within this climate of lawlessness common criminality also flourished.

Only one other incident in national history was similarly threatening to the integrity of the Colombian state. That was the Thousand Days War of 1899–1902, a ghastly conflict in which Liberal revolutionaries attempted to overthrow the corrupt and venal Conservative government in power at that time. That violent episode, like the one examined here, owed its severity and duration to monies earned through foreign sales of the lucrative psychoactive drug coffee. When the war broke out Liberals dominated the coffee trade and its revenues. Liberal party leaders had been able to plant coffee during decades prior to the war because they were shut out of public life by a Conservative party that monopolized all government positions. With the onset of war the Liberals used coffee revenues to buy weapons abroad, bringing them into the country through Venezuela and Ecuador, whose Liberal regimes sympathized with the rebels.[12] Coffee was not an illegal export. But like cocaine it offered an alkaloid rush prized by rich foreigners and for which they paid handsomely.

Not having coffee revenues to draw on in 1899, Colombia's cash-strapped government trembled before the gathering forces of disorder—much as it would a century later. Even with civil war visible on the horizon in 1899, President José Sanclemente was forced to demobilize several army brigades and sell two navy cruisers to raise funds for government operating expenses. The result was predictable. Once the war broke out the weak central government could not prosecute it vigorously. The war dragged on interminably, becoming more brutal over time. At its end two percent of the population lay dead and the country was in ruins. Over its three years Colombia experienced an astronomical annual homicide rate of 466 per 100,000 residents.[13]

The cases of Colombia's two most damaging civil conflicts suggest a corollary to the "iron triangle of violence" thesis: Only when extraordinary amounts of money emanating from abroad are placed at the disposal of anti-state actors can they seriously challenge the authority of Colombia's weak State. Conversely, when law-breakers are denied significant funding from abroad violence and impunity are subject to control through ordinary police measures.

When President Alfonso López Michelsen ended his first year in office in 1975 illegal drug money did not yet constitute a meaningful funding source for anti-state actors. Although there were insurgents in the mountains their numbers were small and the army had them under control. Meanwhile the economy was booming, the National Front being phased out,[14] and the ship of state on an even keel. The M-19 urban guerrillas had announced their birth, but so far all they had done was steal Simón Bolívar's sword. Nothing could slow Colombia's progress, could it?

The answer to this question was clearly "Yes." In fact when Alfonso López Michelsen celebrated his first year in office on August 7, 1975, Colombia's fate was already sealed. The country was on the cusp of a new violence that would over time fill its citizens with anguish and despair.

An incident of November 1975 supplies a metaphor for what awaited Colombia. On the twenty-second day of that month a small plane landed at the Cali airport. Because it had not received proper clearance police searched it and discovered that its cargo was 600 kilos of cocaine destined for sale in the United States. With a kilo of cocaine selling in the States for $45,000, the plane's cargo was worth some $27 million.

The Cali incident touched off a wave of violence in Medellín, where the flight had originated. Over the following week forty people forfeited their lives because of the failed shipment. Known as the "Medellín Massacre," the bloodbath announced the beginning of a new chapter in Colombia's violence.[15]

Rise of the Drug Culture in the United States

"Cocaine is God's way of telling you you're making too much money."
—Remark heard in the U.S. early in the 1970s

Colombia's decade of peace coincided with cultural upheaval and generational conflict in the United States. Social protest was common and persistent during those years, and part of it involved illegal drug use. The country's post–World War II "baby boom generation" came of age during the 1960s, eager to do battle against the nation's social ills. First the baby boomers attacked racism, joining with African American leaders as foot soldiers in the non-violent Civil Rights Movement that had begun the previous decade. Soon they were demonstrating against the nation's ill-fated war in Vietnam. Both the Civil Rights Movement and the anti–Vietnam War protests occurred simultaneously with other social action movements aimed at promoting gender equality, homosexual rights, pacifism, and sexual liberation. At the end of the 1960s social protest in the United States was a diffuse phenomenon joining many seemingly discordant elements. It was a revolt against the biases and prejudices of traditional American society and one of its currencies was illegal drug use by many participating in it.

Money was available to members of the U.S. drug culture. Their country was not only the richest in the world, but it was growing more affluent with each passing day. The U.S. gross domestic product doubled over the years of Colombia's decade of peace, and the world's nations scrambled to sell their products in the American marketplace. The dollar was the king of global currencies and the government constantly assured its citizens that by spending their money they would help strengthen capitalist economies everywhere, thus helping demonstrate the wrongness of communist economic theory. Spending money was patriotic! Life was good for U.S. consumers in general and for purchasers of imported drugs in particular. Improved means of transportation and the convenient proximity of Mexico, Jamaica, and Colombia permitted easy acquisition of imported cannabis and cocaine, and of foreign-made Quaaludes and amphetamines as well. By 1975 illegal drugs flowed into the United States from all corners of the world.

The U.S. drug culture burst suddenly upon the national scene during the decade of the 1960s. Whereas in the first years of the decade Americans in party mode were limited to using tobacco and alcohol, ten years later they could also chose from a pharmacopoeia of psychoactive drugs. Marijuana and heroin were easy to find, as were LSD, Quaaludes, and amphetamines. But best of all, cocaine, was starting to reach U.S. shores in increasing quantity and at ever-more-affordable prices. Cocaine was romanticized in the popular culture, and its astronomical price during the late 1960s and early '70s meant that it was the drug of celebrities and the rich.

It was also lauded for being not addictive and for giving its user both a fabulous high and, some asserted, enhanced sexual prowess. What was not to like about cocaine?

The drug craze that started sweeping the United States during the 1960s was not unprecedented in the country's history. Americans had always been excessively fond of psychoactive drugs, especially those rich in alkaloids. One of the closest students of the phenomenon has called U.S. drug abuse and the country's punitive way of addressing it "the American disease."[16] Americans themselves had addicted the world to tobacco through their lucrative exports of the alkaloid-rich plant from the late 1500s onward. And their own avid consumption of coffee was immensely important to the economic development of Brazil, Colombia, and other tropical countries.

Early U.S. consumption of opium and cocaine became possible thanks to the first wave of economic globalization that reached its peak during the late nineteenth and early twentieth centuries. By the mid–1880s opiates were present everywhere in the United States in paregoric, laudanum, and morphine. After heroin was invented by the German company Bayer in 1898 it was sold over the counter as a pain killer, along with aspirin, invented a year later by the same company. Cocaine was first extracted from coca leaves in 1855, and by 1900 was sold throughout the United States. Medicine cabinets in the U.S. were replete with patent medicines bearing names like Dr. Flint's Quaker Bitters, Ryno's Hay Fever and Catarrah Remedy and Agnew's Powder, which relied on cocaine as their main active ingredient.[17] Bartenders put pinches of cocaine in shots of whiskey and vendors sold it at the doors of taverns and brothels. Ministers and lawyers used cocaine to sharpen their presentations in pulpit and courtroom, and the popular carbonated beverage Coca Cola used cocaine as an ingredient until the year 1903. Marijuana, yet another plant containing alkaloids, grew in popularity after 1910, when Mexicans fleeing revolution in their country helped popularize it.[18]

The easy availability of powerful psychoactive drugs in the U.S., and the growing number of citizens clinically dependent on them, brought the addition of a new word to the English language in 1909. That word was "addict," created to define the several hundred thousand Americans suffering from drug addiction at that time.[19] Three years earlier, in 1906, concern over the growing problem of drug addiction had led to passage of the Pure Food and Drug Act, requiring among other things the listing of ingredients used in patent medicines. That had the effect of abruptly driving opiate-laden patent medicines from the market.

Efforts to control psychoactive drug consumption quickly took a proscriptive turn. In 1914 the Harrison Narcotic Act was passed, sharply limiting the availability of opium, cocaine, and other drugs through a variety of means. At that moment the country was in the midst of wide-ranging reforms collectively known as the Progressive Movement. Progressives were driven by a mix of altruism, Puritanism, moral absolutism, and fear. Their campaign to rid Americans of their bad habits culminated in 1920 with passage of the Eighteenth Amendment to the U.S. Constitution, prohibiting the consumption of alcoholic beverages.

Progressive legislation aimed at proscribing alcohol and narcotics brought increased budgets for the enforcement of anti-drug laws. So many arrests were made in the wake of the Harrison Act and the Prohibition Amendment that by 1932 two-thirds of all inmates in federal prisons were there for drug- and alcohol-related offenses. That marked the historical beginning in the United States of what came to be called the country's "prison-industrial complex."[20]

Although the Eighteenth Amendment was repealed in 1933, the drive to restrict the use of psychoactive drugs and punish those who trafficked in and used them continued unabated. Racial prejudice played a significant role in the process. Opium smoking had been brought into the country by Chinese immigrants during the mid–1800s. It was outlawed in 1909, at the peak of the "Yellow Peril" movement to ban Asian immigration to the U.S. Stringent state anti-cocaine laws were passed during the 1920s after rumors spread that the drug gave African Americans superhuman strength, making them resistant to police bullets. It was also suspected that cocaine made blacks forgetful of their subordinate position in society. The laws were passed at the peak of lynching in the U.S. and murderous rampages of whites through black communities. As Mexican American populations grew during the 1920s and '30s so too did fears of marijuana. Because Americans knew less about cannabis than they did about opiates, they were quick to label marijuana "killer weed" and to believe tales that it fuelled riots of Spanish-speaking immigrants.[21]

No one did more to fan fears about marijuana use than Harry J. Anslinger, director of the Federal Bureau of Narcotics, an agency established by Congress in 1930. During the 1930s, '40s, and '50s, Anslinger lobbied state governments to pass laws restricting the consumption of cannabis. He also published a steady stream of articles bearing titles like "Marijuana: Assassin of Youth," and used Bureau monies to help fund films such as *Reefer Madness*, released in 1936. The movie depicted clean-cut teenagers committing murder after getting high on marijuana. The film helped Anslinger achieve passage of the 1937 of the Marijuana Tax Act, which had the effect of sharply reducing cannabis availability in the U.S. When, in 1940, a government-sponsored study revealed that marijuana smoking does not lead to crime, Anslinger had it suppressed all the while continuing to offer sensationalist and largely false arguments against the drug. During the 1950s his allies in the U.S. Congress passed laws increasing the length of prison sentences for drug offenders, and many states did the same. Thanks to efforts such as these a Kansas jury could hand down a fifty-year prison sentence to a man convicted of selling one ounce of marijuana.[22]

Debate over drug use in the United States possessed a left-right dimension. Conservative politicians gravitated toward proscriptive solutions to the country's problem of drug use and addiction while liberals tended toward the side of decriminalization and clinical treatment of addicts. Conservatives found justification for their position in Christian philosophy, pointing to psychoactive drugs as corrosive of users' moral standards and personalities. Roman Catholics opposed psychoactive drugs on doctrinal grounds, holding that they interfered with the exercise of free will. Liberals and libertarians, on the other hand, opposed the proscriptive bent of anti-drug legislation both as inimical to individual freedom and founded in racist assumptions. In some respects liberal arguments against the punitive approach to drug control drew on the same philosophic principles of justice, fairness, and anti-racism that sustained the Civil Rights Movement of the 1950s and '60s.

U.S. drug culture and the counter-culture movement of the 1960s found their immediate antecedents in the Beat Movement of the 1950s. The Beats were radical iconoclasts who attacked social convention and prejudices at every level and who relied on drugs to help them achieve spiritual enlightenment. The Beat Generation's senior member was William Burroughs, a novelist addicted to the injected heroin-cocaine mixture known as speedballs. Poet Allen Ginsberg combined his study of Zen Buddhism with "pious investigation" of marijuana, LSD, and hallucinogenic mushrooms. Novelist Jack Kerouac was most famous for his novel about an epochal road trip fuelled by near round-the-clock ingestion of marijuana and alcohol. Meanwhile cult figure Timothy Leary became the leading LSD advocate of the '60s, urging the youth of America to let the drug help them "turn on, tune in, and drop out." He touted LSD as "mind candy" and "mental health food." Leary and his Beat contemporaries urged Americans to liberate themselves from bourgeois consciousness while attacking stupidities of the Establishment. For them drug use was a tool for defying society and mounting a revolutionary critique against it.

In the 1960s new figures emerged to promote the use of psychoactive drugs. While it was a marijuana violation that sent him to jail for a year in 1966, novelist Ken Kesey was best known for driving a bus across the U.S. and handing out samples of LSD along the way.[23] Peruvian-born sociologist Carlos Castañeda published a book in 1968 exploring the pursuit of spiritual transcendence through peyote ingestion. Recounting his journey to spiritual enlightenment through the teachings of a Yaqui Indian shaman earned him cult-figure status along with massive book sales. Meanwhile the Beatles extolled LSD, though not explicitly, in their song "Lucy in the Sky, with Diamonds."

The Vietnam War also contributed to rise of the U.S. drug culture. More than a million young men were sent to fight in Vietnam, many of them unwillingly. While there they had easy access to mind-altering drugs, notably heroin, and as a result many returned home addicts. Protests against the war accelerated over the 1960s, helping give rise to the neo–Bohemian hippies whose controlled substance of choice was marijuana. The hippies captured national attention during their 1967 Summer of Love festival in Golden Gate Park. Allen Ginsberg was a guiding light of the hippies, having launched the Flower Power Movement two years earlier. Marijuana smoking was de rigueur at those events. It was endemic in subsequent mass gatherings of young people, such as at the Woodstock rock concert held in 1969. Needless to say, the enforcement of marijuana laws was a daunting task during those years. Although arrests for marijuana possession increased ten-fold between 1965 and 1970, they touched but a tiny percentage of cannabis users.[24] Their arrests did little to reduce the consumption of marijuana.

Early in the counter-culture Movement most marijuana consumed in the United States was grown outside the country, particularly in Mexico. But as demand grew, and as the U.S. increased pressure on Mexico to act against marijuana growers, consumers started looking elsewhere for imports. That soon led to the supplanting of Mexican marijuana by a superior product imported first from Jamaica and then from Colombia. "Colombia gold" was so much better than Mexican cannabis that it quickly gained mythic status in pot consuming circles across the U.S.[25]

Colombian producers responded quickly to the U.S. demand for marijuana. Soon Colombian "mother ships" bearing hundreds of tons of cannabis were anchoring in international waters along the U.S. East Coast, off-loading their cargos, cash on the barrelhead, to U.S. smugglers in high-powered speedboats who delivered it to mainland distribution sites. At the same time major quantities of Colombian marijuana were arriving by air. One daredevil smuggler named Alan Long moved nearly a million pounds into the United States by air and by sea during the 1970s and early '80s. Long transported much of what he brought into the U.S. northward, to Ann Arbor, Michigan. He was so proficient in his work that he single-handedly satisfied the marijuana needs of the greater Ann Arbor community, earning $8 million for himself in the process.[26]

By 1975 an immense amount of marijuana was being smoked in the United States. That year six percent of high school students used pot on a regular basis and twenty-seven percent admitted to using it on occasion. Data released by the U.S. Drug Enforcement Agency in 1978 indicated that forty-two million Americans smoked marijuana. Given that sixty percent of the marijuana smoked in the U.S. at that time originated in Colombia, the Andean nation was supporting the marijuana habit of a consuming public in the U.S. equal in size to its own total population.[27]

Thus Colombia and the United States became locked in a comfortable embrace at the level of marijuana demand and supply. And most Colombians and Americans perceived it to be a benign embrace. By then Americans knew infinitely more about marijuana than they had in the days of Harry Anslinger's film *Reefer Madness.* They had learned that marijuana smoking was a relatively harmless pastime and that their country's draconian anti-pot laws were best obeyed in the breach. One of the best evocations of that liberal moment in U.S. attitudes toward substance abuse was in the 1978 film *Up in Smoke,* a comedy portraying two California hippies who spent their days and their nights smoking joints of monumental size.[28]

At that instant cocaine, too, enjoyed a high level of acceptance by the American public. Just as they had with marijuana, Colombian suppliers acted quickly to satisfy pent-up demand for the alkaloid.

Cocaine had been largely driven out of the U.S. market during the 1920s and subsequently was readily available only to members of the criminal underworld. Until the late 1950s relatively small quantities of the drug were manufactured in South America, principally in Chile, shipments making their way northward to Mafia members based in Cuba.[29] By the 1960s marijuana smugglers like Alan Long had discovered cocaine, but they bought it for personal use. In 1965 the U.S. Bureau of Narcotic and Dangerous Drugs seized a mere seventeen kilos of the alkaloid, and by 1968 the amount seized had increased to only forty-five kilos.

Only during the 1970s did cocaine begin appearing in the U.S. in substantial quantities. Seizures of the drug jumped to 100 kilos in 1970, and reached 400 kilos in 1974. That represented less than three percent of total reaching American shores from Colombia alone.[30] According to figures released by the U.S. government, Colombia's cocaine exports ran between 12,000 and 18,000 kilos over the course of 1975.[31]

Cocaine increased in popularity in part because other drugs had fallen out of favor. By the 1970s LSD was passé, and speed had gained a fearful reputation. By the late '60s the corpses of young amphetamine users were turning up in morgues all over the country. Autopsies revealed that their internal organs had been prematurely aged by the drug. A rash of deaths of celebrities like Janice Joplin and Jimi Hendrix drove home the slogan "speed kills." Quaaludes were also soon pushed aside by cocaine. Unlike Quaaludes, which were also known as "wall bangers," cocaine allowed users to remember their sexual experiences after the fact. Still another source of the drug's popularity lay in its immense profitability. The December 27, 1973, edition of *Newsweek* quoted a DEA agent's remark that "anybody can go down there," buy a kilo of cocaine for $4,000, and sell it in the States for $20,000.

So by 1975 cocaine's reputation was established and its success in the U.S. market assured. No less authority than drug expert Peter G. Bourne had proclaimed the alkaloid to be "perhaps the most benign of illicit drugs widely used today."[32] As in the United States nearly a century earlier, responsible citizens claimed that it let them work harder and live happier lives. Jet setters in the United States and at upscale watering places across the Western world partied the night away fortified by "blasts of blow," the beautiful people's new elixir.

Initial U.S. and Colombian Responses to Illegal Drugs, 1965–1975

"Cocaine, as currently used, usually does not result in serious social consequences."
—1975 U.S. "White Paper on Drug Abuse"[33]

The liberal political mood prevailing in the United States during the 1960s and 1970s played a significant role in the rise of the drug culture there. The first half of the decade was a time of idealism and enthusiasm centering on the country's drive to extend civil rights to its African American minority. John F. Kennedy had set the tone for progressive activism through a call to public service that electrified thousands of young Americans and moved them to volunteer for a range of domestic and foreign social programs. Following Kennedy's assassination in 1963, his vice president, Lyndon Johnson, pledged to continue the fight for racial justice, and to improve the lot of the poorest Americans through his "Great Society" program.

But shortly after taking office in 1965, Lyndon Johnson, now President in his own right, squandered the good will he had earned through his earlier idealism and visionary social programs. He threw his weight behind the military contest in Vietnam, thus giving motive force to the counter-culture movement that celebrated drug use as an element of social protest. Anti-establishment activism of the latter 1960s found its most flamboyant expression in the hippies. That turbulent moment in U.S. history was caught in a 1967 photograph of a young anti-war protester in Golden Gate Park, garlands in her hair, placing a flower in the muzzle of a National Guard soldier's rifle. It was part of that summer's "Flower Power" movement led by hippies and fueled in considerable part by marijuana.

The liberal optimism of the 1960s and '70s had the effect of placing the greatest enemies of marijuana and other proscribed drugs on the defensive. No less personage than Harry J. Anslinger, the man who had criminalized marijuana in the 1930s, told an interviewer in 1972 that earlier when he arrested illegal drug users he was a hero. "Now," Anslinger reflected sadly, "the public thinks I am a rat."[34]

There was one short-lived official attempt to combat drug use during the late 1960s. Richard M. Nixon had been elected President in 1968, in part on the promise that he would conduct a War on Drugs, especially on marijuana crossing into the U.S. from Mexico. Once in office Nixon created a "Narcotics, Marijuana and Dangerous Drugs Task Force," one of whose members was future Watergate burglar G. Gordon Liddy. During summer 1969 the Taskforce directed "Operation Intercept," an attempt to stop marijuana shipments from crossing the Mexican border. The effort did little more than create massive traffic jams at border crossing points. It turned up no contraband marijuana and was soon suspended.[35]

Nixon's departure from the political scene in August 1974 was followed by a notable liberalization of official U.S. attitudes toward psychoactive drugs. During Gerald Ford's short time in office a "White Paper on Drug Abuse" was published suggesting that the government focus its attention on more addictive drugs such as heroin, amphetamines, and barbiturates. Less dangerous and less habit-forming drugs like marijuana and cocaine were not even mentioned in the document's seventy-seven recommendations for controlling drug abuse.[36] The report's publication coincided with the moment that Colombia became the chief supplier of marijuana and cocaine to the United States.

Gerald Ford soft-pedaled his predecessor's drug war in part because when he took office there was a growing nationwide movement to decriminalize personal consumption of marijuana. At Ford's alma mater, the University of Michigan at Ann Arbor, there was massive marijuana smoking, a fact amply illustrated in the history of smuggler Alan Long.[37] In 1972 the Ann Arbor City Council decriminalized marijuana smoking within the city limits. The state of Oregon did the same a year later. Shortly after Ford left office in 1977 similar legislation was introduced in the United States Congress.

Tolerance for marijuana and cocaine use reached its peak during the first year of Jimmy Carter's presidency. One of Carter's first acts was to name Dr. Peter G. Bourne his Special Adviser for Health Affairs. Bourne was a leading advocate of marijuana decriminalization and of the government's focusing its anti-drug efforts on heroin interdiction and opium poppy eradication in producer nations. Meanwhile both he and President Carter lobbied Congress for reducing penalties for cocaine and marijuana possession.[38]

As these events unfolded in the United States most Colombians were indifferent to growth of the illegal drug trade in their own country. Three things accounted for that fact. The first had to do both with the explosive nature of the spread of marijuana and cocaine production and its newness for Colombians. Consequently neither the Colombian public nor its political leadership had much grasp of the size of the new export industry. Certainly they had no inkling of where it would lead them.

A second source of official inaction before the looming threat was the weakness, inefficiency, and susceptibility to corruption of Colombia's government itself. National leaders did not know the magnitude of the new industry because their subalterns told them little about it. The lightness of official presence in outlying areas and its inefficiency when it was present meant that drug producers and exporters had an easy time buying the silence of civil servants at all levels of government, as well as at every level of the police and military. It was simply in the economic interest of Colombian officials not to let their superiors know about the new business that was making them rich through bribes. Meanwhile public officials knowingly received money derived from the drug trade through campaign donations, through family connections, or through outright bribes.[39]

Third and finally, there were too many other issues to be dealt with in Colombia during the decade after the *Violencia*. Carlos Lleras had to see the National Front through to completion, Misael Pastrana dealt with the ongoing hostility of Rojas Pinilla's populist ANAPO movement, and Alfonso López Michelsen worked to cool an overheated economy. All three men confronted ongoing political and social protests in the cities and the armed revolutionary challenge of communist guerrillas in the countryside. Any threat posed by the shadowy, nascent illegal drug trade paled in comparison to these problems.

Colombian and U.S. interests intersected in the area of the communist guerrillas. The two countries were Cold War allies committed to the principle that the Andean nation must not become the hemisphere's second Marxist-Leninist state. As always in U.S. official circles, concerns about illegal drugs were trumped by strategic concerns regarding communism. Only from time to time during the period 1965–1975 did the Americans request Colombian cooperation in drug-related matters. And when they did Colombian help was not always forthcoming. That was the case in 1972 when the Department of Justice requested extradition of Vice-Counsel J.A. Córdoba to face trial in the U.S. for trafficking fifteen kilos of cocaine. Misael Pastrana refused the request and the matter was dropped.[40]

Pastrana himself was similarly rebuffed two years earlier, but by members of his own political class. He had been asked by the U.S. to halt marijuana shipments departing ports on the arid Guajira peninsula. When he ordered departmental officials to do so, politicians of the region wrote him protesting that he had no right to prohibit smuggling in their department. They reminded the President that "it is the only form of subsistence of the majority of the population."[41]

Although Alfonso López Michelsen followed a laissez-faire policy on illegal drugs, the drug trade's baleful influence started to become apparent by the end of his first year in office. In a speech of June 25, 1975, in which he explained why he had just placed Colombia under a state of siege, López cited a wave of strikes in protest of high rates of inflation, and the existence of drug mafias linked to international smugglers who were corrupting both government customs and tax officials and members of the National Police.[42] All the while López insisted, and with justification, that Colombia's growing problem with illegal drugs was rooted in the gringos' failure to control marijuana consumption at home.

It is safe to say that at the end of Colombia's decade of peace neither it nor the United States appreciated the magnitude of the illegal drug trade. Only a few of Colombia's leaders could see the future with any degree of clarity. One of them was Álvaro Gómez Hurtado, a Conservative party leader and journalist. Eleven months after the Medellín Massacre of November 1975, Gómez attended a party where he heard the U.S. Ambassador say that Colombia was sending between one and one-and-a-half tons of cocaine monthly to the U.S., and that Colombia should do a better job of enforcing its drug laws. Not long afterward Gómez published a response in the weekly newspaper *Sábado*. Colombians know they have a problem with illegal drugs, he wrote, but they don't know what to do about it. The country tries to fight the drug trade all the while knowing it's a battle Colombia is bound to lose. Gómez opined that anti-drug laws both in Colombia and the United States had little real impact on illegal drug production in the former country and consumption in the latter. He observed that at the moment there were 700,000 heroin and barbiturate addicts in the United States. Colombia, he admitted, was a "stupendous base of operations" for drug production and smuggling. He pointed to the risible amounts of cocaine seized by national police as evidence of their corruption, and indicted the U.S. for earmarking just $6 million of its $1.7 billion narcotics control budget for anti-drug aid to Colombia.

The main focus of his opinion piece was the drug trade's damage to national institutions, damage much greater than that suffered by the U.S. In the title of his article Gómez expressed a sentiment that Colombian leaders would repeat with growing frequency over the coming decades: "How it costs us!"[43]

CHAPTER 2

The Illegal Drug Hydra, 1970–1983

Colombia Gold

"Within a couple of years traffic in the skies east of Santa Marta would take on the scope of the Berlin Airlift."

—Journalist Robert Sabbag[1]

U.S. smugglers were searching for alternate sources of marijuana even before Richard Nixon's attempt to stop the cannabis flow from Mexico in 1969. It was their country's draconian anti-marijuana laws that drove them to look abroad for supplies, and logically they turned first to Mexico, traditional supplier of pot to gringo traffickers. As demand intensified in the mid–1960s, and as the Mexicans failed to show interest in improving their product or honing their business sense, American smugglers began looking for new sources of supply.[2] Their gaze drifted southward, to the Caribbean and South America, to Jamaica and Colombia especially, two countries known to produce a high-quality product.

Commercial production of marijuana had begun in Colombia during the late colonial period, when hemp was brought from South Asia to supplement native plants traditionally used for rope and burlap. Colombian cannabis had always been known for its psychoactive potency when smoked, although that particular use was limited to members of the lower class, mostly to laborers living in northern Colombia near port cities on the Caribbean coast. There was no record of commercial marijuana cultivation in the country until the 1920s, when modest plantings were discovered in the foothills of the Sierra Nevada de Santa Marta, a towering mountain range between the port cities of Santa Marta and Riohacha. The Catholic Church condemned the use of mind-altering substances, and accordingly Colombia's government prohibited marijuana smoking the nineteenth century. During the 1940s the country's Conservative governments cracked down on cannabis smoking, and by the 1950s there was little commercial marijuana cultivation anywhere in the country.[3]

When North American pot smugglers started showing up in Colombia during the early 1960s they found two promising sources of supply, the first east of the port city of Santa Marta, in the foothills of the mountain range of the same name, and the second 600 kilometers southwest, down the Caribbean coast, around the Gulf of Urabá. The Gulf of Urabá region was dominated by banana plantations owned by the United Fruit Company and therefore enjoyed lively commerce with the United States. Banana ships were constantly in transit between the Gulf's port at Turbo and the U.S. ports of Miami, New Orleans, and Houston. They offered convenient transportation northward for marijuana hidden in banana cargoes. Farther up the coast the Santa Marta region offered many potential advantages for large-scale marijuana production and export, among them a population having historical memory of cannabis cultivation and numerous ports along the Guajira Peninsula offering unobstructed access northward across the Caribbean to the United States. The Guajira region was a relatively sleepy place in the mid–1960s, well described in the novel *One Hundred Years of Solitude* by Pulitzer Prize winner Gabriel García Márquez. The novelist's home town of Aracataca, the Macondo of his novel, lies just eighty kilometers south of Santa Marta, at the edge of the Sierra Nevada foothills.

So the gringo traffickers found early success arranging marijuana shipments with suppliers around the Gulf of Urabá, as well as around the Sierra Nevada de Santa Marta, where people of the region were eager to exchange their cannabis for sorely needed dollars. In this way large-scale commercial marijuana cultivation came to Colombia.

It was not long before Colombians discovered that their country had a lucrative new export product. In February 1966 the Bogotá daily *El Espectador* published an article reporting police seizure of thirty thousand pesos worth of cannabis in the nation's capital. The piece earned a sharp response from journalist Bertha Hernández de Ospina, wife of former president Mariano Ospina Pérez (1946–1950), at the time a journalist writing for the newspaper *La República*. Doña Bertha, as she was universally known, chided *El Espectador* for stating the value of the confiscated marijuana. By so doing, she wrote, "all our bums and idlers" now perceive a brilliant new way to make money. She ended her article musing "What do you think about a little plant that can be easily hidden, that grows anywhere, and that gives such good economic return?"[4]

Doña Bertha's seeming belief that press censorship could keep the criminal element in the dark about the value of illegal marijuana was about as effective as Richard Nixon's plan to keep Americans from smoking the proscribed weed by setting up police roadblocks along the Mexican border. That is to say neither was effective. While radio stations in the U.S. censored song lyrics like "I get high with a little help from my friends," Americans smoked marijuana with abandon. And despite the government's best efforts to cut off supplies, marijuana imports from abroad kept up with demand. At the precise mid-point in Richard Nixon's "Operation Intercept," a two-ton shipment of Colombian marijuana was seized at a Florida airport. At a time when marijuana was selling for $350 per pound, the shipment was worth $1.4 million. If the confiscated marijuana represented ten percent of Colombian marijuana shipments to the U.S. in 1969, shipments from that country already stood at twenty tons. Meanwhile plane loads of pot were arriving daily from Jamaica, along with shipments from elsewhere, by both ship and plane.[5]

Marijuana fever swept the Urabá region during the late 1960s and early 1970s. The Gulf of Urabá and its hinterlands had been a smuggling center since colonial times, when unlicensed merchandise flowed in both directions across the Isthmus of Panama. During the 1950s marijuana and occasional shipments of cocaine, traveling northward from Chilean processing labs, made their way through the Gulf and up the Atrato River toward Panama. Yet not until the marijuana boom of the 1960s was there such intense interest in an illegal export. All around the Gulf of Urabá farmers abandoned traditional crops and took up marijuana cultivation. Many of those working in the banana plantations and on the docks also devoted themselves to the cannabis trade. Members of the Cuna Indian tribe even took out a loan from the Agrarian Bank (*Caja Agraria*) which they ploughed into marijuana cultivation. Ships reaching U.S. ports from United Fruit docks soon were reputed to be carrying as much marijuana as bananas. Official Colombia grew alarmed. So too did the United Fruit Company and the U.S. government. In August of 1971 Misael Pastrana decreed that the Urabá marijuana industry cease. United Fruit cooperated by increasing security on its ships, and the police and armed forces started destroying marijuana crops. The effect of these measures was to push production northeast up the coast to the Guajira Peninsula.[6]

Anti-drug measures in both Colombia and the United States were in part spurred by public reaction against growing drug use, especially by members of the counter-culture movement. Richard Nixon's Operation Intercept followed the 1969 Woodstock rock festival by only a few months, while Misael Pastrana's crackdown on his country's marijuana industry came just a month after Colombia's own version of Woodstock, held June 1971 in Medellín's Ancón Park. Thousands of young people attended the event, which featured rock and jazz bands from Colombia and abroad. A cloud of marijuana smoke hung above the park during the three days of the celebration, which was held in a steady drizzle. It was essentially a hippy celebration held in a stoned ambience of peace and love. Bonfires were lit at night and couples huddled around them wrapped in blankets, smoking marijuana, listening to music, and making love. Over the three days of the event scores of young people were treated at a nearby Red Cross station for drug overdoses, hypothermia, and assorted ailments. Members of the Medellín Fire Department were stationed along the rain-swollen creek flowing through the park to rescue celebrants who fell into it or who were swept away while bathing. At one point a bridge collapsed, dumping several dozen people into the stream. No one was thought to have died, but then no one was sure because most witnesses were stoned at the time.

The rock concert scandalized the citizens of Medellín and of Colombia at large. Newspapers carried photographs of pre-pubescent girls wandering among teenagers who were rolling marijuana cigarettes and consuming pills and hallucinogenic mushrooms. Parents from outside of Medellín filed kidnapping charges against young men who took their daughters to the concert, and the police rounded up and deported foreign hippies who had entered the country illegally to attend the concert. The outcry led to the resignations of Medellín's mayor and the president of the University of Medellín, where a student riot had just taken place.[7]

Growing openness in the use of illegal drugs brought stepped-up attempts on the part of governments to enforce anti-drug laws. The United States, richer and more powerful than the rest of the world, and whose drug culture was the most widespread and anti-drug laws most severe, led the way. A 1970 FBI investigation called "Operation Eagle" revealed for the first time the existence of organized drug rings in Latin America and the Caribbean, a fact underscored by the rising quantities of illegal drugs flowing into the U.S. By 1972 an estimated ton of marijuana was arriving daily from Jamaica, flown into Florida airports. In June 1973 Bureau of Narcotics and Dangerous Drugs (BNDD) chief John Ingersoll reported to President Richard Nixon that an "astonishing variety" of drugs were pouring into the United States. Among those named were heroin, cocaine, amphetamines, hashish, and marijuana.[8]

Ingersoll's BNDD report was part of a ratcheting up of U.S. anti-drug activities that involved replacing his agency with a new, more powerful one. On July 1, 1973, Nixon created the Drug Enforcement Administration (DEA), charging it with vigorously waging his War on Drugs. The DEA quickly went to work crafting two marijuana-related programs, "Operation Buccaneer" and "Operation Condor," whose combined goal was to destroy marijuana plantations in Jamaica and Mexico. The U.S. wrung permission from those two countries to spray their illegal crops with a powerful defoliant called Paraquat, which had the virtues of both killing marijuana and making it unsmokable. By the mid–1970s Jamaican and Mexican production had fallen off sharply.

The twin DEA initiatives came at the precise moment when marijuana smoking reached the height of its popularity in the United States. By the mid–1970s cannabis had been embraced by the middle class. Rolling joints and getting high passed from being a teenage rite of passage to after-work and party time rituals for members of the older generation. The middle class had learned to turn on.[9] Accordingly, the demand for marijuana quadrupled between 1974 and 1978, when the government succeeded in poisoning Mexican and Jamaican marijuana plantations. It was a classic case of states against markets. Would the mighty United States succeed in denying its citizens their marijuana? The answer was a resounding "No!" Richard M. Nixon's victories in Jamaica and Mexico were speedily and painlessly negated in the foothills of the Sierra Nevada de Santa Marta, where Colombian entrepreneurs and U.S. smugglers stepped forward to provide gringos an apparently limitless supply of the best marijuana in the world. Thus it was that U.S. President Richard Nixon and his pot-smuggling fellow citizens set Colombia on the path to becoming the illegal drug emporium of the Western world.

Colombia stood no chance of resisting the swarms of gringo traffickers who descended on Santa Marta and its environs during the mid–1970s. They came paying premium prices and cash on the barrelhead for the region's fabled cannabis. Colombia was poor in comparison to the U.S. Average incomes there were less than a tenth of those in the U.S. Meanwhile Colombians who had money were hard pressed to find anything to spend it on.[10] The country was only beginning to move away from the decades of economic protection and currency control put in place during the 1930s and in succeeding decades to spur industrial development. That economic strategy had worked, for the country did industrialize. But the high tariff barriers made Colombia a country bereft of consumer goods, particularly consumer electronics and luxury goods like imported liquors and cigarettes. So by the 1960s and '70s Colombians were avid both for dollars and for the things dollars could buy.

Colombia's northeastern Caribbean coast, where the great *Bonanza Marimbera* (Marijuana Bonanza) of the 1970s took place, was one of the country's most impoverished regions. That was especially the case in the Guajira Peninsula, a finger of land extending into the Caribbean northeast of the Sierra Nevada de Santa Marta. The Guajira was arid, lightly populated, and historically lacking anything that the world, or Colombians, desired. The only profitable occupation that the people there had ever known was smuggling, especially the smuggling of consumer goods across the border with Venezuela and through ports dotting the department's Caribbean coast. So the people of northeastern Colombia could scarcely have been happier when foreigners descended upon them in the mid–1970s offering top dollar for their world-class cannabis. They embraced the gringo traffickers like long-lost brothers. It was a surreal coming together of the people of Macondo and well-heeled young American traffickers, a bizarre and propitious smugglers' family reunion that seemed to be made in heaven.

The American smugglers did literally descend on northeastern Colombia. At first they arrived in Cesnas, Piper Cubs, and Fairchild turboprops, but soon many of them moved up to DC3s and even larger cargo planes. The Guajira was flat, sandy, and easily adapted to the construction of landing strips for light planes. A report of Colombia's security agency DAS (Departamento Administrativo de Seguridad), published in September 1975, gave the coordinates of 131 clandestine landing strips surrounding the marijuana plantations of the Sierra Nevada.[11] Smugglers from the United States usually arranged their transactions in advance, arriving cash-in-hand to find the marijuana ready for transport and drums of gasoline available for refueling their planes. The gringos came offering technical assistance to marijuana farmers, along with advice on the proper packaging of their product.[12]

The average plane load was one ton, and it took little more than one day to make the round trip from the U.S. to Colombia and back. It was all so quick, easy, and profitable that by late 1976 the planes of smugglers were, as one trafficker recalled, beginning to stack up over the Guajira "like commercial flights over JFK."[13] Meanwhile, though the Colombian government had an inkling of what was going on, it had no way of controlling the trade. Government presence was historically scant in the Guajira, and officials representing the state, police, military, and civilians were liberally paid for their non-interference.

During the boom times of the late 1970s dozens of ships plied the waters between Guajira ports and the Atlantic coast of the U.S., transporting cargo running fifteen tons on average. These mother ships anchored in international waters off the coast of Florida and the Carolinas, off-loading their cargo to U.S. smugglers who paid for the marijuana in cash. So lucrative was the trade that Colombian boat owners could lose four out of five ships and still turn a handsome profit.[14] By 1975 Colombian authorities had identified sixty-four ships dedicated exclusively to transporting cannabis out of twelve ports of embarkation. At the height of the *Bonanza Marimbera* an estimated thirty percent of Santa Marta gold reached the U.S. by ship, and the rest by air.[15] The American Mafia played its role in assisting the marijuana trade. During the late 1970s mob boss Myer Lansky manufactured cigarette boats in North Miami that were capable of transporting up to 3.5 tons of marijuana while outrunning anything owned by the U.S. Coast Guard.[16] Miami wholesaler Donald Steinberg recalled off-loading one 50-ton shipment of Colombia gold that he sold for $25 million, earning himself a profit of $2 million. At his trial in 1984 Steinberg put his earnings after ten years in the marijuana trade at $100 million.[17]

Most Colombians living in the marijuana zone participated in the boom in one way or another. At its height 20,000 to 30,000 agricultural workers tended between 50,000 and 70,000 hectares planted in red-tip and mona, generating annual exports of up to 20,000 metric tons. The most menial field work earned a campesino six times the salary ordinarily paid for agricultural labor.[18] As might be expected, those highest on the economic ladder reaped the greatest rewards. By 1978 there were sixty major exporters in Colombia's northern coastal region, collectively satisfying sixty percent of U.S. marijuana demand. A great many leaders of society were involved. A police commander in Barranquilla reported confiscating five kilos of cocaine from the president of one of the city's leading social clubs, and shortly afterward seizing a large marijuana shipment owned by the brother of Colombia's Vice-Minister of Justice.[19] Perhaps the most spectacular feat of smuggling was carried out in 1976 by the son of a well-to-do Santa Marta family named Juan Manuel Retat. The young man purchased a DC-6 with borrowed money, loaded it with five tons of marijuana, and flew it to Jetmore, Kansas, just north of Dodge City. He landed the plane at night on a three-mile section of highway that his gringo associates had blocked off. They quickly off-loaded the cargo and Retat returned home with a million dollars cash in hand, presumably to live the rest of his life in luxury.[20]

Santa Marta's airport was routinely used for marijuana shipments during the latter 1970s. Its managers turned off airport lights whenever a smuggler's plane landed or took off, everyone who worked there, including members of the police and military, being liberally compensated for their help.[21] Bribery was the order of the day in the countryside where the marijuana was grown. U.S. smuggler Luis García recalled Ciénaga resident Juan Nogera, the owner of well-tended and extensive fields of red-tip marijuana, using stacks of new banknotes to pay tolls at police and military checkpoints so his truckloads of pot could roll through unchallenged.[22] Guerrilla groups were also on the take. When smuggler Alan Long was stopped by communist guerrillas during the early 1970s he was able to buy his freedom, and to keep his truckload of marijuana, by paying the guerrillas with a personal check drawn on his Chase Manhattan Bank account.[23]

U.S. government agencies inadvertently played their role in helping Colombia become Latin America's premier marijuana exporter. In 1971 the Bureau of Narcotics and Dangerous Drugs was ready to extradite Manuel Noriega, head of Panama's military intelligence, for trafficking Colombian marijuana. But the CIA, which employed Noriega as one of its assets, had the U.S. Attorney's office in Miami quash the charge. A year later, when Colombian intelligence agents captured a notorious Barranquilla smuggler with a load of marijuana, he too avoided arrest by producing papers showing he was a CIA employee.[24]

The relationship between top Colombian leaders and the marijuana industry was a complex one. When Alfonso López Michelsen learned that several of his relatives by marriage were named in a CIA white paper on Colombian drug trafficking, López dismissed it as just a list of names containing no proof of guilt. Yet in 1976 López pointed to marijuana and cocaine trafficking as being the source of "social decomposition" in his country, and in 1977 issued a decree allowing the confiscation of land used in producing illegal drugs. In 1978 he dismissed his Minister of Labor because of the man's links to the drug trade. Curiously, that same year found López warning that the marijuana bonanza might end because the gringos were beginning to complain about contaminated shipments.[25]

Top officials in the United States government were also ambivalent about illegal drugs in the late 1970s. U.S. President Jimmy Carter and his top advisor on drug-related matters, Dr. Peter G. Bourne, advocated legalizing marijuana for personal use. Still, in late 1975, Bourne, who at the time headed the Domestic Council Drug Abuse Task Force, handed President Gerald Ford a white paper criticizing Colombians for their role in illegal drug production.[26] The "Bourne Report," as it came to be known, was featured eighteen months later on the CBS television program *60 Minutes* and created a furor in Colombia because it named Liberal party presidential candidate Julio César Turbay as having a nephew involved in cocaine trafficking. Nevertheless some Colombians believed that it was hypocritical for U.S. leaders to criticize them for supplying the illegal drugs that they themselves consumed. Dr. Peter G. Bourne no doubt agreed with them.

Following Turbay's election, the U.S. government pressured him to take action against the marijuana trade, something he did in late 1978 by sending 10,000 soldiers, accompanied by naval and air support, to uproot marijuana growing in the foothills of the Sierra Nevada de Santa Marta. Called *Operación Fulminante,* it led to the arrest of 2,000 people and the seizure of 3,500 tons of marijuana, 486 vehicles, 106 ships and launches, and 125 airplanes. U.S. President Carter congratulated Turbay for his decisive action and urged him to extend the anti-drug operation nationwide.[27]

Colombians were in fact of two minds regarding their lucrative new export. Everyone in the country knew that the drug trade was illegal at every level. At the same time they saw the marijuana trade as relatively pacific and as bringing unparalleled development to an especially backward part of the country. It was something taking place along the far northeastern coast and seemed to be more the gringos' problem than their own. Finally, marijuana was bringing badly needed foreign exchange into the country. Marijuana and cocaine earned Colombia an estimated $2.5 billion in 1980, $1.6 billion of which was deposited in the country's national bank through its *ventanilla siniestra*. Thanks in large part to the illegal drug trade the nation's dollar reserves had swelled from $35 million in 1968 to $5.63 billion in 1981.[28] And when the Americans blamed Colombians for failing to control marijuana production it was hard to disagree with Alfonso López that if the gringo smugglers had not come calling years earlier, and if the U.S. government had done a better job controlling the consumption of marijuana by its own people, then Colombia would not have become the hemisphere's major marijuana exporter.

It was in the spirit of wanting to deal positively with the *Bonanza Marimbera* that Colombian politicians debated the issue during the late 1970s and early 1980s. One prominent advocate for outright legalization of marijuana was Liberal party secretary Ernesto Samper Pizano.[29] Samper remained outspoken on the subject until the early '80s, when the Catholic Church threatened to excommunicate him unless he ceased his campaign. Others were more circumspect, focusing on discovering ways to sanitize the money flowing into Colombia through marijuana sales. Their proposals included granting amnesty to property acquired with drug money prior to 1981, and the awarding of amnesty to the traffickers themselves if they invested their earnings in special government bonds. Late in 1982 Colombia's newly elected president, Belisario Betancur, advocated granting amnesty to marijuana earnings themselves, to "attract hidden capital from wherever it comes, without looking back at its origins."[30]

In retrospect the public debate on marijuana, its possible legalization, and the proper way to deal with its profits was naïve. The weak Colombian state was simply not in a position to legalize cannabis without approval of the United States, and that approval would never be forthcoming, certainly not during the 1980s when public and official views in the U.S. grew more hostile toward illegal drugs with each passing day. The shift back toward harsh proscription of illegal drugs began in the U.S. in 1978, when parents across the country started organizing against marijuana, the smoking of which had become widespread among their children. This "parent's movement" against marijuana and other drugs was part of a general shift toward conservative politics in the U.S., highlighted by the return to power of the Republican Party in 1981 under the leadership of Ronald Reagan.[31] One of Reagan's first acts was to renew the War on Drugs that his co-partisan Richard Nixon had first declared a decade before.

Also lessening the significance of debates on marijuana revenues was the fact that by the 1980s they were being dwarfed by earnings from the cocaine industry. But this fact had not yet registered in the consciousness of most politicians. When Colombian leaders did perceive the magnitude of the violent and disruptive cocaine trade a few years later, it was impossible to consider taming it through simple grants of amnesty.

In any event there was little need to fret about marijuana earnings over the decade of the 1980s. The bonanza was coming to an end. Recreational drug users in the United States had turned from marijuana to cocaine as their controlled substance of choice. Cocaine had suddenly become abundant and relatively cheap everywhere in the U.S., and bales of Colombian marijuana sat unsold in Miami warehouses. *Operación Fulminante*, and an accompanying U.S.

campaign known as Operation Stopgap, designed to disrupt marijuana shipping in the Caribbean, had a dampening effect on cannabis production around the Sierra Nevada de Santa Marta, driving production southeast into the Eastern Llanos and southwest into the department of Cauca on Colombia's Pacific coast.[32] Colombia gold was also being adulterated, and it was becoming increasingly dangerous for unarmed American smugglers to travel to Colombia with large amounts of cash in hand. Finally, Americans were beginning to grow their own marijuana. Doña Bertha was correct when she wrote in 1966 that the plant that could be easily grown and hidden anywhere. During the '80s cannabis devotees in the U.S. developed seedless marijuana appropriately named "sinsemilla," and started growing it clandestinely in their homes and family gardens, in woodland glades and in national parks. All of these events sent Colombia's marijuana industry into a twenty year decline that by the year 1999 reduced estimated earnings on the crop to a paltry five million dollars.[33]

So by the early 1980s marijuana was becoming passé, and cocaine Colombia's drug of the future. As usual, national officials both in Colombia and the United States were slow to recognize that fact. But citizens closer at hand knew better. And they were worrying about it. In August of 1983 a Liberal party conference of delegates from national territories was held in Mitú, a small town near the Brazilian border in the province of Vaupés. Delegates to the meeting knew that coca plantations and cocaine laboratories were appearing throughout Colombia's relatively unpopulated southeastern provinces. They were equally aware that their country was abjectly unprepared to deal with the corrupting power and violence of cocaine production. They concluded that the best way to protect themselves from the frightening new industry was by legalizing coca growing—and perhaps cocaine manufacture—in Colombia's Amazon watershed.[34]

Cocaine Comes to Colombia

> "At the beginning of the 1970s the city of Cali, and I think you could say the same for all of Colombia, was predisposed to convert itself into the paradise of cocaine, the best business in the world."
>
> —Employee of the Cali Cartel[35]

Colombia entered into cocaine export for the same reason it entered the marijuana trade. Strangers came looking for the illegal commodity, offering to pay handsomely for it. Beyond that there were notable differences in Colombia's marijuana and cocaine businesses, and they collectively explain why the one was a fleeting part of the country's economic profile and the other became an ongoing aspect of it.

The first difference has to do with the nature of the export itself and the way it is manufactured and marketed. Marijuana is not a tropical plant, but rather a weed easily grown in any climate zone. Dried and smoked like tobacco, its alkaloids are delivered to consumers simply and directly. Cocaine is the highly refined derivative of the tropical coca plant. More than two hundred kilos of coca leaves are required for the manufacture of a single kilo of cocaine. Therefore cocaine is mass-produced only when it can draw on tens of thousand of hectares planted in coca, tended by thousands of campesinos, known as *raspachines*, who deliver the leaves to processing centers usually located near the fields. There the coca leaves are transformed into the paste from which cocaine is made.[36] The paste becomes cocaine in laboratories, or "kitchens," that may or may not be near the source of coca leaves. All of this implies considerable involvement of labor, physical facilities, chemical ingredients, technological know-how, and transportation resources, brought together within an armed setting and in a climate of secrecy owing both to the industry's illegality and its lucrative nature. And this describes only cocaine manufacture. It says nothing of the complex fiscal infrastructure supporting the endeavor, the complicated and dangerous delivery of the finished product to market, the banking of profits, or the remission of profits to those running the business. Cocaine manufacture is, in short, vastly more complex than marijuana production.

The cocaine industry became rooted in Colombia's heartland, whereas the country's *bonanza marimbera* was an ephemeral phenomenon taking place in one of the country's peripheral regions. The cocaine business was in Colombian hands almost from the start, unlike the marijuana trade, which followed the traditional pattern of Third World raw material exports controlled by foreigners who realized most of the profit. For these reasons the cocaine industry penetrated Colombian society much more thoroughly than did the marijuana business. As an immensely profitable enterprise initially centered in the country's principal cities, its largess was spread to many not directly involved in the trade, to members of the business community and to public officials at all levels and in all branches of government and administration.

As an illegal endeavor the cocaine industry attracted criminals from its earliest days. Within the business they enjoyed comparative advantage over the rest, many of them flourished spectacularly. The most cold-blooded and violent among them earned the nickname "cocaine cowboys." Thus Colombia's cocaine enterprise was from the onset violent in a way that the marijuana trade was not.

The cocaine industry became a cash cow for Colombia's revolutionary guerrilla groups. The country's first coca plantations and large-scale cocaine kitchens were located in frontier regions under guerrilla control, as were a significant number of cocaine processing installations. Guerrilla groups, most notably the country's largest, the FARC, wasted little time tapping into the cocaine business, which soon supplanted kidnapping and extortion as its chief moneymaker. Guerrilla expansion was simultaneous with and took place in many of the same places coca grew and cocaine was produced. The cocaine industry therefore invigorated the guerrillas' revolutionary project in a way the marijuana trade never did.

In all these ways cocaine subverted Colombia more thoroughly than did marijuana. It also generated much more money and over a much longer period of time, making its disruptive effect greater over time. The cocaine industry was a cancer growing in Colombian society, corrupting it as it spread. Like cancers afflicting the human body it attracted little attention at first, eventually invading and attacking vital organs of state and society.

Colombia's cocaine and marijuana industries were capitalist enterprises par excellence, enjoying explosive growth that fed on demand so powerful as to be undeniable. In this regard they stand as ideal examples of the demand-supply dynamic at the core of market capitalism. Money talks, and the money offered by American drug users was available instantly and in quantities undreamt of by Colombians at any previous time in their country's history. The illegal drug trade illustrates the trouble states have in controlling markets, particularly illegal ones. The U.S. government has historically been unsuccessful in keeping its citizens from consuming proscribed substances. It took the Colombian government an exceedingly difficult quarter-century to reduce its drug traffickers' ability to freely supply the gringos the drugs they demand. At the outset neither government perceived the magnitude of the illegal enterprise until years after it had exploded upon the scene. Eventually the two states were able to bring the illegal drug trade under control, but only after a fashion and at great expense to both.

U.S. failure to control illegal drug use by its people has a long history. Ever since the U.S. led the world in outlawing opiates and cocaine, first at the Hague Convention in 1912, and later at the League of Nations during 1919-20, recreational drug users in the U.S. and the world happily circumvented national prohibitions. During the 1920s legal cocaine and opiate production for medical purposes totaled thirty tons per year; another one hundred tons were legally manufactured and found their way into the hands of users.[37] Save during World War II, when Asian and Latin American supply routes for opiates and cocaine were disrupted, the drugs were readily available to consumers in the Americas and elsewhere. Cole Porter thought nothing of introducing his 1934 tune "I Get a Kick out of You" with the words "I get no kick from cocaine." Although the lyrics were changed after the U.S. government demonized selected drugs in the 1940s and '50s, Americans continued to consume cocaine and all the others as well. Following World War II a significant quantity of illegal drugs consumed in the U.S., particularly cocaine, passed through Cuba, where Mafia dons like Santos Traficante, Jr., in company with local traffickers, transshipped supplies produced in Chilean laboratories. After Fidel Castro's takeover of the island in 1959 most of the Mafia and Cuban traffickers shifted their operations to Miami.

Prior to the rise of the U.S. drug culture relatively small amounts of cocaine were consumed in the United States, usually by members of the Mafia elite and by Bohemians like novelist William Burroughs.[38] But the 1960s found cocaine gaining in popularity, first among members of the artistic community, especially musicians. During the middle years of the decade rock groups like the Beatles and the Rolling Stones experimented with the drug and popularized it through some of their songs. Other trend-setters followed their lead. Actor Dennis Hopper, who co-starred in the 1969 box office hit *Easy Rider,* selected cocaine as the drug praised by the Mexican trafficker who handed it over to the Americans, referring to it *"pura vida!"* Hopper, who referred to cocaine "the king of drugs," later took credit for having popularized it in the United States.[39] Around the year 1969 anti-drug agents in the United States started hearing rumors of Colombian involvement in the cocaine trade. But they dismissed them. One former BNDD employee recalled that when the subject of possible Colombian cocaine production came up everyone in his office dismissed it as being "beyond them."[40]

Agents of the BNDD could be forgiven for not knowing about Colombia's entry into cocaine manufacture. Although in 1969 small amounts of the drug were already being made in the country, Colombia had no prior history of significant cocaine manufacture.[41] Agents could likewise be excused for their ignorance of Colombia's entrepreneurial tradition and of those who best exemplified it, the people of Antioquia, known everywhere in the country as the *paisas.* Antioquians were renowned in Colombia and elsewhere for their industrious nature, qualities that during the 1930s had earned them the label "the Yankees of South America." Their department was prosperous within the Colombian setting, a center of gold and nickel mining, coffee production, and textile manufacturing. So it is hardly surprising that when the cocaine industry rose in Colombia *paisas* were closely associated with it.

Two chemists from Medellín, brothers named Tomás and Hernán Olózaga, pioneered cocaine manufacture in Colombia. From the late 1940s they processed morphine, heroin, and cocaine for sale to the Mafia in Cuba. As the amounts they sold were small they attracted little attention. That changed in 1959 when Fidel Castro came to power in Cuba, bringing the island under intense U.S. scrutiny. Less than five months after Castro's success, on May 22, 1959, Bogotá's *El Espectador* published a five-column front-page story on the Olózaga's arrest at their home in Medellín's well-to-do El Poblado neighborhood, charged with selling five pounds of heroin to Cuban traffickers for $350,000. The article also detailed the brothers' long history in the illegal drug trade. While they made cocaine chiefly with Peruvian paste, some of their paste came from Colombia's traditional coca growing region of Tierradentro, in the department of Cauca. Their heroin was made from opium gum imported from Asia and brought into the country through Ecuador.[42]

Little more was heard on the subject of cocaine in Colombia for another ten years. It was only at the end of the 1960s, as demand for the drug grew in the United States, that *paisa* contraband traders operating out of the Colón, Panama, free-trade zone were asked by Americans whether they had cocaine. When the Colombians said no, the gringos followed with the question "Why not?"[43] With the drug selling in the U.S. at the time at up to $45,000 per kilo, it was a question the *paisas* were soon asking themselves.

Antioquia was well suited as a center of Colombia's early cocaine trade. It had access to the outside world through the Gulf of Urabá, used by *paisa* merchants since colonial times for the transport of illegal merchandise. They had also smuggled goods to and from Panama across the Isthmus of Darien, making use of the Atrato River which linked the Isthmus and the Gulf of Urabá. In modern times smugglers increasingly flew their merchandise in, using DC-3s and DC-4s for the transport of untaxed cigarettes, liquors, and electrical appliances. Contraband activity increased markedly after Carlos Lleras Restrepo imposed strict import and currency controls in the mid–1960s. So at the time foreign drug traffickers started asking for cocaine Colombian contraband runners already had a well-established transportation network featuring clandestine airports extending from Antioquia across the Andes to the Eastern Llanos and into the Amazon watershed. They also had links with members of the Emerald Mafia headquartered in Bogotá, with whom they worked to move contraband gemstones out of the country. Paisa contraband runners had links as well with officials at the custom house in Turbo, the chief port of the Gulf of Urabá, and with money changing houses and betting parlors in Medellín.[44] They were, in short, perfectly positioned to add cocaine to their line of illicit merchandise.

Still other external factors eased Colombia's entry into the cocaine trade. As with the case of marijuana, during the late 1960s young American traffickers descended upon the country in search of the drug. At first they had trouble finding it. In 1969 the trafficker Antonil was able to locate just a single cocaine kitchen in the southern part of the country. It was operated by an Ecuadorian who had taught the locals how to make paste from locally grown coca. A year later, in 1970, Antonil was able to buy a small quantity of the drug in a Bogotá alleyway. But it was cocaine legally manufactured in the city by the pharmaceutical company Merke. At that time about the only available Colombian-made cocaine was that pilfered by employees of Merke, along with that provided by functionaries working at the Colombian Ministry of Health or obtained from local physicians. It sold at a bargain price of $8,000 per kilo.[45] In 1970 a young New Yorker named Zachary Swann vainly wandered the beaches of Santa Marta, his finger on his nose, searching for someone who would sell him cocaine. Swann repeated that tactic on the beaches of Barranquilla, again without success. At length he made contact in Barranquilla with a Colombian who took $3,000 in exchange for a half-kilo of cocaine heavily adulterated with borax, aspirin, and amphetamines. In 1971 Swann visited Bogotá where, after considerable effort, he was able to buy several kilos of cocaine that he smuggled back to the U.S. Swann's brief career in the cocaine trade ended when he was arrested in the U.S. in 1972. By that time, however, aspiring foreign cocaine traffickers were swarming into Colombia hoping to duplicate their colleagues' earlier success in marijuana-producing areas along the Caribbean coast.[46] Unfortunately for them police had no trouble spotting the would-be drug smugglers and arrested them in droves. By 1973 ninety-six mostly young and mostly gringo traffickers languished in Colombian prisons.[47] They had learned the hard way that cocaine was not simply there for the taking.

Cuban and Chilean traffickers learned a similar lesson during 1970 and 1971. Each had hoped to eliminate the other by making Colombians into their junior partners in the cocaine trade.[48] But the Colombians swiftly pushed them aside and took over the business. Chilean traffickers suffered an additional blow following the September 1973 coup led by Augusto Pinochet. One of the dictator's first acts was to deport them to stand trial in the United States. A few of those fortunate enough to escape made their way northward, finding work in Medellín, Cali, or Bogotá.

By 1971-72 Colombians understood fully that the gringos were avid for cocaine, and that they could provide it for them. Two of the first to do so were an established Medellín contraband merchant named Alfonso Gómez, known as "El Padrino" (The Godfather), and the head of a Cali car theft ring named Gilberto Rodríguez Orejuela. By the mid–1970s the two emerged as Colombia's leading cocaine traffickers.

Alfonso Gómez used his numerous clandestine landing strips to transship Chilean cocaine and Bolivian paste through the Amazon River town of Leticia. He flew the paste to Bogotá where he had built a laboratory to process it. The cocaine was sent from there to Antioquia where it was transferred to larger planes that flew it to Matamoros, Mexico and then smuggled into the U.S.[49] According to the national security agency DAS, cocaine paste first started moving through Leticia in 1971. By 1973 more than a ton of paste was smuggled annually through the Amazon River port city.[50]

Gilberto Rodríguez Orejuela began his career at the same time as Gómez, but under less propitious circumstances. He had no airplanes at his disposal and therefore no easy access to either Chilean cocaine or Bolivian paste. So he started by smuggling paste in from Peru, at the time South America's greatest producer of both coca leaf and paste. Initially Rodríguez used mules (drug smugglers) to transport a few kilos at a time to Cali, where he established a cocaine kitchen. One of his most proficient assistants was an attractive and petite young woman nicknamed "La Chiqui" who made over a dozen trips to Lima, successfully returning each time with several kilos of paste, some of which she transported in her vagina. Soon Rodríguez perfected the technique of driving to Peru via the Pan American Highway, and returning with ever larger loads hidden in his car. The ploy worked until 1975 when he was arrested in Lima and charged with possession of 200 kilos of paste.[51]

As Rodríguez Orejuela, Alfonso Gómez, and others like them labored to send ever-larger shipments of cocaine northward, they dispatched friends, family members, and business associates to the United States to handle cocaine distribution, collect payments, and remit their earnings. They also made use of hundreds of mules. One observer remembered them as like "an army of ants" traveling to the United States carrying small quantities of cocaine hidden in their clothing, taped to their bodies, hidden in their shoes and in double-sided suitcases, and in their stomachs.[52] Once in the U.S. some mules stayed on to coordinate distribution, remit profits, and to deal with competitors. One of the most competent was twenty-nine year old Griselda Blanco, who arrived in New York in 1973 and supervised the violent removal of Cuban distributors from the city. She thus repeated what the Cubans had done to gringo distributors during 1971 and 1972. Police in New York had some idea of the turf war raging on city streets, and they noted that by 1973 more cocaine than heroin was being sold in the city.[53] The reason became clear a year later when Griselda Blanco was indicted by a Brooklyn Federal Court, charged with distributing 150 kilos of cocaine. Soon thereafter Blanco jumped bail and fled to Miami, where she quickly earned the reputation as the top cocaine distributor and assassin in the U.S.[54]

Not all of Colombia's early cocaine traffickers had criminal backgrounds. Medellín's Jorge Luis and Fabio Ochoa came from a middle-class family having no prior link to either contraband or narcotics. As young men they worked in a family restaurant located near the Medellín stockyards. At length Jorge Luis moved to Miami where he opened an import-export furniture company and enrolled in classes at a nearby college. When one of his teachers asked for help in buying cocaine, he had his brother Fabio locate a half-kilo of the drug and send it to Miami hidden in the heels of shoes worn by a relative. At the time it hardly seemed like a criminal act, and in later years Fabio Ochoa insisted that he was a businessman and not a criminal.[55] It's fair to point out that in the United States at the time cocaine was viewed as not a particularly dangerous drug, and government officials had a liberal attitude toward its consumption. Later, when Fabio Ochoa joined with other traffickers to fight extradition to the U.S., he blasted the Americans as having lured Colombians into supplying them cocaine and then ungratefully turning on them. The logic of his argument notwithstanding, the Ochoa brothers soon became important cocaine traffickers and founders of what would later be known as the Medellín Cartel.[56]

Ochoa could also have blamed members of Medellín's business community for encouraging his trafficking. Many of them quietly bought into the cocaine business by purchasing shares in shipments, a system known as *apuntería*, which brought a return of between 40 and 50 percent receivable almost immediately. Cocaine trafficking was a stupendous business. In the mid–1970s the drug flowed into the United States virtually undetected, reaching consumers with apparently limitless funds for purchasing it. In 1977 U.S. trafficker Jorge Jung easily found a dealer in Los Angeles who begged him for as much cocaine as he could supply at a price of $37,000 per kilo. His suppliers in Medellín scrambled to comply and soon were sending between fifty and a hundred kilos weekly into southern California. Within four years the flood of cocaine reaching Los Angeles had become a torrent. The host of the 1981 Academy Awards ceremony remarked that the film industry's greatest revenue earner that year was Colombia, the country, not the studio. It was a common practice to cut high-quality cocaine, thereby doubling its value. Thus a kilo of cocaine selling for $40,000 in New York or Boston reached the street having earned the retailer $80,000, this at a time when the dollar was the world's most powerful and prized currency. At those prices Colombian cocaine was literally worth its weight in gold. The twenty, fifty, and hundred dollar bills exchanged for the drug averaged three times the weight of a kilo of cocaine, forcing traffickers to find inventive ways of banking the cash or sending it home.[57]

At first Colombia's cocaine *nouveaux riches* sent the cash home hidden in freight. One of Gilberto Rodríguez Orejuela's associates remembered waiting on the docks of Colombia's Pacific Ocean port city Buenaventura, along with the redoubtable "La Chiqui," to receive a shipment of electric appliances crammed with smuggled currency. Jorge Luis Ochoa, of the Medellín trafficking group, sent cash back hidden in crates of furniture and in hollowed-out table legs. When the flood of U.S. currency became too great, the traffickers turned to money laundering, banking the cash and transferring it to legitimate businessmen in exchange for peso deposits at home. They started investing in real estate, expensive cars, and jewelry, both at home and in Miami. They also favored the four-door Toyota SUV, which the locals soon christened narco–Toyotas.[58]

By the mid–1970s Colombia's cocaine industry was well established. Cocaine kitchens had proliferated across the country and the sky was filling with planes transporting loads of paste into the country from Peru and Bolivia. Peru's coca leaf harvest totaled a staggering twenty million kilos in 1974, and Bolivia's crop was not far behind that.[59] Meanwhile Colombians began growing their own coca in increasing quantities, mostly in Vaupés, Caquetá, and Putumayo, all part of the Amazon watershed. In 1974 and again in 1979, newspapers carried reports of the army destroying fields of coca in Vaupés. Meanwhile, five hundred kilometers to the west along the Caguán River, in the department of Caquetá, settlers viewed coca as a new source of wealth for their frontier region.[60]

From the beginning Colombia's cocaine traffickers had dreamt of the day they could control all aspects of production, which implied substituting domestically produced paste for that imported by air. Planting coca and chewing its leaves had never been a tradition in Colombia. But coca was a tropical plant and Colombia a tropical country. Thus there was no problem with growing it there. And paste was easy to make in the field. It was only necessary to soak the coca leaves in an alkaline solution such as lime, causing them to release their fourteen alkaloids, one of which was cocaine. After the leaves were soaked for a day, kerosene was introduced which absorbed the alkaloids and allowed the leaf pulp to be strained out. Sulfuric acid was then added to precipitate the salts held in the kerosene solution, one of which was cocaine sulfate. The kerosene was then siphoned off and lime added to it to neutralize the acid, a process which left a grayish residue called paste, or *pasta*.

Once paste was delivered to a cocaine kitchen it was subjected to further processing to create cocaine base, at a 2.5 to 1 paste-base ratio. The base was then dissolved in ether and mixed with hydrochloric acid and acetate, resulting in the creation of cocaine hydrochloride.[61] By the time Colombians had started processing substantial amounts of domestically produced paste in the mid–1980s, it sold for $600 per kilo. Meanwhile a kilo of base sold for $1,800 and a kilo of cocaine for $6,000.[62] Still most of the paste refined in Colombian laboratories continued to be flown in from Peru and Bolivia. This would continue to be the case until the decade of the 1990s.

The year 1976 was important in the history of Colombia's cocaine industry, for it marked a generational shift among Antioquian traffickers. It also coincided with increased police pressure on the traffickers as well as a spike in drug-related violence. In February 1976 Alfredo Gómez, along with several of his associates and numerous body guards, flew from Medellín to Bogotá to meet with their associates in the emerald mafia. Called a "summit" of drug capos, it was held in response to their concern over growing police pressure both in Colombia and the United States. The U.S. Drug Enforcement Agency had recently opened an office in Bogotá, staffing it with a Puerto Rican agent named Octavio González. A month earlier, January 1976, police in New York had arrested their key distributors, men and women associated with Griselda Blanco, now in hiding in south Florida. When the Antioquian traffickers adjourned their meeting and prepared to board planes at Bogotá's El Dorado, police appeared and a gun battle ensued. One policeman and one body guard were killed in the shootout. All of the capos were arrested and taken away to jail. On the way to jail yet another gunfight erupted as other body-guards tried, unsuccessfully, to free their employers. Although the capos were soon released the pressure proved too much for Alfredo Gómez, a diabetic with a weak heart. Gómez soon retired from the drug and contraband trade and moved away to Cartagena. He left behind one of his body guards, a twenty-five-year old with an extensive criminal background named Pablo Escobar. By the late 1970s Escobar emerged as a recognized member of Medellín's trafficking community, and by the early 1980s as the group's preeminent figure.[63]

Another key moment in the Medellín group's rise also took place in 1976, far to the north of Colombia in the U.S. state of Massachusetts. That's where former marijuana smuggler Jorge Jung was living when he received a phone call from former cellmate Carlos Lehder, inviting him to come visit Lehder in his home town Armenia, in the heart of Colombia's coffee country. Like Jung, Lehder had just been released after serving two years in the Federal Correctional Institution at Danbury, Connecticut, on a charge of marijuana smuggling. While cellmates, Jung told Lehder of how before his arrest he had flown large cargos of pot out of Mexico and across the U.S. to New England. As Jung spoke, Lehder worked out the puzzle that had bedev-iled Colombian traffickers throughout the early years of the 1970s: How could they introduce significant amounts of cocaine into the U.S. market? Suddenly Lehder understood. All he and his colleagues needed to do was pay American pilots to fly their product straight from Colombia into the United States. Daredevil gringo pilots like Jung could provide Colombian traffickers a pipeline running straight from the coke labs of Antioquia into the nostrils of rich Americans. As the Colombian in the bunk above him explained his idea, Jorge Jung suddenly knew, as he later recalled in the memoir of his drug-smuggling years, "I was going to get so fucking rich it was beyond belief!"[64] Not long after Lehder contacted him in 1976, Jorge Jung in fact became very rich.

Lehder and Jung put the plan into effect immediately. By 1977 the Colombian had estab-lished himself in the Bahamas, on a small island called Norman's Cay, just 250 miles southeast of Miami, and had started receiving shipments from Medellín, flown in by American pilots recruited with the help of Jung. Lehder established contact with a hairdresser in Los Angeles, also with Jung's help. The hairdresser promised him access to members of the entertainment industry and many others willing to pay several hundred dollars for a gram of high-quality of Colombian coke. It was a potentially vast market. Lehder rented a house in Beverly Hills and began receiving initial shipments, the first delivered to him by mules. Meanwhile he recruited pilots, purchased airplanes, and worked out the logistics of large-scale delivery. One of the first cocaine deliveries was made by Lehder's mother, who brought him eight kilos hidden in her suitcase. When Jung chided Lehder for using his own mother as a mule the Colombian replied testily "Everybody has to work, and she wanted a free trip to Disneyland."[65]

Soon Lehder no longer needed his mother's services. In August 1977 he began direct air deliveries of cocaine to the United States. The first 250 kilo shipment was provided by Pablo Escobar and flown into South Carolina by way of the Bahamas. It was then taken to southern California by land and quickly sold for $10 million. The transaction earned Lehder and Jung a million dollars each.[66] It also made Lehder famous among Colombian cocaine traffickers.

In 1976 cocaine muscled past coffee as Colombia's most lucrative export, and 1977 saw cocaine earnings outstripping coffee sales by half.[67] Cocaine production was now being estimated in tons rather than kilos and was gathering momentum fast. Between 1975 and 1977 the amount exported jumped from something approaching twenty tons to around fifty tons.[68] The year 1976 found Colombian cocaine flowing into the United States by air, land, and sea. Ever-larger caches of the drug were discovered on ships of the nationally owned Flota Gran Colombia line, as well as on ships of the national navy. When the Colombian Navy's flag ship *Gloria* reached U.S. waters to participate in that country's bicentennial it was found to be laden with cocaine hidden in a score of places. The ship's officers were implicated in the smuggling operation.[69] After Lehder and Jung opened U.S. skies to cocaine flights dozens of American pilots signed on to earn the $400,000 to $1 million salary paid for a successful flight, some of them offering their own planes for use by Colombian traffickers.[70]

Happily for U.S. and Colombian drug traffickers neither of their governments was aware of the scope of their activities or had an inkling of their implications. One of the few public figures who did was young Liberal party reformer Luis Carlos Galán, who, in a speech of 1977, blasted what he termed his country's "three great mafias," contraband traders, emerald smugglers, and drug traffickers.[71] Colombians listened to him with indifference, thus guaranteeing that the cocaine industry would have time to consolidate itself.[72]

Nor were Colombians especially concerned over the rash of drug-linked crimes that became apparent by 1976. Between 1973 and 1975 the people of Medellín had started finding the bodies of murder victims appearing around the city, and during that period homicide rates increased by ten percent per year. Most of the victims were thought to be mules who had somehow angered their employers.[73] The "Medellín Massacre" of late 1975 raised eyebrows, yet was seen by most as something limited to the criminal underworld. Violence increased notably in 1976, the same year DEA chief Octavio González was assassinated in his Bogotá office. His murderer, who was a U.S. citizen and a DEA informant, was himself shot dead as he fled the scene.[74] At about the same time there was an ominous development within the Medellín-Bogotá cocaine trafficking group. A spate of killing broke out among its members in what would soon be called the "Cocaine Wars." The blood-letting ultimately claimed the lives of hundreds of traffickers, in both Colombia and the United States over nearly ten years' time. The drug trade spawned violence even in remote parts of the country. Settlers in frontier areas like Caquetá watched in dismay as coca growing and cocaine-making began in their midst. As one of them remarked unhappily, "where there's coca there's violence."[75]

Drugs, Violence, Impunity

"The younger of the two girls, six-year-old Yadid, had been brought forward and executed in the same manner. It had not been so simple with seven-year-old Zuleika. She had clasped her hands to her face, and her body had tensed and flinched, as a rifle bullet slammed into her right temple.... After more than half an hour, with the child still moving, they had shot her again, this time above her left eye. Terror had contorted her face as she died."
—Journalist David McClintick on the 1982 execution of the children of trafficker Carlos Jader Álvarez by M-19 guerrillas[76]

Colombia's *Violencia* of 1947–1965 was mostly about politics and only secondarily about money. The new violence of the 1970s was mostly about money. Because illegal drugs earned unprecedented amounts of wealth, they generated most—if not all—of the new violence. As always had been the case, Colombia's iron triangle of violence and impunity stood at the heart of the growing lawlessness that drug money spawned. Once the new violence became generalized the country's weak state could not control it. The state's inability to protect its citizens grew in proportion to the burgeoning violence.

Before illegal drugs and the violence that followed in their wake, kidnapping presented the quickest route to substantial earnings for Colombian lawbreakers. And it was the left-wing guerrillas, often working in collaboration with ordinary criminals, who provided this preamble to the country's new drug-related violence. Almost immediately upon formation of the FARC and ELN in the mid–1960s, both groups seized upon kidnapping as the easiest means to raise the cash needed to build a revolutionary army. Unlike drug trafficking, an activity driven by market forces, the guerrillas' money-raising project was violent at the outset because it involved a capital crime. Sadly for Colombia, the guerrillas' kidnapping initiative and the country's illegal drug industry emerged nearly simultaneously. They inevitably intersected. A synergy of violence resulted from the coming together of kidnapping and the illegal drug trade, magnifying the disruptive force of each activity. Even worse, paramilitary action against guerrilla kidnappers and anyone seen to be associated with them became an inextricable part of this witches brew of Colombian drug money-inspired violence.

Kidnapping was negligible in Colombia prior to its "boom" starting in 1980.[77] In 1954 Colombia was scandalized when five-year-old Nicolás Saade, son of the vice-consul of Syria living in Barranquilla, was kidnapped for ransom. The crime was resolved in a matter of hours when police killed the man who carried out the kidnapping and rescued the boy unharmed. Later it was learned that a brother of the vice-consul had commissioned the boy's abduction. Although Colombia was sunk in the bloody *Violencia* at the time, people could scarcely believe that the life of an innocent child was placed at risk in such a manner.[78]

In little more than a decade after the Nicolás Saad incident in Barranquilla kidnapping was on the way to become routinized in Colombia. The father of Colombia's kidnapping industry was a campesino of southern Huila named Pedro Antonio Marín. His *nom de guerre* was Manuel Marulanda Vélez, but his nickname was "Tirofijo" (Sure Shot), for his prowess with a rifle.[79] One of Marulanda's first important projects after founding the FARC in 1964 was to plot the abduction of a wealthy industrialist named Harold Eder. During early 1965 Marulanda infiltrated his followers into Cauca where Eder had a vacation home, at length capturing him there and extracting a substantial ransom from the elderly man's family.[80] Other lucrative kidnappings followed and the practice was institutionalized at the FARC's Fourth Plenary Meeting in August 1969, where the kidnapping of "important personalities of the enemy, or of rich industrialists" was recommended to the group's members.[81] Other guerrilla groups followed the FARC strategy and started aggressive fundraising through kidnapping and extortion.

Colombians not formally associated with the guerrillas frequently assisted in their kidnappings. Later called "godfathers of the guerrilla" by paramilitary leader Carlos Castaño, who declared war on them, these guerrilla auxiliaries helped select victims, lent logistical support, and in some cases even helped negotiate the size of ransom payments—all in exchange for a percentage of the take.[82] Members of the criminal underworld collaborated too, especially when they sympathized with the guerrillas' cause. That was the case with Jorge Santacruz Londoño, a leader of Cali's Los Chemas gang. In 1969 Santacruz helped his friend Luis Fernando Tamayo, a founder of the ELN, in the kidnapping of two Swiss citizens, netting $700,000 in ransom. The money helped Los Chemas launch what eventually became Colombia's Cali drug cartel. Santacruz later had Tamayo murdered so he could keep all of the ransom money.[83]

Twenty-year-old Pablo Escobar also used kidnapping to raise the money, allowing him to launch his career in drug trafficking. His victim was a *paisa* industrialist named Diego Echavarría, whom he seized and murdered near Escobar's home town of Envigado in 1971. Although Escobar was never charged with the crime he was widely believed to have been its author and chief beneficiary, to the extent that his admirers in Envigado's criminal underworld started referring to Escobar as "Doctor Echavarría," or simply *El Doctor*.[84] Kidnapping contributed to Escobar's rise in an indirect way. Antioquia's first notable drug smuggler, Alfonso Gómez, hired twenty-five-year-old Escobar as one of several body guards among whose tasks was keeping the capo from being kidnapped. Thus Escobar had traveled with Gómez to the summit of drug kingpins held in Bogotá in February 1976. That allowed him to glimpse the world of the country's cocaine trafficking elite.

Political leaders and the general public played their own indirect role in the rise of kidnapping. Colombians were ambivalent toward kidnapping, especially when carried out by guerrillas. When a rash of kidnappings spread panic in Antioquia during 1974 and 1975, President Alfonso López Michelsen made a secret trip to the department to reassure members of the business community that the crime wave did not represent an authentic social problem. It is not known whether his words calmed the *paisa* leaders, though in a speech given three years later López was at pains to minimize kidnapping as significant new public order problem. López admitted that during his presidency 324 kidnappings and 417 extortionate kidnappings had taken place, but he assured his listeners that the crimes were nothing out of the ordinary and had nothing to do with terrorist or guerrilla activity.[85] As López Michelsen downplayed the significance of kidnapping many left-leaning Colombians accepted the guerrilla's logic that kidnapping was an acceptable way of relieving the oligarchy of its ill-gotten wealth.[86] Others not necessarily of the left wrote off the spate of kidnappings as a function of the general social decline spawned by an illegitimate political system. Meanwhile, political leaders were reluctant to take the guerrillas to task for their kidnappings because they hoped that if they treated them with humanity they might lay down their arms. When Belisario Betancur was elected President on a peace ticket in 1982, by which time the guerrillas' kidnapping policy was common knowledge, the subject was not even brought up during peace negotiations for fear of angering the guerrilla and upsetting negotiations.[87] This left Colombians at risk from kidnapping little choice but to fend for themselves.

Members of the country's burgeoning cocaine mafia used threats and violence to advance their industry. Pablo Escobar Gaviria provided a model for the violent trafficker, using his talent for mayhem to rise to the top of the Medellín trafficking group. First Escobar hurried his old patron Alfonso Gómez into retirement by having those in charge of Gómez's money laundering operation murdered. Once Alfonso Gómez lost heart and removed himself from the scene Escobar stepped into his shoes.[88] The young man surrounded himself with others like himself, recruited from the streets of Envigado and Medellín, and he installed them in a café on the southern outskirts of the Antioquian capital. They were blindly loyal to Escobar, fearless, and willing to carry out any task that he assigned. Variously called *sicarios* (hired assassins), *pistolocos* (crazy triggermen), and *gatilleros* (trigger men), they specialized in drive-by shootings carried out from the backs of motorcycles. Griselda Blanco had perfected the technique during her years in the United States, and it was she who taught it to Escobar. The assassins worked as a team, a driver and a passenger. Their weapon of choice was the MAC-10 machine pistol. Motorcycle assassins (*asesinos de la moto*) carried out spectacular shootings in Medellín during the 1970s, working with lists handed to them by their employers. The demand for trigger men was such that a school for training them was established near Medellín in 1980. By 1981 Medellín had recorded 500 drive-by shootings from motorcycle.[89]

The marijuana business also had its share of violence. In one incident three Guajira traffickers were killed in factional fighting. Afterward, as the three were taken to be buried, gunmen opened fire with machine guns, killing twenty people in the funeral procession. A notorious trigger man from the marijuana zone boasted having seventy kills to his credit, most of them beggars, prostitutes, and homeless people gunned down in the streets of Barranquilla. When his employers grew tired of his excesses they ordered him shot seventy times, once for each of his victims.[90]

As Colombia's guerrilla and drug-inspired crime and violence spiraled upward during the 1970s and early '80s the country's inefficient legal system became ever more dysfunctional. As early as 1972, *El Tiempo* had editorialized that foreign traffickers liked doing business in Colombia because it appeared to be "a country without laws."[91] And that was in a decade when 60 percent of homicide cases led to arrests. Twenty years later Colombia's legal system was in effect non-functioning, with just 20 percent of homicides leading to arrest, 6 percent to trial, and only 4 percent to conviction. Making matters worse, most crimes were not even reported, and the ones reported became bogged down in a legal system that functioned with excruciating slowness. In 1983, a year when nearly 90 percent of crimes committed in Colombia went unreported, 1.2 million criminal cases awaited action while 24,000 of 30,000 prisoners had no idea when their cases would be heard.[92]

The character of guerrilla and drug crime had much to do with this erosion of Colombia's already insufficient system of criminal justice. Families of kidnap victims were warned that if they informed police of the crime their loved one would be executed. When the police were called in the kidnappers usually executed the captive before fleeing. Extortion was rarely reported because its purpose was, after all, the purchase of security for a set fee. Thus the very people who were victimized both hindered law enforcement agents and encouraged extortionists and kidnappers. The national government declared negotiating with kidnappers to be illegal early in the 1980s, but the law was widely ignored.

Pablo Escobar's technique of dealing with criminal prosecution also damaged Colombia's legal system. Early in his career he adopted the strategy of assassinating those playing a role in his prosecution, whether witnesses, arresting officers, or court officials. Escobar also had his henchmen destroy incriminating court documents. Later he refined his system to include bribing judges to dismiss charges against him. Judges who refused his money were killed. It was a strategy known as "money or lead" (*plata o plomo*).[93]

No armed group benefited more from Colombia's turbulent late 1970s and early 1980s than did the M-19. Populist in nature and sprung from the stolen 1970 presidential election, the group captured the popular imagination as the communist guerrillas never did. The M-19 proclaimed its presence when its founders stole Bolívar's sword in 1974, promising to hold it until national politics became less corrupt and more in keeping with the Liberator's ideals. They went on to stage a series of riveting operations that included the kidnapping and execution of a labor leader in 1976, the distribution of pilfered milk to children in poor neighborhoods during 1977, the theft of weapons from an army base in 1979, the capture of diplomats attending a reception at the Embassy of El Salvador in 1980, and a successful 1981 military offensive in the southern part of the country carried out in collaboration with the FARC and the ELN.

A flamboyant *costeño* named Jaime Bateman Cayón founded the M-19. Bateman, who famously opined that "revolution is a fiesta," took pride in his organization's unpredictability and esprit. For him the M-19 was both a social cause and an expression of Colombian nationality. Bateman and the other leaders of M-19 took pride in the fact that they did not even know the number of their followers, or the details of their operations. M-19 leaders reveled in an operational atmosphere described as "folkloric disorder."[94]

Flexibility and populism without a fixed ideological center were the M-19's strengths. The movement could appeal to patriotism without being too specific, yet it easily found common cause with the communist FARC and ELN, carrying out joint operations with them as circumstances dictated. Yet there was a derivative quality in the M-19's tactics and operations. The group embraced the FARC strategy of kidnapping as a revenue earner, going on to demonstrate great proficiency in the practice. As urban guerrillas the M-19 studied and emulated the tactics of Uruguay's Tupamaro and Argentina's Montoñero urban guerrillas groups, even hosting a Montoñero consultant named Paco during early 1976.[95] In March of that year they kidnapped, subjected to a "people's trial," and then executed Colombian labor leader José Raquel Mercado on the charge that he had betrayed the working class. That was a reenactment of the 1970 Tupamaro's kidnapping and execution of U.S. agent Daniel Mitrione, dramatized in the popular 1973 Costa-Gavras film *State of Siege*. Seizure of the Salvadorian Embassy by the M-19 in 1980 was likewise modeled on another famous action of foreign revolutionaries, the Nicaraguan Sandinistas' capture of their country's parliament building in 1978. The M-19 copied the Sandinista mass kidnapping down to the detail of their eventual evacuation to Cuba following release of the captives. But the M-19 did the Sandinistas one better, flying away to Cuba with a large sum of money in hand, having extracted a considerable ransom from governments of the hostage diplomats.

The M-19 provides an excellent illustration of the violence-producing interplay between revolutionary action and illegal drugs. One of Jaime Bateman's childhood friends was marijuana trafficker Jaime Guillot Lara. Sympathetic to Bateman's movement, Guillot allowed the M-19 to smuggle weapons into Colombia on ships that he used for marijuana transport. He also lent the guerrillas his money laundering expertise, showing them how to use banks like the World Finance Corporation to help them move funds abroad for the purchase of weapons. Guillot, who retired from drug smuggling in 1982 and prudently fled to Cuba, also helped Bateman purchase armaments on the black market.[96] The fruits of Guillot's help were evident in a 1981 operation that stands as one of Colombia's most spectacular cases of weapons smuggling. Early that year M-19 operatives had traveled to Europe where they purchased a ship named the *Karina* and loaded it with a hundred tons of rifles and ammunition purchased in Belgium. They then sailed it to Colombia's Pacific coast via the Panama Canal, after off-loading several tons worth of the weapons in the Guajira. That portion of the cargo was loaded on a hijacked plane and flown to the FARC stronghold of Caquetá. At length someone in Panama informed the Colombian government about the *Karina*, and a navy gunboat apprehended and sank it. Of the Caquetá shipment, most of the weapons made their way into hands of the FARC, though the army did manage to seize 230 Belgian FAL assault rifles along with 27,000 rounds of ammunition.[97]

The same year as the *Karina* incident the M-19 began viewing drug traffickers as a poten-tially rich source of funds for their revolutionary struggle. Accordingly in October and Novem-ber of 1981 they kidnapped several traffickers and members of their families. Carlos Lehder was seized just outside his hometown of Armenia. A few days earlier M-19 cadres had kid-napped three children of the trafficker Carlos Jader Alvarez near their home in northern Bogotá. Lehder was able to escape, though he received a gunshot wound in the process. The Jader Alvarez children were not so lucky, ending up captives in the highland town of Gachalá, sixty-five kilometers northeast of Bogotá. On November 12, M-19 kidnappers seized Marta Nieves Ochoa, the sister of Jorge Luis Ochoa, on the campus of the University of Antioquia in Medellín. Her family was sent word that she would be released upon payment of a twelve million dollar ransom. Ochoa refused the demand. Rather, he called for the help of his friends and allies in the cocaine trafficking community. A few days later his closest associate, Pablo Escobar, hosted a meeting to address the kidnapping problem at his hacienda Napolés in south-eastern Antioquia. Over 200 attended, and Carlos Lehder, recovering from the bullet he had taken while escaping from kidnappers a month before, presided over the event. Those in atten-dance had begun calling themselves "the kidnappables" (*los secuestrables*). Among them were José Santacruz Londoño, enforcer of the Cali trafficking group, and Fidel Castaño, an Escobar associate who by that time had dedicated his cocaine-derived fortune to ranching and to fight-ing the FARC guerrillas, who two years earlier had kidnapped and murdered his father.[98]

The meeting resulted in formation of an organization the traffickers named *Muerte a Secuestradores* (Death to Kidnappers), or MAS. Each of those attending subscribed a million pesos ($33,000) to formation of an army charged with pursuing the M-19 until such time that they released Marta Nieves Ochoa. Pablo Escobar's anger against the guerrilla group was only slightly less than that of Jorge Luis Ochoa, Carlos Jader, and Carlos Lehder. Just a few months before the rash of kidnappings Escobar had met with M-19 leaders, donating $16,000 to their cause and saying to them "I am a man of the left." Now he felt betrayed by the guerrillas and vowed to punish them.[99]

December 3, 1981, was the day selected to announce the existence of MAS. It was a Sun-day, and Cali's America soccer team was hosting Medellín's team Nacional. Just before the con-test began a small plane circled the stadium and dropped thousands of leaflets describing MAS and giving a hair-raising description of the fate awaiting the kidnappers if they failed to imme-diately release Marta Nieves Ochoa. Among the things in store for them were their public exe-cution, and the murder of their family members and friends. A month later Carlos Lehder expanded on the content of the flier, publishing a document in which he blasted the M-19 for damaging the nation's economy and causing productive Colombians to flee the country. Iden-tifying himself as an ex–kidnap victim he called for the construction of a special prison for kidnappers equipped with the latest model electric chair from the United States, but equipped with a trap door at the bottom that would drop cadavers into an automatic incinerator.[100]

During the last weeks of 1981 and on into January of 1982 an army of some 200 heavily-armed *sicarios* fanned out over Medellín in search of M-19 members and anyone belonging to their support network. Most of the operation was carried out in and around Medellín, though other MAS contingents were active in Bogotá, Cali, Armenia, and elsewhere. Pablo Escobar put his own top gunmen in command of the organization, young men with nicknames like Arcángel, Yuca, Pinina, and Chopo. In short order they captured a dozen top leaders of Medel-lín's M-19 cadre, and tortured and killed scores of the group's lesser figures. As the slaughter gathered momentum frantic M-19 leaders begged Panama's Manuel Noriega and Venezuela's President Carlos Andrés Pérez to help mediate the conflict. Thanks to their help Marta Nieves' ransom was reduced to a modest $532,000, and the young woman was released unharmed on February 16, 1982. But by that time scores of M-19 members and sympathizers lay dead.[101]

Colombians were impressed with the expeditious way the traffickers had dealt with the Marta Nieves kidnapping, especially the way their army of *sicarios* had hunted down guerrillas the authorities had been unable to catch for years. It sent the message that the best route to handling the guerrilla might well be the paramilitary one, and it highlighted the ineptitude of the country's legally sanctioned police forces.

Unfortunately for Carlos Jader Álvarez MAS was not able to free his children. Jader was one of Colombia's lesser traffickers and therefore could not call on international figures to mediate his problem. Even worse for him, authorities in the United States had recently penetrated his trafficking organization, seizing monies he had planned to use to ransom his children. At length their M-19 kidnappers grew tired of waiting for the money executed the children of Jader Alvarez, in April 1982. Their deaths did not go unpunished. By late 1982 Jader Alvarez had tracked down and captured those behind the crime, undergraduate students enrolled at Bogotá's National University. When it became clear that the children were in fact dead Jader had his men take the kidnappers to a remote part of the Eastern Llanos, chain them to trees, and leave them to be devoured alive by creatures of the forest. It was a sad commentary on the state of law enforcement in a country where an aggrieved father was forced to exact a monstrous form of justice on behalf of his slain children.[102] The incident also serves as a metaphor for the interplay of guerrilla and drug violence making life increasingly dangerous for Colombians as the 1980s began.

The Cartels' Golden Moment, 1978–1983

> The complex became operational in 1983 with the arrival of laboratory technicians, camp supervisors, and a general manager. They began producing more than four tons of cocaine per week, and twenty tons per month. Whenever they topped those production quotas workers were treated to chicken dinners.
> Description of the Medellín cartel's Tranquilandia complex.[103]

Life was good for most Colombian cocaine traffickers during the interval of 1978 to 1983. Production increased exponentially each year, and lax control in both the U.S. and Colombia made manufacture and shipment of their product relatively easy. By then exports were being measured not in hundreds of kilos but rather in hundreds of tons. At last supply was catching up with demand, with Colombian cocaine dominating 75 percent of the U.S. market. Cocaine wasn't the only drug being exported. In 1982, an estimated 70 percent of the marijuana imported by the U.S., and 80 percent of Quaaludes, came from Colombia.[104]

Even better things were in store for foreign consumers of Colombian cocaine. Members of the Medellín group were constructing a cocaine-manufacturing facility in the eastern part of the country that significantly rationalized and expanded their export operation. In keeping with the high spirits of the moment they called it Tranquilandia (Tranquil Land), a place guaranteed to keep gringo consumers abundantly supplied with their beloved blow, which at the time was still considered a relatively benign drug in the United States. A psychology text published in 1980 assured students that consumption of the drug two to three times per week "does not create serious problems."[105] Pablo Escobar, the Ochoas, and Carlos Lehder were help-ing the gringos and in the process making themselves stupendously rich.

By the early 1980s members of Colombia's trafficking elite were among their country's wealthiest citizens. They owned fleets of airplanes tasked with flying Bolivian and Peruvian cocaine base to their laboratories, as well as dozens of trucks smuggled it into the country via the Pan American Highway. Scores of flights departed Colombia weekly for multiple desti-nations in the U.S. One American smuggler recalled that some clandestine strips resembled "miniature O'Hares in Chicago." Neither the U.S. nor the Colombian government was yet aware of precisely what was going on. When law enforcement seized a two-ton shipment of cocaine at Miami International Airport in March 1982, it was seen as an "early indication" of the magnitude of Colombia's cocaine trade. At that moment cocaine shipments from there were running upwards of 200 tons annually.[106]

The lot of Colombia's leading trafficker Pablo Escobar could hardly have been better. Having erased most record of his youthful indiscretions, Escobar was lauded for his good works in and around Medellín, especially for his construction of low-cost housing for the city's poor. In 1982 Escobar won a place in the national congress. Friends in high places whis-pered to him that some day he might even become President. Why not? Up to the year Escobar was elected to Congress as a *suplente*,[107] the government of Bolivia had been in the hands of the country's leading cocaine traffickers.[108] Escobar's colleague Carlos Lehder had progressed from using his mother as a mule in 1977, to purchasing an island in the Bahamas that he used as his base for smuggling ten tons of cocaine into the U.S. between 1978 and 1983. Lehder, too, had political ambitions. He founded a populist, anti-imperialist movement in 1982, and he announced his intention to use it to unite Latin Americans against the gringo oppressor.

Other leading traffickers focused more narrowly on business. By 1983 Jorge Luis Ochoa was anticipating the moment when the Tranquilanda complex would allow him send two tons of cocaine to the United States per week. In Cali José Santacruz Londoño was already shipping between 2,500 and 3,000 kilos of cocaine monthly to Panama, where it was reshipped to Tampa, Florida, in lots ranging up to 400 kilos each.[109] And the Medellín and Cali groups were not the only ones manufacturing cocaine and shipping it to U.S. and European destina-tions. By the early 1980s other trafficking families were operating out of Bogotá and Leticia, along the Caribbean coast and the Armenia-Pereira axis and elsewhere in the country.[110]

By early 1983 there seemed little reason to think that the good times would not last. There were a few lurking dangers to be sure, such as the extradition treaty that Colombia had signed with the U.S. in 1979. But public opinion ran strongly against the treaty and neither President Julio César Turbay nor Belisario Betancur had shown any interest in acting on it. Betancur's new Attorney General Rodrigo Lara Bonilla was making noises about coming down hard on the traffickers but during the first months at his post Lara had not acted on his words. Liberal reformer Luis Carlos Galán continued to rail against drug corruption, but he was far from wielding effective political power. In the meantime leading traffickers were wealthy and powerful, and tolerated by Colombians. Most citizens of the country saw the trade in cocaine and marijuana as neither dangerous to the country nor particularly evil. Best of all for the traf-fickers, they had friends in high places. Presidential candidates solicited their campaign con-tributions, befriended and protected them. The future appeared rosy.

One trafficker remembered 1978–83 as when Colombia bombarded the U.S. with cocaine and the U.S. bombarded Colombia with money. He meant it literally. After 1977, when Carlos

Lehder had shown how it was done, all of the leading traffickers used American pilots to fly large shipments of cocaine into the U.S. virtually undetected. Most famous among them was a young Louisianan named Barry Seal, a Vietnam War veteran who started flying for the Medellín group in 1981. Between that time and 1983 Seal made over a hundred flights between Colombia and the U.S., dropping his cargo over his farm near Baton Rouge, where it was collected by colleagues and turned over to the Colombians who handled distribution. Seal flew at night, and so low over the Gulf of Mexico, at what he called "sea-spray height," that he was never apprehended. During his career he flew over five tons of cocaine and hundreds of thousands of Quaaludes into Louisiana, earning some $50 million for his trouble.[111]

Jorge Luis and Fabio Ochoa made similar use of Florida pilots Jon Roberts and Mickey Munday, who initially retrieved cocaine dropped into the ocean off Miami. Later they moved their operation to an airport near Lakeland, in north-central Florida. They flew some thirty-eight tons of cocaine into Lakeland between the late 1970s and the mid–1980s, earning $2 billion for Pablo Escobar and his colleagues. The Medellín group paid the men $3,000 for each kilo reaching the hands of their agents in Florida.[112] Meanwhile the Rodríguez Orejuelas of Cali were working in association with the Meneses Organization, anti–Sandinista traffickers that received shipments from them for transport into Southern California. In 1981 alone Norwin Meneses and his relatives sold nearly a ton of cocaine in the Los Angeles area, earning $54 million.[113]

Panama was of great importance to Escobar and the rest during the golden moment of cocaine trafficking, especially after Manuel Noriega took control of the country following Omar Torrijos' death in mid–1981. The Panamanian strongman would do anything for money, and the traffickers had plenty of it. Noriega allowed trans-shipment of Colombian cocaine for a fee, and used Panamanian Defense Forces troops to escort plane loads of drug money to the country's national bank for deposit. Lax banking regulation made Panama Latin America's money laundering haven. Billions of dollars poured into the country, with Noriega keeping a percentage of it in commissions. In 1979 the Medellín group's accountant in the U.S., Ramón Milian Rodríguez, worked out an elaborate means of shipping cases packed with dollars to Panama for deposit in the country's national bank. The plan worded perfectly until May of 1983, when Noriega betrayed Milian to the DEA. Milian was subsequently sentenced to a long prison term.[114]

International events played into the traffickers' hands during the late '70s and early '80s. Neither the United States nor any other country of the region hesitated using drug money when it was in their interest to do so. U.S. intelligence services knew of Manuel Noriega's trafficking and in 1972 even recommended his assassination. Yet the U.S. government found it prudent to keep Noriega on the payroll as a valuable intelligence source on Cuban activities. Noriega's help became all the more valuable to the U.S. at the end of the 1970s, when the left-wing Sandinista regime came to power in Nicaragua. During the early 1980s Noriega allowed weapons and cocaine to reach the counter-revolutionary Contra rebels in Nicaragua. Meanwhile he helped Pablo Escobar ship cocaine through the Nicaraguan capital in collaboration with the country's Sandinista government.[115]

Cocaine played an ongoing role in U.S. foreign policy during the Contra War in Nicaragua. At one point Oliver North argued that money seized in anti-drug operations should be used to purchase weapons for the Contras. Ramón Milian did the same, offering to use drug money earned by the Medellín group for the purchase of Contra weaponry as part of a plea bargain with the U.S. government.[116]

Nor was Cuba immune to the lure of drug dollars. When Colombian traffickers began large-scale air transportation of cocaine, they received over-flight rights from the Cuban government, along with permission to refuel their planes on the island. Badly in need of foreign exchange, Cuba also provided banking services for traffickers like Jaime Guillot Lara, who had good anti–American credentials. There was evidence that the renegade World Finance Corportion simultaneously laundered drug money for Guillot on behalf of the M-19, revenues from M-19 kidnappings, and monies earmarked for weapons purchases by the guerrilla group.[117] At the same time the bank worked both for Castro's government and anti–Castro groups operating out of Florida, and for Miami-based Mafia dons such as Santos Trafficante, Jr.[118] It was a tangled web having drug dollars at its center. When it came to illegal drug money everyone was on the take.

Back home the traffickers continued to thrive. Official Colombia played its part, sometimes unwittingly. One of Julio César Turbay's final official acts before leaving office was to make ether a duty-free import, this just as the massively ether-dependent Tranquilandia complex was beginning its cocaine bombardment of the United States. And one of Belisario Betancur's first official acts was to grant tax amnesty to narco-dollar earnings. A Bank of the Republic official explained his reasoning: "Why should we drive all this money into the black market and into foreign banks?"[119]

Major politicians made liberal use of drug money to finance their campaigns during the 1982 election. Former President Alfonso López Michelsen, then candidate for a second term, met privately with Pablo Escobar and other leaders of the Medellín group, coming away with a substantial donation from them. The meeting was held in a downtown hotel and arranged by Ernesto Samper, campaign manager for López. Pablo Escobar's cousin Gustavo Gaviria and members of the Ochoa clan favored Belisario Betancur, donating the equivalent of several million dollars to his campaign. Some of the candidates suspected they were receiving "hot money" derived from the illegal drug trade and acted accordingly. López hurried away from his meeting with Escobar after just five minutes. Later during his visit to Medellín he failed to attend a lavish reception Escobar had prepared for him at Hacienda Napolés. Some politicians openly befriended the traffickers. Liberal Alberto Santofimio Botero welcomed Pablo Escobar into his Liberal Renovation movement after Escobar was expelled from the New Liberalism movement headed by Luis Carlos Galán. The man with whom Escobar won election as *suplente,* Jairo Ortega, had been the lawyer of Santofimio's friend, senior Medellín trafficker, "El Paorino" Alfonso Gómez. After the 1982 election it was estimated that ten percent of new congress members had received campaign donations from drug traffickers.[120]

Members of the business community, and of Colombia's most prestigious families, were equally happy to receive monies from the traffickers. They readily sold their family mansions and country estates to the drug mafia, invested in cocaine shipments, and attended the lavish parties thrown by Escobar to celebrate the arrival of cocaine shipments in the U.S. Businessmen in Medellín and elsewhere also helped the traffickers launder their money. They allowed them to deposit drug money in their Miami bank accounts, reimbursing the monies at home in Colombian pesos. They likewise paid traffickers in pesos for property purchased with drug dollars in Miami, and they encouraged traffickers to invest in Colombian-owned businesses in the U.S. Even the smugglers of contraband helped launder drug revenues. At one point Pablo Escobar bought the business of Colombia's largest smuggler of Marlboro cigarettes, thus converting the sale of contraband Marlboros into a money laundering operation.[121]

The Medellín trafficking group led the way in rationalizing and improving the cocaine industry. Pablo Escobar had paste dryers installed in Bolivia to help cut transportation costs, even as he sped import substitution by having Peruvian coca planted in jungles of the Orinoco and Amazon watersheds. He and the Ochoa brothers improved efficiency and increased profits by assigning specialized tasks to themselves and to their principal associates: Escobar bribed public officials and supervised the importation of chemicals used in cocaine processing, the Ochoa brothers oversaw air transportation of the product to the United States, Gonzalo Rodríguez Gacha supervised the Tranquilanda manufacturing complex in Caquetá, and the loquacious Carlos Lehder managed Tranquilandia's cocaine kitchens and handled the group's press releases.[122] Meanwhile new product lines were being developed in Colombia and the U.S. to help stabilize prices and maintain consumption levels. Early in the 1980s Colombians started smoking *bazuco,* a highly addictive form of cocaine base, while in the U.S. crack cocaine was invented and instantly became the craze in urban ghettos.

As these developments took place officials in both Colombia and the United States remained astonishingly unaware of the magnitude of the cocaine industry and its social impact. This was in spite of the fact that by the early 1980s illegal drugs had come to represent 5.3 percent of Colombia's gross domestic product, outpacing coffee's 4.5 percent and petroleum's 1.9 percent. In the U.S. law enforcement officials were the first to become aware of the flood of cocaine and to observe the violence it generated. In 1984 the police chief of Los Angeles had denounced the cocaine trade and the problems it brought, proclaiming the situation to be "totally out of hand." That year an estimated 18,000 shipments of cocaine, marijuana, and Quaaludes were flown into the U.S., with only ten percent of the shipments being intercepted by authorities.[123]

Of all those who flourished during the golden moment of cocaine trafficking, Carlos Lehder was the most flamboyant. Lehder had returned home to Armenia late in 1978, his Bahamas operation well established and generating millions of dollars annually. Lehder began spending his money with abandon. He built a Bavarian-motif theme park on the outskirts of Armenia, featuring a large nude statue of John Lennon. Angered when the DEA placed his Norman's Cay operation under surveillance at the end of 1981, he printed leaflets reading "Nixon-Reagan Drug Enforcement Agency Go Home" and had them dropped over Nassau during the Bahamas' independence-day celebration in July 1982. That same year found him contributing generously to Liberal party candidates and joining other traffickers in attacking the 1979 Colombo-U.S. extradition treaty. Lehder's campaign against the treaty and his effort to convince the Colombian public that cocaine trafficking was an honorable profession were transformed into a political movement during 1983. On March 11 of that year Lehder launched his National Latin Movement, an odd amalgam of anti-imperialism, populism, and nationalism, seasoned with crypto-fascism and a hint of violence. Through speeches, and through his party newspaper *Quindío Libre,* he portrayed himself as a friend of the poor and a supporter of guerrilla groups battling for social justice. He compared drug traffickers to the 1920s whiskey smuggler Joe Kennedy, father of U.S. President John F. Kennedy, and he advocated legalizing personal consumption of marijuana and cocaine. During July 1983 Lehder traveled to Bogotá where he attempted to debate Justice Minister Rodrigo Lara Bonilla on the floor of Congress. He had planned to accuse Lara of hypocrisy for attacking cocaine traffickers in public while snorting the alkaloid in private.[124]

Lehder's strident attacks on the United States and members of his country's political establishment made him a person of particular interest in law enforcement and political circles. Just as he was launching his National Latino Movement, officials from the U.S. Drug Enforcement Agency were entering into conversations with Colombian counterparts aimed at bringing him to Tampa, Florida, for trial under terms of an indictment issued there in 1981. Yet none of that had been made public when Carlos Lehder flexed his political muscles in early 1983.

Like Lehder, Pablo Escobar was at the height of his power and prestige during early 1983. In April he was featured on the cover of the country's leading news magazine, *Semana*, which characterized him as a *paisa* Robin Hood who had risen from humble beginnings to become of one of Medellín's leading philanthropists. The closest the magazine came to suggesting that his wealth came from drugs was its remark that the origin of Escobar's fortune was the subject of considerable speculation.

Pablo Escobar was also outspoken in his opposition to the extradition treaty. To that end he enlisted the help of model and television personality Virginia Vallejo. Together they sponsored anti-extradition forums and participated in meetings of the Liberal Renovation movement, along with its founder and presidential hopeful Alberto Santofimio Botero. Santofimio had been the first to encourage Escobar's own presidential ambitions, and the *Semana* piece did nothing to lessen the *paisa* trafficker's sense of self-importance.

Escobar's rise had been meteoric from the moment when Jorge Luis Ochoa asked him for help in rescuing his kidnapped sister. As soon as Escobar's paramilitary army MAS secured the girl's safe release in February 1982, the grateful Ochoas organized a lavish dinner in his honor at a restaurant in south Medellín. The cream of the city's elite attended, along with the famous and the infamous of Antioquia's drug trafficking, contraband, and paramilitary community. Among them were Escobar's trafficking partners Gustavo Gaviria, Pablo Correa, and Gonzalo Rodríguez Gacha. Contraband importer Jaime Cardona Vargas, known as the Marlboro King, was there along with trafficker-turned-rancher and remorseless pursuer of EPL and FARC guerrillas Fidel Castaño. So too was Griselda Blanco, taking a break from her job as enforcer of the Medellín group's Miami office.[125]

Escobar's election to Congress occurred just a month after the dinner. Not long after that came an invitation from the Spanish Socialist Workers' Party to attend the inauguration of the country's new socialist president, Felipe González. Escobar traveled to Spain in late 1982 with Jairo Ortega, the man for whom he was *suplente,* and his political patron Alberto Santofimio. When he returned home Escobar was granted a U.S. visa, and in early 1983 he toured the United States with his wife and children, visiting Disney World, the Grand Canyon, and Washington, D.C.[126]

Not long after his return home Escobar was approached by an envoy from M-19 founder Jaime Bateman. The guerrilla leader knew of the *paisa* trafficker's earlier admiration of the M-19 and wondered whether there was hope for reconciliation—this despite the fact that Escobar had supervised the slaughter of the group's Medellín members barely a year earlier. Escobar assured the envoy that he had put the episode behind him as soon as the M-19 released Marta Nieves, and therefore welcomed the meeting. It never took place because Bateman died in a plane crash shortly after his overture to Escobar. When Escobar learned of the accident he sent his own planes to help search for survivors.[127]

In short, everything seemed to be going Pablo Escobar's way in mid–1983. He had power and prestige. Already one of the country's wealthiest men, his fortune swelled with each passing week. He owned nineteen residences in Medellín, each equipped with its own heliport, as well as rural holdings along the Magdalena River totaling thousands of hectares.[128] His real estate and business interests in Miami were extensive. At that instant there seemed to be little threatening the future of Escobar and Colombia's other cocaine magnates.

CHAPTER 3

The Cartels' War Against the State, 1984–1994

The Extraditables

"Pablo Escobar knew that he was just one misstep away from life behind bars in the United States. His hatred of extradition was a matter of both personal survival and national pride."

—Journalist Mark Bowden[1]

March 10, 1984, was an important date in both Colombia and United States, for that was when both countries at last grasped the scope of the Colombian cocaine industry. On that March day national police swooped down by helicopter on the Tranquilandia processing complex in far southeast Colombia, where they seized nearly fourteen tons of cocaine and destroyed laboratories that would soon have been producing over three tons of the alkaloid per month.[2]

It is little short of astonishing that neither country was fully aware of the cocaine boom in Colombia until nearly a decade after it had begun. By that time trafficking groups in Medellín and Cali had built a sophisticated and wildly profitable enterprise sending 200 tons of cocaine into the U.S. annually, most of it by air, and virtually undetected.[3] The first use of the word "cartel" in regard to the Medellín trafficking group had appeared in a DEA document a year before the Tranquilandia raid. U.S. officials had had their first inkling that Colombia was a major cocaine producer in March 1982, when Customs agents found two tons of the drug aboard a cargo plane at the Tampa airport that they traced to the Medellín cartel.[4]

When the good times ended for Colombia's drug mafia, they did so with lightning speed. During the latter part of 1983 Carlos Lehder and Pablo Escobar became wanted men, and by mid–1984 all of Colombia's leading traffickers had fled the country because of a nationwide crackdown on illegal drugs. From 1984 onward the threat of extradition to and incarceration in the United States hung over their heads. Pablo Escobar and his colleague José Gonzalo Rodríguez Gacha decided to oppose extradition openly, through bribes and threats, and, failing that, through violence and terror. As Escobar famously remarked, "Better a tomb in Colombia than prison in the United States." Members of the Cali cartel chose to oppose the state and its laws by funneling money to public officials, particularly those serving in the nation's congress.

53

They also used drug money to buy the cooperation of officers serving in the police, in the military, and in DAS and other national security agencies.

Both strategies ultimately failed. By 1993 both Escobar and Rodríguez Gacha were dead and the following year found Cali Cartel chief Gilberto Rodríguez Orejuela negotiating his surrender. He and many other members of the country's leading trafficking groups were eventually extradited to stand trial in the United States.

The Cartels' war against the State punished Colombia and drove violence to levels not seen since the *Violencia* of the 1940s and '50s. But unlike the *Violencia,* which led to the suspension of democratic rule, Colombia's drug violence of the 1980s and early '90s ended by strengthening democratic institutions. That was all to the good, for the long and bloody fight against the cartels was merely the opening act in a decades-long struggle pitting Colombia against the illegal drug trade and its attending guerrilla and paramilitary violence.

* * *

Pablo Escobar's fall from grace came suddenly during August and September of 1983, although his quick passage from admired upstart politician to hunted criminal was prefaced by a series of developments in the area of law enforcement dating back to 1981. That year two new anti-drug law enforcement entities were created, one in Colombia and the other in the United States. In 1981 Colombia transferred drug enforcement activities from the army to the police, at the same time creating a new police branch specialized in drug-related matters, Dijín, or Dirección Central de Policía Judicial e Investigación. At about the same time the U.S. opened Centac 26 in Miami, an investigative unit tasked with gathering information on the illegal drug trade in south Florida, and on the shocking drug-related violence that had rocked the city for more than three years. Thanks to its work, particularly through the electronic monitoring of telephone calls and short-wave radio communication, U.S. law enforcement agencies were able to arrest a great many traffickers and bring the cocaine wars under control by the latter 1980s.

Agents working in Dijín and Centac 26 quickly and rather easily compiled information on the leading lights of Colombia's drug industry, sharing it with officials in their respective governments. Thus it was that by 1983 Pablo Escobar's name was well known to law-enforcement agents both in Colombia and the United States, as were the names of most of his peers. Carlos Lehder was even better known and more hotly pursued than Escobar. Recently indicted by a Federal court in Jacksonville, Florida, Lehder was considered at the time to be Colombia's leading cocaine trafficker. July 1983 found a team of U.S. law enforcement officials, led by a U.S. Federal attorney, meeting secretly in Bogotá with their Colombian counterparts and attempting to arrange Lehder's extradition. The flamboyant Armenia native had made their work easier through his many public statements, especially the one he made in a Caracol Radio interview of June 28, 1983. During the interview he had bragged of "helping out" with Colombia's drug smuggling bonanza, thereby bringing much needed foreign exchange into the country. He took credit for keeping small-time smugglers from being "trapped like flies" in U.S. airports, "with their little suitcases and little boxes," without ever stating that it was he who had pioneered large-scale delivery of cocaine to the United States by air. Admissions such as these convinced Colombian authorities to issue an arrest warrant for Lehder on September 2, 1983. When he learned of it Lheder fled to the Eastern Llanos where he announced that he had joined the guerrillas to fight for social justice and oppose American imperialism.[5]

Unlike the talkative Lehder, Pablo Escobar worked hard to hide his criminal past. But like Lehder he opened himself to public scrutiny when he became active in politics early in the 1980s. That is why on August 16 and 17, 1983, he attended Chamber of Representatives sessions, in which recently appointed Minister of Justice Rodrigo Lara Bonilla debated Representative Jairo Ortega, the man for whom Escobar served as backup congressman, or *suplente*. The debate centered on the "hot money" that traffickers had spread so liberally among political candidates in elections the previous year. Lara, of the New Liberalism movement headed by José Antonio Galán, had launched a crusade against the corrupting influence of drug money in politics. Jairo Ortega answered him by producing photocopies of a million peso check that a trafficker named Evaristo Porras had contributed to Lara Bonilla's own political campaign. As the debate grew more heated Lara raised the name of *suplente* Pablo Escobar, accusing him of being one of Colombia's leading cocaine traffickers. It was the first time anyone in Colombia had stated openly what many people either suspected or knew to be a fact. Lara's words, however, set events into motion that ended Escobar's political career within a few weeks, and subsequently ended Lara's own life.

Eight days after the Lara-Ortega debate Bogotá's *El Espectador* published an exposé of Escobar's youthful criminal activities in Medellín, following it on September 6 with a front-page piece on the 1976 Envigado arrest of Escobar and his cousin Gustavo Gaviria for trafficking cocaine. Congressman Escobar reacted to the piece by ordering his men to buy up all copies of the newspaper in Medellín, Puerto Boyacá, and Puerto Triunfo.[6] Events moved quickly and crushingly against him after that. In the United States the ABC and CBS television networks picked up on the growing scandal, holding Escobar and Carlos Lehder up as examples of traffickers' infiltration of Colombian politics. The programs were widely reported in the Colombian press. Meanwhile judicial officials in Medellín re-opened the case of the two DAS agents who had arrested Escobar in 1974, and who were assassinated by the trafficker's *sicarios* in 1977. On September 23, Judge Félix Zuloaga ordered Escobar's arrest in connection with the killings. Then, two days later newspapers recounted a 1974 automobile theft attributed to Escobar, a case dismissed because two material witnesses in it were murdered before the case went to trial. One week later Judge Félix Zuloaga was assassinated in downtown Medellín. Hard on the heels of that public records linking Escobar to the case Zuloaga had been investigating were burned.

These revelations moved Escobar's political patron, Alberto Santofimio Botero, to ask Escobar to resign from his Liberal Renovation movement. By the end of September Congress started debating whether it should expel Escobar, doing so on October 26. That removed Escobar's immunity from arrest. Meanwhile justice minister Lara Bonilla impounded fifty-five aircraft owned by leaders of the Medellín Cartel. In October Lara informed Colombians that six of the country's professional soccer teams were either wholly or partly owned by drug traffickers. On November 17 Colombia's Natural Resources Institute fined Escobar for illegally importing exotic animals for the zoo he had built at Hacienda Napolés. On January 20, 1984, Pablo Escobar announced his retirement from public life.[7]

Most Colombians greeted these events with ennui. They tended to agree with the traffickers' contention that illegal drugs were more a problem for the United States than for Colombia. And they harbored an understandable dislike of U.S. demands that Colombia crack down on illegal drug production while doing little to stem the use of drugs among its own citizens. President Belisario Betancur was of the same mind. When he took office in mid–1982 he refused to sign extradition requests from the United States, and in late 1982 complained of the "Olympic disdain" with which the U.S. treated Colombia.[8] At the time Colombians were interested in the guerrillas, specifically in Betancur's efforts to reach a peace accord with them, something that had been his chief campaign plank in the 1982 election.

The end of Pablo Escobar's political dreams led him to refocus his attention on his main activity, the export of cocaine. In early 1984 he convened an important meeting of traffickers at one of his properties near Medellín. The meeting at Hacienda Doradal was to chart the Medellín trafficking group's course in the immediate future. With the Tranquilandia complex complete Medellín's traffickers planned to push exports to the United States to above 100 tons per year. That would significantly increase Colombia's total annual export of the alkaloid. Transportation dominated the discussions, namely how to increase drug flows to the United States through the use of larger airplanes. The trafficker summit was actually a series of meetings whose high point was a lavish luncheon hosted by the Ochoa brothers at a posh restaurant called Kevin's Disco, in the mountains overlooking Medellín. A buffet featuring quail eggs dipped in honey awaited guests, and the event culminated when a priest baptized the son of Rafael Cardona, the cartel's principal Miami operative. All leading cartel members were present, along with their several hundred heavily-armed bodyguards housed in an immense tent adjacent to the restaurant.[9]

Business and a baptism were featured themes of the drug summit. But the matter uppermost on everyone's minds was Pablo Escobar's recent series of setbacks. How, they wondered, would the cartel's chief enforcer respond to them? They knew that he was furious about his reverses and they worried that Escobar would respond with violence that they would all have cause to regret. Most knew, for example, that during the events of the past September he had contracted the assassination of Justice Minister Lara Bonilla, and of Lara's adviser Edgardo González Vidales. All hoped Escobar might be convinced to cancel the contracts.

Masked foreboding pervaded the meeting which outwardly was full of good humor and exquisite cordiality. Each man present knew that a harsh word, or even a raised eyebrow, might be interpreted as an order to kill by one of *El Patrón's* henchmen. Among those present were non-traffickers, most of them lawyers, bodyguards, and selected *sicarios*, such as Escobar's chief lieutenant Carlos Mario Castaño ("El Chopo").[10] Senior trafficker Santiago Ocampo was one of the first to speak. He advised the younger men to keep a low profile, to stay out of politics, and to avoid antagonizing the state. The Ochoa brothers and most other cartel members heartily agreed with him, and several of those present opined that if the cartel started murdering public officials it would bring the wrath of the state down upon them all. The conversation was a kind of minuet having life or death consequences. Escobar's henchman El Chopo broke the mood by wisecracking "Calm down, boys. If the state comes down on us then we'll just kill it too!" The remark brought hearty if uneasy laughter.[11] All present knew both that the subtle form of debate taking place had long-term implications for their mutual enterprise, and that Escobar would do what he wanted to do, probably violently.

In choosing to take up arms against the state Pablo Escobar was squarely within Colombian political tradition. Since the time of national independence Colombians had risen against governments they loathed, in the end usually negotiating favorable terms with the State they could not overthrow by force of arms. As he prepared his own war against the nation Pablo Escobar had studied Belisario Betancur's strategy to grant amnesty to guerrillas, some of whom had fought the state with blood and fire for two decades. He, Escobar, viewed himself as a political rebel not unlike the guerrillas, as a man of the left who had used his own money to build low-cost housing for the poor. So if he used terror against the nation, by assassinating its minister Lara Bonilla for example, he would be well within the tradition of Colombian rebelliousness. One hundred years of national history instructed Pablo Escobar that if he made greater society suffer enough it would eventually prevail on political leaders to forgive his crimes and, most importantly, not to extradite him to the United States.

The fact that he had long acted with impunity also shaped Escobar's thinking. Since the kidnap-murder of industrialist Diego Echavarría in 1971, widely attributed to him, Escobar had never been convicted of a crime—this in spite of the fact that over the past thirteen years he had routinely resorted to bribery, extortion, and murder of all those who had opposed him. His most recent victim was Judge Gustavo Zuloaga, murdered fewer than five months before for daring to re-open legal proceedings against Escobar. So in preparing his campaign of violence *El Patrón* included in his calculation the understanding that he could rely on Colombia's notoriously lax legal system and his phalanx of lawyers to help him avoid paying the price for future crimes.

Final among the reasons Escobar opted for violence was his confidence that the people of Antioquia would protect him from outsiders sent from Bogotá to prosecute him. He had a popular following in Medellín's poor barrios, and many public officials and police were on his payroll. And those not his supporters were terrified of his gunmen. Escobar's physical surroundings protected him as well. The cartel leader rarely strayed from his home turf, terrain extending from the barrios of Medellín to his extensive land holdings scattered throughout the Middle Magdalena region of Antioquia. These redoubts guaranteed him shelter in time of need. All this reinforced Pablo Escobar's conviction that violence against the state was his best option.

When the Medellín cartel adjourned its February 1984 conference all of its members were confident that even if they weren't entirely in harmony with one another on operational matters, their easy access to the U.S. illegal drug market would continue as it always had. They had little inkling that cocaine trafficking was about to become much more difficult, and that their giant cocaine processing plant in the southeastern jungles was targeted for attack. Their unsuspected but onrushing problem had begun ten weeks earlier, when one of their operatives in the United States foolishly placed a fifty-five metric ton order for ether at a plant in New Jersey, paying for it with $400,000 in cash. It was the sort of mistake made by someone whose illegal business had never been seriously scrutinized by law enforcement agencies. Legitimate ether orders were normally below one ton, while illicit ones for cocaine manufacture might run to between ten and twenty tons. A fifty-five ton order was unprecedented. A year earlier DEA agents had come to understand the importance of ether to cocaine production and had instructed manufacturers to let them know of suspicious purchase requests, particularly any made by Colombians. Thus the New Jersey ether manufacturer tipped off the DEA, which attached electronic homing devices to the bases of several ether canisters and monitored their movement southward to their stopping place in Colombia's southeastern wilderness. When the DEA station chief in Bogotá visited Dijín commander Colonel Jaime Ramírez on March 6, telling him they had located a huge cocaine production facility in the Amazon jungle, his response was "You must be kidding."[12]

The Tranquilandia raid took place on Saturday, March 10, 1984. As the Dijín helicopters prepared to land they were greeted by a few bursts of gunfire from the small force of FARC guerrillas hired to protect the site. The guerrillas quickly retreated and a few employees at the facility escaped across the nearby Yarí River. Otherwise only a few lower-level workers were caught, men and women who by their accents were identified as recruited from the streets of Medellín. Neither Rodríguez Gacha, who directed the Tranquilandia complex, nor Carlos Lehder, who ran its laboratories, or any other trafficker of consequence, was apprehended. Dijín learned soon afterward that an informant within the agency had leaked word of the raid twenty-four hours before it occurred. Members of the cartel had visited a brother of Dijín chief Ramírez on March 9, offering him three million dollars if he would convince his brother to call off the raid. At that moment Jaime Ramírez was at a police base directing preparations for the operation, code named "Yarí '84." A week later the Dijín informant's mutilated body was discovered near Bogotá along with those of two female companions.[13]

What police forces found at Tranquilandia was the world's largest cocaine processing facility. It was housed in a complex of settlements containing warehouses, laboratories, dormitories, aircraft and landing strips, scattered through clearings along the northern bank of the Yarí River, bearing the names Villa Coca, Coquilandia, Pascualandia, and Tranquilandia I, II, and III. All of the sites had been abandoned in haste, for large quantities of cocaine and much else besides had been left behind at the fourteen laboratories making up the complex. Along with nearly fourteen metric tons of cocaine and fifteen tons of cocaine base, the police discovered 11,800 containers of ether and large stores of acetone and other chemicals. Four small airplanes were confiscated along with fuel for them; numerous weapons were seized, including nineteen machine guns and ammunition for them. Documents were discovered linking the complex to the Medellín cartel and to the FARC.[14]

Officials in Colombia and the United States were delighted with the destruction of Tranquilandia, none more so than U.S. ambassador Lewis Tambs. When sent to Bogotá by the Reagan administration Tambs was instructed to search for evidence connecting Colombia's communist guerrillas with the drug trade, something he could now do. His instructions were part of the U.S. effort to subvert Nicaragua's left-wing Sandinista regime, part of the North Americans' historic Cold War commitment to oppose communism at every turn.[15] Not long after "Yarí '84" the undiplomatic Tambs coined the term "narcoguerrilla," earning him the anger of many Colombians, among them President Belisario Betancur, whose peace initiative with the guerrillas appeared to be bearing fruit. As for the guerrillas, FARC spokesman Jacobo Arenas brushed off charges of his group's involvement with the traffickers. He likened it to picking up a cash-filled wallet that one finds lying in the street.[16] When Pablo Escobar was interviewed shortly after the raid and asked about Medellín cartel links with the FARC he denied them, saying the question offended his personal dignity.[17]

All this was an unwelcome distraction for Belisario Betancur, who was only weeks away from what appeared to be an epochal cease-fire with the FARC. Yet Betancur's problems intensified five days after the Tranquilandia raid when M-19 guerrillas attacked Florencia, 225 kilometers northwest of Tranquilandia. The M-19, which had links with both the FARC and the Medellín cartel, had only recently established itself in the province of Caquetá, whose capital was Florencia. Their plan was to emulate the FARC's success in building rural cadres and cashing in on the department's growing cocaine industry.[18] The army drove the M-19 from Florencia with relative ease and the President's negotiators were able to sign a truce with the FARC on April 28, 1984. All hoped and many believed the agreement would usher in a new era of peace for Colombia. But then Pablo Escobar's assassins murdered Minister of Justice Rodrigo Lara Bonilla.

Lara's murder, which took place on the last day of April, 1984, had the signature of the Medellín cartel. It was carried out by two young men on a motorcycle, the passenger armed with a machine pistol that he used to extinguish the justice minister's life. The killing, the first of a sitting minister in the history of the country, shocked Colombians and jolted Belisario Betancur out of relative complacency about the illegal drug trade and its implications for Colombia. Within hours of Lara's murder Betancur had declared a state of siege under which the army and police could arrest anyone involved in the illegal drug trade. Accordingly traffickers could be arrested on sight, tried in military courts, and given long jail terms. When he announced the extraordinary measures in a May 1, 1984, radio address to the nation, Betancur referred to drug trafficking the most serious problem that Colombia had ever faced in its history, and he called for a "great national mobilization" against the traffickers. It was precisely the reaction that Santiago Ocampo, the Ochoa brothers, and most of the others had feared. Now the national spotlight was full upon them and no trafficker was safe in either person or property.

Colombia's trafficking community was shocked by the government's swift reaction to the Lara murder, none more so than Pablo Escobar. He had killed many times before and there had never been much official reaction. Just two weeks before the Tranquilandia raid Escobar's men had assassinated Lara Bonilla's adviser Edgardo González on a street in northern Bogotá and little was said about it. But now the whole country was up in arms and his arrest seemed imminent. It was time to flee.

Luckily for the drug kingpins, Panama's dictator Manuel Noriega provided them sanctuary. He had done so, at the bargain rate of four million dollars in October 1983, just as Pablo Escobar's criminal past was being revealed and his immunity from prosecution ended by Congress. So within hours of Lara Bonilla's assassination all of Colombia's leading traffickers, save Carlos Lehder who remained in the Eastern Llanos, had installed themselves in hotels in Panama City, from which vantage point they anxiously monitored the government offensive unfolding against their interests back home. They were especially horrified when Belisario Betancur, never a friend of the extradition treaty, announced that he would take full advantage of its provisions. One of his first official acts after declaring the state of siege was to sign the extradition order for Carlos Lehder.

Coincidentally, former President Alfonso López Michelsen had arrived in Panama City just as the traffickers began their exile there. López was in town as part of a team of international dignitaries sent to monitor Panama's election of that year. No sooner than his luggage was delivered to his room than his telephone rang. It was Jorge Ochoa asking for a meeting. It was a worried and apparently frightened Pablo Escobar and Jorge Ochoa who met with Alfonso López in a suite at the Panama Marriott on May 4, 1984. López knew the two men personally, having met with them in a Medellín hotel two years before when receiving their contribution to his presidential campaign. Escobar and Ochoa now wanted López to return the favor by telling Belisario Betancur that they were not involved in the Lara Bonilla assassination, that they wanted to return home as soon as possible, and that they would cease drug trafficking in exchange for amnesty and a promise from the government that they would not be extradited to the United States. López did as they asked and within three weeks Colombia's Attorney General Carlos Jiménez Gómez met secretly with the exiled traffickers, who then numbered some one hundred and included José Gonzalo Rodríguez Gacha. Jiménez López received the traffickers' six-page proposal to the government of Belisario Betancur. In it they pledged to quit the cocaine trade, to remit their foreign-held monies to Colombia, and to assist in the rehabilitation of their drug-addicted fellow citizens. All they asked in exchange was the lifting of the state of siege, a promise of amnesty for past crimes, and written assurance that they would not be extradited to the United States. They also asked that Betancur inform the U.S. government of their promise of good behavior.[19]

It is not known what parts of the agreement, if any, the Betancur government was willing to accept, for it was the United States held the key to the agreement's fate. And the U.S. dismissed it out of hand. Furthermore, the American embassy leaked word of the meetings and set off a firestorm of criticism forcing Betancur to publicly reject the initiative. U.S. interference at the presidential level also spoiled careful police work by the DEA aimed at bringing down the Medellín cartel. The cartel's premier pilot, Barry Seal, had become a DEA informer early in 1984 and was providing extensive and detailed information on the group's operations. On June 25 of that year Seal managed to film the off-loading of a large shipment of cocaine at the airport in Managua, Nicaragua, capturing on film an assistant to Sandinista Minister of the Interior Thomas Borge, as he helped none other than Pablo Escobar, and pilot Barry Seal, off-load the cargo.[20] Sunk in a covert war against Nicaragua's Sandinista government, the Reagan administration was unable to resist scoring political points against the enemy regime by leaking the Managua airport film to the press. That not only ended Seal's usefulness to the DEA but was his death sentence. A cartel hit team assassinated Seal in Baton Rouge in February 1986. No longer would Colombian traffickers entrust foreigners, least of all gringos, with intimate details of their operations.

By July of 1984 Escobar, the Ochoas, Rodríguez Gacha, and their fellow traffickers had departed Panama and slipped back into Colombia. By year's end leaders of the Medellín and Cali cartels were living openly in their respective cities, plotting how to rebuild their fortunes. The two preceding months had been hard on them. Barry Seal and the DEA had ruined the Medellín group's plan to make Nicaragua a new center of cocaine manufacture, and the U.S. government had filed indictments against leading cartel members for trafficking cocaine through Nicaragua. Manual Noriega had seized their Panama cocaine processing complex in the Darien rainforest, only narrowly escaping assassination afterward by Escobar's *sicarios* thanks to the timely intercession of his friend Fidel Castro.[21] Back in Colombia legal proceedings continued to move apace against cartel leaders. Superior Court Judge Tulio Manuel Castro Gil issued preliminary findings against Escobar, Rodríguez Gacha, and the Ochoas for the Lara Bonilla killing on August 14, following it with a formal indictment of them as material authors of the crime in October. At that moment five arrest warrants were pending against Escobar, including two dating back to the 1977 murder of the DAS agents in Medellín. The anti-drug crackdown had resulted in the seizure of sixty-three metric tons of cocaine and bazuco, the confiscation of 144 of the cartel's airplanes, and the destruction of eighty-four cocaine kitchens. Additionally, some 1,500 metric tons of marijuana were seized in the northern coastal region, and Belisario Betancur ordered the marijuana fields sprayed with the toxic defoliant Paraquat, sending the country's marijuana industry into permanent decline. Meanwhile the Dijín was hot on the trail of Carlos Lehder, coming close to capturing him on several occasions.[22]

Despite all this the Medellín cartel had little trouble recouping its losses and returning to the offensive in its battle against the Colombian state. Key to this was continued strong demand for cocaine in the United States and Europe. In July 1984 Jorge Ochoa sent four tons of cocaine to Los Angeles for use by visitors to the Summer Olympics, and that same year Cali cartel's José Santacruz Londoño set up several cocaine labs within the United States. In Central

America CIA agents turned a blind eye as Contra rebels helped move Colombian cocaine northward through Honduras and into the United States to help fund their insurgency against the Nicaraguan government.[23] Not long after returning to Colombia from Panama, Jorge Ochoa and his childhood friend Gilberto Rodríguez Orejuela and their families relocated to Madrid to better direct growing cocaine shipments to the countries of Western Europe.[24]

The destruction of Tranquilandia had the effect of strengthening the alliance between Escobar and Rodríguez Gacha. José Gonzalo Rodríguez Gacha lost a great deal of money in the Dijín raid and he was eager to resume cocaine production in eastern Colombia. This time he would be more careful, putting more space between his laboratories. And he would do a better job of hiding and protecting them. While he reestablished coca plantations and cocaine kitchens in Caquetá, he started building other installations north of there, in the departments of Guaviare and Meta, which lay closer to his home department of Cundinamarca. Rodríguez Gacha and Escobar continued to pay the FARC to help them guard their cocaine kitchens. Up to 1984 it was money well spent. On October 12, 1984, a FARC unit fought off a police detachment sent to raid one of the Caquetá labs. By late 1984 Pablo Escobar owned a 500 hectare coca plantation in the southeastern jungles, complete with its own laboratory and 100-man FARC column that both provided protection and helped with production. El Patrón visited the facility on December 24, 1984, so he could pay Christmas bonuses to its workers.[25]

So the loss of Tranquilandia was damaging but hardly devastating to Colombia's leading cocaine exporters. In a U.S. indictment handed down against them in early 1985, the Medellín group was charged with supplying twenty-five tons of the alkaloid to American users between the years 1981 and 1984. All things pointed to their continuing to meet to meet the robust demand for their product in the U.S. Although a kilo of cocaine rose to $27,000 in Miami following the Tranquilandia raid, its price had fallen back to $14,000 per kilo by year's end.[26] Better yet from the standpoint of the traffickers, crack cocaine had suddenly become the drug of choice in U.S. urban areas, driving up both the price and demand for cocaine.

As cocaine production recovered, Escobar intensified his struggle against all those who wanted to see him jailed for his crimes. His strategy against them was the same as ever, combining the best legal defense money could buy, and a strong offense featuring bribes, threats, and violence. A key task of his legal team was to supervise the massive bribery of public officials.[27]

Once the traffickers' negotiations with the government collapsed in July 1984, everyone taking part in the prosecution of Pablo Escobar, up to and including President Belisario Betancur, started receiving threats from Escobar's operatives. In late October someone phoned Tulio Castro Gil, the judge who had indicted Escobar in connection with the Lara Bonilla assassination, offering him a large sum of money in exchange for his dropping the case. The caller warned Castro Gil to consider the offer carefully, saying his boss had executed judges before. Castro Gil rejected the bribe and was assassinated in Bogotá nine months later.[28]

Similar pressure was leveled against representatives of the U.S. government in Colombia. Escobar sent word that his men would soon begin assassinating embassy staff and any Colombians or Americans working for the DEA. He underlined his threat with a November 26 bombing outside the gates of the U.S. embassy that killed a hapless female street vendor. At about the same time DEA agents in Medellín noticed they were being followed by men presumed to be Escobar *sicarios*. The trafficker's offensive produced almost immediate results. By the end of the year the DEA had closed its Medellín office and Ambassador Lewis Tambs and his family had fled Colombia, never to return.[29]

The year 1985 began with Belisario Betancur telling the nation he was steadfast in his war against the drug trade, which he termed a "filthy and degrading business," conducted by "bad sons of Colombia" who merited swift and rigorous punishment.[30] He acted on his words on January 5 by sending five Colombian traffickers to stand trial in the United States, the first ever extradited under terms of the 1979 treaty. Principal among them was businessman and owner of the Nacional Medellín soccer club Hernán Botero Moreno, accused of laundering $55 million through a Florida bank in 1981. The public was aghast, even angered, over television images of the heretofore respected Botero being led to and from his trial in shackles. They watched with morbid fascination as one of the lesser figures was condemned to fifteen years in a federal prison in a trial lasting just three months. Under Colombia's Napoleonic system any good lawyer could drag out a trial for years, usually getting his client off with little more than a slap on the wrist. But from the traffickers' point of view the events unfolding before them were indeed a serious and life-threatening matter. Belisario Betancur held fast to his extradition policy throughout the first half of 1985. By September six Colombian nationals had been extradited to the U.S., nine more were in jail awaiting extradition, and 105 requests from the Americans for "provisional arrest" of traffickers preliminary to extradition were pending.[31]

The extraditions created panic among cocaine traffickers throughout Latin America. For fifteen years they had suffered no sustained opposition from any government, not from even that of the Unites States, which had long sent mixed signals about the cocaine trade. The U.S. had tacitly permitted, even encouraged, the flow of cocaine through Central America when it knew monies earned from drug sales would help Contra rebels fighting to overthrow the leftist regime in Nicaragua. The executive branch of the U.S. government had thwarted DEA efforts to arrest Honduran trafficker Juan Ramón Mata Ballesteros, operator of an airline that flew Andean cocaine into Mexico and military supplies back to the Contra insurgents. The CIA and Department of Justice went so far as to close the DEA office in Tegucigalpa in 1983 to protect Mata Ballesteros' operation. At the time the Honduran trafficker was responsible for handling between one-third and one-half of Colombian cocaine reaching the U.S. He was integral to what drug agents called the "Mexican trampoline," by which Mata transported the drugs through Central America to members of the Guadalajara Cartel, which then "bounced" them into the western United States. DEA agents referred to Mata Ballesteros and his CIA-protected airline SETCO as key to the "explosion" of cocaine moving through Mexico and into the U.S. during the middle and latter 1980s.[32]

But now the United States was turning its fury against the traffickers. U.S. pressure was behind the arrest in Spain of Jorge Ochoa and Gilberto Rodríguez Orejuela in November 1984. During 1985 and 1986 the U.S. worked tenaciously, although unsuccessfully, to have both extradited from Spain.[33] And the U.S. gave strong support to Colombia's Dijín in its hot pursuit of Carlos Lehder.

The struggle to jail drug kingpins in the United States was an aspect of the historic contest pitting states against markets. It was all the more riveting during the latter 1980s, because at that moment the might of the United States was unrivaled in the world and its anti-drug laws the most punitive of any major power. When America began seriously addressing its illegal drug problem, the Cold War was drawing to a close, enhancing its status as global leader. At home the crack epidemic had started to ravage urban ghettos reviving historic fears among the white majority of drug-crazed blacks doing them harm. All of this is to say that even if Pablo Escobar had not ordered the killing of Justice Minister Lara Bonilla in 1984,

Colombia and the U.S. would have soon begun cooperating to send the traffickers northward for trial. Both countries were beginning to perceive the illegal drug industry's threat to national institutions.

During January and February 1985, police intelligence throughout the Americas picked up word that leading traffickers were plotting to punish the Americans for their extradition campaign. In late 1984 U.S. interests in Colombia were bombed, and by early the following year the names of U.S. Embassy personnel were circulated among *sicarios* on the Medellín cartel's payroll. The international trafficking community was offering sums as large as $300,000 for the kidnapping of any DEA agent. Meanwhile plans were being laid in Colombia to free Jorge Ochoa and Gilberto Rodríguez by dynamiting a wall of the Spanish prison where they were being held. Traffickers registered a notable success on February 7, 1985, when they kidnapped Enrique Camarena, Mexico's leading DEA agent, in Guadalajara. Camarena's mutilated body was found a month later in a field east of the city. Juan Ramón Mata Ballesteros was implicated in the crime. He fled Mexico and was captured in Cartagena by Colombian authorities a month after the killing.[34]

A day after the kidnapping of Enrique Camarena in Mexico, the Medellín cartel bombed the offices of Xerox, IBM, and Union Carbide in Mexico. From his jungle hideout in the eastern part of the country Carlos Lehder, who was now proclaiming himself a member of the M-19, warned that he would use that group to strike at all U.S. interests in Colombia. Intelligence sources indicated that Lehder met with Jorge Ochoa's brothers, along with Peruvian, Bolivian, and Mexican traffickers in Tabatinga, Brazil, a smuggling village on the Amazon River just east of Leticia. There they spoke of coordinating the anti-extradition struggle.[35]

It was during this foment in the trafficking community that Pablo Escobar was presented with a godsend. The M-19 approached him and asked for help in carrying out another of the spectacular operations that had been their trademark, one that would yet again capture the public imagination and humiliate the government.

The M-19 was also in turmoil during early 1985. Since the previous year the group had been in on-again, off-again peace negotiations with the government, but their refusal to lay down their weapons—and the army's tireless attacks on them as a result—led the M-19 to return to "total war" against the government in June 1985. Colombians on the left, and there were many of them, were disappointed. They had just witnessed the FARC's formation of a political party, the Union Patriótica (Patriotic Union), or UP, and they had hoped it might spell the end of the guerrilla war and the beginning of a viable left political alternative to the discredited traditional parties.

Money, and a common loathing of the political status quo, had always been the token uniting interests of El Patrón and the M-19. Leaders of the guerrilla group's war faction had wracked their brains during a recent congress in Havana as to how to stage their next act of revolutionary theater in such way that Escobar would finance it. At length Álvaro Fayad came up with the idea of seizing Colombia's Supreme Court building, the Palace of Justice (*Palacio de Justicia*), and staging a mock trial of Belisario Betancur there.[36] Yet when Iván Marino and Álvaro Fayad sat down with Escobar in July 1985 they presented the project as related to "the extradition thing."[37]

At least two meetings took place between Escobar and the M-19 leaders. The first one, with Carlos Pizarro, was held at a village just south of Escobar's Hacienda Napolés, and the second, with Marino and Fayad, at the hacienda itself. There the guerrillas sketched their decision to storm the Palace of Justice, located across the Plaza de Bolívar from the National Congress, and just two blocks from the presidential palace, and when in control of the building charge the President of Colombia with violating the previous year's cease-fire agreement. Their point made, and the public yet again impressed with their revolutionary panache, the rebels doubtless planned to fly away to Cuba along with the court's justices. Escobar heard them out and said he would bankroll the operation only if two of his men could go along to burn court records pertaining to extradition and kill the justices who supported the extradition treaty. Fayad and Marino rejected Escobar's demand. Eyewitnesses to the meetings never heard the guerrilla leaders say they would burn the court's archives and murder the justices, though Iván Marino did accept the two million dollars Escobar had offered for performing those tasks.[38] Escobar also paid for the rifles, ammunition, and explosives that the guerrillas used in the attack, and allowed planes flying the weapons into Colombia to land at Hacienda Napolés. He also contributed rifles and ammunition from the cartel's arsenal. Unfortunately for the guerrillas, the anti-tank rockets Escobar promised failed to arrive in time to be used in the Palace of Justice attack.[39]

The assault on the Palace of Justice took place shortly before noon on the morning of November 6. All initially went as planned. M-19 members who had infiltrated the building's support staff, seemingly through those working in the building's cafeteria, helped them drive their weapons-laden truck into the building's parking garage. Four police and security guards were killed there, along with two of the judges' chauffeurs. Meanwhile other guerrillas stormed in through the building's front door, shouting *Viva Colombia!* and *Viva la paz!*, killing the building's supervisor and an elevator operator along the way, and making their way to the third floor where the Justices had their offices. All told, forty-one guerrillas took part in the assault.[40]

Little else that day went as the M-19 had planned. They thought that by holding the Justices hostage Betancur would negotiate with them and within a few hours they would all leave the building safely, their grievances fully aired. The military thought otherwise. Pablo Escobar had warned Carlos Pizarro that the military would never let the President decide strategy when the Palace of Justice was taken, and that was precisely the case. The army and police had known the guerrillas were planning a violent act in downtown Bogotá, though they did not know precisely where or when. So when the court building fell they were ready to take action, which they did within three hours of the takeover. Twenty-seven hours later it was all over. The army parked a tank in the front door of the building and used it to help troops to blast their way in, ultimately killing all save one of the guerrillas. The courts records were burned and all but one of the Justices favoring the extradition treaty were executed by the guerrillas.[41] Along with Pablo Escobar millions of Colombians watched the Palace of Justice incident on television. The trafficker was delighted with the way the event unfolded, for it meant his gunmen would have to kill only the remaining pro-extradition justice, Hernando Baquero Borda.[42] Accordingly, Baquero was murdered by motorcycle assassins nine months later. In the attack, carried out on July 31, 1986, one of Baquero's bodyguards and a bystander also died.

The Palace of Justice incident traumatized Colombians, and remained an ongoing subject of polemic and debate. Supporters of the M-19 denied that the Medellín cartel was involved in any way, but most Colombians thought otherwise. Foremost among them were *El Espectador* editor Guillermo Cano and television journalist Jorge Enrique Pulido. In weeks following the tragic events of November 7 and 8, Cano and Pulido led the capital's press corps in analyzing the relationship between the M-19 and Pablo Escobar, deducing that the trafficker's hand was indeed present in the events surrounding the Palace of Justice tragedy. The reports angered Escobar, who remarked to his henchman Jhon Jairo Velásquez that the two newsmen should be added to the list of leading Colombians to be killed.[43] Cano was murdered by Escobar's *sicarios* a year later, and Pulido survived until being cut down in 1989.

The reputation of the M-19 was sullied by the Palace of Justice assault, and so too was that of the national army. Eleven of those rescued from the court building, ten cafeteria workers and the one surviving guerrilla, a university student named Irma Franco, were taken away never to be seen again. Soon it was revealed that they were interrogated under torture by army intelligence and then executed and buried in a secret location.[44] Nor did Belisario Betancur escape the opprobrium that Colombians heaped upon all involved in the Palace of Justice affair. He was blamed for doing nothing to stop the army assault on the building that destroyed it and that claimed the lives of at least fifty innocent people trapped there. Relatives of those victims showed their anger by boycotting a mass held in honor of the victims that Betancur attended. Incredibly, less than a week after the nightmare of the Palace of Justice, another 20,000 Colombians died when the town of Armero was destroyed by a mud avalanche that roared down upon it from the nearby Nevado del Ruiz. Again the state and its president were faulted for responding ineffectively during the attempt to rescue the few who survived that tragedy.

As 1985 drew to a close Belisario Betancur was the lamest of lame duck presidents. He entered office in 1982 buoyed by the campaign slogan "Yes he can!," but recent events had made that early optimism a cruel joke. Only the prospect of an upcoming presidential campaign, and the knowledge that a new group of leaders would soon be manning the ship of state, permitted any hopefulness to penetrate the gloomy national mood. The only Colombians who seemed to be doing well were the traffickers. Twelve days after the Palace of Justice attack indictments handed down in the U.S. showed that over the preceding five years the Medellín cartel alone had sold fifty-eight tons of cocaine in the U.S., at a street price of $17.4 billion.[45] News of the indictment angered Escobar and his colleagues, but they were pleased by another event taking place the day of its release. Their assassins at last caught up with Dijín chief Colonel Jaime Ramírez, who had led the costly Tranquilandia raid. Cartel *sicarios* shot Ramírez to death before his wife and children, as they sat in traffic returning to Bogotá from a weekend holiday.

The New Violence

"The bodies came down the river like logs adrift. They floated by so putrefied and disfigured, and there were so many of them, that the commander of the riverine base at Barrancabermeja, and mayors of towns along the river, decided not to collect any more dead from the river."

—Recollection of the Middle Magdalena River
hinterlands during the late 1980s[46]

Colombia's New Violence was at once simple and complex. It was simple in that it flowed from illegal drug earnings and complex because it was immensely varied in its detail. Another complicating factor was that while this violence can be placed in five categories, those categories overlapped, bled into one another, and changed over time. The first category was the cartels' war against the State, the subject of the present chapter, extending from the mid–1980s to the early 1990s. The second was intra-trafficker violence taking place within and among discrete groups and spilling over to touch family and friends of the drug dealers. The third involved traffickers and guerrillas, while the fourth had to do with traffickers and paramilitary groups. The fifth category was violence associated with the common criminality which vastly proliferated in Colombia when the war against the cartels stretched the country's legal system thin.

Of the first category of Colombia's New Violence, the cartels' war against the State, it should be observed that Colombia's struggle to defend its integrity before the drug mafia's offensive is unprecedented in the history of modern democratic states.[47] Recent political history finds no other case of a democratic nation founded under the rule of law whose people were more hard-pressed by a small criminal minority determined to bend them to their will. The discussion of that struggle has much to do with the weakness and flawed character of democratic rule in Colombia. The state did ultimately prevail over the murderous Escobar and Rodríguez Gacha and their henchmen, but only with difficulty and with the help of extra-state players.

The greater world community was also to blame for the traffickers' relative successes against the Colombian state. The traffickers' vast wealth and formidable armed power were founded in market forces operating within a globalized economic system poorly managed by its constituent nation states. The United States deserves both praise and blame in this context. U.S. cocaine consumers made the traffickers wealthy through their purchases of that illegal drug, its lax gun laws helped arm them, and its insistence that traffickers be sent to the United States for trial led them battle the Colombian state in hopes of avoiding that fate. At the same time U.S. technical assistance at length helped the Colombian government prevail over the powerful cartels— and later and over the communist guerrillas who used illegal drug monies to help finance their operations.

In the final analysis, though, it was Colombians working within their country's legal structure who did the most, and who paid the greatest price, in winning the war against the cartels. Brave and dedicated officials who refused to accept bribes from the traffickers helped preserve the ideal of the rule of law in Colombia. They often forfeited their lives for this steadfastness. Those judges, police officers, political leaders, their family and friends and supporters, were the heroes of their country's eventual triumph during the cartels' war against the State.

The second category of Colombia's drug-related new violence was that taking place within the trafficking community, and it fell into three sub-categories. First was intra-group violence involving leaders or employees of a single drug family, network, or cartel. Second was violence between cartels. And third was violence incidental to the drug trade.

Intra-group violence was a consistent feature of Colombia's illegal drug industry. This study has already mentioned the wave of killing attending Medellín's rise as the center of the country's cocaine trafficking during the 1970s. Cali soon followed with equally shocking increases in violent deaths, as its traffickers established that city as Colombia's second cocaine-exporting metropolis. Neither was Bogotá spared the spiraling violence associated with illegal drugs. It was the vendetta between families along the Bogotá-Medellín trafficking axis that touched off the Cocaine Wars mentioned above in chapter two, which spilled over into the streets of New York and Miami during the latter 1970s and early 1980s, alerting U.S. law enforcement officials to the cocaine boom. Violence attended the marijuana bonanza along Colombia's northern Caribbean coast, and was a notable feature of life within the country's emerald mafia. José Gonzalo Rodríguez Gacha, of Pacho, Cundinamarca, just south of the emerald mines of Boyacá, began his career as an emerald mafia gunman. He first made his reputation by helping slaughter members of leading smuggling families in massive assassinations carried out in Bogotá and Miami during the Emerald War of 1973.[48] But the cocaine trade quickly outstripped emerald smuggling as a producer of violence. The same history of intra-group bloodshed was repeated in southwestern Colombia. By the mid–1980s the people of Valle began noticing that most burials were of young men involved in the rising cocaine business, whose mutilated bodies began appearing in ever greater numbers around the department.[49]

Colombians often use the word "mafia" to describe trafficking and smuggling families and groups. While the country's criminal organizations were sui generis, having little organic connection with the Italo-American crime families, leaders like Pablo Escobar did study Mafia techniques and made use of them in his organization. Mafia protocols became generalized throughout Colombia's trafficking community. For example, when a contract was let for assassinating a member of the group it was to be kept secret. Thus many victims died unaware that they had been targeted, although many of those around them knew they would soon be killed.[50]

As in the Mafia crime families of Italy and the United States, internecine warfare within Colombian trafficking groups was a constant. Early 1987 witnessed one such blood-letting within the Medellín cartel, touched off when the Ochoa brothers reportedly lost a major cocaine shipment in the U.S. and failed to reimburse several minor traffickers who had piggy-backed their shipment on that of the Ochoas. Dozens of Ochoa family members and associates were kidnapped as a result, and some twenty of them murdered. Among them were two brothers-in-law of Jorge Ochoa and two of his oldest associates, Pablo Correa Arroyave and Pablo Correa Ramos. As young men the Correa cousins, along with Pablo Escobar, had led the Medellín gang known as Los Pablos.[51] Deaths from the 1987 intra-cartel war eventually ran into the hundreds and even claimed the lives of two Panamanians close to General Manuel Noriega, who had come to Medellín to purchase cocaine.[52]

By 1987 law enforcement was paralyzed in Medellín. That year's cartel war represented just one facet of violence that had accelerated throughout 1986, when murders in the city averaged ten per day. At the end of 1986, 20,000 murders remained unsolved in Medellín and DAS agents there were so afraid of assassination that they ceased investigating capital cases and simply forwarded them on to Bogotá. DAS agents sent from Bogotá to investigate cases in Medellín were easily identifiable by their accents and instantly became the targets of cartel assassins.[53]

Of all intra-cartel wars the most costly in terms of human life was the one that devastated the North Valle Cartel between 2003 and 2005, ultimately claiming several thousand lives. An idea of its savagery is suggested by what happened when a leader of one of the competing factions, Víctor Patiño Fómeque, was extradited to the United States and began talking to the authorities there. His enemies back in Colombia retaliated by murdering thirty-five of his family and friends. At length, U.S. authorities allowed twenty of Patiño's family members to seek refuge in the United States.[54]

Colombia's most notable example of war between trafficking groups was that between the Medellín and Cali cartels. It started late in 1987 at a summit meeting of leading traffickers called by Pablo Escobar and held at a luxurious resort near Palmira, Valle. The Medellín group had long wanted to streamline cocaine export, and had called the meeting with their chief competitors to propose that they, Medellín, handle all shipments to the exterior, charging a ten to thirty percent fee for the service. At the time Escobar, the Ochoa brothers, and Rodríguez

Gacha were among the wealthiest men in Latin America and were growing continually richer by sending multi-ton shipments of their product abroad.[55] Cali's leaders came to the meeting with another agenda, that of rejecting Escobar's offer and challenging Medellín's supremacy in the international cocaine trade. Cali had been at odds with Medellín ever since Escobar had ordered the assassination of Rodrigo Lara Bonilla in 1984, bringing the state down on the trafficking community as never before. They had watched Escobar's subsequent campaign of terror with increasing disapproval and had noted the way leaders of the Medellín cartel were pursued ever more closely by Colombian and U.S. authorities. Jorge Ochoa had only narrowly escaped extradition to the United States following his arrest in Spain late in 1984, successfully fighting off that peril through Spain's court system and managing to return home in July of 1986. Ochoa had easily bribed his way out of custody in Colombia, remaining at large ever since. Meanwhile Pablo Escobar was being hotly pursued by the authorities. So in the eyes of Cali's leaders the men of Medellín were in no position to dictate terms.

The Palmira cartel summit of November 20–21, 1987, was in fact the beginning of the end for Pablo Escobar and the Medellín cartel. Cali sent the message that they intended to challenge the *paisas* for dominance by having Jorge Ochoa arrested at a highway toll booth as he neared the meeting place.[56] Just as Escobar received the news that his closest associate was in police custody, he learned something else that infuriated him. A confidante of the Rodríguez Orejuelas visited his room and told him that his employers had decided Medellín's day was done and that it was Cali's turn to dominate the cocaine trade. Escobar left the meeting abruptly muttering "so this is war, then."[57]

Medellín became almost unlivable during the cartel war of 1988, and the situation in Cali was only slightly better. The year began when a massive car bomb in Medellín destroyed Pablo Escobar's luxury apartment building, Mónico, killing the building's guards, injuring one of the trafficker's children, and destroying his collection of luxury automobiles in its parking garage. Escobar retaliated by sending his *sicarios* to Cali, where by mid-year they killed more than sixty members of the competing group's employees. He also had several of Rodríguez Orejuela's drug stores bombed and later sent his leading gunman, whose nom de guerre was Tyson, to lead a team that was to machine gun Cali cartel leaders as they attended a soccer game. Nineteen died in the fusillade, although the chief targets escaped unharmed. As the war dragged on Cali's leaders went so far as to hire British mercenaries, sending them by helicopter to Hacienda Napolés, where they were to murder Escobar. The plan also miscarried when the helicopter was forced down by bad weather.[58]

The cartel war ran for years, efforts by both groups to end it notwithstanding. The Cali group even asked José Gonzalo Rodríguez Gacha's help in mediating the dispute. Rodríguez Gacha was perhaps not the best choice as peacemaker, for he was even more sanguinary than Pablo Escobar. Rodríguez was reportedly seen in the New York City area conferring with agents of Cali. But his overtures came to nothing. If there was a winner in the war it was Cali. None of its leaders died in the war, while both Escobar and his ally Rodríguez Gacha had met their ends by 1993.[59]

Along with trafficker violence aimed at the state, and that linked to inter-cartel warfare, there was a category of drug-related bloodshed that can be called incidental, or peripheral. It included violence against enemies outside of the illegal drug community, including the "social cleansing" of social outcasts, the settling of scores of a personal nature, murder and mayhem for hire, and violence that can only be described as spontaneous, or random.

Much of this miscellaneous cartel-related violence was directed through "offices," or "collection offices" (*oficinas de cobro*), where gunmen and bodyguards gathered to await orders and to receive payment for services rendered, and where non-traffickers could have their complaints brokered. The first of these "offices" was established by Pablo Escobar near his home town of Envigado, and soon thereafter a school was established nearby where his gunmen received advanced training. One Isaac Guttnan ran the training facility, which was located near the village of Sabaneta.[60] Eventually all significant trafficking groups had their own *oficinas de cobro* that in some respects duplicated functions of local police stations.[61]

All trafficking groups had enforcers in charge of discipline internal and external to their organizations. For the Medellín cartel Pablo Escobar was first serve this function; later both Escobar and José Gonzalo Rodríguez Gacha were the Medellín group's strong-arm men. Cali made use of an exceedingly violent group of associates from municipalities in northern Valle, men who later collectively came to be known as the North Valle cartel. Among the most infamous were Iván Urdinola, Diego Montoya, and Henry Loaiza.

Urdinola, Montoya, and Loaiza were traffickers who became major land owners in northern Valle, turning that part of the department into a private bastion where they acted with impunity. They had no need for *oficinas de cobro* because they themselves were so proficient in the exercise of violence, and because they usually operated in concert with local police and military. That sort of cooperation had a long history in northern Valle, dating back to times of the *Violencia,* and even before.[62] Northern Valle was where Gustavo Rojas Pinilla, as military commander of Valle del Cauca, had recruited conservative assassins known as *pájaros* (birds). Rojas and other military officers made use of *pájaros* recruited from Northern Valle after the *Nueve de Abril* (1948) and on through the early 1950s. Rojas Pinilla maintained contact with notorious *pájaros* from the region, such as León María Lozano ("El Cóndor") even during the years he served as President of Colombia (1953–57).[63]

As enforcer for the North Valle cartel, Iván Urdinola had a special room in his hacienda where his enemies were interrogated and then murdered. His technique was to first ask his prisoner whether he worked for the DEA or the guerrillas. Then regardless of the answer he executed him with an electric chain saw. One of his men would collect the remains and dispose of them in the nearby Cauca River. Urdinola's associate Juan Carlos Ramírez ("Chupeta") preferred giving his victims a chance to escape and then hunting them down and killing them. Drug traffickers weren't the only violent residents of northern Valle. Early in the 1990s thieves stole one prominent rancher's prize bull and sold it to a local butcher. The aggrieved landowner soon apprehended those involved in the theft, up to and including the butcher who slaughtered the animal, and his clients who purchased the meat, and had them all tortured and murdered.[64]

One of Colombia's most notorious acts of peripheral narco-violence during the late 1980s took place in northern Valle where the M-19 attempted to establish a front in the municipality of Trujillo. Never a group to learn from previous mistakes, the M-19 had planned to finance its North Valle operation by kidnapping traffickers and members of their families, and by controlling a popular cocaine export corridor to the Pacific down the Garrapata River. The experience ended even more disastrously for the guerrilla group than had its 1980 attempt to extort money from leading cocaine traffickers, or their 1985 seizure of the nation's Supreme Court building. When the guerrillas entered the region of Trujillo they stupidly challenged the North Valle trafficking community and, particularly, its two most ruthless leaders: Henry Loaiza and Diego Montoya.

The bloodletting began in Trujillo January 15, 1989, when cartel operatives, accompanied by local police, murdered a student, said to be an M-19 member, who was home on vacation. Thirteen similar killings took place over the course of 1989, with others following at an increasing tempo over the course of that year and on through 1990 and 1991. March and April of 1990 marked the most intense phase of what became known as the Trujillo Massacre. Sixteen separate incidents took place over that span of time, several of which rose to the level of massacres, defined as the killing of six or more people. The most ghastly slaughter took place on the first of April, when Henry Loaiza and Diego Montoya supervised the execution of sixteen campesinos in a rural part of the department, decapitating them with chain saws. Afterward one of their men, Daniel Arcila Cardona, loaded the body parts on a truck and disposed of them in the Cauca River. Two weeks later henchmen of Loaiza and Montoya, accompanied by local police, murdered Trujillo's priest, who earlier had led a march protesting the massacre. Three other church workers died with him.[65]

Daniel Arcila quit the North Valle cartel not long after the April 1, 1990, incident, testifying to authorities and giving full information about the violence taking place in and around Trujillo. Sadly for Arcila the cartel captured him in May 1991. On the fifth day of that month they called together a large number of fellow traffickers, as well as soldiers from Batallion Palacé in Buga, and police from nearby Tuluá, to witness his execution. It took place in a leisurely fashion and with a chain saw. Henry Loaiza and Diego Montoya performed the execution, later having Arcila's remains tossed into the Cauca River. By the time the Trujillo Massacre ran its course, some 300 had died.[66]

Self-defense and the desire to protect trafficking infrastructure were hardly the only sources of peripheral drug-related violence. The fact was that wherever money from trafficking flowed violence inevitably followed. Where it flowed most abundantly its attending violence was most intense. Medellín and Cali were notorious during the latter 1980s as places where traffickers did what they wanted thanks to the impunity that their money bought, and the fear that their *sicarios* inspired in local populations, especially at the level of the judiciary. Petty crime flourished in such settings, leading to the establishment of parallel systems of criminal justice running from death squads made up of off-duty policemen to the henchmen of drug traffickers sent out to kill those seen as undesirables.[67] It is instructive that in May 1986, as internal strife racked the Medellín cartel, the Cali cartel was conducting extensive "social cleansing" within the department of Valle del Cauca. Attorney General Carlos Jiménez Gómez publicly denounced the spate of nocturnal killings in Cali, saying they had the aspect of a dirty war.[68] The senselessness of this bloodshed was illustrated by a spate of killings of independent garbage collectors called *basuriegos,* guilty of nothing more than being ragged, dirty, and poor.[69]

Peripheral violence included that having no discernable motive. As easy money paid for any vice in nocturnal Cali, where cocaine, bazuco, and marijuana were consumed freely in the city's many night clubs and discos, and heavily-armed young men cruised the streets in new SUVs with beautiful young women at their sides, little more was needed to invite death. During those years a great many young *caleñas* never returned alive from their dates with trigger-happy boyfriends. Reasons for the murders were many. But the truth was, as a student of that violence later discovered, "no one wanted to remember their deaths."[70]

Trafficker involvement with guerrilla groups, and with anticommunist paramilitary groups, constitutes the third category of Colombia's drug-related New Violence. Although it varied in specific detail it was uniform in that it centered on money. The relationship was invariably productive of violence. The case of the M-19, discussed above, amply illustrates this. So too was the traffickers' relationship with the FARC. The communist, campesino guerrilla movement began its involvement with illegal drugs indirectly, by levying a tax on coca cultivation in Meta and Caquetá. This began in 1982, and the guerrillas also began contracting their cadres out to the Medellín cartel to protect its properties in eastern Colombia. In 1983 José Gonzalo Rodríguez Gacha reached a formal agreement with FARC leaders under which he could operate in FARC-dominated areas in exchange for paying taxes ranging between ten and fifteen percent of the value of his product. But the FARC soon reneged on the deal. In December 1983 members of Front 1 of the FARC raided one of Rodríguez Gacha's laboratories in Vaupés, making off with nearly 200 kilos of cocaine, a half-million dollars in cash, and fifteen rifles. Late the following year they attacked a Tranquilandia laboratory, kidnapping sixteen people and releasing them only after receiving 600 kilos of cocaine, twenty-five million pesos, and quantities of ether and acetone. That attack touched off low-level warfare between the trafficker and the guerrillas extending from the remote eastern jungles to more populated parts of the country. Rodríguez Gacha soon became proficient in striking at what he perceived to be a soft FARC target, the guerrilla group's political party, the Unión Patriótica, or UP.[71]

The FARC had proclaimed the UP's birth in 1984, launching the party with great fanfare in June 1985. When UP candidates campaigned for office in 1986 congressional elections the trafficker viewed them to be members of the FARC and therefore legitimate targets in his war against the guerrilla group. Rodríguez Gacha's *sicarios* started killing UP members and by the end of 1986 had assassinated 300 of them. In December of that year a member of the UP Directorate, Alvaro Salazar, met with Rodríguez Gacha to hear him propose that if the FARC would stop attacking his cocaine production facilities he would halt his killing of UP members. At the meeting Salazar heard the trafficker explain that the FARC had been "very lacking" (*muy faltones*) in honoring their 1983 agreement with him. He said that FARC cadres had taken over three of his cocaine kitchens valued at several million dollars each, and had wrecked others. They had also stolen his merchandise, waylaid one of his men and stolen money from him. Gacha told Salazar that FARC commanders said they were powerless to do anything about it. All he wanted, the trafficker complained, was for the FARC to "let him work."[72]

Álvaro Salazar took Gacha's request to FARC commander Luis Morantes ("Jacobo Arenas"). He had an ally at the meeting in Guillermo Sáenz Vargas ("Alfonso Cano"), a member of the guerrillas' Directorate. Sáenz warned Morantes that if the FARC did not reach some sort of an accord "with the Mexican" it might push him into an alliance with the army, which would add to the guerrillas' problems.[73] Morantes refused to negotiate with Gacha, saying he welcomed war with him. "This guy is a criminal," opined the FARC leader.[74] It was a fateful decision. Morantes' action had the effect of solidifying the link between the Mexican and paramilitary leaders of the Magdalena Medio region. It also meant that the killing of UP members would continue until the group had lost 2,800 of its members and ceased to exist as a political party.[75]

José Gonzalo Rodríguez Gacha was a businessman skilled in manufacturing cocaine and exporting it to the United States. His colleagues in Medellín knew that, which is why at their meeting in early 1982 they had put him in charge of directing the Tranquilandia manufacturing complex. As well as pioneering the mass-production of cocaine, Rodríguez Gacha was inventive in smuggling it into the United States. He was one of the first to ship the drug through tunnels under the U.S.-Mexican border, and he specialized in sending simultaneous plane-loads of cocaine northward. On a single night during the early '80s he dispatched seven heavily-loaded cargo planes to the U.S., several of which returned stuffed with dollars. The Mexican was one of those traffickers who weighed his dollar receipts rather than counting the bills individually. He brought such a flood of the U.S. currency into the Magdalena Medio region of Colombia that prostitutes there started accepting dollars only for their services.[76]

During his early years in Pacho, Cundinamarca, a town located south of the emerald zone of western Boyacá, Rodríguez Gacha worked for Víctor Carranza and Gilberto Molina, heads of the Emerald Mafia. It was Carranza and Molina who had introduced him to the Medellín trafficking group. By the mid–1980s Rodríguez Gacha served as a sort of bridge between the Medellín cartel and the Emerald Mafia.[77] That became important to Gacha when his manufacturing facilities in the east came under increasing pressure from both the FARC and government anti-drug agents, for it sped the transfer of his cocaine kitchens into the Middle Magdalena region.

Late in 1984 an event took place that had profound implications for Colombia's drug-related violence. In December of that year paramilitary forces under the command of Henry Pérez intercepted one of Rodríguez Gacha's cocaine shipments not far from Puerto Boyacá. A meeting between the two men followed and within months the two were united in an alliance that benefited both: Rodríguez Gacha would buy armaments for the paramilitary and Pérez and his men would protect the trafficker's cocaine production facilities from FARC and ELN guerrillas operating in the region. The alliance worked well. Within three years Rodríguez Gacha was manufacturing cocaine at some forty locations throughout the Middle Magdalena, exporting as much as two tons of cocaine weekly. The now well-armed paramilitary forces were killing a great many guerrillas and expelling them from zones where they had been dominant for years. By 1986 the guerrillas, who had been supreme in Puerto Boyacá and its hinterlands during the late 1970s and early '80s, were seriously weakened. To celebrate that fact Henry Pérez and his allies erected a billboard at the town's entrance reading "Welcome to Puerto Boyacá, land of peace and progress: anti-subversive capital of Colombia."[78]

José Gonzalo Rodríguez Gacha and Henry Pérez were drawn to one another by a shared hatred of the FARC. Their initial meeting was thus described as "love at first sight."[79] Both men were Conservatives and hence predisposed to dislike any left political ideology, and both had suffered years of persecution at the hands of the FARC. That experience had led Henry Pérez and other campesinos around Puerto Boyacá to arm themselves against depredations of the guerrillas' Front 9, which by the early 1980s had begun massive extortion and kidnapping of farmers such as themselves.[80] Thus it was with a certain élan that the two set off in pursuit of communists across the breadth of the Middle Magdalena region.

Involvement with the paramilitary of Puerto Boyacá helped Rodríguez Gacha achieve several goals. As well as providing him a safe haven for continuing his production of cocaine at an industrial level and punishing the guerrilla group that had wronged him, it helped realize the dream of every Colombian drug trafficker: the Middle Magdalena region gave him a corridor to the sea through which he could move his product virtually unimpeded. Thanks to help from the paramilitary, along with that of his colleagues in the Emerald Mafia—who were themselves Conservatives and anticommunists—he could ship coca paste into the Middle Magdalena via eastern Colombia and through the emerald district, turn it into cocaine, and send it on to foreign markets through the lower Cauca region of Antioquia and across the department of Córdaba to the Gulf of Urabá and to other points of egress along the Caribbean coast. By the latter 1980s there were only a few guerrilla strongholds along that route that had yet to be reduced. The Castaño brothers had already established their own paramilitary force in Córdoba, greatly reducing the guerrilla presence there. Rodríguez Gacha and his paramilitary colleagues bent to the task of further reducing FARC strength in such places with effectiveness that pushed Colombia's violence to appalling new levels.

It was during 1987 that the Mexican, along with his colleagues Pablo Escobar, Víctor Carranza, and Henry Pérez, conceived the idea of hiring foreign mercenaries to instruct their forces in advanced war-making techniques. Unlike the guerrillas, who for over twenty years had sent their best fighters for advanced training in Cuba, the Soviet Union, China, and Vietnam, the narco-paramilitary would train their men at home. Agents were dispatched to Amsterdam and other European sites where they recruited mercenaries who began work in late 1987. The mercenaries were led by retired British and Israeli army officers, senior among them the Israeli Yair Klein. The first training of a select group of *sicarios* took place at a camp Rodríguez Gacha had dubbed Fantasy Island, a property he owned in the Magdalena River north of Puerto Boyacá. Other training sites were Cincuenta, located in Putumayo near the border with Ecuador, and base Uno, near Cimitarra, Santander. Smaller training camps were established on property owned by Pablo Escobar and Fidel Castaño.[81]

The initial training group consisted of twenty men selected by Rodríguez Gacha, twenty by Henry Pérez, and five each from Pablo Escobar and Víctor Carranza. One additional trainee was the Mexican's teenage son Freddy. Courses lasted from two to three months and the mercenaries instructed trainees in weaponry and explosives, and in tactics and strategies of irregular warfare. Other training sessions took place at the Putumayo camp, with Henry Pérez, Rodríguez Gacha, and others attending a graduation ceremony there during mid–1988.

Consequences of the advanced paramilitary training were immediate. In March 1988 a call came from Córdoba asking that some of the better graduates be sent to "solve a problem" relating to FARC growth around Turbo, Antioquia, on the Gulf of Urabá.[82] Thirty-four men soon set out for the region, several of whom brought their wives along to cook for the group. During the month they were in the region they executed some one hundred of Turbo's residents, on the suspicion they were either FARC members or sympathizers.[83] The worst single mass bloodletting of 1988 took place in Segovia, Antioquia, a town lying squarely in the corridor Rodríguez Gacha and others were clearing for drug shipments. On November 11, a paramilitary group led by Alonso de Jesús Baquero, known by his nom de guerre El Negro Vladimir, entered the main plaza of Segovia where he directed the massacre of forty-three people. The town had been selected because it was both a FARC stronghold and a place where the UP had made gains in recent elections. Thirty carefully selected men accompanied Baquero that day, and they chose their victims from a list of names El Negro Vladimir had compiled during visits to Segovia over the previous two weeks.[84]

By the time of the Turbo and Segovia massacres El Negro Vladimir had earned the reputation as Puerto Boyacá's most ruthless paramilitary leader. Recruited by the FARC when he was eleven years old, he had spent seven years with them, finally deserting at age eighteen because he and another guerrilla had fallen in love and had a child. The couple fled the *campo* to a nearby town, which happened to be Puerto Boyacá. It was there in June 1985 that he was taken in by Henry Pérez and his paramilitary forces, quickly earning favor for the skill with which he hunted down his former colleagues. But Alonso de Jesús Baquero did not limit himself to killing guerrillas. He also fought the state. In early 1989 he brought the wrath of the nation down upon the paramilitaries when he directed the murders of eleven government officials traveling to investigate a mass killing near Puerto Boyacá two years earlier. Baquero's killing of the government investigators, which took place on January 18, at a place called La Rochela, in Santander, led to sharp criticism of government-sanctioned self-defense forces, as well as to the arrest of Baquero in August 1989. El Negro Vladimir was subsequently sentenced to thirty years in prison, the maximum penalty allowed under Colombian law.[85]

The case of Alonso de Jesús Baquero reveals that by the late 1980s Colombia's new violence had entered a new phase. The combination of revolutionary guerrillas, anticommunist paramilitaries, and illegal drug monies created an explosive cocktail that accelerated Colombia's civil disorder. Narco-guerrilla-paramilitary violence became an ongoing feature of life in many of Colombia's outlying regions throughout the 1990s and into the first years of the twenty-first century.

The fifth and last category of Colombia's new violence consisted of the common criminality that took wing as drug-related violence drove the country's criminal justice system into near collapse. Colombian police records from the early 1980s revealed shocking increases in common crime coupled with failure to apprehend those responsible for it. Even worse, half of all Colombians had suffered personal attacks or material losses at the hands of ordinary criminals, while nearly a third of those victimized failed to report the crime out of fear of retaliation by the criminals themselves, along with knowledge that there was only a remote likelihood that the police would help them in any event. The people of Colombia were trapped in what was described as "a non-functional criminal justice system."[86]

Impunity and rising rates of violence in Colombia led the European-based human rights organization Pax Christi to carry out an inquiry on the subject in 1988. The group concluded its study by blaming the Colombian government for allowing abuses of human rights to take place, and recommending that European nations suspend all aid to the country. Pax Christi further recommended punishing Colombians by imposing an economic boycott of their country, to be effective until such time as the massacre of civilians ceased. Illegal drugs were not mentioned in the study's conclusions. Nor was there mention of cocaine consumption in Europe or the illegal drug revenues flowing from European consumers into the hands of the country's perpetrators of violence.[87]

* * *

By the latter 1980s most Colombians were aware that violence levels were rising, although many of them remained untouched by it. They read in the press and saw on television reports of nocturnal social cleansing in Cali, drug wars in Medellín, and massacres in places like La Rochela, Segovia, Urabá, and Trujillo. But they saw them as isolated and unrelated. Most Colombians continued to see the growing violence as rooted in social inequality and defects in the nation's political system, conditions many believed gave rise to and possibly justified the revolutionary guerrillas. This was the insistent and convincing message they had been taught by academics and pundits for twenty years and more. President Virgilio Barco entered office in August 1986 convinced that social inequality lay at the heart of the new violence.[88] Yet he was troubled that his country was by that time routinely described as the world's most violent nation not in a declared state of war.[89] He was also aware that homicide rates had more than doubled between 1972 and 1986, rising from a relatively low level of nineteen per hundred thousand to the troubling rate of forty-seven. All indications were that such rates would soon exceed the 1972 rate by three or four times.[90] None of it seemed to jibe with the country's fiscal stability and ongoing economic progress. With this in mind the new President commissioned a study of the causes of the violence during early 1987, to be carried out by leading social scientists at the National University in Bogotá. Before the year was out the commission returned its report, confirming Barco's belief that "Colombians kill one another more because of the quality of their lives and their social relationships than to arrive at control of the State."[91] Make Colombia a more democratic and egalitarian place, the social scientists argued, and the country will become a less violent place. Nowhere in the study was there an explicit linkage between the country's spiraling violence and the international drug trade. It would be a while yet before such a connection became clear to Colombians.

Democratic Responses to the Violence

"If in 1987 or 1988 many started thinking that the country would fall apart completely, that it was on knife-edge, by 1990 the question was how much it could resist the Cartel chiefs, and what horrific acts might they still cause. Judicial institutions, still inefficient, began to recover."
—Historian Jorge Orlando Melo[92]

Virgilio Barco entered the presidency at a significant juncture in Colombian history. Political reform was long overdue, and the new president came into office committed to beginning the process of revamping national institutions so as to make the country's democratic system more open and transparent. He also pledged to find ways to lessen the social inequality that he believed lay at the heart of Colombia's notorious violence, this in his inaugural message of August 7, 1986. He went on to say that he considered the illegal drug industry to be the greatest threat to national institutions, and he promised to deal vigorously with it under national law. He was referring specifically to the bilateral extradition treaty with the United States, which he, Barco, had helped draft in 1979.

Unfortunately for Virgilio Barco, there was little consensus about national drug policy, either within his administration or among the general public. Some of his advisers argued that the traffickers should receive amnesty in exchange for their promise of future good behavior, a solution in line with the traffickers' own proposal to the government in 1984. Their advice was also similar to offers then being made to the guerrillas in exchange for demobilization. Barco himself, and others among his advisers, favored the hard line, meaning cooperation with U.S. anti-drug efforts, particularly at the level of extradition. For them the traffickers were criminals who should be held accountable for their acts. Outside of government the public remained largely indifferent to the illegal drug issue. Many even viewed the cocaine industry as a good thing because of the economic boost they believed it gave to the economy. And most Colombians continued to see drug use as chiefly a U.S. problem. They resented the Americans' demand that Colombian traffickers be sent to suffer exemplary punishment in the U.S. while they themselves were unable or unwilling to halt the consumption of illegal drugs in their own country.

Key national institutions were also divided, even fragmented, by pressures the illegal drug trade exerted on them. The legislative branch of government was thoroughly infiltrated by drug monies that legislators had received both in the form of bribes and as campaign contributions.

Thus the traffickers had a significant group in both houses of congress predisposed to give them a favorable hearing. Colombia's judicial branch was similarly compromised by the traffickers, with judges and other court officials living in terror of being killed by cartel assassins if they enforced anti-drug legislation, or under pressure to accept bribes for not prosecuting traffickers and not enforcing anti-drug laws. Among armed forces, the military, particularly the army, was compromised by the traffickers' money. Army officers were also inclined to overlook the misdeeds of traffickers who fought the guerrillas. After José Gonzalo Rodríguez Gacha declared war on the FARC he was given the nickname *El Intocable*, "the Untouchable One," for the way the military protected and even befriended him. Asked about this in the mid–1980s, Rodríguez Gacha replied "The military gives them medals. I give them money and dead communists."[93]

Across the country many departmental and municipal police forces were on the traffickers' payrolls. This was especially the case in Cali and Medellín, where leading drug dealers ran little danger of arrest as they went about their daily business. This put other law enforcement agencies not so compromised at a severe disadvantage. DAS was forced to close its office in Medellín because the generalized state of impunity there made its officers easy targets, and agents of the independent police drug unit Dijín lived under constant threat of assassination.

If Colombians were divided over the danger the illegal drug industry presented to society, and whether or not illegal drug money subverted national institutions, the traffickers were divided over how to deal with society and the state. Most accepted that their business was illegal and did their best to minimize contact with the state and its law enforcement agencies. Most major traffickers wanted to co-exist peacefully with the state and used their wealth as a powerful tool to help achieve that. Only a few, notably Pablo Escobar and José Gonzalo Rodríguez Gacha, preferred to challenge the state outright. Escobar gambled that if he could terrorize state and citizens, and avoid capture, he would eventually force them to forgive his crimes and guarantee that he would not be extradited. He in fact won that bet.

During the first six months of Virgilio Barco's presidency Pablo Escobar launched an all-out effort to thwart the state's anti-drug initiatives. His lawyers worked overtime to lobby against the extradition treaty, whose legality was being debated by the Supreme Court. As his lawyers bribed and cajoled, other of his employees kept up a barrage of threats to members of the judiciary and their families. Yet others continued to assassinate his enemies, most notable among them Dijín head Jaime Ramírez and *El Espectador* investigative reporter Luis Roberto Camacho, both of whom died in November 1986. Escobar's strategy paid off on December 13, when a terrified Court voided the 1979 extradition treaty on a technicality. Escobar was delighted, and his newspaper *Medellín Cívico* trumpeted the court's action to be a triumph for the Colombian people. But his happiness was premature. One day later, on December 14, Virgilio Barco reinstated the extradition treaty under terms of another international agreement dating from 1980. Escobar answered the President with an act of terror as shocking as his 1984 assassination of Justice Minister Lara Bonilla: his *sicarios* murdered the man who had been a thorn in his side since 1983, Guillermo Cano. It had been Cano who, through his newspaper *El Espectador*, had launched the exposé that turned the cartel chieftain into a fugitive. And it was Cano whose crusading editorials against the illegal drug industry had given heart to Colombians who opposed the traffickers.[94]

With Cano's assassination the battle was again joined between Pablo Escobar and the Colombian State. The day after the newspaperman's death Virgilio Barco declared a state of siege, featuring a host of new sanctions against the traffickers, and he published a "most wanted" list of 128 traffickers, fifty-six of whom had already been indicted in the U.S. That was just one of several blows to Escobar extending into early 1987. During the first months of that year U.S. authorities seized his properties in Miami, and those of his colleague Rodríguez Gacha. Just as word of the confiscations reached him came the arrest of Carlos Lehder and his quick extradition to the United States. It was the first extradition of a major Colombian trafficker and as such strengthened Escobar's resolve. He ordered his agents step up their combination of bribes and threats against judicial officials, with the result that during the middle months of 1987 the courts awarded him a stunning series of favorable decisions. They dismissed all charges against him, including those implicating him in the assassinations of Lara Bonilla and Guillermo Cano. Meanwhile the Supreme Court struck down the President's extradition power yet again. Former President Carlos Lleras Restrepo expressed the anger of many Colombians by blasting the climate of impunity and terror reigning in the country, and calling for constitutional revisions that would rehabilitate the rule of law in Colombia.

On November 20, 1987, Escobar received another blow when his colleague Jorge Ochoa was arrested while traveling to the Medellín-Cali cartel meeting in Valle del Cauca. That unleashed another legal battle between cartel lawyers and government officials, the latter group desperately seeking legal grounds for extraditing Ochoa to the U.S. where he would stand trial for a host of drug-related offenses. But with the 1979 extradition treaty a dead letter, and there being no other way to legally send Ochoa out of the country to stand trial, the trafficker's lawyers at length won his release. As if to rub it in Escobar had a team of *sicarios* kidnap and murder the nation's Attorney General, Carlos Mauro Hoyos Jiménez. Hoyos had worked hard with the Americans to effect Ochoa's extradition, for which Escobar and his supporters had branded him a traitor. Hoyos had heightened their anger by pronouncing himself fully in favor of extradition because he perceived that the nation's justice system "was powerless to control the traffickers."[95]

The legal system's impotence before the traffickers was indeed pathetic. Not only were the courts unable to extradite Jorge Ochoa in late 1987, they had not even been able to prosecute him on a pending civil offense once Spain returned him to Colombia in August 1986. Ochoa's lawyers simply bribed the presiding judge to dismiss the case, allowing Ochoa to go into hiding.

Jorge Ochoa's release from jail in December 1987 angered the United States and led it to threaten economic sanctions against Colombia for insufficient cooperation in its anti-drug campaign. Colombian officials turned back the threat and Virgilio Barco redoubled his effort to educate the Americans on the seriousness of Colombia's drug war and of U.S. responsibilities in it.[96] Meanwhile members of the American public had at last become aware of the gravity of the illegal drug trade and the crime and violence it engendered. A national presidential campaign was underway during 1988, and Americans reacted favorably to the promise of candidate George H.W. Bush to renew the War on Drugs declared by Presidents Nixon and Reagan. Early in the year Senator John Kerry chaired hearings on the drug problem that provided hair-raising detail on the illegal drug trade, especially as it involved Colombia, and the corrupting role it had played in the recent Contra War.[97] A series of news magazine features appeared at the same time bearing titles like "The Drug Thugs" and "Drugs, Money, and Death," while in Miami the trial of Carlos Lehder was widely reported. In June 1988 Lehder was sentenced to serve multiple life sentences in a federal penitentiary. A CBS-*New York Times* poll released in mid-year revealed that 48 percent of Americans viewed drug trafficking as the most important international problem affecting the nation. At that same time U.S. prisons were beginning to fill with a largely African American population sent there by harshly punitive legislation passed two years earlier during the crack epidemic in urban ghettos.[98]

During 1988 Virgilio Barco and those in his administration kept up their pressure on Escobar and Rodríguez Gacha. In July Escobar was indicted for his involvement in the recent paramilitary massacres in Turbo and Segovia, Antioquia. Ten months before, Minister of Justice Enrique Low Murtra had charged Rodríguez Gacha with the October 1987 assassination of Unión Patriótica leader Jaime Pardo Leal. There was little response from the Medellín cartel during 1988, as its leaders were preoccupied with the war against their rivals in Cali.

As 1989 began Escobar and Rodríguez Gacha were ready to renew their offensive against the state. The cartel war of the previous year had decreased in intensity thanks to mediation by Rodríguez Gacha. Both men felt renewed confidence in their ability to achieve their goals through terrorist acts carried out by the thousand mercenary-trained *sicarios* on their payrolls. Colombia's legal system continued in a state of paralysis, with lawyers refusing to serve as judges and even rejecting appointment to the Supreme Court. As though flaunting his invincibility, Rodríguez Gacha, at the time one of Latin America's wealthiest men and Colombia's largest landowner, attacked Gilberto Molina and Víctor Carranza, his former associates in the Emerald Mafia. On February 26, 1989, and in typically brutal fashion, he had Molina, six of Molina's body guards, and twelve guests massacred as they attended the emerald don's birthday party in Sasaima, Cundinamarca.[99] They were but nineteen of the estimated 3,000 killed during the Medellín cartel's ambitious attempt to take control of the Emerald Mafia.[100] Rodríguez Gacha's murder of Gilberto Molina was the act of a man supremely confident in his ability to dominate all others through violence—everyone from the emerald zone's capos to the state, the constitutionally recognized repository of armed force for the Colombian people.

The actions taken by José Gonzalo Rodríguez Gacha and Pablo Escobar during 1989 can only be understood in terms of Colombia's iron triangle of violence. That is, they harked back to Colombia's tradition of rebellion against a state perceived at once as weak and illegitimate. The kings of cocaine may have rebelled against the state for motives different from those of the guerrillas, but they despised it and scorned its ineptness for many of the same reasons as did the guerrillas. For Escobar the state was beneath contempt, the corrupt servant of what he perceived to be a political and economic oligarchy. By this view he was justified in fighting a war against it while absolving himself of guilt for having slaughtered scores of its employees. Only this interpretation helps one make sense of his bitter complaints against the nation as it attempted to punish him for his countless crimes. "We do not accept, nor will we ever accept … the violation of all our rights," screamed Escobar as the authorities closed in on him during the latter months of 1989. "We are ready to confront the traitors!"[101] Such declarations were possible only in a country whose lawbreakers viewed impunity as the norm and the enforcement of national law as an infringement of their rights.

Pablo Escobar and Rodríguez Gacha seemed supremely confident as they renewed their war against the state in 1989. On the last day in May their men narrowly missed killing DAS chief Miguel Maza Márquez with a car bomb. In early May cartel gunmen murdered Antioquia's Governor Antonio Roldán. That was the same month Virgilio Barco's new Justice Minister Mónica de Greiff resigned, remarking as she did so that she was not cut out to serve in time of war. Threats to the judiciary continued. On August 16, Judge Carlos Valencia was assassinated after having ratified lower-court indictments of Escobar, leading 4,000 judges to call a strike the next day to protest their vulnerability at hands of the traffickers. Early on August 18, cartel *sicarios* machine gunned Antioquia's police chief, Waldemar Franklin Quintero, whose agents had recently seized 2,000 kilos of Escobar's cocaine.[102] But all of that was merely a prelude to the crime that at last would herald the end of the Medellín cartel: the killing of presidential candidate Luis Carlos Galán.

Like so many other victims of the cartel's war against the state, Galán had long been an enemy of the traffickers and a supporter of extradition. By August 1989 it was a given that he would be Colombia's next president, which was why Escobar and Rodríguez Gacha agreed he must be killed. Accordingly, several of their *sicarios,* fresh from the Paradise Island mercenary training course, followed Galán to a campaign rally at a town outside of Bogotá, where they shot him to death on the afternoon of August 18.

No other act of cartel terror produced a more powerful response than did Galán's murder. Virgilio Barco declared a state of siege and ordered the authorities to seize the property of traffickers all over Colombia. The homes of Escobar and Rodríguez Gacha were raided and their family members interrogated. The government seized more than 200 homes and haciendas of traffickers, some 100 of their airplanes and helicopters, thirty of their yachts, and some 600 weapons. Thousands were arrested and the President began signing extradition orders. By year's end over twenty traffickers had been sent to stand trial in the United States. In an unprecedented step Barco invited the United States to aid in the search for Galán's murderers. By September a specialized U.S. military intelligence unit called Centra Spike was installed at the U.S. Embassy in Bogotá, where it began surveillance of the electronic communications of both Pablo Escobar and Rodríguez Gacha.[103]

The drug kingpins fought back with great savagery. When the National Police formed a new group called the Search Force (*Bloque de Búsqueda*), sending its 200 men into Medellín to pursue him, Escobar's *sicarios* hunted down and killed thirty of them within the first two weeks. On November 27 the cartel leaders bombed a Cali-bound passenger plane, killing all aboard. A week after that they detonated a truck bomb in front of DAS headquarters in Bogotá, killing sixty-three people and injuring another 600, and destroying the skyscraper housing the intelligence agency. Escobar sent large numbers of his men to Bogotá where they terrified the citizenry by setting off scores of pipe bombs. Car bombs exploded in hotels and at corporate offices in Bogotá, Medellín, and other cities.

Despite their best efforts the "total war" against the state was not going well by Escobar and Rodríguez Gacha. On two occasions during October 1989 Escobar narrowly escaped capture by the police Search Force. A month later U.S. intelligence traced Rodríguez Gacha to a hilltop cabin southwest of Bogotá. The mission to bomb the cabin was called off at the last second for fear that a stray bomb would fall into a village lying just beyond the target. Hearing the approaching airplane, Rodríguez Gacha was able to escape. But his luck did not hold. Enemies in the Cali cartel had placed a spy in his inner circle, and with that person's help Colombian and U.S. forces traced the trafficker and his son to the Caribbean coast, where electronic surveillance pinpointed their location. Hot pursuit followed, with Gacha and his son Freddy fleeing military helicopters along the edge of coastal mangrove swamps in a speed boat. At length the boat put in near Tolú, the helicopters landed, and in the ensuing gunfight Gacha and his son died. Defiant to the end, the Mexican took his own life.[104] Now only Pablo Escobar was left. No longer could he seek refuge in Panama, as he had in 1984. The United States had invaded that country five days after Rodríguez Gacha's death, easily capturing Manuel Noriega and sending him to the U.S. to stand trial for drug trafficking.

Colombians were in a post-traumatic yet hopeful frame of mind as 1990 began. Their police forces had just killed one of the two traffickers who had put them through a nightmare of violence during the preceding five months. And the government was in the process of signing a peace agreement with the M-19 and EPL guerrillas, and with two smaller insurgent groups. Those positive developments were accompanied by steady progress toward fundamental political reform. The public and the government were united in their hope that a new national constitution could open the political system as never before, and effect reforms designed to lessen the impunity that reigned in the country. Accordingly, and in quick succession, congress approved the calling of a constituent assembly to approve rewriting of the constitution. The public approved their decision and work on the new document began in early 1991.

Pablo Escobar viewed these developments with great interest. His goal was, as it had always been, to use negotiation, bribery, threats, and violence to bend state and society to his will, to the end of forcing it to forgive his crimes and protect him from extradition. Thus a bloody dialogue took place between Pablo Escobar and the Colombian state extending through 1990 and to June 1991.

Over the months of negotiation leading up to the drafting of the new national constitution, Escobar's spokesmen both inside and outside of the government lobbied hard for a provision in the new document banning the extradition of Colombian nationals. Meanwhile his lawyers advanced the argument that Escobar was a political, rather than an ordinary, criminal. As such he would enjoy the same rights as the guerrillas who offered peace in exchange for forgiveness of past crimes and limited time in jail. A group of distinguished citizens calling itself "The Notables" helped Escobar negotiate with the government. Former Presidents López Pumarejo and Turbay Ayala led the group, along with Medellín mayor Juan Gómez Martínez. It worked with Barco's Secretary General Diego Montoya Vélez to broker a deal between the state and the Extraditables, as Escobar and his colleagues called themselves. The prospect of such distinguished citizens serving as intermediaries for one such as Pablo Escobar struck many Colombians as additional proof that their government was not just inept, but that it had lost its moral compass.[105]

As former national presidents argued against extradition, Pablo Escobar made brilliant use of terror to break the will of Colombians and their leaders. Late in 1989, and on into 1990, he pursued a campaign of kidnapping members of prominent Antioquian families, a son of Diego Montoya among them. At the same time Escobar announced that he would pay $4,000 for every police officer murdered in Medellín, double that if the agent killed was an officer. The assassinations began immediately. By March the number of police agents killed numbered 75, and by June it reached 180. Because many of the gunmen were members of gangs from the city's poor neighborhoods, the police started retaliating with indiscriminate killing of teenaged men living in such places. All of this played into Escobar's hands, as he knew it would. As the months passed a popular groundswell developed to grant the trafficker anything he wanted in exchange for peace. Even new President César Gaviria changed his hard line on extradition when Escobar's men kidnapped several of Colombia's most distinguished citizens shortly after his inauguration August 7, 1990. One of them was Diana Turbay, the daughter of President Turbay Ayala. By year's end Gaviria had agreed to all of Escobar's terms, including his demand that if he surrendered he would be housed in a prison designed to his specifications.[106]

By January 1991 Pablo Escobar was the only Medellín cartel member not to have accepted the government's generous amnesty offer. Fabio Ochoa had turned himself in the previous month, remarking that going to jail would let him awaken from the "nightmare" that his life had become.[107] His brothers Jorge and Juan gave themselves up a month later. But Escobar, who was still hotly pursued by the Search Block and mistrustful of the police who thoroughly hated him, continued his war. By that time his *sicarios* had murdered 475 police officers in Medellín. When police there killed two of his men in late January he retaliated, having hostage María Montoya executed and detonating a car bomb as fans surged out of Medellín's soccer stadium. On February 3, hostage Diana Turbay died during a police attempt to free her, probably at Escobar's order. Even as the Constituent Assembly worked to draft the country's new constitution, which was all but guaranteed to contain the no-extradition clause that he coveted, Escobar authorized the April 30 assassination of former Justice Minister Enrique Low Murtra.

All the while Escobar's lawyers liberally bribed members of the Constituent Assembly to make doubly sure they approved Article 35 of the new document, banning extradition. The article passed handily on a vote of fifty-one in favor, thirteen against, and five abstentions. Colombians were so thoroughly tired of the extradition issue and the violence surrounding it that even Assembly members who had refused Escobar's bribes voted for the measure. Most of the Colombian public applauded their action.[108]

Article 35 was approved on June 19, 1991, and on the following day Pablo Escobar turned himself in at the prison especially constructed for him on the side of a mountain overlooking Medellín. Not long afterward he appeared before a judge and read a statement in which he confessed to once having helped ship 400 kilos of cocaine to France and the Middle East. At the end of the typed statement he denied ever waging war against the Colombian government. He said his only crime against the state had been to fight extradition through legal means and in the press.[109]

Moment of Hope

"It would take Colombia at least a decade to regain confidence in its ability to confront criminal organizations. And when it broke up the Medellín cartel the cost paid by Colombians was enormous."
—Lawyer Miguel Silva[110]

Colombia breathed a collective sigh of relief in July 1991 when the new constitution was completed and went into effect. The Constitution of 1991 was born of a long spell of disillusionment with the bitter partisanship that touched off the *Violencia* in the 1940s and led to suspension of democratic governance during the 1950s. The Constituent Assembly that wrote the new constitution reflected Colombia's hope that new political parties would emerge to challenge the traditional Liberal and Conservative parties' monopoly on power. That desire appeared on its way to fulfillment when the constituent assembly was elected in December 1990. Nineteen of its sixty-four members were drawn from members of the M-19, which only months before had been a revolutionary group fighting to overthrow the government. When the Constituent Assembly began its work in February 1991, one of its co-chairs was, incredibly, the leader of the M-19.[111]

Those epochal developments on the national political front were mirrored by astonishing changes on the international scene. Collapse of the Soviet Union in late 1991 led pundits to announce the "end of history," claiming that democracy and capitalism had definitively triumphed in their long struggle against communism. Meanwhile a wave of neoliberal economic reform swept the world, carrying Colombia along with it. Trade barriers were lowered, state-owned companies sold, and free trade was held out as a panacea that would help close the gap between rich and poor.

All these events produced a climate of optimism in Colombia well-nigh unprecedented in national history. The opening of the political system, as well as wide-ranging reforms written into the new constitution, seemed to herald a new day. Suddenly ethnic and religious minorities were empowered, regional autonomy enhanced, and individuals granted unprecedented new civil rights. Many believed that these reforms would lead to an end of the decades-long insurgency of the FARC and the ELN. Those two oldest and most powerful guerrilla groups surely would follow the M-19 and EPL by demobilizing and sending their leaders into the democratic political fray. And best of all, at least for now, the violent traffickers' confrontation with state and society had ended. Rodríguez Gacha's death, Pablo Escobar's incarceration, and the Ochoas' surrender to the authorities had apparently dismantled the Medellín cartel. True, the Cali cartel emerged from its war with the Medellín group virtually unscathed and greatly strengthened. But the point was made that traffickers who violently defied the state did so at mortal risk to themselves.

Colombians had only slightly mixed feelings about the new constitution's Article 35, prohibiting the extradition of foreign nationals, a measure widely seen as their nation's response to the United States and its assumption that Colombia must dance to whatever tune it played. To many the provision was a guarantee that the recent horrors of Escobar's violence would not be repeated. The people had given him what he wanted. Only a few saw the prohibition of extradition as surrender to narcoterror. So at last the country enjoyed a moment of peace. Guerrilla conflict seemed to be ending. Economic and political changes at large in the world promised greater openness, freedom, and economic prosperity. And best of all Pablo Escobar was out of sight and mind, locked safely away in his prison. Or was he?

Pablo Escobar was not contrite when he began his incarceration in June 1991—far from it. Rather, he viewed the few years he would spend in jail as a temporary inconvenience, and he planned to go on managing his trafficking operation while imprisoned. Running illegal enterprises from prison was a time-honored tradition in Colombia. Just as Escobar began serving his sentence his associates successfully delivered 1.4 tons of cocaine to Spain.[112] Not only did he continue shipping cocaine to Europe and the United States, but he also imposed a tax on fellow traffickers running between $100,000 and $300,000, depending on the size of the shipment, and payable monthly.[113] He justified this by depicting himself as an industry pioneer who had brought the enterprise to its present state of success through great personal sacrifice. His army of *sicarios* remained intact, so collecting these taxes was not in doubt. Escobar remained in close contact with his colleagues by telephone and through personal visits. Under terms of his incarceration he was allowed visitors and meal delivery, and other creature comforts as well. The trucks bearing this constant flow of items were equipped with compartments hidden beneath the floors providing ample space for unauthorized visitors. Liberal bribes to those guarding the prison guaranteed that the trucks would not be searched with much vigor. The result was that over the first three months of his confinement Escobar received more than 300 visitors. Meanwhile a steady stream of trucks and construction workers made their way up from Medellín bearing building materials and luxury household items that soon turned the prison into something akin to a spa.[114]

As the public learned these details they started referring to his jail as the Cathedral. Located on a wooded mountainside on a piece of land purchased from one of *El Patrón's* front men, it was staffed not by prison guards but rather by his own henchmen. Anyone not connected with Escobar's organization was kept outside, more to guard against the trafficker's enemies than to keep him inside. A soccer field was built outside, and there was space for fiestas and special events. Large-screen televisions were installed and Escobar's men were housed in a dormitory building set apart from their chief's main residence. In the evening whiskey flowed, marijuana was smoked, and pornographic videos were viewed. A steady stream of beautiful women made their way up the mountain from Medellín to help inmates pass their hours of tedium. For many years the trafficking community had patronized Colombia's national beauty contests, helping contenders improve their chances by financing their plastic surgery. It was understood that the capos would later be able to inspect the surgeons' work first hand. A procuress in Medellín screened female visitors to the Cathedral and helped set their gratuities. At length the service became so popular that Escobar installed a statuesque model nicknamed *La Mona* (The Blond) in a guard post outside the prison to help handle the flow of overnight female guests. A small jail cell was constructed under the prison's main building where *El Patrón* could hold anyone who displeased him.[115]

Details of life in the Cathedral soon became common knowledge within Colombia and without, turning earlier satisfaction over Escobar's surrender to ashes. Once again the notorious killer had mocked the nation and its people and made them look like fools. In January 1992 César Gaviria examined photographs of the Cathedral's luxurious new living quarters and became furious. He began plans to move Escobar to the nearby Itagüí maximum-security prison.

Escobar, too, was having second thoughts about his accommodations. But his concern had to do with his own personal security. Word reached him during March 1992 that the Cali cartel had attempted to buy three large bombs pilfered from a military arsenal in El Salvador. He also learned that the same British mercenaries who had tried to kill him at Hacienda Napolés during June 1989 had again been contracted by Cali to bomb the Cathedral.[116] All the while the number of others planning to kill Escobar increased rapidly. Not long after his incarceration Escobar had paramilitary leader Henry Pérez murdered because he had learned that Pérez worked with DAS chief Maza Márquez and the Cali trafficking group during their war against Rodríguez Gacha. In having Pérez killed Escobar made enemies of the paramilitaries of Puerto Boyacá, a town lying just across the Magdalena River from his land-holdings in Antioquia.[117]

As the first year of his captivity drew to a close money problems started plaguing Escobar. Although his organization continued shipping massive amounts of cocaine to the United States, significant quantities were being seized by police tipped off by Escobar's enemies.[118] At the same time traffickers in Valle del Cauca were taking away an increasing share of his business. Making matters worse, his colleagues in Medellín were showing a growing disinclination to pay the taxes he demanded. As the months went by Pablo Escobar grew increasingly angry and paranoid. Finally, in June of 1992, he learned that two of his oldest associates, members of the Moncada and Galeano trafficking families, had failed to tell him about a twenty million dollar cache of U.S. currency that they had earned ten years earlier. Furious, Escobar summoned

William Moncada and Fernando Galeano to explain their actions. Only minutes into the meeting Escobar had the two men seized, tortured, and murdered. He then had his men hunt down and kill as many of the two men's employees as they could find. Within three days fifteen of them lay dead. That action, typical of *El Patrón*'s way of doing business, proved to be a colossal mistake.[119]

Within a few days of the Moncada and Galeano murders Pablo Escobar knew it was time to leave the Cathedral. On the third day of July a small plane dropped leaflets over Medellín charging him with the spate of murders. It was the same method Escobar himself had used to announce the formation of MAS eleven years earlier, and it said that his enemies were organizing against him. Escobar knew all too well the ruthless efficiency of such groups and the definitive nature of the justice they exacted. Within days of the leafleting of Medellín he received word that the government was planning to remove him from the Cathedral and send him to a real prison. Thus early on July 22, 1992, with Special Forces troops already on the way to remove him, Pablo Escobar fled the Cathedral.[120] The ease with which he did so caused the nation and its Chief Executive again look foolish and impotent. At the international level Colombia was a laughing stock.

Narcoterror returned to Colombia in the months following Escobar's escape. But this time the forces arrayed against him included the trafficker's own former associates, chief among them Fidel Castaño. The paramilitary leader had been an associate of Escobar's since the 1970s, and was the man chosen by Escobar in 1981 to direct MAS. But Castaño had been a friend of both William Moncada and Mario Galeano. And as an ardent anticommunist Castaño had never been happy with Escobar's frequent assertions of his leftist sympathies and his aid to groups like the M-19. During the months after Escobar's escape Castaño worked with the Galeano and Moncada families, and with leaders of the Cali cartel, to create a military organization capable of destroying Pablo Escobar and his gang. Under his leadership a five million dollar reward for Escobar's capture was raised from within the trafficking community, and it was soon matched by another two million dollars provided by the Colombian and U.S. governments, the latter through funds provided through DEA, FBI, and CIA budgets.[121]

As Fidel Castaño and his colleagues built their paramilitary army the government reconstituted the Search Force and sent its 1,500-men into Medellín yet again. Its arrival, on top of knowledge of Castaño's actions, was too much for a number of Escobar's top lieutenants, who turned themselves in during the months of September and October 1992. Those who didn't began to die. One of the first and most important of Escobar's henchmen killed was "Tyson" Muñoz, one of Medellín's most feared assassins and the man who had led the machine gun attack on Cali cartel soccer fans two years earlier. When members of the Search Force blew the door off his apartment in a Medellín skyscraper on October 28, they did so with such vigor that the door flew across the apartment and through a window, falling into the street below. The *sicario* was killed while attempting to flee. By year's end troops of the Search Force had raided thousands of buildings in and around Medellín, killing and capturing scores of Escobar's men.[122]

Escobar fought back as he always had, with a campaign of terror. Thanks to the paramilitary training that his men had received during 1988 and 1989, they were proficient in the use of car bombs, which they started using to blow up government buildings and businesses, particularly in Bogotá. Emulating Carlos Lehder, Escobar tried to wed his struggle against the state with that of the guerrillas, namely with the ELN, which had fronts in the *comunas* (poor neighborhoods) ringing Medellín. In January 1993 he announced the birth of a new guerrilla organization which he dubbed Antioquia Rebelde (Rebel Antioquia), that he hoped would unite gang members, ELN cadres, and his own *sicarios* as a bulwark against both state and paramilitary forces. But just when Escobar announced existence of Antioquia Rebelde he committed a new act of terror that led the ELN to disavow its link with the trafficker's new revolutionary organization. On Saturday morning, January 30, one of Escobar's men attempted to blow up the Bogotá skyscraper housing Colombia's Chamber of Commerce. When he discovered that the Chamber's parking garage was closed on Saturday he drove around the block and parked at the entrance of a pedestrian mall full of families buying school supplies for the upcoming academic year. The powerful blast killed twenty-one people, a number of them infants and children, and maimed over a hundred more. Pablo Escobar had always shrugged off the deaths of innocent bystanders killed in his campaigns against the state, saying "innocent people die in every war."[123] But the callousness of the January 30 attack united Colombians against him as never before.

One day after the ghastly bombing in Bogotá a letter was published that heralded the end of Pablo Escobar and the Medellín cartel. Its author was Fidel Castaño, and it announced the formation of a paramilitary group called the "Persecuted by Pablo Escobar" (*Perseguidos por Pablo Escobar*), or the PEPES, a well-armed and well-financed group organized through meetings with Antioquian industrialists, politicians, and ranchers, all anxious to stop the kidnapping and killing of people by Pablo Escobar and the "demented criminals" employed by him.[124] Fidel Castaño's younger brother Carlos recounted a dramatic moment in one of those meetings when someone voiced the fear that if they helped arm the new organization Escobar would have their families killed. Fidel Castaño replied "If Pablo kills your family for helping us, I will kill every last one of his relatives if they help him." The room fell silent and at length someone said "Then this is the end of Pablo Escobar!"[125]

In February 1993 the PEPES intensified their destruction of the Medellín cartel. By that time their organization had two divisions, one to gather intelligence on the structure of Escobar's group and the other to capture, interrogate, and then kill its members. Heading the PEPES' military arm was Diego Murillo, known as "Don Berna," who had been a Galeano family enforcer since the 1970s. Murillo and his men used an apartment located in Medellín's fashionable El Poblado neighborhood for their questioning of Escobar's associates. They invariably tortured and then killed them. During an especially intense phase of the anti-cartel operation, and with the cooperation of military forces engaged in what they called Operation Green Ruana, Don Berna had several of Escobar's henchmen hurled from military helicopters into the jungles of the Chocó.[126] In the early months of 1993 the PEPES murdered several of Escobar's lawyers, among them his chief spokesman Guido Parra, explaining that the lawyers' work for *El Patrón* had rendered them little better than common criminals. As Escobar's lawyers and some 300 members of his organization were being eliminated, *El Patrón*'s property was being destroyed. Dozens of his mansions and commercial enterprises were burned. The PEPES threatened and harassed Escobar's family members, burned his collection of antique cars, and even castrated his prized stallion Terremoto. All the while Escobar, in deep hiding, sent letters to Prosecutor General Gustavo de Greiff bitterly denouncing the PEPES' violations of his rights, employing the logic of counter-elites throughout Colombian history who fought the state while holding it to high standards in protecting their own civil rights.

Ordinary Colombians were dismayed by the tactics of the PEPES but pleased with their results. So too were officials of the United States, who made it a point to see that U.S. intelligence quickly made its way into the hands of the PEPES. Ambassador Morris Busby complained to César Gaviria about the group's human rights violations, but he did nothing to stop his government's support of them. DEA chief Joseph Toft complained that by helping the PEPES carry out their work he and his colleagues had "sold their souls." But his sentiment was based more on the fact that the group was also being helped by the Cali cartel rather than in any concern over Colombian-on-Colombian human rights abuses.[127]

As his organization was decimated before his eyes Escobar grew ever more desperate. Although he had offered a bounty of $27,000 for each Search Force officer assassinated, he had fewer *sicarios* capable of acting on the offer. Escobar's end was near by November 1993. The United States had made sure that his wife and children remained in Colombia, first denying them visas for travel to the U.S., and then arranging for them not to find refuge in Germany. In November the PEPES started murdering Escobar servants and family retainers, forcing the trafficker to send his family away to the greater safety of Bogotá. It was his concern for them that led to his death. By the first of December the Search Force had staged some 10,000 raids in Antioquia. Forty-seven of its officers had died carrying them out, but in so doing the special police force had the satisfaction of killing 129 of Escobar's men and capturing 132 others. The United States collaborated with electronic intelligence focused on monitoring the trafficker's telephone calls. It was one of those calls that finally betrayed *El Patrón*. On December 2, 1993, Escobar remained on the phone too long while speaking with his wife, thus giving the U.S. spy plane overhead time to pinpoint his location in a Medellín apartment building. Commander of the Search Force, Colonel Hugo Martínez Poveda, and his men attacked the building and flushed Pablo Escobar out and onto an adjoining rooftop, where he was killed. Thus ended the trafficker's campaign of terror that claimed hundreds of Colombian lives over nearly ten years' time.

The story of Pablo Escobar's and José Gonzalo Rodríguez Gacha's war against the state illustrates the effectiveness of anti-state terrorism in Colombia, while that of the PEPES reveals the effectiveness of paramilitary anti-terror terror. Another lesson contained in the bloody episode was that Colombo-U.S. collaboration in the area of law enforcement creates a synergy helpful in bringing violent anti-state challenges to a satisfactory conclusion. And it contains within it the story of a Colombian public steadfast before the traffickers' outrages and certain that their democratic state would eventually prevail over both José Gonzalo Rodríguez Gacha and Pablo Escobar.

Traffickers in Valle del Cauca emerged from their war against the Medellín cartel greatly strengthened in terms of their share of the cocaine export market. By U.S. estimates, in 1994 illegal drug dealers there, grouped under the rubric "Cali cartel," shipped most of the some 300 tons of cocaine reaching the U.S. from Colombia. While U.S. estimates of Colombian cocaine production and export varied greatly, generally over-estimating both, there was no doubt that some seventy-five percent of the cocaine reaching the United States came from Colombia, sent there by traffickers located in the Valle del Cauca.[128] To the despair of U.S. anti-drug warriors, Colombia was supplying seventy-five to eighty percent of the cocaine reaching the United States from Latin America, in the process earning twenty-five billion dollars annually. As the U.S. War on Drugs intensified cocaine prices fell, meaning that increasing amounts of the drugs were entering the country. By 1994 cocaine could be bought for as little as $10,000 per kilo in some parts of the U.S., down from $55,000 per kilo twelve years earlier.

Total cocaine imports from Latin America were estimated as running from 243 and 340 tons, while some estimates put the total at 400 tons.[129] The much-heralded War on Drugs was obviously being lost in an abject fashion.

Paradoxically, destruction of the Medellín cartel also spelled the end for the Cali trafficking group. The fall of Escobar, Rodríguez Gacha, and their *sicario* armies not only demonstrated that the drug cartels could not defeat the state, but suggested that the Valle del Cauca trafficking network would go the way of the Medellín group. Fully a year before the death of Pablo Escobar, U.S. electronic monitoring of trafficking operations in Miami brought indictments of members of the Urdinola-Grajales organization in northern Valle. Information uncovered on its leaders, most notably Iván Urdinola, enabled Colombian authorities to speedily arrest and try leading traffickers of Valle and send them to prison. The year 1993 found Miguel Rodríguez Orejuela petitioning the United States government for amnesty in exchange for surrendering to Colombian authorities. In October 1994 his brother Gilberto contacted Colombian authorities offering to have the entire Cali trafficking group surrender in exchange for reduced prison sentences. His arrest in Cali eight months later spelled the end of the Cali cartel.[130]

These events of the early 1990s did not mean that Colombia's ordeal was over. The illegal drug industry did not go away once the Medellín and Cali cartels were dismantled. Statistics revealed that Colombia remained awash in illegal drugs, both cocaine and, increasingly, heroin, and that Colombian traffickers continued to bombard the United States and Europe with those commodities. The industry's vigor is illustrated by the size of Gilberto Rodríguez Orejuela's trafficking organization at the time of his arrest on June 9, 1995. It included 1,500 employees handling cocaine sales and shipment, ninety-six retired army and police personnel on his payroll, nine members of the national congress reporting directly to him, and thousands of other Colombians employed in the host of functions integral to running a multi-national enterprise.[131] In other words, vast amounts of money continued to be made by successors of the original cartel leaders.

Happiness in Colombia dissipated quickly following victory in the country's war against the cartels. Not only did the illegal drug trade pass into the hands of other dangerous armed groups, but Colombia entered a period of political turmoil flowing from the Cali cartel's massive use of drug money to buy political favor during the 1994 presidential campaign. This was especially devastating because it led the United States to sharply cut its aid to Colombia. These difficulties centered on the country's new president, Ernesto Samper, whose campaign managers had accepted millions of dollars from members of the Cali group. Joseph Toft touched off the scandal when he made public cassette recordings of traffickers in Cali discussing the transfer of funds to Samper's campaign. Toft, who had just ended his tenure as Colombia's DEA chief in Colombia, returned to the United States where he repeatedly damned the country as a "narcodemocracy." Toft's actions, and the narco-cassette scandal, soured bi-national relations and severely weakened the Samper presidency.[132]

All of this took place at a time when the country's remaining communist guerrillas, especially the FARC and the ELN, were rapidly gaining strength. The long war against the cartels had distracted the Colombian government from its anti-guerrilla campaign, and the weakness of the state during Samper's presidency further encouraged the guerrillas. As the state failed to check the guerrillas' advance, anticommunist paramilitary groups organized to oppose the revolutionaries. And as the guerrilla-paramilitary struggle intensified during the 1990s, and continued on into the first years of the twenty-first century, illegal drug revenues played an ever more significant role in financing both groups' operations. In this sense Colombia's victory over the cartels marked but a single step in the journey toward controlling the country's illegal drug industry and its attending violence. The moment of hope following the cartels' defeat was all too brief.

CHAPTER 4

The Guerrillas' War Against the State

Introduction: Guerrillas and Drugs

"The drug mafia influenced the modernization of the guerrilla, aided in their contacts with arms traders, and, on occasion, served as their intermediaries."
—Former EPL member Alvaro Villarraga[1]

Colombia's guerrillas and illegal drug traffickers appeared at the same moment in history and shared notable similarities over the four decades of the two groups' rise and decline as threats to state and citizen. Along with the fact that both groups appeared during the first half of the 1960s, the guerrillas and the traffickers passed their first decade of activity little noticed by the average Colombian. The guerrillas were few in number and located far from centers of national life. The earliest drug dealers, who dealt in marijuana, were located on the country's northeastern Caribbean coast, an impoverished region far from the nation's heartland.

When the Colombian public did start paying attention to the guerrillas and the traffickers around 1975 they reacted similarly to both, with calm and a degree of unconcern. The average citizen was not initially disturbed by either group, despite the fact that the insurgents were dedicated to overthrowing the government by force of arms and in spite of the fact that the traffickers were acknowledged to be criminals. A substantial portion of the population saw the guerrillas as representing a legitimate popular response to social inequality, and to the country's flawed political system, while they viewed the marijuana traffickers as introducing a new non-traditional export seemingly on the verge of legalization, and bringing new economic life to one of the country's most backward regions even as it swelled foreign currency reserves.

This benign perception of guerrillas and traffickers reversed over the ensuing twenty-five years. By the beginning of the twenty-first century both groups were universally viewed as dangerously disruptive of national life and meriting both vigorous attack by the armed forces and exemplary prosecution by the judicial system.

The guerrillas and the traffickers were similar also in their disregard of the Colombian State and its citizens. Members of both groups perceived the State as their principal enemy and therefore a target of unremitting attacks. This made life hard for ordinary people caught in the crossfire. Traffickers were little concerned when innocent bystanders died, dismissing their deaths as collateral damage in their fight for survival. The guerrillas were even more callous. They viewed their fellow citizens as convenient sources of revenue via extortion and kidnapping for ransom. At the same time the FARC, the oldest of the country's communist guerrilla groups, routinely forced hapless young men and women into their ranks when they saw it convenient to do so.

Guerrillas and traffickers were alike in that they enjoyed substantial early success in their wars against the Colombian state. By the late 1980s Pablo Escobar and José Gonzalo Rodríguez Gacha had instilled such fear in the public that Colombians were willing to forgive anything if only they would halt their ghastly terrorist acts. And by the late 1990s the guerrillas were at the height of their drive to overthrow the Colombian government. By 1998 public order had deteriorated to such an extent that Colombians elected a president pledged to offer the FARC substantial concessions in exchange for peace. They looked on expectantly as newly-elected peace candidate Andrés Pastrana approached the FARC in a most abject fashion. But leaders of the nation's largest guerrilla group, flush with monies from their illegal drug dealings and equipped with the finest weaponry money could buy, brushed aside Pastrana's peace overtures and stepped up their war against an enemy they perceived as timorous and malleable, and therefore subject to defeat.

Colombia's weak state and intractable terrain were keys to the rise of both the guerrillas and the traffickers. These interconnected factors had always stood at the core of the country's periodic outbreaks of violence, and the two groups-in-arms profited from them in equal measure. Unlike the earlier violence, the presence of vast illegal drug wealth passing into hands of guerrilla and trafficking counter-elites lent Colombia's strife of the 1980s and 1990s an intensity that previous civil wars had lacked. The presence of near unlimited funding through illegal drug sales allowed the two groups to whipsaw the nation and its institutions, severely weakening and damaging both in the process. During the 1980s and early 1990s Pablo Escobar and José Gonzalo Rodríguez Gacha attacked the judicial and political systems with blood and fire, while the Cali cartel used its wealth to subvert those same branches of government, and the police and military as well. At the same time the guerrillas, increasingly buoyed by their own illegal drug revenues, moved ahead with their revolutionary project. The Colombian state lost control of ever larger portions of its national territory and levels of lawlessness increased. So too did illegal drug production. By the late 1990s Colombia's citizens and state were being swept into a maelstrom of illegality and violence formed by the latter's inability to control substantial parts of national territory, regions where the guerrillas and the manufacture of illegal drugs flourished in equal measure.

Their link to the greater world was another feature shared by the guerrillas and the traffickers. The country's communist insurgents based their philosophy on the writings of Marx and Lenin, drew heavily from the works of Mao Zedong, Ho Chi Minh, and, most importantly, those of Fidel Castro and Che Guevara. The burst of revolutionary enthusiasm seen in Colombia during the early 1960s was a direct consequence of Castro's success in Cuba in 1959, a fact that instantly made Colombia a front in the Cold War. Hence the guerrillas appearing in Colombia during the 1960s were fundamentally different from those of earlier years, nearly all of whom found inspiration in the philosophies of nineteenth century liberalism and conservatism, and whose links with their co-ideologists in other countries were tenuous at best.

Illegal drug trafficking was another exotic import within the context of Colombia's greater history. As has been explained above, the country had no history of supplying illegal drugs to the international market prior to the 1960s, when the first North Americans started arriving in search of high-quality marijuana, the "Colombia gold" fabled among gringo pot smokers. Ten years later Americans descended upon Colombia again, this time in search of cocaine. At their behest Colombia quickly became the leading producer of that lucrative commodity.

A final and defining similarity in the guerrillas and traffickers was the extent to which they drew the United States into Colombian affairs. The U.S. had always exercised influence in the country, but never so much as when Colombia became synonymous with illegal drugs and guerrilla insurgency. It was not lost on Colombians that both the guerrillas and the traffickers were in large part a function of U.S. power and wealth: the former drew on deep-seated hatred of U.S. imperialism and economic domination of Latin America, while the latter were fed by the seemingly insatiable demand for illegal drugs among well-heeled U.S. consumers. In the end the United States played a significant role in helping Colombia tame both the guerrillas and the traffickers.

Colombia's guerrillas benefited both directly and indirectly from the illegal drug trade. The M-19 was the first of the country's revolutionary groups to systematically make use of drug monies and the help of friendly traffickers to purchase weapons in international markets. It was the good luck of the Maoist EPL guerrillas to establish themselves in Córdoba, a department important in the export of marijuana during the 1970s and 1980s, and cocaine from the 1980s onward. And FARC guerrillas had drugs literally thrust upon them. Beginning in the late 1970s the Medellín cartel started paying members of the group's cadres to protect cocaine kitchens located in the equatorial jungles of southeastern Colombia. In 1982 the guerrilla group began taxing the *campesinos* who were growing coca for the Medellín group, a practice the FARC continued into the twenty-first century, by which time it had replaced both the Medellín and Cali cartels as Colombia's largest single cocaine producer. The only guerrilla group to resist financing its operations with drug revenues, the ELN, ultimately paid a high price for its high-mindedness. Not having drug wealth to draw on forced it to earn revenues almost entirely through extortion and kidnapping, making the ELN ever more hated as time went on and hastening its decline as an effective fighting force.

As well as benefiting them directly, illegal drugs helped Colombia's guerrillas in indirect ways. Virtually wiped out in a successful military operation in 1973, the ELN was able to rebuild when units of the national army, previously devoted to pursuing the ELN, were withdrawn and were sent away to destroy marijuana plantations during the administration of President Julio César Turbay (1978–1982). The same dynamic was seen in the area of law enforcement and criminal justice. Never strong or efficient, the nation's law enforcement became nearly non-functional during the onslaught of drug-related violence and criminality during the 1980s. This gave guerrilla groups an ever freer hand in recruiting new members and expanding their spheres of operation. The combined weight of illegal drug and guerrilla activity sent the country's law enforcement into virtual collapse by the late 1980s, the time when the FARC and ELN entered their period of greatest growth.

Perhaps the illegal drug industry's greatest indirect aid to the guerrillas came through its immense power to corrupt. From the 1960s onward Colombians were made aware, through the news media and personal observation, that public officials happily accepted money from traffickers, often in exchange for letting them pursue their criminal activity. Corruption had always been a feature of the nation's political system and helped explain the public's low opinion of their public servants. When drug money started surging through Colombia's economy, and growing numbers of politicians were added to the traffickers' payrolls, the nation's political system sank further into ill repute. Not coincidentally, Colombia's political nadir, 1994–1998, coincided with the FARC and ELN guerrillas' time of greatest vigor.

Colombia's guerrilla groups benefited indirectly from illegal drugs even when they decided to cease being guerrillas. This was the case between 1989 and 1991, when the M-19, the EPL, and several lesser insurgent groups signed peace agreements with the government. Coming at the most intense moment of the state's war against Pablo Escobar and Rodríguez Gacha, the grateful national government accepted their surrender under the most generous of terms. Not only were members of the two groups not held accountable for past crimes, many of which were horrific, but they were welcomed back into civil society with open arms. M-19 leader Antonio Navarro was elected by popular vote to help draft the country's 1991 constitution, while EPL leader Francisco Caballero was given a diplomatic posting in Europe.

Neither the FARC nor the ELN sued for peace during the Cartel War. Instead they used the years of the late 1980s and early '90s to greatly increase their troop strength and spheres of operation. And the FARC went on to become Colombia's largest single cocaine exporting organization as well. Just as the FARC and ELN were beginning what both believed to be their final campaign to seize the Colombian state, the national government was thrown into near-paralysis following revelations that illegal drug money had thoroughly penetrated its presidential and congressional branches. The scandal continued throughout the presidency of Ernest Samper, leading the United States to levy sanctions against Colombia during the last two years of Samper's four-year term, 1997 and 1998. Those years marked the height of the guerrilla offensive, a time when policymakers in the U.S. and elsewhere perceived the FARC to be on the verge of making good on its long-standing promise to replace the country's political system with a radical socialist one. With illegal drug production reaching unprecedented levels, and with FARC cocaine sales running hundreds of millions of dollars per year, there was real fear that a Colombian communist narcostate would destabilize northern South America and perhaps Central America and Mexico as well.

The remaining portion of this chapter traces three phases in the evolution of Colombia's revolutionary guerrillas. It sketches their slow initial growth between the 1960s and early 1970s, their appearance as a disruptive force in national life from the latter 1970s into the early 1990s, and their emergence as a significant threat to national institutions during the latter 1990s and first years of the twenty-first century. The following discussion makes clear the close correspondence of guerrilla successes in Colombia and growth of the country's illegal drug trade. Guerrillas and illegal drugs appeared simultaneously upon the Colombian scene. In many respects their relationship was a symbiotic one.

The Guerrillas During Colombia's Decade of Peace, 1965–1975

"Guerrillerismo and its fate in Colombia show concretely that the abstract defense of violence is in itself insufficient to guarantee a program which will serve as a revolutionary guide to the masses, and of the masses."
—Historian José F. Ocampo, 1975[2]

During the interval 1965–1975 Colombia's guerrillas were not merely an insignificant threat to the prevailing order, they seemed to be headed toward extinction. By 1975 Colombian

Marxists gloomily judged the guerrilla effort a failure. Meanwhile, anticommunists breathed sighs of relief that the revolutionary threat had seemingly passed. In 1975 the few remaining members of the ELN were hiding out in the mountains of northeastern Colombia. The FARC was only beginning to recover from the loss of most of its men and munitions during battles with the army during 1973.[3] The recently founded EPL lived a precarious existence, under furious military attack in the far-away mountains of northern Antioquia and southern Córdoba. And the M-19 had done little more than announce its existence by stealing a sword once owned by Simón Bolívar.

Yet while Colombia appeared to be a place where revolutionary guerrillas could not flourish, it was also condemned by history to have them. In the earliest days of the Cold War Marxist-Leninists perceived Colombia to be a country ripe for proletariat revolt. It suffered notable social inequality and had a stormy political history, and it possessed a militant Communist party and a vocal, left-leaning labor movement. Furthermore, just as the Cold War began in 1947 the country entered its slide into the *Violencia*. Thus it was that twenty-one-year-old Fidel Castro thought he might be part of Latin America's first proletariat uprising when, on April 9, 1948, he joined the massive riot known as the *bogotazo*, which destroyed major portions of Bogotá's city center. The incident was touched off by the assassination of Liberal party chief Jorge Eliécer Gaitán on a downtown street. It sparked a Liberal uprising against Conservative president Mariano Ospina Pérez and ultimately left over a thousand dead. The city's Liberal police force joined rioters, along the way handing Castro a rifle and inviting him to help them overthrow Ospina. The young Cuban found a place on a hill overlooking the national defense ministry and fired on it several times, hoping to kill someone of importance.[4]

The *bogotazo* and its echoes in towns and cities elsewhere in Colombia did not bring down the government of Ospina Pérez, although it did accelerate the *Violencia* and lead to formation of Liberal guerrillas a year later, in 1949. Still the *bogotazo* was essentially a Liberal revolt against Conservative rule that had few overtones of proletariat uprising.

Communism in fact had little chance of prospering in Colombia, a Roman Catholic country whose people are intensely entrepreneurial and who believe property ownership to be a God-given right. Once the Cold War started all of the country's leaders, Liberals and Conservatives alike, joined the anticommunist block led by the United States. Colombia was the only Latin American country to send troops to fight in the Korean War. During the mid–1950s the country was led by General Gustavo Rojas Pinilla, a rabid anticommunist who had received military training in the United States. When he became president Rojas declared the country's Communist party illegal and in 1955 sent the army into mountains south of Bogotá to wage a scorched earth campaign against campesinos whom he believed to be communists. For all these reasons communist gains in Colombia were minimal during the *Violencia* and in the decade following it. It was only after the country's army, police, and judicial system were attacked and weakened by the illegal drug industry that the revolutionary left could prosper.

Fifteen years before illegal drugs became a problem in Colombia members of its revolutionary left attempted to emulate Fidel Castro's revolutionary success in Cuba. Those who took up arms and went into the mountains after 1959 were in fact squarely within a national tradition extending back to the earliest days of the republic. Colombia's intractable terrain, upon which the hand of the government had always rested lightly, offered inviting shelter to counter-elite revolutionary forces. That was a key reason it had experienced armed uprisings over the entirety of the nineteenth century, many of which took on the character of guerrilla insurgencies at some point in their history. Most of those revolts were led by Conservatives aiming at toppling a Liberal regime in Bogotá, or Liberals taking up arms against Conservative governments that they viewed as oppressive. Most were short-lived affairs and only a few rose to the level of full-blown civil wars. The last of them, the War of the Thousand Days (1899–1902), cost the country dearly, especially near its end, when guerrilla warfare was its chief feature.

The formation of armed partisan cadres was a feature of twentieth century Colombian life in decades preceding Castro's Cuban Revolution. When tensions rose after the Liberal victory in the presidential election of 1930, leaders of both of the nation's traditional parties periodically called on their followers to take up arms. Conservative violence against Liberals in North Santander during 1932 led young Liberal leader Jorge Eliécer Gaitán to help arm his fellow party members. After a massacre of Conservative party activists by Liberal police in early 1939, Conservatives party leaders voted to help arm partisan self-defense forces. And when political violence spiraled out of control ten years later, when the Conservatives were again in charge of national politics, Liberal party leaders helped organize and arm partisan guerrillas who numbered 4,500 by 1953.[5]

During the gloomy years of the *Violencia,* Liberals reached out to members of the country's small Communist party for help in confronting national police who had been turned into what were essentially Conservative shock troops.[6] Thus as the *Violencia* raged Communist party members were present in numerous Liberal guerrilla organizations and in several discrete groups of their own.[7]

The power-sharing National Front accord of 1958 spelled the end of the *Violencia.* Liberal president Alberto Lleras Camargo presided over demobilization of the remaining Liberal guerrillas and the hunting down of *violentos* who had turned to banditry. In the end only a few small communist groups remained, living in scattered and remote agricultural communes, the largest of which was located in extreme southern Tolima, a region known as Marquetalia.[8] The Communist party had accepted the amnesty offered to all guerrilla groups when the National Front went into effect. But it continued to oppose the National Front, which it viewed as oligarchic and undemocratic. For these reasons communist leaders did not order their followers in the countryside to disarm. Rather, they announced that the scattered groups would be non-aggressive settlements promoting the "armed colonization" of party members.[9]

Fidel Castro's overthrow of the Cuban government took place just four months after the National Front went into effect. During his first year in power Castro began a thoroughgoing land reform program that led the United States to levy punitive sanctions against Cuba. The U.S. soon moved from sanctions to a plan of armed intervention carried out by Cuban exiles during April 14–17, 1961—the abortive Bay of Pigs operation. These events vastly energized members of Colombia's revolutionary left, among them a young man named Antonio Larrota.

Larrota had been active in the Colombian Communist party during the late 1950s but was expelled for failure to follow party policy, as well as for his anarchist tendencies. In January 1959, following a student protest over an increase in bus fares, he joined with others to form a revolutionary group called MOEC, the Worker, Student, Campesino Movement (Movimiento Obrero Estudiantil Campesino). Not long after that he traveled to Cuba, where he witnessed Castro's early reform activities and the Bay of Pigs attack. Those events inspired Larrota to return to Colombia, where he hoped to emulate Castro by establishing a revolutionary stronghold in Cauca, in company with the Liberal guerrilla-turned-bandit Adán de Jesús Aguirre ("El Águila"). Unfortunately for Larrota the Colombian government had learned of his activities and had offered a cash reward for his capture. This led Aguirre to murder him in mid–1961 in order to collect the money. That ended one of the earliest attempts to spark Castroite revolution in Colombia.[10]

At the same time Antonio Larrota met his fate in southern Colombia, his brother Ramón and a physician named Tulio Bayer were attempting to establish a revolutionary presence in the country's Eastern Llanos. Along with former Liberal guerrilla Rosendo Colmenares, they located their headquarters in the village of Santa Rita, on the Vichada River, some forty kilometers upriver from its confluence with the Orinoco. Their fates were similar to that of Antonio Larrota, though not as definitive. Army forces entered Santa Rita in October 1961 and arrested the three men and their followers, all of whom were subsequently given short prison terms. Ramón Larrota soon escaped and renewed his attempt to foment revolution. December 7, 1961, found him writing Cuba's Minister of Industry, Ernesto "Che" Guevara, asking Guevara to tell Fidel Castro that he and others continued to work toward freeing Colombia from Yankee imperialism and oligarchic rule, and that they would appreciate their help in the endeavor.[11]

At the moment Ramón Larrota was writing Che Guevara, Colombian-Cuban relations reached their breaking point. Throughout 1961 the government of Alberto Lleras Camargo had received reports that Cuba was sponsoring revolutionaries such as the Larrotas. Then late in November Conservative Party leader Álvaro Gómez blasted the Lleras government for allowing more than a dozen communist enclaves, which he termed "independent republics," to exist in over a dozen places throughout the countryside. Gómez' speech, along with the subversive actions of the Larrotas and others like them, and pressure from the United States, led Lleras to sever relations with Cuba on December 10, 1961. Just a week after that Fidel Castro delivered his famous "I am a Marxist-Leninist" speech.[12]

By early 1962 Colombia's military was making plans to eliminate the communist "independent republics," starting with the oldest and largest of them, Marquetalia. The communists of Marquetalia had been on a war footing long before it learned of the military campaign being planned against them. For six years they had fought a running battle against Liberal groups occupying territory in the region of Chaparral, just north of their commune. The Liberals were led by Gerardo Loaiza and referred to themselves as "*limpios*," meaning that they weren't sullied by communism. The communists were led by the charismatic Jacobo Prías Alape ("*Charronegro*"). The source of the dispute between the two groups was both territorial and ideological. Loaiza's *limpios* disliked the communists because they failed to respect private property, were not professing Catholics, and insisted on "breaking the hierarchical unity of the family," meaning that they advocated equal rights for women. The communists, on the other hand, criticized the Liberals for being undisciplined, prone to banditry, and obsessed with the notion of private property.[13]

Events in the *limpio*-communist warfare came to a head early in 1960, when three Liberal guerrillas entered the village of Gaitania, which was Marquetalia's chief settlement, asking to speak with *Charronegro*. When they came face-to-face with the communist leader they murdered him and then fled. What followed was the most intense phase of the war between the Liberal and the communist guerrillas of southern Tolima, resulting in the deaths of some fifty of the former and twenty-five of the latter, Gerardo Loaiza among them.

With the death of Prías Alape leadership of the communists passed to his lieutenant, a thirty-year-old campesino from Génova, Caldas, named Pedro Antonio Marín, nicknamed *Tirofijo* (Sureshot) for his skill with firearms. Marín, who had taken the *nom de guerre* Manuel Marulanda Vélez, for the labor leader killed by Conservative police in 1951, was commander of the Marquetalia colony when the Colombian army began making plans to destroy it.

The attack on Marquetalia was part of a multi-pronged military operation known as *Plan Lazo*, developed in consultation with the United States Southern Command headquartered in Panama. While the overall thrust of the operation was to stamp out the *Violencia* in all parts of Tolima, the Americans, and many members of the Colombian military as well, were especially interested in eliminating the Marquetalia settlement, which they perceived as disturbingly similar to the one Fidel Castro had founded in the Sierra Maestra mountains of eastern Cuba and from which he launched his successful revolutionary movement just a few years earlier.

When Colombia's army launched Operation Marquetalia during May and June of 1964, it did so in a way that was both definitive and excessive. Air force jets were called in to bomb and strafe the forested and largely unpopulated mountains and valleys of the region. Then on June 14 several thousand troops invaded Gaitania itself. But apart from a few skirmishes with *Tirofijo*'s rear guard the army forces found little of interest when they seized the settlement. Its forty-five families had long since slipped away to join their friends living in the communal settlement of Rio Chiquito, some fifty kilometers to the southwest in the department of Cauca. A year later, when the army attacked Rio Chiquito, the communists escaped a second time, trekking eastward across the valley of the Madgalena River, over the Eastern Cordillera of the Andes, and losing themselves in the jungle fastness of Meta and Caquetá.[14]

Manuel Marulanda Vélez and his followers gave up the idea of establishing permanent settlements following their defeats of the mid–1960s, adopting instead a strategy of hit-and-run guerrilla attacks. In 1966 they formally constituted themselves as the FARC, the Revolutionary Armed Forces of Colombia (Fuerzas Armadas Revolucionarias Colombianas), locating their center of operations in the mountains and jungles of Colombia's southeastern frontier zone.[15] Early in the 1970s they attempted to establish a second front in Marulanda Vélez' home department of Quindío, in the center of the country's coffee zone. But that brought a crippling attack by the army and yet another retreat into the country's southeastern jungles. No other significant FARC actions took place until the latter years of the 1970s. At its 1974 meeting in Meta the group's leadership vowed to continue the struggle but opined that they were happy to have lived to fight another day. At that moment the FARC consisted of some 750 men under arms, about the same number as ten years earlier.[16]

If the FARC suffered ongoing setbacks during Colombia's decade of peace, the fate of the ELN was much worse. The Ejército de Liberación Nacional (National Liberation Army) was born when university student Fabio Vásquez Castaño traveled to Cuba during 1962 in search of military training. Fidel Castro's government obliged him, and by 1964 Vásquez was back in Colombia launching his guerrilla group. Six months after its founding, on January 7, 1965, the ELN launched its first operation, an attack on the village of Simocota, Santander. They killed three of the town's police officers, losing one of their own members during the assault, robbed the town's agrarian bank of four thousand pesos, and left a manifesto promising to make Colombia a country worthy of virtuous citizens. The Simocota Manifesto ended with the words "Liberty or death!"[17]

At first fate appeared to smile on the ELN. The success of the Simocota raid attracted the charismatic priest Camilo Torres to its ranks, along with a number of student leaders from the Industrial University of Santander. But Torres was killed in an army ambush within months of his joining the ELN, in February 1966, and the group went on to pursue an ill-advised expansion into the lower Cauca River region of Antioquia. There, in the *municipio* of Anorí, during 1973, the army trapped and killed most of its members. The loss at Anorí seemed to spell the end for the ELN. Through the remainder of the 1970s the ELN was dispirited and adrift, and consisted of only a few score members.[18]

The unsuccessful early history of the FARC and the ELN was duplicated by the slightly younger Popular Liberation Army, EPL (*Ejército Popular de Liberación*). The EPL was the military arm of the Marxist-Leninist/Communist Party (PCML), a Maoist guerrilla force that combined the Chinese notion of "prolonged popular war," and Che Guevara's thesis that the inevitable proletariat uprising was properly begun by establishing *focos*, or small revolutionary enclaves in rural zones. But initial PCML attempts to apply Guevara's *foco* theory during 1967–68 were disasters. Their first sites in the department of Valle were quickly located and destroyed by the Colombian army. Other *focus* established in northeastern Antioquia and in the neighboring department of Córdoba managed to survive, but just barely. The EPL passed the decade of the 1970s rent by internal divisions and narrowly avoiding destruction by the government.[19]

The EPL's attempt to duplicate Mao Zedong's success in the Colombian countryside was clearly a failure. The country's rural population had only recently emerged from the *Violencia* and was hardly anxious to enter a new spell of bloodletting under the leadership of young men from the cities steeped in revolutionary theory they had learned in books. To be sure, rural Colombians suffered from the historic inequality of land ownership that condemned most of them to lives of poverty, ignorance, and poor health. Only recently, during the late 1960s, President Carlos Lleras Restrepo had set massive, largely peaceful land invasions into motion through his formation of a rural union called the ANUC (*Asociación Nacional de Usuarios Campesinos*). But Misael Pastrana, who succeeded Lleras in 1970, dismantled ANUC. Only the FARC remained stable over time, thanks to its origin as a campesino agricultural commune initially dedicated to self-defense, rather than to any grand scheme of peasant revolution. Were Colombia not on the verge of becoming the western world's leading illegal drug emporium it is likely that the country's revolutionary guerrillas would have been successfully contained by the country's small and under-funded military.

Guerrilla Advance During the Illegal Drug Boom, 1975–1993

"The link with the drug trade established by the farc revealed itself as a better and more stable source of revenue than the kidnapping and extortion practiced at an industrial level by the ELN."

—Political scientist Román D. Ortiz[20]

The mid–1970s were a time of recuperation and slow but steady expansion for Colombia's communist guerrillas. Leaders of the oldest and largest of them, the FARC, had always known that it must grow to prosper. Soon after its founding in the mid–1960s FARC leaders began sending mid-level cadres into strategic parts of the country under orders to establish fronts, or operational units, capable of existing on their own, optimally made up of thirty or more fighters. By 1978 the FARC counted 750 combatants distributed among some ten fronts.[21]

The FARC established one of its first fronts in the Middle Magdalena River region, the centrally located natural corridor linking the jungle fastness of southeastern Colombia, where the group had its headquarters, and the country's Caribbean coast. Following a "corridor to the sea" strategy developed at its Fifth Conference in 1974, the insurgent group turned the Middle Magdalena town and surrounding territory of Puerto Boyacá into one of its bastions. By 1980 six of its fronts operated in the region and wielded considerable influence. Virtually all political office holders in the town and surrounding *municipio* were members of the Communist party, which at the time was the FARC's political voice. All of them had been vetted by commanders of FARC fronts operating in the area.[22] The FARC enjoyed similar success in the hinterlands of the Gulf of Urabá, in the extreme northwest of Colombia. Lying at the Caribbean end of the "corridor to the sea," Urabá gave the guerrillas an ideal entry port for weapons and munitions.

The ELN was far behind the FARC in rebuilding its fortunes. Almost wiped out at Anorí, Antioquia, in 1973, the group first tried to return to its original home in western Santander, but found FARC fronts already established there. So the handful of surviving ELN members continued on northward into the department of Bolívar, and a few explored a region to the east, across the Eastern Cordillera, in the intendancy of Arauca.

Luckily for the ELN it was joined in 1974 by a defrocked Spanish priest named Manuel Pérez. "El Cura Pérez," as he became known throughout Colombia, was a tireless organizer who played a major role in rejuvenating the Castroite insurgent group. Thus by September 1975 the ELN was sufficiently strong to remind Colombians that it still existed, and to exact a measure of revenge for the Anorí defeat, by assassinating General Ramón Rincón, who had played a key role at Anorí, on a Bogotá street.[23] Still, it limped through the remainder of the 1970s divided by deadly internal squabbles. The ELN reached its low point in 1978 when it possessed just thirty-six men and women under arms.[24]

Farther still from constituting a significant fighting force was Colombia's third communist guerrilla organization, the EPL. The Maoist group remained holed up in the mountains of southern Córdoba, barely surviving in the face of repeated military operations against it. Yet several factors combined to keep it in the field, among them leader Francisco Caballero's friendship with and help from the ELN's new leader Manuel Pérez, the inspiration they drew from Maoist writings, including those of Albanian leader Enver Hoxha, and the timely swelling of its ranks by deserters from FARC Front 5. By July 1978 the group had enough men to attack and briefly hold the village of Puerto Libertador on the upper San Jorge River in southeastern Córdoba.[25]

Several events of the mid–1970s combined to sustain and encourage Colombia's guerrillas. The year 1975 witnessed the humiliating defeat of U.S. forces by communist guerrillas in North Vietnam. In 1976 Cuba adopted a new constitution under which that country would be officially organized as a Marxist-Leninist state. And in Colombia a general strike in September 1977, marked by a bloody government response, sent many militants to join the guerrillas. Finally, and most importantly, there was the rise and success of the M-19.

The M-19 brought new life to Colombia's armed insurgency through its daring and creativity, and its skill in promoting its revolutionary acts as motors of democratic reform and social justice. In 1975 the M-19 captured headlines by kidnapping Sears executive Donald Cooper and receiving a million dollar ransom for his release. The money financed its kidnapping and execution a year later of labor leader José Raquel Mercado, accused by the M-19 of betraying the cause of the workers. A year after that, in August 1977, several dozen M-19 members escaped Bogotá's La Picota prison, using dynamite to blow a hole in the prison wall. All the while the M-19 maintained a high profile and attracted new members by doing things such as hijacking milk trucks and distributing their contents to children in city slums. Its skilled use of publicity at a time of social and political unrest increased public sympathy for all of Colombia's revolutionary movements.

As the illegal drug trade gathered momentum during the 1970s it came to play an ever more significant role in guerrilla successes. The jail break of M-19 militants in 1977 had in fact been engineered by a notorious French heroin-turned-cocaine trafficker Laurent Fiocconi. During 1974 Fiocconi had escaped from a U.S. federal prison, where he was serving a sentence for heroin smuggling. He made his way to Bogotá, where he married a Colombian woman and then was adopted by a Colombian national named Hernando Rojas. Fiocconi subsequently killed his adoptive father, became involved in the rising cocaine industry, and was arrested in Bogotá for possession of chemicals used in cocaine processing.[26]

Marijuana played a major indirect role in advancing the guerrillas' cause during the last years of the 1970s. The election of Julio César Turbay in 1978 was attended by a scandal involving his links to the country's booming marijuana industry. Resulting pressure from the United States, and from his own constituency inside Colombia, led the newly installed president to mobilize the army and send it away to the north coast to uproot and destroy several hundred thousand hectares of cannabis. That severely depleted government troops in areas where they were normally present, relieving pressure on the guerrillas and making it easier for them to increase recruitment and operations. The M-19 led the way in both areas. As soon as the army announced Operación Fulminante, departing for the marijuana plantations during November 1978, M-19 members rushed to complete work on a 75-meter tunnel running from a sympathizer's home in a neighborhood adjacent to Cantón Norte, the army's base in Usaquén, just north of Bogotá. The tunnel extended to the armory of the base, and through it the guerrillas removed 5,000 rifles and other military hardware. That audacious theft, announced to the nation on January 2, 1979, embarrassed the military, vastly increased the prestige of the M-19, and heartened all of the country's revolutionary insurgents.[27]

As the M-19 was building its tunnel in Usaquén the FARC was concluding its Sixth Conference, held on the Río Duda in western Meta. The meeting was important for the decision made there to establish a FARC front in each of Colombia's twenty-one departments, with priority given those in the south that had access to the Pacific Ocean. Commanders of already-established fronts were sent away with orders to help finance the ambitious expansion by stepping up fundraising in areas under their control, this through the collection of voluntary contributions from poorer campesinos (*cuotas*) and protection money (*vacunas*) from wealthier ones. The plan was successful; it allowed the FARC to increase its fronts from nine to seventeen by the time of its important Seventh Conference in 1982, and to increase its fighting force by 25 percent, from 750 to 1000 men.[28]

Yet another important event in Colombia's worsening guerrilla violence was the kidnapping, torture, and assassination of Minister of Government Rafael Pardo Buelvas in September 1978. A small group called Workers' Self-defense Organization, or ADO (*Organización Autodefensa Obrera*), carried out the brutal act in reprisal for the killing of protestors by police during the general strike of one year earlier. Pardo Buelvas' murder scandalized Colombian society and led new President Julio César Turbay to issue a decree titled the National Security Statute, giving the military a free hand in detaining suspected subversives and trying them before military tribunals. The measure was effective in that it led to the arrest of the ADO leaders and, following the Cantón Norte weapons theft, most of the M-19 leadership as well. But the Security Statute was also highly unpopular in Colombia, a country whose military had traditionally been held in check by civil authorities. It also subjected the country to international criticism led by the human rights organization Amnesty International, which reported numerous cases of prisoner abuse during the nearly four years that the provision was in effect. Critics charged Turbay and his Minister of Defense, General Luis Carlos Camacho Leyva, of conducting an Argentine-style Dirty War in Colombia under the aegis of the defense decree. They also likened Turbay's security provision to the harsh National Security Doctrine imposed by Brazil's military during the late 1960s, and adopted by Uruguay and Argentina during the 1970s.[29]

The jailing of dozens of M-19 members following the weapons theft led the populist insurgent group to stage its most spectacular operation up to that time, seizure of the Dominican Embassy in Bogotá during March 1980. M-19 guerrillas held the building and sixteen diplomats who had been attending a reception there—one of whom was the U.S. ambassador—for two months. They demanded the release of their jailed comrades, a million dollars ransom in exchange for the hostages, and safe passage to Cuba. During the incident they argued that their acts were political in nature, and called for a national dialogue on the violence. That would become a key point in all subsequent conversations with the guerrillas, especially as it related to the granting of amnesty for crimes committed in the course of revolutionary actions. The M-19 also raised hopes by calling for peace talks with the government that they claimed might lead to eventual peace and their return to civil society.

At length Turbay agreed to all of the demands save that of releasing the jailed M-19 leaders. At the end of April, after sixty-one days occupying the embassy, the guerrillas were allowed to fly away to Havana where they were received as heroes. Two months later several key M-19 figures jailed in La Picota prison escaped by disguising themselves as prison guards.[30] In July 1980, M-19 leaders Jaime Bateman and Iván Ospina, who had been in Putumayo during the embassy takeover, arrived in Cuba at that country's invitation, to help celebrate that country's 1959 revolution and to receive Fidel Castro's personal congratulations for their successes.

The M-19 embassy takeover of 1980 proved signally important to Colombia's guerrilla movement. It revealed that a handful of committed revolutionaries could engage directly with the government and come away victorious in a manner unimaginable during the gloomy years of the early 1970s. The civil war could be fought in ways other than through frontal confrontations with the military.

As M-19 leaders considered their next moves the FARC was modifying its own strategy. Throughout its previous fifteen years of existence the country's largest guerrilla group had avoided direct engagement with the Colombian army on the theory it would lose any firefight with the better armed government troops. But with their fortunes improving, and a significant number of government forces still committed to the marijuana eradication effort near the Caribbean coast, the FARC decided to adopt a more aggressive strategy of seeking out and engaging the army's anti-guerrilla units. Thus in August 1980 members of a FARC front numbering more than a hundred fought a twenty-three man army patrol, killing three and capturing its other members. It was the first time any guerrilla group had enjoyed that level of success against the country's regular army.[31] The incident shaped future FARC strategy as well. Two years later, at its Seventh Conference, the campesino guerrilla force officially embraced the aggressive offensive stance that it would maintain for the next twenty years.

Early 1981 was marked by a flurry of new M-19 activity. During January the group sent units across the lightly guarded Ecuadorian border into the frontier intendancy of Putumayo, and through the Pacific Ocean port of Tumaco into the department of Nariño. This "invasion of the south," employing weapons shipped through Cuba and Panama, led Colombia to again sever relations with Cuba, in March 1981. Meanwhile the M-19 took steps to beef up the weaponry of fighters in its new Southern Front. In May 1981 its agents in Belgium, flush with money from the recent embassy hostage-taking, purchased several hundred tons of rifles and munitions on the black market and a ship for transporting them, the *Karina*.[32] The *Karina* incident, the M-19's opening of its Southern Front, and recent FARC successes in Meta and Caquetá, all intensified pressure on the government to enter into peace talks with the guerrillas in hopes of halting the escalating violence.

Within months of his taking office in 1978 it became clear that Julio César Turbay's hard line against the guerrillas had merely strengthened them. New recruits were joining the M-19 and other insurgent groups at accelerating rates, and levels of violence were increasing. The M-19 was especially effective in shaping public opinion through news releases stressing the political character of their acts, and portraying the government and armed forces as undemocratic imperialist lackeys and oppressors of the people. Their criticisms grew sharper once arbitrary arrests and prisoner abuse became commonplace under the state of siege in effect throughout Turbay's presidency, and under the new National Security Statute. Criticism of the government and its heavy-handed policies resonated not only with the Colombian public but also with foreign governments and international human rights organizations. By the midpoint in his presidency the din of criticism was so great that Turbay let it be known he supported a law granting amnesty to all of those in arms. Congress accordingly produced an amnesty law in March 1981. But the guerrillas rejected it because it did not apply to guerrillas accused of capital crimes or to those in jail and awaiting trial.

Once it was clear that the new law was a failure, public figures and editorial writers of leading newspapers repeated their calls for conversations with the guerrillas and the drafting of a more lenient amnesty law. The president responded in September 1981 by appointing a peace commission headed by former president Carlos Lleras Restrepo. One of the commission's first acts was to modify the National Security Statute provision allowing the preventive detention of those suspected of terrorist acts. That modification regulated the terms of preventive detention to prohibit torture and other forms of inhumane treatment of detainees.[33] Meanwhile prestigious public figures, including the members of Turbay's peace commission, agreed that unless the government accepted the guerrillas' thesis that their crimes were of a political nature and not subject to prosecution under normal criminal statutes, then little progress toward peace would be forthcoming. That conviction, and the increase in violence during 1981, ratcheted up pressure on the government to draft a more lenient amnesty law.

A new amnesty law was passed by Colombia's congress in February 1982, but it too was rejected by the guerrillas, who disliked its requirements that hostilities be suspended while demobilizations took place, that the groups involved identify their members, and that they accept certain guidelines for their reincorporation into civil society. This was discouraging to the president's peace commission, which resigned en masse a month after the second amnesty law was passed. In a letter to Turbay they cited intransigence on the part of the guerrillas—

the M-19 had ended a communication to them with the phrase "To power through arms!" They were also critical of intransigence on the part of the armed forces. The president responded with a letter of his own, in which he cited the military's complaint that the commission had focused too narrowly on achieving peace with the M-19 while seemingly ignoring the fact that it was only one of several groups under arms.[34] At that moment Turbay's presidency was nearing its end. Rather than pursue the peace initiative he lifted the state of siege of June 20, and five days later Belisario Betancur was elected on a pro-peace platform.

Public support for peace talks had built throughout Turbay's presidency, and by the time of the 1982 presidential campaign 70 percent of Colombians surveyed believed that the incoming government should continue trying to come to terms with the guerrillas. All candidates in the contest had strong pro-peace planks in their platforms, that of Conservative Party candidate Belisario Betancur being the strongest. Betancur won the election with a strong plurality of votes, thanks to the fact that Alfonso López Michelsen and Luis Carlos Galán had split the Liberal vote.[35]

Belisario Betancur's plan for peace with the guerrillas was exceedingly open-handed. During the presidential campaign he had advocated a blanket amnesty for those in arms against the state, with no preconditions other than that the guerrillas lay down their weapons and return to civil life. To help achieve this he appointed a peace commission immediately after his August 7 inauguration. Among its members were a representative of the Communist party and a demobilized former member of the M-19. Amidst a flurry of negotiations in which most of the groups in arms participated, congress passed Betancur's amnesty law on November 19, 1982, and the president signed it on the following day.[36] As that process neared its completion the government released nearly 300 imprisoned guerrillas, including almost all of the M-19 leadership, on their promise that they not return to the field. But most of the M-19 members took up arms again.

The response of M-19 commander Jaime Bateman was disappointing. Three days after the president had signed the amnesty law Bateman rejected it, saying it should have been accompanied by thoroughgoing political and social reforms. His actions were in part influenced by the fact that his group's second front in southern Colombia had recently been armed by weapons from the *Karina*, while Bateman had come to believe that recent guerrilla advances in Nicaragua and El Salvador pointed toward similar success in Colombia. Bateman also drew confidence from the support of Fidel Castro, Manuel Noriega, and Daniel Ortega. And Bateman was in the process of reestablishing good relations with Pablo Escobar and the Medellín cartel, thus insuring his group invaluable internal support for his anti-state activities.[37] The FARC's response to Betancur's amnesty program was more promising. That group entered into negotiations with the government's peace commission early in 1983, saying they might consider laying down their arms in the near future. But in the end the FARC proved little more forthcoming than the M-19. The FARC renewed its war early in 1983, establishing fronts in new geographic regions. These discouraging developments led the chairman of Betancur's peace commission to resign in early May, causing negotiations to be suspended.

Meanwhile the president's peace initiative was meeting stiff resistance from the nation's military. The army, which had enjoyed cordial relations with Julio César Turbay, was skeptical of Belisario Betancur from the moment he became the leading peace candidate in the 1982. Military leaders held that the guerrillas would never bargain in good faith with the government and could only be made to do so through military action. The generals also spoke for Colombians living in parts of the country under guerrilla influence, where extortion and kidnapping had become ongoing features of life for all except the poorest citizens. Betancur's own Minister of Defense, General Fernando Landazábal, was his most troublesome military critic during the first years of his presidency. Landazábal and his colleagues were furious when Betancur freed hundreds of jailed guerrillas just months into his presidency. By the end of Betancur's first year in office they were pressuring him to let them renew their offensive against the insurgents. In January 1984 Landazábal granted a radio interview in which he accused the guerrillas of negotiating with the government in bad faith, and he promised that the armed forces would never let the insurgents take the government by force of arms. Ten days later Betancur sacked his defense minister, thereby reminding the generals that they were not permitted to intervene in political matters.[38]

Late 1983 Belisario Betancur resumed his peacemaking efforts. He reconstituted his peace commission and met personally with M-19 leaders while on official trips to Spain and Mexico. Suddenly in March 1984 the FARC came to term with government, agreeing to a one-year cease fire to begin the following month. The country's largest guerrilla group also announced it was forming a political party that would promote its reform programs within the setting of democratic politics. It launched the Unión Patriótica party the following year. These developments caught the M-19 by surprise. Initially it denounced the FARC for insufficient commitment to its revolutionary ideals. But the FARC's truce brought pressure on the M-19 to make a similar gesture, which it did in declaring a cease fire during late August 1984. The EPL and radical Worker's Self-defense Organization (ADO) followed suit within days. Belisario Betancur and his supporters breathed a sigh of relief when all of the accords had been signed. The agreements seemed to be proof that two years of often frustrating negotiations with guerrillas had been worth it. Mid-way through Betancur's presidency only the ELN continued to reject the government's peace overtures.

Colombia's military vehemently opposed the entirety of Betancur's peace program. The day Belisario Betancur was elected president someone in the army, probably General Landazábal, wrote a bitter denunciation of the way his country's civil population failed to understand the gravity of the guerrilla menace. His essay, circulated anonymously in military circles, expressed the writer's conviction that the country would never respond effectively to the guerrilla challenge until the public elected decisive civilian leaders. The writer warned that hasty moves toward peace on the part of the government would simply encourage the guerrillas.[39] Especially troubling to the military was the national policy separating the military and civilian spheres. The principle of military autonomy was spelled out in 1958 in the "Lleras Doctrine," formulated by the first National Front president Alberto Lleras Camargo. His separation of military from civilian decision-making was an outgrowth of Gustavo Rojas Pinilla's dictatorship of 1953–57. But for a nation suffering a burgeoning insurgency it made little sense to the military that it should be isolated from policy decision-making concerning the guerrillas. And it seemed unfair that in the face of growing civil disorder the military's budget and armed force should remain proportionately one of the smallest in all Latin America. The 1.5 percent of GDP allotted to the Colombian military was less than half that of other countries in the region, and Colombia's three soldiers per 1000 population was half that of the largest states of the region, Brazil, Mexico, and Argentina.[40]

Ultimately events supported the view of Colombia's military leaders. As the Colombian people and their new President worked for peace the guerrilla intensified their war. Among insurgent groups the FARC was best positioned to take advantage of the breathing space offered by Betancur's peace initiative.

The FARC concluded its important Seventh Conference, in May 1982, shortly before the election that brought Betancur to power. Its steady growth, along with appearance of new revenues from illegal drugs, enabled the guerrillas to formalize the shift to an offensive strategy taking shape since their 1980 ambush and seizure of an elite army anti-guerrilla unit. Called the New Form of Operating (NFO, *Nueva Forma de Operar*), it envisioned surrounding the national capital with a force of 16,000 armed fighters, cutting the city's food supply, and thereby causing a general uprising against the government. When that came to pass FARC leaders would emulate both Fidel Castro and Daniel Ortega and ride triumphantly into Bogotá at the head of their rebel army.[41] The NFO was fanciful when announced, as the FARC's total armed force consisted of just 1,000 men. Yet thanks to the peace initiative of Belisario Betancur the FARC grew virtually unimpeded for four years, more than tripling by 1986, to 3,600 fighters.[42]

The encirclement and seizure of Bogotá was part of the FARC master plan for eventual triumph drawn up at the 1982 meeting. Called the Strategic Political-Military Plan (*Plan Estratégico Político Militar*), it projected continuation of the insurgents' early "centrifugal strategy" of continuously spinning new fronts out into key parts of the nation. The plan was spectacularly successful, for it allowed the FARC to increase its fronts from seventeen to thirty by Betancur's last year in office.[43] The FARC made no effort to hide its grandiose scheme. When the Seventh Conference adjourned the group had added the letters "EP"—*Ejército Popular* (Popular Army)—to its name, to indicate that it had transformed itself into a peasant army. Over the ensuing twenty years the FARC-EP would continue to expand, faithfully following the strategy outlined in 1982.

Money derived from illegal drug sales figured prominently in FARC planning. Its decision to tax coca farmers and drug traffickers was formalized at the Seventh Conference. There was also general agreement at the meeting that the commanders of fronts operating where cocaine kitchens operated could steal from the traffickers when convenient.[44]

The cocaine boom created certain anomalies in FARC-held parts of eastern Colombia, for it made extortion and kidnapping less important than in other regions of the country where drug monies weren't abundant. When newspaper reporters from Bogotá visited the headquarters of FARC Front 15 in the jungles of Caquetá, a site of major cocaine manufacture, they discovered an idyllic setting in which 300 men and several score women and children bathed and swam in limpid river water, watched the latest movies on Betamax videos, and participated in community theater productions under electric light supplied by two generators. Meanwhile their leaders toasted visitors with champagne. All of them were equipped with the best light weaponry available at the time. The guerrillas were open about receiving money from drug dealers but professed ignorance as to how their benefactors came by the money.[45]

Of Colombia's major insurgent groups the only one having scruples against financing operations with drug money was the ELN. The Roman Catholic moral strictures that the group embraced condemned psychoactive drug use as an affront to human dignity. This rejection of drug-related financing helps explain ELN weakness up to 1983. But the ELN had good luck that year thanks to a major oil discovery in the intendancy of Arauca, where it had recently established its Domingo Laín Front.

The ELN's approach to the Caño Limón-Coveñas oil field was as paradoxical as it was lucrative. On one hand the group's hatred of what it viewed as imperialistic exploitation of Colombia led it to attack the pipelines carrying the oil on its way to world markets. The ELN's first dynamiting of the Caño Limón pipeline took place in 1984, and its sabotage of the pipeline would continue incessantly into the twenty-first century. In 1986 the ELN proclaimed an all-out military offensive against oil-exporting companies, warning "Wake up Colombia ... they are stealing our oil!"[46] At the same time the ELN had entered into a lucrative relationship with the German and Italian corporations contracted to develop the oil fields. In 1983 the ELN kidnapped four engineers working for the Manessmann Corporation, ultimately receiving a $4 million ransom for their hostages, a promise that an additional $4 million would be invested in local infrastructure projects and that company vehicles would bear the signs reading "Manessmann has a heart for children." Thanks to monies received from Manessmann and other foreign corporations, received through extortion and as ransom payments received in exchange for kidnapped company executives, the ELN quickly moved from being an insurgent group on the brink of extinction to Colombia's most affluent guerrilla group by the mid–1980s. In 1985 the ELN had 800 well-armed members whose per capita wealth outstripped that of all other groups in arms.[47] Its new wealth allowed it to establish fronts in Valle, Córdoba, Magdalena, North Santander, and in the Lower Cauca River region of Antioquia. By the mid–1980s the ELN had the satisfaction of driving representatives of the Colombian state out of Anorí, the site of its near annihilation ten years earlier.[48]

The EPL, like the ELN, drew major revenue from kidnapping. But unlike their straight-laced sister group, Córdaba's leading guerrilla organization had no qualms about using the drug industry to help supply it with money and armaments. By the 1980s Córdoba had become a major export point for both marijuana and cocaine. It had a Caribbean coastline and was strategically located between the Gulf of Urabá to the southwest and the Gulf of Morrosquillo to the northwest, both bodies of water favorite points of departure on the Caribbean for drug laden ships and launches. The department was also dotted with airports, many of them clandestine, which collectively witnessed thousands of drug-related flights from the late 1960s through the remainder of the twentieth century. As in the case of the FARC, the EPL collected fees from traffickers for protecting their shipments, and levied taxes on them as well. Those monies were then used to pay for weapons, ammunition, and supplies that were smuggled back into Colombia on the traffickers' ships and airplanes.[49]

EPL leaders welcomed Belisario Betancur's peace initiative as giving them a way to enter politics while continuing their revolutionary activities. The strategy served them well, for by 1985 it was able to hold its Third Conference and move forward with plans to turn its followers into a true *campesino* army. Its membership had grown 300 percent, to some 450 well-armed fighters.[50]

By the mid–1980s a resurgent EPL was sowing terror throughout the rich agricultural and ranching zone around the department's capital of Montería, kidnapping widely and indiscriminately. Founded in 1967 by students at the Universities of Cartagena and Córdoba, the EPL quickly embraced kidnapping as its chief source of funding, on the logic that any Colombian not actively supporting the group was an enemy and thus subject to "retention" by the group's members.[51] Around 1980 the EPL had welcomed to its ranks a virtuoso kidnapper, one Antonio Martínez Pastrana. Known throughout the region as "El Viejo Rafa" (Old Rafa), Martínez had served the EPL during the 1970s as an informant and messenger. It was his love of kidnapping and his skill at it that quickly made him an economic mainstay of the EPL. By the mid–1980s "El Viejo Rafa" was known throughout Córdoba's Alto Sinú region for his ploy of developing a near paternal relationship with the ranchers and farmers he was extorting only to later kidnap them. "El Viejo Rafa," who was widely believed to have supernatural powers, had his headquarters in Ayapel, in extreme eastern Córdoba, not far from the Cauca River. Throughout early years of the 1980s businessmen, ranchers, and farmers trekked to the remote village to deliver up their *vacunas* to him. While the police knew where the EPL leader lived and what he was doing they were afraid to venture into his domain.

Only members of Córdoba's trafficking community were safe from Martínez Pastrana's attentions. El Viejo Rafa refrained from extorting or kidnapping them, or even irritating them. Instead he became their business partner, doing nothing more than taxing marijuana and cocaine shipments departing their clandestine airports and using their help in arming and sup-plying his troops.[52] In this regard he was more intelligent than leaders of the M-19, who had attempted to extort money from the traffickers.

Like the EPL, the ELN, and the FARC, the M-19 had prospered over the first three years of Belisario Betancur's peace initiative. Yet none of Colombia's insurgent groups had been more disingenuous than the M-19 in dealing with the president. It had been the populist and nationalist group's call for national dialogue and peace talks in 1980, during the embassy hostage-taking, that had first excited Colombians and set forces into motion that carried Betan-cur to power two years later. But when Betancur offered the M-19 unconditional amnesty in November 1982, its leader Jaime Bateman flung the offer back in his face, opening new fronts and carrying the war into rural areas. The M-19's duplicity was a function of its misperception of its own power and influence and of its demonstrated ability to raise money to finance its operations. In the end those same qualities sent it into decline and ended its time as a fighting force.

The M-19's rise and decline as a guerrilla group serve as a case study of the dynamic rela-tionship existing between Colombia's revolutionary insurgents and illegal drug money. Although kidnapping and extortion were the guerrillas' initial source of funding of all major guerrilla groups, illegal drug revenues soon became the most important source of funding for all save the ELN. Those monies paid for impressive growth and increasingly audacious and violent attacks on state and citizenry. The guerrillas' relatively easy early successes and increas-ingly violent actions ultimately led to a national reaction against them. The M-19 both over-estimated its own power and the persuasiveness of its revolutionary message, and misread the public mood.[53] Its leaders interpreted the Colombian public's longing for peace, and Belisario Betancur's generosity of spirit and civility, as timidity and weakness. Hence when they took the Palace of Justice they naively believed that Belisario Betancur would walk there from the presidential palace and submit himself to a mock trial for his supposed betrayal of the peace process. The M-19 members who conducted the operation likely anticipated flying away to Cuba after the operation, a substantial ransom in hand, as they had done following their seizure of the Dominican Embassy some five years before. Nor did the M-19 accurately gauge the depth of the military's anger against them. All these errors of perception came to a head when they seized the Supreme Court building. The military brushed aside the president who had refused to consult with them and went on to kill the M-19 attackers. Colombians criticized the military's brutality in retaking the Palace of Justice. But the debacle also sullied the image of the M-19 and paved the way to the group's dissolution as a fighting force.

It was the unenviable task of Virgilio Barco, who succeeded Belisario Betancur in the presidency, to lead the government against insurgents bent on overthrowing it, as well as against drug lords who used terrorism to bend it to their will. To Barco's credit he fought both the guerrillas and the traffickers with greater success than had either of his two predecessors. At the same time he significantly furthered reform of Colombia's political system and presided over demobilization of what had become the country's third-largest guerrilla group, the M-19. When he took office Barco announced a "plan of national rehabilitation" aimed at the country's poorest *municipios,* founded on the notion that by reducing poverty and inequality he would remove the guerrillas' chief reason for existence. At the same time he required that peace-making activities be under government auspices, and that talks with insurgent groups be held in designated areas. He also required complete demobilization of guerrilla forces in exchange for government aid in helping ex-guerrillas re-establish themselves in civil society.[54]

Initially Barco's peace effort met with little success. Ten months after his inauguration the FARC, still claiming to honor its cease-fire proclaimed during the administration of Belisario Betancur, ambushed an army column in Caquetá, killing twenty-seven soldiers and wounding forty others. The event prompted Luis Morantes ("Jacobo Arenas") to remark laconically that "these kinds of incidents are natural in a truce of this sort."[55] Virgilio Barco and the Colombian people did not see it that way. The FARC ambush marked the definitive end of the cease-fire that had ostensibly been in effect between the government and the FARC since mid–1984. Shortly after the Caquetá ambush, in September 1987, the FARC hosted a meeting bringing together leaders of the M-19, EPL, ELN, and two smaller guerrilla groups to form the umbrella Coordinadora Guerrilla Simón Bolívar (CGSB), whose goal was to better coordinate the insurgents' military operations. Over the several years of its existence the CGSB did coordinate a few joint operations, such as one launched in October 1988, when a joint FARC/ELN/EPL force overran and annihilated a small contingent of troops at army base in Urabá, in what they termed the Battle of Saiza. It was the CGSB's answer to a peace plan released by Virgilio Barco one month earlier.[56]

The M-19 did not participate in the Battle of Saiza, though at the time it remained a member in good standing of the CGSB. At that moment the M-19 was moving quickly toward coming to terms with the Colombian government, a process that when completed would make the non-communist insurgents the first guerrilla group to demobilize.

A number of factors forced the M-19 to demobilize, first among them its decline as a fighting force. Founded as an urban guerrilla group, it had dwindled to fewer than a thousand combatants as a result of ongoing operations against them by the Colombian army, and by the tarnishing of its image after their seizure of the Palace of Justice. By 1988 the remnants of the M-19 lived a miserable existence high in the mountains of northeastern Cauca, far from the cities that were the setting of its earlier notable actions. Over the five years since the Palace of Justice assault the group had not carried out any notable operation, and between 1983, when Jaime Báteman died in a plane crash, and 1988, it had lost seven of its leaders in combat. At a time when the FARC and ELN were flourishing the M-19 had become irrelevant, with many Colombians uncertain whether it remained an organized force. Still in spite of its decline the M-19 retained its ability to capture the attention of the Colombian public through daring acts. That was the case on May 29, 1988, when it kidnapped Conservative party leader Álvaro Gómez, killing his two bodyguards and dragging Gómez away to spend two months imprisoned in a house in western Bogotá, not far from the city's airport.[57] In explaining the kidnapping M-19 leader Carlos Pizarro cited recent massacres carried out by paramilitary forces in Urabá and Córdoba, killings he linked to the government of Virgilio Barco. By kidnapping Alvaro Gómez, whom Pizarro characterized as a typical representative of the "oligarchic regime" running the country, he would call attention to the "dirty war" starting to take shape alongside the ones being waged by the drug traffickers and the guerrillas.[58]

But there was much more to Carlos Pizarro's decision to kidnap Alvaro Gómez than concern over the recent spate of paramilitary depredations. That became clear a few days after the act when Pizarro issued a series of communiqués demanding public discussion of its grievances in exchange for which it promised a cease-fire and the speedy release of Alvaro Gómez. When Virgilio Barco grudgingly agreed to the meetings, the M-19 released Gómez. Not long afterward, on September 1, 1988, Barco released a Peace Plan that he and his advisers had been working on since early in the year. It was detailed and specific, and spelled out precisely how insurgent groups would lay down their weapons and reintegrate their members into civil life. Shortly after that Pizarro, speaking on behalf of the CGSB, responded positively to the president's plan.[59] Events moved rapidly after that. In December Virgilio Barco announced that the M-19 would soon enter into peace talks, and a month later conversations between M-19 leaders and government negotiators took place in southern Tolima, not far from the FARC birthplace of Marquetalia.

Political considerations were uppermost in the minds of M-19 leaders when they started their move toward demobilization. Political reforms long advocated by the group had started taking hold in Colombia, first in March 1988, when the country held its first-ever mayoral elections.[60] In them the Unión Patriótica party, which had been founded by the FARC three years before, won sixteen of the country's nearly five hundred mayoral posts. Later that year the national congress began debating reform of the national constitution, and at year's end Virgilio Barco told the nation that he supported further opening the country's democratic system at every level of government. Not long after that he responded to a chief demand of the M-19 by striking down a law permitting the military to arm citizen self-defense groups, a practice widely criticized as promoting paramilitary activity. All this convinced the M-19 to lay down its arms, a decision made all the easier by the group's lack of a deterministic political ideology. Meanwhile the FARC damned the M-19 for having "passed over to the side of the government."[61]

In October 1989 Carlos Pizarro announced that he would run for president in Colombia's upcoming elections. It was a remarkable statement coming from a man still technically in revolt against the government he now proposed to lead by winning a democratic election. Still the announcement was welcomed by Colombians reeling from Pablo Escobar's terroristic assault on state and society. The government's peace talks with the M-19 continued through the remainder of the year, and in January 1990 a final peace accord was signed between Pizarro's group and the Colombian government. On March 9, 1990, Pizarro met with President Virgilio Barco and heard the President say "Welcome to democracy."[62] The M-19 turned itself into a political party, the Alianza Democrática M-19, and on May 27 won 12.4 percent of the presidential vote, that being the largest ever polled by a candidate of the left.[63] But Carlos Pizarro Leongómez was not his party's candidate; rather the person receiving the unprecedented vote was his second-in-command, Antonio Navarro Wolff. Pizarro had been assassinated a month earlier by a teenager hired by paramilitary leader Carlos Castaño. At the time Castaño was locked in combat with the M-19 leader's one-time associate Pablo Escobar, and he had reasoned that because of the long association between the M-19 and the Medellín cartel a Carlos Pizarro victory would also be a victory for Pablo Escobar. As paramilitary leader Carlos Castaño put it, "Carlos Pizarro had to die."[64] Thus Pizarro joined tens of thousands of other Colombians who paid the ultimate price for involvement in the lucrative and bloody illegal industry.[65]

Demobilization of the M-19 was watched intently by Colombia's other insurgent groups, but none more closely than the EPL, whose stronghold was in the mountains of southern Córdoba. By 1990 the Maoist group had been virtually eliminated as a military force and was anxious to lay down its weapons. In that the EPL had been wealthy and flourishing just five years before, the story of its rapid demise is instructive of what was soon to come in Colombia at large.[66]

The EPL began its rise in 1978, the year it had the good luck to receive an infusion of FARC deserters and new weaponry as well, most notably claymore mines effective in ambushing military patrols. That year also marked the beginning of cocaine's golden age, when ever-larger quantities of the drug flowed northward, most of it dispatched from airports in Córdoba. The late 1970s also marked the FARC's arrival in nearby Urabá, just west of Córdoba across a low range of mountains called the Serranía de Abibe, where it gained converts among workers in the region's banana plantations and in the unions that represented them. Córdoba's wealth and strategic location, near Panama and Colombia's historic smuggling routes, was another feature of Córdoba that made it attractive to the guerrillas. The department also possessed some of Colombia's best land, well-watered fields of cassava, yam, rice, corn, and most other food crops native to lowland Colombia. But the department's chief product was cattle, over three million head in the 1980s, which grew fat on the department's rich grasslands and tropical savannas.

Movement of communist guerrillas into the department of Córdoba was exceeded only by that of drug traffickers with ties both to the Medellín cartel and to marijuana growers of the Santa Marta-Guajira region. The traffickers flocked to Córdoba because of its many airports, twenty-three legal and thirty clandestine ones, most of which were given over to drug flights during the 1980s.[67] Many of the flights undertaken by the Medellín cartel's ace pilot Barry Seal departed airports located in Córdoba. One of the largest was located in the central part of the department on *finca La Mireya,* owned by one of Colombia's most important traffickers and money launderers, César de Moya Cura. Moya's farm was near the town of Buenavista, on the main highway linking Montería and Medellín.

Drug traffickers descended on Córdoba with a vengeance during the late 1970s and early '80s, quickly buying up the best grazing lands the department had to offer. Their method of acquiring them was direct: they approached owners, cash in hand, offering several times what the land would have been worth on the open market. "Either accept our offer today," the traffickers would tell landowners, "or next week we will buy it from your widow."[68] In this manner drug traffickers soon became the owners of Córdoba's best cattle lands.

EPL guerrillas lived in harmony with the traffickers. Both groups lived outside the law and therefore shared a common enemy. Traffickers viewed the *vacunas* they paid the guerrillas a small price to pay for the insurgents' driving the police out of many *municipios* across the department. Guerrilla leaders were often guests at lavish weekend parties thrown on the drug barons' estates, such as the one held in December 1986 to celebrate the assassination in Bogotá of pro-extradition journalist Fidel Cano. EPL kidnapping specialist El Viejo Rafa was especially welcome at such events, for he was good company and enjoyed the music, drink, and feminine companionship available in abundance at trafficker galas. The EPL leader had become so friendly with César de Moya that by 1985 he had turned the settlement of La Mejor Esquina, which lay near his ranch, into one of the staging areas for his kidnapping expeditions and a depository for the money and goods that he extorted from ranchers and businessmen not involved in the drug trade.[69]

Things could hardly have been better for the EPL at the end of the first half of the 1980s. Money flowed into their coffers from every corner of Córdoba. Its estimated earnings from extortion, kidnapping, protection money, and taxes on drug exports were running between 300 and 450 million pesos monthly at mid-decade.[70] But that was also the moment that Fidel Castaño and his brothers arrived in Córdoba and declared war on the EPL. What followed was a dirty war pitting paramilitary forces commanded by the Castaños against the EPL and its FARC and ELN allies operating in the department, details of which are contained in the following chapter. Suffice it to say here that what ensued was a bloody war in Córdoba and in the neighboring region of Urabá, at the end of which the EPL emulated the M-19's example and demobilized, late in 1991. Its members entered civil society under the banners of their new Hope, Peace, and Liberty party (*Esperanza, Paz y Libertad*). With demobilization of the EPL only the country's two largest insurgent organizations, the FARC and the ELN remained in the field.

Colombians took heart from the fact that four of their six principal insurgent groups had demobilized or were in the process of doing so at the time President César Gaviria took office in August of 1990. Furthermore, the cartel war was winding down. Gonzalo Rodríguez Gacha was dead and Pablo Escobar hotly pursued by the authorities. With the end of the Cold War, and significant political reform taking place before their eyes, they were beginning to think that peace might soon return to their country. Peace and prosperity appeared to be the way of the world in the early 1990s, a time when leaders everywhere were preaching the neoliberal gospel of unending prosperity within a climate of democracy. Colombia embraced neoliberalism during the early 1990s. State-owned businesses were privatized, tariffs lowered, and competitiveness became the word of the day. When he took office on August 7, 1990, Gaviria seemed thrice blessed: the economy was prospering, the Cartel War was winding down, and the guerrilla movement seemed to be running out of steam. In his inaugural address he promised to wage a decisive and integrated war against the drug traffickers, and he held out the hope of success in both areas by the end of his term.

Unfortunately for César Gaviria, neither the FARC nor the ELN showed any sign of accepting the government's offer of peace. They had enjoyed steady growth throughout the 1980s and early '90s. Sheltered by the towering Eastern Cordillera of the Andes, and having their headquarters in the lightly-populated and remote eastern portion of the country, neither group had yet experienced the military and the paramilitary pressure that had driven their sister organizations to the bargaining table. Rather, the FARC and ELN had followed the dual strategy of engaging with the government even as they fought its armed forces. Over the five years that the FARC's 1985 truce was in effect its forces averaged more than 100 military engagements per year, with 200 taking place in 1990 alone. The ELN had been even more active, carrying out more than 400 military actions during 1990, many of them in the form of attacks on oil pipelines.[71] Colombia's two remaining guerrilla groups were growing stronger, not weaker. They saw no reason to lay down their arms.

During the first months of César Gaviria's term Colombians looked forward to the December 9 plebiscite that would approve the drawing up of a new national constitution and select members of the constitutional convention that would carry out that task. Had the FARC and the ELN demobilized they would have seen their leaders take part the country's most significant act of political reform. They chose to fight instead, stepping up attacks as the plebiscite approached. The most serious action took place on November 11, when 500 FARC and ELN guerrillas staged a joint operation aimed at overrunning a military base near Tarazá, located in northeastern Antioquia on the Cauca River. Three-hundred guerrillas attacked the base while the others stormed police stations in Tarazá, and in nearby Cáceres, on the east bank of the river. Army reinforcements reached the base the next morning, driving the attackers away, but not before all of the post's officers and thirteen soldiers were killed.[72] The government retaliated a month later, destroying the FARC headquarters at Casa Verde, Meta, located not far from the village of La Uribe. The attack forced the FARC to withdraw farther eastward, to the plains of the Yarí River, sixty kilometers north of where the Medellín cartel had built its cocaine processing complex Tranquilandia ten years before.

The FARC and ELN stepped up their attacks after the army assault on Casa Verde. Although FARC leaders had been in conversations with the government since the time of Virgilio Barco's peace initiative of mid–1988, the talks were merely a diversionary device. The ELN never committed to peace talks, though its leaders did participate in meetings with the government held under aegis of the CGSB between 1990 and 1992, first in Caracas and then in Tlaxcala, Mexico.[73] Between 1988 and 1990 the ELN experienced its time of greatest growth, reaching 2,600 troops in the latter year.

By mid–1992 the FARC and ELN were fighting government troops in seven departments, and the ELN was increasing its attacks on exports from the Caño Limón-Coveñas oil fields. The ELN explained its actions as geared to keep valuable natural resources from being exploited by multinational corporations, and because it had not been consulted regarding how oil revenues were to be used.[74] Between 1986 and 1996 ELN attacks on oil pipelines totaled 985.[75] October 1992 witnessed a spike in guerrilla activity caused by the approach of the country's first-ever election of governors, another step toward political decentralization. These measures, aimed at increasing democratization, had the effect of heightening the guerrillas' campaign to control local government and thus capture its revenue stream. The process of increasing political influence through coercion and violence at the local level is termed "armed clientelism" by students of Colombian politics.[76] The violence peaked during the week before the October 1992 elections when FARC urban militias burned busses in Bogotá while the group's Front 55 cut off the country's main highway to the Eastern Llanos. In several outlying parts of the country guerrillas stormed towns and assassinated members of their police forces. All of this took place in the chaotic months following Pablo Escobar's escape from the Cathedral.

Colombians who just months earlier perceived public order to be improving, were bitterly disappointed yet again. The peace that seemed within reach just months earlier had vanished in a miasma of violence. Homicide rates in the country were the world's highest, reaching levels that far surpassed those of the worst years of the *Violencia*.[77] And the guerrillas were very much part of the mix. In response, a group of left-wing artists, journalists, and intellectuals, led by Nobel Laureate Gabriel García Márquez, published a November 1992 open letter to the FARC and ELN. In it they accused the guerrillas of having become an historical anachronism, going on to blast their kidnapping, extortion, and drug trafficking. They warned that FARC and ELN activities were generating both paramilitary activity and excesses by the nation's armed forces. They ended warning the guerrillas that their actions were ruining Colombians' "shared dream of a democratic and happy society."[78] But the guerrillas were deaf to the entreaties of these distinguished citizens. By 1992 leaders of the FARC and ELN were arrogant in their belief that they could triumph through military means, and their wealth made them impervious to arguments founded in any notion of the common good. The ELN was establishing new fronts in rural areas, and militia groups in Medellín and other cities. It was flush with money extorted from petroleum companies, and its movement into new regions gave the group access to public monies as well. Two months before García Márquez and the others denounced guerrilla excesses, the ELN launched its ambitious "Eagle Flight Offensive," the first phase in its plan to expand its seventeen fronts from company to battalion strength.

The FARC was in even better financial shape than the ELN. In 1993 its income from kidnapping and extortion was $23.2 and $10.4 million respectively. And it earned a great deal more through its involvement in the illegal drug trade. During that same year its revenues from cocaine sales were $92.6 million. It earned an additional $11.5 million from sales of heroin. From that moment until the first years of the twenty-first century the FARC was Colombia's greatest exporter of cocaine.[79] By 1994 FARC troop strength stood at 9,500, with some 38,000 Colombians serving in non-combat roles, providing a wide range of logistical services.[80] At that moment the insurgents projected launching their definitive offensive to overthrow the Colombian government in the year 1997.[81] Within this setting commanders of thirty FARC fronts gathered in Caquetá during April 11–18, 1993, for the group's Eighth Conference. It was the most important meeting in FARC history, for it was there that Colombia's largest guerrilla organization finalized its plan to seize control of the country.

The Guerrilla Offensive of 1994–2002

"We're going to be in power!"
—FARC commander Guillermo Sáenz
("Alfonso Cano"), April 2000[82]

The FARC's Eighth Conference was in part a response to César Gaviria's declaration of all-out war on insurgent groups early in his presidency. FARC leaders were so certain of victory that they drafted a list of reforms to be implemented once they were in power. Social democratic on the whole, they included pledges to devote half of the national budget to social programs, to pursue progressive taxation and economic protectionism, and to restrict natural resource consumption to domestic use only.[83]

At the military level the FARC expanded on its New Form of Operating, first spelled out at its Seventh Conference of 1982. It proposed the creation of operational units of up to 1,000 troops capable of seizing fixed military installations and inflicting significant defeats on the national army. Five regional blocks were to be created under unified command, and urban militias were also to be formed. Plans were announced as well to upgrade weaponry and improve officer training at their military school located in the Llanos del Yarí. Five new fronts would be positioned around Bogotá and tasked with tightening the group's encirclement of the capital. By the time of its 1993 congress the FARC had evolved sufficiently to assign specific tasks to its numerous fronts. Forty-four percent of them were designated combat fronts, fifteen percent explosives units, and forty-one percent non-combatant units.[84] FARC leaders continued to believe that guerrilla pressure on the national capital would lead *bogotanos* to rise up and join them in overthrowing the government.[85]

In early 1994 the FARC aggressively engaged in establishing control of the Urabá region of Antioquia and Chocó. The group's longstanding goal had been to secure a corridor to the sea along which they could send weapons and supplies to their redoubt in the southeastern part of the country. That task became easier following EPL demobilization during 1991. As early as 1992 the FARC joined EPL dissidents who had refused to lay down their weapons moved into the parts of Urabá and Córdoba vacated by the EPL. Soon they started killing ex–EPL members, whom they branded traitors to the revolutionary cause. During 1992 alone more than sixty demobilized EPL members died in this manner.[86] With the FARC's 1994 offensive Urabá slipped into full-scale civil war. Ex-EPL members, dubbed "hopeful ones" (*esperanzados*) after their political party Hope, Justice and Liberty, formed small self-defense groups called "popular commands" (*comandos populares*) and joined forces with military and paramilitary forces. Within this setting, on January 23, 1994, the FARC entered Barrio Obrero in Apartadó, an invasion barrio established on a *finca* called *La Chinita*, and massacred thirty-six ex–EPL members.[87]

The *La Chinita* massacre and the violence throughout Urabá were catalysts for three important developments: first, they revived paramilitary activity there; second, they caused many of those having left-wing connections to flee the area; third, they led President César Gaviria, on February 11, 1994, to permit the formation of militias to help citizens protect themselves against the guerrillas. The program, called Convivir, was implemented during the first months of the administration of Ernesto Samper, in late 1994. Samper's Defense Minister, Fernando Botero, launched Convivir during November 1994 amidst an ongoing FARC offensive in Antioquia, Córdoba, Meta, Putumayo, and Caquetá. In launching Convivir, Colombia admitted that it was unable to protect its citizens from the guerrillas. The program was hotly debated during November and December of 1994. Those on the left criticized it as state promotion of paramilitarism. Colombians on the right praised it as an alternate way of confronting the growing communist insurgency.[88] A survey taken late in the year showed that 78 percent of Colombians approved of Convivir while only 16 percent opposed it.[89]

Colombia's guerrillas were angered by Convivir, which they correctly judged would make their task more difficult. They were already complaining about paramilitary growth throughout Colombia, which had been termed "explosive" by Defense Minister Botero.[90] Yet while in late 1994 Colombia's guerrillas were unhappy about the citizens' militia program, they were mightily pleased with a brewing scandal that showed signs of crippling the administration of Ernesto Samper. The scandal of course involved illegal drugs.

In the midst of Samper's 1994 presidential campaign DEA chief Joe Toft, who was stationed in Bogotá, released cassette recordings of Gilberto Rodríguez Orejuela discussing donations to the campaign, which was being managed by Fernando Botero. Toft had worked to bring down the Medellín cartel during the Barco and Gaviria administrations, but became depressed following Pablo Escobar's death because he knew the Cali cartel had replaced the Medellín group as chief cocaine supplier to the U.S. He was filled with both anguish and disgust when he learned that during early 1994 the Cali traffickers lavished money on politicians opposed to extradition and holding liberal positions on the matter of illegal drugs. Foremost among them was Ernesto Samper. In his youth Samper had advocated legalization of marijuana, and in 1982 he had recruited campaign donations from the Medellín cartel when campaign manager for Alfonso López Michelsen.[91] DEA chief Toft knew all of this and in mid–1994 made sure everyone else did as well. When he left Colombia a few months after Samper's inauguration he branded the country a "narco-democracy."[92]

The "Narco-cassette scandal" followed Ernesto Samper throughout his presidency and condemned his regime to ineffectiveness. Fernando Botero and other Samper confidants were disgraced and eventually jailed, and there were ongoing rumors that the president would either resign or be replaced through a coup.[93] Opposition to Samper increased during 1995, with the United States threatening to withdraw support from Colombia unless Samper fought the Cali cartel with the same dedication that his predecessors had pursued Pablo Escobar. Álvaro Gómez denounced Samper's presidency as illegitimate and called for the president's overthrow; he was assassinated late in 1995, apparently on orders of someone in the North Valle cartel.[94]

Samper's problems intensified over the course of 1996, one of the most violent years ever recorded in Colombia.[95] One month after former Minister of Defense Fernando Botero testified "Yes, he did know," when asked whether Samper was aware of the massive campaign donations from the Cali cartel, the United States decertified Colombia, saying, in effect, that Colombia was no longer a partner in good standing in the war on drugs. The burdens attending that action, especially in the area of U.S. cooperation with the nation's military, increased Colombia's difficulties just as the guerrilla offensive was moving into high gear. Worse was soon to come. On June 12 Colombia's "Narco-congress" exonerated Samper from involvement in the drug money scandal, leading the U.S. to take the unprecedented step of revoking the president's visa for travel there. Two months later, as Samper prepared to travel to New York to deliver an address at the United Nations on dangers of international drug trafficking, nearly four kilos of heroin were found hidden on the presidential jet. It would have been comic opera were not so many Colombians dying at the time. Such was Samper's state of mind as he left for his speaking engagement at the United Nations that he claimed to have carried a cyanide capsule in his back pocket which he planned to swallow if the Americans violated his diplomatic immunity and tried to arrest him.[96]

The U.S. campaign to punish Colombia continued on into 1997 when it decertified the country a second time. Colombia's erstwhile old friend and ally did so despite the fact that by that time most leaders of the Cali cartel were either dead or in jail. These American actions also aggravated effects of the Asian currency crisis which had plunged Colombia and other Latin American countries into sharp economic decline. The falling peso and attendant woes forced Samper to declare a state of economic emergency early in 1997.

The FARC observed this national misery and humiliation with relish and with growing conviction that their time of victory was nigh. When Guillermo Sáenz ("Alfonso Cano") was asked in early 1996 whether the FARC intended to negotiate with Samper's peace commissioners he replied that his group would never deal with representatives of such a weak government. Two years later a FARC cadre asked Víctor Sáenz ("El Mono Jojoy") why he was talking with the government "if we're winning the war and have almost defeated the state." The question was well founded: between 1996 and 1998 the FARC inflicted sixteen consecutive defeats on the national army. Those successes enhanced the image of the FARC, especially in Western Europe.[97] Among the victories were several in which the guerrillas overran military bases in southeastern Colombia almost without opposition. Wounded soldiers were executed and the rest taken hostage. When the anti-narcotics base at Las Delicias, Putumayo, was overrun during August 1996, Manuel Marulanda sent along a cameraman to film the attack for recruitment purposes. The high mountain base Cerro Patascoy in Putumayo near the border with Nariño was taken in fifteen minutes in December 1997. Prior to overrunning the army base at Miraflo-res, in Guaviare, FARC commanders purchased 200 grilled chickens with which to reward troops after what they knew would be an easy victory.[98] Meanwhile army operations met with scant success. A major operation of September-October 1997 was a costly failure, netting one guerrilla captured and two cows killed.[99] At that time relations between the military and the government could hardly have been worse. In July 1997 Samper fired army commander Harold Bedoya after the general blasted the president as incompetent. That moved another high-ranking officer to resign saying that he could not serve a government that was illegitimate. These acts raised fears that a military coup was imminent.[100]

Ernesto Samper limped through the remaining months of his presidency, eventually transferring power to Andrés Pastrana in August 1998. The new president's task was unenviable. Colombia's military was dispirited by the unbroken string of defeats stretching back over two years, and there was nationwide criticism of its lack of a viable strategy to defeat the guerrillas.[101] At that moment the FARC was at the height of its power. During the 1998 presidential campaign both leading candidates agreed to withdraw all government presence from an extensive portion of Meta and Caquetá in exchange for the guerrillas' entering into peace talks. The FARC raised hopes of peace by embracing the idea of a safe haven under its exclusive control, something it had promoted since the presidency of Belisario Betancur. But for the FARC peace talks were only a means to the end of victory over the Colombian government. As the group's high command talked peace during mid–1998, its agents were in Europe arranging a massive weapons purchase with Russian arms trafficker Viktor Bout, the weapons to be paid for with equally massive quantities of cocaine.[102]

Andrés Pastrana was a peace candidate, much as Belisario Betancur had been sixteen years earlier. There were many similarities between the two presidents' ill fated attempts to deal with the guerrillas. Like Betancur, Pastrana had no well-articulated plan for peace. Rather, he hoped that his good will and that of the majority of Colombians who had voted for him would soften the hearts of the guerrillas. But as in the case of Betancur the guerrillas looked on Pastrana and his supporters as weaklings ripe for manipulation. The FARC had convinced the peace camp that it was ready to lay down its arms, all the while treating the talks as simply a continuation of its war "by all possible means." The ELN was more forthright. It simply refused to speak meaningfully with the government. Both the FARC and the ELN believed their success in recent years meant that "objective conditions" were right for their long-awaited overthrow of a political system they perceived as venal, corrupt, and unfair. The guerrilla's bad faith doomed Pastrana's peace presidency from the beginning, just as it had that of Betancur sixteen years earlier.

Colombia was a society at cross-purposes in 1998. That was the norm in a country whose citizens had rarely achieved consensus over nearly two centuries of national life. But internal division was a dangerous luxury in a country where the legal edifice undergirding public order was threatened by a revolutionary insurgency and where widespread impunity was buoyed by a flood of illegal drug money.

The national military was aware of the gravity of the situation and strongly opposed the new president's plan to grant the FARC a safe haven in exchange for the promise to talk peace. But, seemingly incredibly, they were not consulted on the matter. This was in keeping with the forty-year policy of keeping the military out of political decision-making.

International opinion was mixed on the subject of Pastrana's peace plan. United States officials were against ceding territory to the FARC. Such was their dismay over Colombia's failure to control cocaine production, and so great was their fear that the country was becoming a failed state and a menace to its surrounding region, that the U.S. saw it in its best interest to embrace Pastrana and help him in any way possible—never mind that the U.S. had vastly aggravated Colombia's plight during 1994–98 by punishing Ernesto Samper and his government. Thus before Pastrana was sworn into office he met with U.S. President Clinton, who greeted him warmly and pledged $289 million to help Colombia fight illegal drugs.

Western European governments, especially the social democracies, were also supportive of Pastrana's peace plan, though not its military aspect. They tended to sympathize with the guerrillas, whom they viewed as radical social reformers promoting the common good. It was a view that the guerrillas had advanced since the 1960s, one that many Colombian and foreign academics promoted as well.

A great many Colombians opposed Pastrana's peace plan, and the country's paramilitary forces did so violently. In some respects the paramilitaries were the mirror image of the guerrillas. Like the insurgents they knew the government could not protect ordinary citizens living in rural areas. Iconic leader of Colombia's paramilitary forces in 1998 was thirty-five-year-old Carlos Castaño, who had sworn vengeance on the FARC after its members had kidnapped and murdered his father.[103] Castaño's mission was to kill the guerrillas and their sympathizers, and he had supporters throughout Colombia, especially among rural landowners who had always been the guerrillas' chief targets for extortion and kidnapping.

Upon taking office Andrés Pastrana started acting on his earlier promises to the FARC. He ordered the arrest of Carlos Castaño and moved against army officers accused of collaborating with the paramilitary. On October 14, he ordered all state presence removed from a 42,000 square kilometer region in the heartland of southeastern Colombia. During the same month he announced a "Marshall Plan" for rural Colombia, to be paid for with a World Bank loan. Increased attention to rural development was one of the FARC's many demands.

Colombia's military vigorously protested Pastrana's creation of the Cleared Zone (*Zona de Despeje*), but obeyed his order to end military presence there. By December 1998, the FARC was in full control of the extensive area, greater than the combined size of the Netherlands and Belgium.

But even as arrangements were being made for establishing the Cleared Zone the FARC made it clear that it did not intend to suspend the civil war while talking peace with the government. On November 1, 1998, one thousand of their troops fell upon Mitú, the departmental capital of Vaupés, killing or capturing the town's small garrison of 250 soldiers and wiping out its police force. They were driven out three days later by army Special Forces rushed in by helicopter, but not before the center of Mitú was destroyed and many of its residents lay dead.[104]

The Mitú attack was like a bucket of cold water in the faces of Colombians who had hoped the government's many concessions would pacify the FARC. Subsequent events further dashed their hopes. The FARC's intention to pretend to talk peace while pursuing military objectives became clearer on January 7, 1999, when Andrés Pastrana and a large entourage traveled to the FARC's new unofficial capital of San Vicente del Caguán to begin talks with the group's supreme leader, Manuel Marulanda Vélez. The much-heralded event was a fiasco. Marulanda failed to appear, leaving Colombia's president sitting under the tropical sun beside an empty chair. When a FARC official did at length appear it was not even a member of the group's secretariat, but rather "Joaquín Gómez," the guerrilla commander whose forces had overwhelmed the army's Las Delicias and Patascoy bases during 1996 and 1997. Pastrana's humiliation was all the greater when, shortly after his return to Bogotá, Marulanda warmly received former Nicaraguan president Daniel Ortega in San Vicente del Caguán, accepting from him the Order of César Sandino, an honor awarded to world leaders who had shown "exceptional service to their nation or to humanity." Later that same day Marulanda's lieutenant Víctor Suárez ("El Mono Jojoy") blasted Andrés Pastrana as "an oligarchic dauphin and neoliberal."[105]

Still Pastrana persevered in his attempts to placate the FARC. In April 1999, he fired Generals Rito Alejo del Rio and Fernando Millán, accused by the guerrilla and human rights groups of aiding anticommunist paramilitaries. In early May, the Colombian President rushed to San Vicente del Caguán when he learned that Manuel Marulanda and his top lieutenants had agreed to meet with him. The chief theme treated at the meeting was the FARC's demand that the government grant it additional territory in exchange for helping local *campesinos* substitute legal crops for coca. Meanwhile the ELN was demanding that the government grant it a cleared zone in the south of Bolívar.

While these conversations were in progress the guerrillas intensified their effort to overthrow Pastrana. Both the FARC and ELN stepped up their programs of extortion and kidnapping to raise additional funds for their armies. The FARC multiplied its surprise roadblocks, known as *pescas milagrosas* (miraculous fishing trips), at which cadres sometimes used laptop computers to verify the bank accounts of victims thought worthy of being held for ransom. The ELN favored mass kidnappings, which were even more lucrative. On April 12, 1999, they hijacked an airplane and marched its passengers away to jungle prisons. A month later they did the same to ninety-five people attending mass at a church in Cali. ELN leader Nicolás García explained the group's action, saying "the rich must sometimes live the consequences of the war ... [and] we must finance the war."[106]

The FARC and ELN also stepped up attacks on army and police installations, the former group guided by its desire to secure corridors of cocaine export. Just a month after Víctor Suárez had blasted Pastrana as a neoliberal oligarch, he ordered that three American peace activists held by the FARC be executed. The Americans had strayed into a part of northeastern Colombia where the guerrillas and paramilitaries were fighting for dominance over cocaine export routes into Venezuela.[107] During May 1999 Russian cargo planes owned by the weapons trafficker Viktor Bout began delivery of the 10,000 AK-47s ordered a year earlier and paid for with cocaine. Well-armed FARC columns inflected heavy casualties in many parts of the country, and in late May Marulanda Vélez hardened his position by demanding that the large *municipio* of Cartagena de Chairá be added to the Cleared Zone.[108] Elsewhere insurgents battled paramilitary groups, causing thousands of civilians to flee their homes in the countryside.[109]

Illegal drug sales constituted a growing proportion of FARC revenues. By the end of the 1990s and into the first years of the twenty-first century Colombian cocaine production rose to unprecedented levels, with much of it controlled by the guerrillas. During 1999 the FARC earned an estimated ten to twelve million dollars per month from cocaine they shipped out from some seventy clandestine air strips located in territory under its control. The guerrilla group was active in 63 of 174 *municipios* where illegal drugs were produced.[110] An estimated billion dollars in drug monies were earned by the FARC in one fourteen-month span during 1998 and 1999.[111] Drug exports were the responsibility of Tomás Medina Caracas ("El Negro Acacio"), a virtuoso kidnapper and commander of FARC Front 42, headquartered in Viotá, Cundinamarca.

This remarkable success in drug trafficking was in part a function of U.S. coca-reduction programs in Peru and Bolivia earlier in the 1990s, the effect of which had been to drive cultivation of the plant into Colombia's Amazon watershed. By 1999, seventy percent of the hemisphere's coca was grown in Colombia. As Colombia lost control of ever greater swaths of national territory coca cultivation spread into new areas. By the late 1990s FARC-controlled Putumayo surpassed both Guaviare and Caquetá in coca production. Meanwhile a coca boom was taking place in the south of Bolívar and in North Santander's Catatumbo region, both areas under guerrilla control. This expansion took place amidst an aerial fumigation program in effect from the time of the Gaviria administration. Despite fumigation, coca plantings were moving toward their peak of 169,800 hectares in 2001. By one estimate cocaine production rose to 839 metric tons that year.[112]

The FARC's political profile was at its height during the three years the Cleared Zone was in existence. More than twenty-three thousand visitors trekked to San Vicente del Caguán during 1999 and 2000 alone, and once there they listened, usually sympathetically, to representatives of the guerrilla group. Peace activists were warmly received. Females among them were handed red carnations and all were treated to skits dramatizing the FARC's struggle on behalf of the poor. The Pastrana government encouraged such visits in the hope that contact with those concerned over Colombia's plight would broaden the guerrillas' perspective and make them more inclined to peace. Perhaps the most improbable visitor to the Cleared Zone was the President of the New York Stock Exchange, who explained the virtues of free markets and neoliberalism to bemused FARC leaders. All the while the civil war continued and the lot of Colombians worsened. Kidnappings surged toward 3,000 in 1999, making Colombia the "kidnapping capital of the world." Impunity surged to 95 percent, meaning that just 5 percent of crimes were subjected to prosecution.[113]

Kidnapping skyrocketed as the guerrilla offensive moved apace during the period 1994–2002. That crime, referred to by the guerrilla as "retention," began to spike in 1996 when it surpassed 1,000 victims. In 1998 kidnappings numbered more than 3,000, and the crime reached its peak in 2001 when 3,524 people were taken away and held for ransom.[114] The FARC surpassed the ELN in kidnappings as its drive to topple the national government accelerated. Its roadblocks went from 17 in 1998 to 67 in 1999, ultimately reaching 113 in 2001. Foreigners were prime targets. Between 1996 and 2001 the FARC derived $632 million from ransoms paid for foreign kidnap victims. By the latter 1990s kidnapping generated 36 percent of FARC revenues compared to 54 percent from illegal drug sales.[115]

The Colombian public was in anguish during those years. Newspaper scion Francisco Santos organized a movement named País Libre (Free Country), which presided over numerous mass demonstrations. Millions across the nation participated in the ¡No Más! March of October 1999, and by the end of the year Colombians were begging the FARC to suspend their offensive, including their attacks on remote towns in Huila and Tolima and their assassination of soldiers home on leave. Termed "the silent war" by the weekly news magazine *Semana*, there were sixty such murders for the year by late November 1999.[116] In mid–December the FARC announced a Christmas truce, halting all illegal activities save kidnapping, extortion, and drug sales.

The year 2000 began with FARC confidence at an all-time high. Their drive to surround Bogotá had progressed well, though not without a few military setbacks. There had been heavy losses during the FARC's retreat from Mitú in late 1998, and during its assault on Puerto Lleras, Meta, in mid–1999. But for the Colombian military such successes were not commonplace. Still reform of the national military was under way and troop strength slowly increasing. Yet the average citizen found it hard to appreciate those changes. The public was more attuned to news of military failures, such as when a nervous army patrol opened fire on high school students during a field trip in August of 2000, killing many of them. Tragic news like that was paralleled by disconcerting reports from the FARC. In late April 2000 the group proclaimed its Law 002, which formalized its longstanding kidnapping policy. The law ordered Colombians having a patrimony in excess of one million dollars to begin making payments to the guerrillas or else be subjected to kidnapping.[117] FARC spokesman Víctor Suárez ("El Mono Jojoy") told reporters of the new law. He was the same FARC commander who informed Colombians in December 1998 of a fearful new weapon in the group's arsenal. It was a rustic mortar developed with the help of consultants from the Irish Republican Army. Its shell was a shrapnel and dynamite-clad propane gas tank shot from a length of aluminum tubing. Although wildly inaccurate, the mortars were capable of leveling buildings upon impact. Throughout 2000 the FARC used these weapons to good advantage, wreaking extensive damage to remote villages. Police stations were the guerrillas' principal targets. Once the police were subdued, their stations often reduced to rubble around them, ambulatory policemen were marched off to jungle prisons while survivors unable to walk were executed.

As the FARC tightened its encirclement of Bogotá training courses were developed for the future administrators of the nation. During 2000 bright mid-level cadres were sent to study public administration at schools established in the Cleared Zone. Part of the curriculum involved watching videos of the Sandinistas' triumphal entry into Managua during July 1979.[118] FARC leaders such as Guillermo Sáenz ("Alfonso Cano") were buoyed by the triumphal tour of European capitals recently completed by FARC public information chief Luis Devia ("Raul Reyes") and two of his aides. European leaders had received Devia like a head of state and had listened respectfully to his prediction of imminent overthrow of the Colombian government by the FARC.[119]

Things grew worse in Colombia. The FARC stepped up its forced recruitment of campesino children into its ranks, some of them as young as twelve years of age. Farm families in FARC-dominated areas began fleeing the countryside as a result. As the new millennium dawned as many as thirty percent of FARC forces were young women, many of whom had joined the group voluntarily.[120] Complicating matters was a new U.S. aid package called Plan Colombia, first announced by Andrés Pastrana in early 2000. The effectiveness of new attack helicopters provided to the Colombian military through Plan Colombia led both the FARC and the ELN to intensify their attacks on national infrastructure, blowing up electric towers, bridges, hydroelectric generating plants, dams, and aqueducts. Over the course of 2000 a total of 383 electric towers were destroyed across Colombia in FARC and ELN attacks.[121] At the same time battles between the guerrillas and the military raged in northwestern Antioquia and the Chocó. In mid–October, 400 FARC attacked and destroyed much of Dabeiba, Antioquia, while 500 members of a combined FARC/ELN/ERG (Ejército Revolucionario Guevarista) force, also using home-made mortars, attacked and destroyed public buildings in Bagadó, Chocó, and kidnapped thirty-five of the town's residents. Four helicopters sent to repel the attack were ambushed and destroyed and all fifty-three soldiers on board killed.[122] As military actions intensified so too did the national debate over Plan Colombia. Many argued that the U.S.-backed military aid program merely worsened the conflict. Civilians continued to stream out of the countryside and cries for peace intensified. During both 2000 and 2001 homicides in Colombia approached 35,000.

The year 2001 witnessed intensified fighting between the guerrillas and the paramilitary. On May 2, FARC and paramilitary forces converged on the town of Bojayá, Chocó, located in a strategic zone of drug export and weapon import. During the battle a FARC mortar fell through the roof of the town's church, killing 112 of the mostly women and children huddled inside. In the northwest part of the country the FARC fought the ELN for control of money extorted from oil and mining companies. Massive kidnapping for ransom continued. In one well-planned FARC operation fifteen residents of a Neiva apartment building were rounded up at gunpoint, loaded onto trucks, and driven away to prisons in the Cleared Zone.[123] Peace marches continued across the country. Many Colombians despaired that they were trapped in a civil war that had no end.

As 2001 drew to a close FARC leaders continued to speak of their imminent success. They had driven national police from 17 percent of Colombia's thousand *municipios*, while a third of all *municipios* had seen their *alcaldes* flee to departmental capitals. Forty percent of the country's *municipios* had suffered some form of guerrilla violence over the course of the year. A survey taken in December 2001 revealed that 41 percent of Colombians wanted to leave the country.[124]

Violence flared again after January 20, 2002, the day the FARC announced the end of its holiday truce. That was a blow to a group of European Union and Western Hemisphere nations that had asked the FARC to remain in the peace process. Over the thirty days that followed the guerrilla group staged 117 operations, including attacks on military installations, laying mine fields, and blowing up energy towers, oil pipelines, and bridges. Late in January the citizens of Meta, where the FARC had been purging *municipios* of government presence, 200,000 citizens marched banging sauce pans and shouting "Freedom! Freedom!" Indians in southern Colombia staged similar demonstrations, while international organizations protested human rights violations by paramilitary groups.[125]

By mid–February it was clear that the peace initiative launched by Andrés Pastrana nearly four years before had come to nothing. It was obvious too that when Pastrana's removed state presence from the Cleared Zone he had merely fed the FARC's conviction that it could overthrow his government. Two events provided Pastrana the excuse he needed to reclaim the guerrilla's safe haven. Late on February 19 a woman in labor, her unborn child, and their attendants, died when the ambulance rushing them to a clinic plunged into a river in northeastern Antioquia. Less than an hour earlier FARC operatives had dynamited the bridge they attempted to cross. A few hours after that incident FARC guerrillas hijacked an airplane in Neiva, flew it to the Cleared Zone, and kidnapped several of its passengers. Among them was Peace Commissioner Jorge Gechem Turbay. Pastrana described these two events in a televised address to the nation on the evening of February 20. He ended the somber talk by announcing that the army had been sent to drive the FARC from the Cleared Zone.[126]

The FARC had word of what was coming. Weeks earlier Víctor Suárez had ordered 6,000 heavily armed troops out of the Zone, charging them with continuing the guerrilla offensive. A paroxysm of violence followed. Three days after Pastrana's speech FARC guerrillas kidnapped Liberal politician and presidential candidate Ingrid Betancourt as she and several companions drove toward San Vicente del Caguán. Six weeks after that, on April 4, they attempted to assassinate Liberal presidential candidate Alvaro Uribe Vélez. Days later, on April 11, ELN guerrillas kidnapped fourteen members of the Departmental Assembly of Valle.[127]

CHAPTER 5

The Paramilitary Offensive

Introduction: Civil Defense and Impunity

"All Colombians, men and women not involved in the call to compulsory military service, may be used by the Government in acts and works contributing to the reestablishment of normality."
—From a 1965 law authorizing the arming of citizen militias[1]

Colombia's paramilitary movement, which reached its peak during 2000–2001, was born of guerrilla expansion during the late 1970s, and of the national government's failure to adequately protect its citizens from guerrilla depredations. Paramilitary groups initially had the character of legally constituted citizen militias trained and in part armed by the military. But as the guerrillas gained strength paramilitary groups did also. Like the guerrillas, the paramilitaries began acting with impunity, thereby placing themselves outside the parameters of Colombian law.

The country's first notable paramilitary groups were organized in centers of early guerrilla strength, the Middle Magdalena River region, eastern Antioquia, and Córdoba. As the guerrillas multiplied during the 1990s, so too did the paramilitary. Both groups used illegal drug revenues to finance their military operations, settling into parts of the country strategically important to cocaine export. The traffickers, the guerrillas, and the paramilitaries therefore tracked one another in terms of geographic incidence.

When Álvaro Uribe won the presidency in 2002 and effectively attacked the guerrillas, the paramilitaries lost their *raison d'être*. Three years into Uribe's first term most of the country's 18,000 paramilitary fighters had demobilized. Meanwhile most of their leaders had entered prison voluntarily to stand trial for their crimes.

The following chapter places Colombia's paramilitary phenomenon in historical context, and goes on to examine the country's recent paramilitary experience. It concludes with a summary of paramilitary demobilization during the first term of President Álvaro Uribe Vélez (2002–2006).

* * *

Throughout most of Colombia's history uprisings against the government were a function of the citizens' understanding that they could rebel against the state with little fear that the state would retaliate against them quickly or effectively. The government's historic weakness and inability to control its territory resulted in a habit of "easy" rebellion against inept governments that were habitually inattentive to the needs of their citizens. The country's history is replete with uprisings by citizens angry over the state's sins of omission or commission. Sometimes their rebellions appeared justified and sometimes not. The relative ease with which citizens took up arms against Bogotá had the effect of making Colombians at once critical, idealistic, and bellicose. Citizens of that country have been famously sensitive to what they consider attacks on deeply-held values, values initially enshrined in platforms of the country's Conservative and Liberal parties. As late as the mid–twentieth century Colombians fell into bloody conflict along conservative-liberal lines, decades after those philosophies and the political parties inculcating them had ceased to be significant elsewhere in Latin America.

Philosophical differences separating Colombians can be traced to the ancient debate in moral philosophy concerning the right and the good. The question is whether human society is best oriented toward the defense of immutable rules and institutions, or whether its standards should be dynamic and flexible, geared toward the achievement of human happiness at the most generalized level possible. The right and the good were at issue in Colombia during the 1930s, when Conservatives argued that property ownership was an absolute right and therefore not to be infringed upon, while Liberals reasoned that property possesses a social function outweighing the protection of ownership under the theory of Natural Law. Colombian Liberals won that debate at the ballot box, going on to carry out modest land reform on the strength of their victory. Political fortunes reversed during the 1940s when Conservative defenders of immutable principles of social organization took control of the government. Disagreements centering on the right-good debate became more heated as the decade progressed and resulted in the breakdown of Colombia's political system during 1949. Events of that year were driven by the demagoguery of political leaders, especially of extreme right-wing Conservatives, who claimed that the Liberals and their allies in the Communist party intended to turn Colombia into a communist state that would take away their God-given rights.

The paranoid ravings of Conservative demagogues, coupled with the intemperate responses of their Liberal counterparts, intensified Colombia's *Violencia*, which began in 1947. When Conservative President Mariano Ospina Pérez moved toward imposing martial law in late 1949 the country's Communist party ordered its members to take up arms to defend themselves against the government. The Communists' call to citizen self-defense was emulated by leaders of the Liberal party, and soon both groups had thousands of armed followers roaming the countryside doing battle with the Colombian army and police. Most of those guerrilla forces demobilized when the joint Liberal-Conservative National Front government became operational in 1958. But the communist guerrillas whose party leaders were excluded from National Front power-sharing, remained under arms. When the decade of the 1960s began a few hundred of them lived in scattered communal agricultural settlements in remote mountainous parts of the country.[2]

At any other time in Colombian history a few tiny enclaves of armed *campesinos* might have been of little concern. But those weren't normal times. Fidel Castro had just come to power in Cuba after leading a small revolutionary force into the capital from a distant mountain redoubt. Castro's exploit in Cuba, coming at the height of the Cold War, brought Colombia's communist enclaves into the national consciousness. The abortive U.S.-backed invasion of Cuba in April 1961, coupled with Conservative party leader Álvaro Gómez's call that the settlements he called "independent republics" be destroyed, led the Colombian army to launch a desultory raid on the largest of them, Marquetalia, located in southern Tolima, in January 1962. The communists easily evaded the soldiers, returning to their homes once the troops withdrew. But the exercise infuriated Marquetalia's leader Manuel Marulanda Vélez ("Tirofijo") and set him on the offensive. Soon Marulanda's followers launched what would become a decades-long policy of self-financing through extortionate kidnapping. During 1963 his followers seized a farmer and held him for ransom. They also stopped a bus and kidnapped several passengers. In December 1963 one of Marulanda's men hijacked and air taxi and then destroyed the Air Force helicopter sent in pursuit, killing the helicopter's pilot and co-pilot. That angered the Colombian military and made their full-fledged attack on the "independent republic" of Marquetalia inevitable.[3]

The invasion and occupation of Marquetalia took place during May and June 1964, and drove Manuel Marulanda's small group out of the region and over the Central Cordillera into the Rio Chiquito region of northeastern Caldas. There they reconstituted themselves as a guerrilla force pledged to overthrowing the national government. In mid–1965 it held its First Conference in Rio Chiquito, there proclaiming itself the Southern Bloc of Colombia's communist self-defense forces.[4] Two years later it adopted the name Revolutionary Armed Forces of Colombia (*Fuerzas Armadas Revolucionarias Colombianas*, or FARC).

Once the followers of Marulanda organized themselves their need for funds became acute. That is why as soon as they arrived in Rio Chiquito they arranged the kidnapping of industrialist Harold Eder, seized at his vacation home not far from Marulanda's hideout, on March 21, 1965.[5] Colombians soon learned that Eder had died of a gunshot wound received not long after being taken away by his captors. In the meantime the victim's wife had delivered two million pesos to Marulanda's men, a sum totaling nearly $200,000 in 1965 dollars. Eder's seizure was just one of several such kidnappings that took place in southern Colombia during 1965.[6]

Not long after the Eder incident Manuel Castellanos, president of one of the country's largest interest associations, the Society of Colombian Farmers (*Sociedad de Agricultores de Colombia*, or SAC), wrote President Guillermo León Valencia asking him to permit citizen self-defense against the "wave of kidnappings" taking place in southern Colombia.[7] Valencia answered in late December 1965 with Legislative Decree 3398 authorizing the arming of civilian self-defense groups.[8] Three years later, in 1968, the decree became National Law 48. These legal provisions were an ominous sign that new sources of violence were beginning to afflict Colombia. As the 1970s progressed violence levels started rising throughout the nation, particularly where the guerrillas and the drug mafias were most active. Guerrilla-related violence first became notable in the armed groups' initial areas of expansion, the Middle Magdalena/eastern Antioquia regions, and just to the northwest in the department of Córdoba and adjoining lands around the Gulf of Urabá. Early drug-related violence was most intense in and around Medellín. A wave of kidnapping there had moved President Alfonso López Michelson to visit Medellín to reassure civic leaders in 1975 that he would protect them from the "social decomposition" beginning to afflict their city. But he did not offer such assurances to rural-dwelling Colombians who were starting to suffer at the hands of guerrillas. They were literally out of sight and mind of national government officials, and living in places where the hand of the government rested but lightly. That is why they began to arm themselves.

Paramilitary Growth During the 1970s and 1980s

Before killing him they insulted him repeatedly with something that was impossible
for a campesino like him: "Oligarch son-of-a-bitch." Later they made him kneel
and shot him in the back.
—Carlos Castaño, on his father's execution by FARC guerrillas[9]

One of the FARC's first operational decisions was to establish fronts northward along the
Magdalena River, through northeastern Antioquia and Córdoba, and into the frontier region
around the Gulf of Urabá. Accordingly, the FARC established Front 4 in the Middle Magdalena
during 1965, and Front 5 in Urabá. Both fronts prospered. The guerrillas sent their most skilled
organizers into the two lightly-populated regions. As places of recent settlement they lacked
in social services and were poorly administered by the government. Within that setting FARC
organizers had little trouble convincing the locals that their destiny lay with the Communist
party and its program of giving political voice to society's downtrodden, arguments that helped
them win a series of local elections during the 1970s. Thus FARC-supported candidates dominated local government in numerous towns in northeastern Antioquia and the Middle Magdalena. In Puerto Boyacá, at the geographic center of the Middle Magdalena, the mayor and
municipal council were all Communist party members, as they were in several other towns
along that part of the river.

These successes encouraged the FARC, which was still smarting from the setback it had
suffered in 1973 when the Colombian army turned back its attempt to expand into the country's
Coffee Axis, the region in the Central Cordillera extending from Quindío northward into
Antioquia, where most of the country's coffee is grown.[10] When the guerrilla group held its
Sixth Conference in the jungles of Meta in 1978, it had rebuilt its membership and increased
the number of its fronts. The founder of Front 4, Ricardo Franco, had been instrumental in
launching Fronts 11 and 12 in southern and central Santander, Front 22 in northwestern Cundinamarca, and Front 9 in Quindío. Inspired by Franco's success FARC leaders decreed that
fronts must be established in each of the country's twenty-three departments. But that expansion required more money than the group had needed prior to that time. FARC cadres were
sent away from the Sixth Conference with the following admonition: "Get money by whatever
means necessary so we can start buying some real weapons."[11]

FARC guerrillas become more aggressive after the Meta conference. Whereas during the
group's early days it had politely asked campesinos to pay quotas and better-off ranchers and
farmers to pay protection money, those demands were not excessive. After 1978, however, the
FARC's demands became greater and more threatening. Kidnapping became commonplace and
demands for ransom increased in amount. Colombia's first paramilitary forces took shape
within that setting.

The first notable figure in Colombia's paramilitary movement was a campesino named
Ramón Isaza, who lived just west of Puerto Triunfo, on the Antioquian side of the Magdalena
River and an hour south of Puerto Boyacá. Isaza had put himself in danger when he rejected
the increasing demands of Front 9 commander Gentil Duarte. So Duarte ordered Isaza kidnapped. When word of this reached Isaza he traveled to the military base up river at Puerto
Berrío, where on February 22, 1978, he met with an officer named Faruk Yanini Díaz. Yanini
supplied Isaza with seven rifles and sent him home with the words "Defend yourself, because
it's impossible for the army to give each Colombian a soldier for his personal protection."[12]

Thus Ramón Isaza was prepared when guerrillas from Front 9 approached his farm. Isaza and several of his sons, along with a few relatives and neighbors, fired on them and drove them away. The act made Isaza locally famous and set him on the path to forming one of the first citizens' militias in the Middle Magdalena region. Six of Isaza's eight sons became leaders of his paramilitary army which ultimately comprised five fronts and numbered almost a thousand men. Known as "the Paisa Tirofijo," and "El Viejo," Isaza and his men were eventually charged with killing over 600 campesinos they had identified as FARC members or sympathizers. Those killings were not the result of massacres but rather of selective killings. "My order was to kill them one-by-one," one of his men later said, going on to explain, "we always threw their bodies into the Magdalena River." Isaza used many means to seek out his victims, including giving candy to children in exchange for information on guerrilla sympathizers.[13]

At the time Ramón Isaza organized his paramilitary force south of Puerto Boyacá, another farmer, Gonzalo Pérez, started doing the same thing north of the river town. His *finca San Vito* was thirty kilometers from Puerto Boyacá, and close to Puerto Berrío, Antioquia. When FARC Front 4 commanders started ratcheting up their demands for money in the late 1970s, he and his neighbors first tried reasoning with them, going as far as offering to pay their *vacunas* in installments. But it was to no avail. In 1978 Gonzalo Pérez contacted his son Henry, a taxi driver in Bogotá, and asked him to find weapons for defense of the family farm. But when Henry Pérez visited the military base in Medellín the commanding officer there told him the army had no clear strategy for dealing with the FARC and could not give him any weapons. The younger Pérez returned from his mission empty-handed and with the understanding that he and his father must find their own way to deal with the guerrillas.[14]

Colombia's military in fact needed civilian help during the late 1970s and early '80s. A strong anti-establishment mood was at large in the country, with much anger directed against President Julio César Turbay for his hard-line policy against the guerrillas. At the moment the guerrillas were in an ebullient mood, buoyed by the ongoing successes of their dashing colleagues in the M-19. Flamboyant M-19 operations such as their theft of military weapons in late 1978, and their seizure of the Dominican Embassy in early 1980, had swelled the ranks of Colombia's numerous insurgent groups even as they heightened calls for the government to answer their reform demands. As internal criticism of Turbay mounted at home the United States began pressuring him to militarize Colombia's anti-drug effort. Turbay responded by sending thousands of soldiers far from the nation's heartland on a multi-year mission to destroy extensive marijuana plantations along the northern Caribbean coast; this severely depleted military forces just as they were most needed in places like the Middle Magdalena region. The best the military could do was place army battalions in Puerto Boyacá and in Segovia, the latter located west of the Magdalena River in the mountains of eastern Antioquia. It did so in early 1979, designating the former Battalion Bárbula, and the latter Battalion Bomboná. The new battalions were poorly staffed and limited in their ability to pursue the highly mobile FARC columns circulating freely through the countryside.

In 1980 the army's ranking officer in the Middle Magdalena region, General Daniel García, learned that Gonzalo Pérez was organizing an anti-guerrilla militia just down the river from his headquarters at Puerto Berrío. Over the course of that year García sent members of his staff to meet with Pérez and to offer him help. Thus in January 1981 army officers from Puerto Berrío presided over a ceremony held at *finca San Vito*, during which the self-defense force of Gonzalo and Henry Pérez was formally installed pursuant to Law 48 of 1968. In addition to supplying equipment to the militia group, the army trained its members at battalions Bárbula and Bombóna, and subsequently made use of its members as guides in anti-guerrilla operations. The Middle Magdalena self-defense movement grew rapidly after the FARC kidnapped and murdered a well-liked rancher of the region in mid–1981. One resident later remembered it as a pivotal instant in the history of Puerto Boyacá: "I went and told my compadre: 'Either we organize or we're screwed!'"[15]

The Middle Magdalena entered full-scale civil war during the early and middle years of the 1980s. Members of the Isaza and Pérez paramilitary groups not only helped guide soldiers from nearby army bases, but pursued FARC guerrillas and supporters on their own, frequently using intelligence supplied by the military. Their strategy proved to be effective. By the mid–1980s the FARC's hold on the region was broken. "It was horrible but we won," a resident of Puerto Boyacá later recalled.[16]

During the early years of paramilitary organization around Puerto Boyacá, Henry Pérez played an ever more important role in coordinating and institutionalizing the paramilitary effort there. He reasoned that it was not enough to simply arm citizen militias, even militias capable of coordinating their activities with the national military. What the younger Pérez envisioned was a complex structure that would integrate the anti-guerrilla and military efforts, participate in local politics, and aid in the region's socio-economic development. Thus he became the father of what later came to be termed *parapolítica* (paramilitary politics). Pérez found an enthusiastic ally in Liberal politician Pablo Emilio Guarín, a man who shared his belief in an integrated approach to regional self-defense. Another who agreed was the mayor of Puerto Boyacá, Luis Alfredo Rubio. Their organizational effort took on a note of urgency during 1981 and 1982, as a pacifist mood gained ground in the country. Belisario Betancur was elected President on the strength of his promise to make peace with the guerrillas. The new president's soft-line position, coupled with mounting guerrilla aggressiveness, moved many Colombians to embrace the idea of citizen self-defense. Betancur's peace initiative, which included his order to the army to sharply restrict its anti-guerrilla operations, and his release of several hundred jailed guerrilla leaders in late 1982, did much to boost the organization of paramilitary forces. In early 1983 leaders of the Middle Magdalena region came together to launch the Farmers and Cattleman's Association of the Middle Magdalena (*Asociación Campesina de Agricultores y Ganadores del Magdalena Medio*, or ACDEGAM). The umbrella group's expressed aim was to coordinate citizen self-defense and to become involved in a host of other civic activities, both in Puerto Boyacá and in the surrounding region. Eventually ACDEGAM funded thirty schools in four Middle Magdalena departments, where teachers taught a patriotic and anticommunist curriculum and instructed their students in military arts. It maintained a clinic for ACDEGAM associates, provided technical support for agriculture and ranching, and even sponsored highway construction projects. In mid–1984 the self-defense cooperative was given legal recognition by the government of Boyacá. Two years later ACDEGAM's leaders were promoting a new organization called Common Front (*Frente Común*), aimed at uniting anti–FARC *municipios* along the Magdalena from Cundinamarca, Tolima, and Caldas in the south, through Boyacá, Antioquia, and Santander along the river's lower reaches. In May 1988 the association hosted a forum for yet another new organization, called the Anti-Subversive Alcalde's Front (*Frente de Alcaldes Antisubversivos*).[17]

ACDEGAM was looked upon as a model organization of its sort by the mid–1980s. None other than peace President Belisario Betancur acknowledged its effectiveness, although he was apparently ignorant of its dirty war in the countryside, when he visited Puerto Boyacá in 1985 and gave fulsome praise to the peace and prosperity that he perceived throughout the region. In a speech delivered in the town's plaza he lauded ACDEGAM's guiding light Pedro Emilio Guarín, whose good works, Betancur said, were reflected in faces of the town's residents, faces full of "the happiness, tranquility, and plenitude of peace."[18]

Puerto Boyacá provided Colombia's first model of successful regional paramilitary organization against guerrilla insurgents. But it was two campesinos from Antioquia, Fidel and Carlos Castaño, who led in uniting the nation's paramilitary groups. They did so first during the latter 1980s and early '90s in northwestern Colombia: from the Chocó and Urabá up the Caribbean coast to the Guajira Peninsula, and throughout the Bajo Cauca as well—a region extending from northeastern Antioquia across the southern portions of the departments of Sucre and Bolívar. Not long after, during the latter 1990s, Carlos Castaño turned Colombia's paramilitaries into a nationwide confederation. The Castaño brothers became dedicated enemies of the guerrillas after the FARC kidnapped and murdered their father, Jesús Castaño, in 1979.

Jesús Castaño and Rosa Gil married and raised a family of twelve children on a farm outside of Amalfi, in the mountains of northeastern Antioquia, eighty-five kilometers northeast of Medellín. Their *finca* consisted of 250 hectares and supported 150 dairy cattle. The large family, typical of rural Antioquia, lived modestly on sales of milk and other dairy products to Medellín and surrounding towns. Theirs was a typical middle-class campesino existence, even down to the day in 1964 when eldest son Fidel, then sixteen, borrowed 2000 pesos from a merchant in Amalfi and left home to seek his fortune. Happily for the family Fidel returned five years later with money in hand. He repaid the loan, bought a half-interest in his father's farm, and opened a bar in nearby Amalfi. The family prospered. Soon they bought another farm fifty kilometers northeast, on the upper reaches of El Bagre River, near Segovia. By the late 1970s *El Hundidor* boasted 600 head of cattle.[19]

Like many of his neighbors Jesús Castaño tolerated the FARC when its members first began appearing in the countryside, expounding their ideas of good government, justice, and egalitarianism. He let them camp on his land and on occasion sent them gifts of milk and other farm products. But in the late 1970s came the FARC directorate's call to increase the group's cash flow. Accordingly, in June 1979, four members of Front 4 seized Jesús Castaño at *El Hundidor* and sent the family a note demanding twenty million pesos for his release (approximately $200,000). Over the next two months Fidel and other family members rushed to gather the money from savings, donations from family and friends, and a loan from the Agrarian Bank. They used the services on an acquaintance from Remedios named José Tobón to help them negotiate a lower ransom with the kidnappers. The agreed-to sum was delivered to the kidnappers in late August 1979. Weeks passed and then a second note arrived demanding a second payment, this time fifty million pesos. Again Fidel Castaño struggled to collect the money, once more using the mediation services of José Tobón. By borrowing against *El Hundidor* he raised thirty of the fifty million and had it sent to the FARC. Intermediary Tobón assured the family that it would have Jesús Castaño home by the Christmas holidays. Time passed and no word came from the guerrillas. Finally on February 7, 1980, the Castaños received a third note demanding yet another fifty million pesos. Suspecting correctly that his father was already dead, Fidel Castaño responded with a note reading, "I've never had that much money. But if I ever did I would spend it fighting you."[20] He more than fulfilled his promise.

Over the following year Fidel Castaño gathered information on the kidnapping, eventually learning details on his father's execution and the identity of those involved. His task became easier when a Front 4 member named Gilberto Aguilar defected to Castaño's paramilitary group, giving a full account of Jesús Castaño's death. This information in hand, Fidel Castaño began his campaign of revenge.

The first kidnapper to die was one Conrado Ramírez, who had been seen by farm workers among the guerrillas taking Jesús Castaño away. Fidel, along with his fifteen-year-old brother Carlos, reported this fact to soldiers headquartered in Segovia. Ramírez was arrested by the military and bound over to a local magistrate. But the magistrate was a FARC sympathizer who quickly released Ramírez, telling the Castaños that their testimony was biased, and based only on hearsay evidence. With that Fidel and Carlos Castaño armed themselves and set out to dispense their own justice. A few days later they cornered Conrado Ramírez in Segovia and executed him. As Fidel Castaño's younger brother Carlos recalled it, the act "enchanted the whole town." Everyone in Segovia knew who was responsible for the murder, and why. Yet when authorities investigated no one told them who had killed Conrado Ramírez.[21]

At about the time the Castaños pursued their father's murderers they began serving as guides for soldiers of the local army detachment. During these missions they never took part in formal engagements, but rather searched out and killed FARC members afterward, usually at night, as they found them relaxing in towns around the area. Soon they were joined by others who had reason to hate the guerrillas. By late 1980 their paramilitary group numbered ten: two of its members were cousins of the Castaños and four others were workers from *El Hundidor*. Carlos Castaño increasingly led the group's military operations while his brother was tasked with raising money and supplies. It took money to outfit the armed force and the Castaños were mere campesinos. But there was money to be made in Colombia at the time, the "golden moment" of cocaine export to the United States, when drug-consuming gringos "bombarded" Colombia with cash. And in those early days of the country's cocaine boom a majority of the dollars landed in Antioquia. Thus one understands how it was that, in the words of Carlos Castaño, his brother became a "money-making machine" following their father's death.[22] Fidel Castaño's acquaintance with Pablo Escobar was vastly useful in his fundraising effort. The elder Castaño became an associate of what soon became the Medellín cartel. Fidel Castaño so impressed Pablo Escobar—Castaño was, after all, at war with the FARC's Front 4 at the time—that Escobar put him in charge of his own paramilitary army, Death to Kidnappers, or MAS, following the M-19's kidnapping of Martha Nieves Ochoa in November 1981. Fidel Castaño handled his task so expeditiously that Martha Nieves was released by the M-19 in early 1982. The thirty-year-old campesino from Amalfi was doubtless well paid for his work.[23]

Not long after heading up MAS, Castaño and his military force joined with the Middle Magdalena paramilitaries. In 1982 their group, which by then had grown to fifty, traveled southeast through the mountains and across the Magdalena River valley, to Puerto Boyacá. There they reported to Battalion Bárbula and were sent on to Puerto Triunfo and the paramilitary force of Ramón Isaza.[24] Isaza welcomed the *paisas* and listened with interest to their accounts of anti–FARC operations in the mountains northeast of Medellín. Isaza and his men were even more interested in hearing Fidel Castaño's description of how Pablo Esobar's MAS had annihilated Medellín's M-19 guerrilla front just a few months earlier.

Through the latter months of 1982 and into early 1983 the men from Amalfi participated enthusiastically in the dirty war raging in and around Puerto Boyacá. Because they were new to the region the Castaños could send selected men into FARC strongholds where, as Carlos recounted, "we eliminated them one-by-one."[25] But early in 1983 the Castaños and their paramilitary army, by then numbering 100, were forced to flee the Middle Magdalena. Pressure had built on the military to sever its links with the bloodthirsty outlanders. Consequently during late 1983 several members of the Castaños' force died in skirmishes with army patrols. That led Fidel to consult with Carlos; the two decided to continue their war against the guerrillas elsewhere and on their own terms. They poured over maps at length selecting a site on the upper Sinú River, some 300 kilometers northwest of Puerto Boyacá, in the department of Córdoba. They bought land on the left bank of the river, near the town of Valencia. Their key acquisition was a ranch called *Las Tangas,* 100 kilometers south of Montería and on the approach to the *Nudo de Paramillo,* a mountain fastness long the domain of FARC and EPL guerrillas. *Las Tangas* was also 100 kilometers east of San José de Apartadó, a key town in the strategically important Urabá region and a FARC stronghold.[26] The early 1980s was an ideal time to become a landowner in Córdoba, but only if one arrived there with significant personal protection. At that time the department was home of the Maoist Popular Liberation Army (*Ejército Popular de Liberación,* or EPL), and many of its farms and ranches lay abandoned by their owners. The insurgents had driven land prices down by 70 to 80 percent.[27]

The EPL was founded in the mid–1960s by students at the University of Córdoba and the University of Cartagena. Quiescent over the first fifteen years of its existence, the Maoist group came to life late in the 1970s at the height of enthusiasm for armed revolutionary action in Colombia. The EPL held its First National Conference in 1981, a meeting that concluded with leaders commanding followers to raise money to pay for the group's expansion. In this way they emulated the FARC leadership's action of three years earlier. EPL members responded, carrying out scores of kidnappings, mostly of rural landowners and businessmen from Montería and other towns across the department.[28] EPL cadres also formed strategic alliances with the cocaine and marijuana traffickers who abounded in Córdoba. By the mid–1980s both the EPL and the FARC earned money protecting extensive coca plantations owned by traffickers around the village of El Dos, located just west of Turbo on the Gulf of Urabá. The guerrillas offered traffickers protection in exchange for cash and munitions. At that moment there was little or no military presence in Córdoba, for the department had been relatively pacific up to the 1980s. As conditions steadily worsened citizens of Córdoba complained to Belisario Betancur about guerrilla depredations in their department. Betancur, at the time in the midst of his peace offensive with the guerrillas, sent his personal secretary Alfonso Ospina to meet with Córdoba's leaders. Ospina effusively informed the locals that "Nothing is going on around here, these guerrillas are just pathetic," words that flabbergasted his audience.[29]

Over the three years that followed guerrillas and drug traffickers had the run of Córdoba. By the mid–1980s local politics too had fallen under control of the allied outlaw groups.[30] Córdoba was, in short, a place ripe for the sort of leadership that Fidel Castaño was about to give it. When he settled there in 1984 he and his men were already skilled in the art of irregular counter-insurgency warfare, in both rural and urban settings. And the structure of his paramilitary group was becoming ever more complex. Fidel had taken charge of financial matters, while Carlos was positioning himself to head up military operations. Brother Vicente was the group's comptroller. Carlos Castaño was not on hand when Fidel moved their force to its new home, for in mid–1983 his brother had sent him to Israel to undergo a year of military training at a private school located in Tel Aviv. While at the school the younger Castaño met members of the Colombian armed forces, among them a junior officer named Rito Alejo del Río. A dozen years later del Río would become an invaluable ally to Carlos Castaño when he assumed command of his family's paramilitary army.[31]

Over the course of 1984 Fidel Castaño stocked *Las Tangas* with cattle and bought other land farther west, around the Gulf of Urabá. His ranches prospered and at the end of the decade he bragged that had he wished he could have sold 450,000 calves at Medellín's livestock auction. Meanwhile he pursued the task of destroying the guerrillas in Córdoba, chiefly by eliminating members of their civilian support network. One of his first acts was to dispatch his lieutenant Carlos Mauricio García Franco ("Doble Cero") and six others to the Urabá port of Turbo on orders to assassinate the members of a gang trafficking weapons to the EPL. In three days the group returned to *Las Tangas* leading pack animals burdened with weapons and ammunition taken from their victims. The three members of the gang who had survived the attack, "Leonidas," "Adonay," and "El Ñato," fled the area, never to be seen there again.[32]

Carlos Castaño harbored special hatred for those in civilian society who helped the guerrillas, "Godfathers of the Guerrilla," as he called them. Some time after his brother's attack on the EPL's weapons supply network in Turbo, and following his military training in Israel, the younger Castaño carried out a similar but more ambitious operation against a prominent cocaine trafficker named Gustavo Escobar Fernández. While not related to Medellín cartel founder Pablo Escobar, Gustavo Escobar did share Pablo Escobar's fondness for the guerrillas. He was an important ally of EPL leader Bernardo Gutiérrez. Even though Gustavo Escobar traveled in armored cars and was surrounded by a heavily armed bodyguard, the younger Castaño eventually managed to have him assassinated in Bogotá's El Dorado airport.[33]

By 1985 the Castaños were ready to launch the Córdoba War. Carlos Castaño had prepared himself by orchestrating a series of lighting attacks on FARC members and sympathizers during the last week of 1984. He and his men fanned out through Medellín, Amalfi, Segovia, Remedios, and San Carlos, and carried out twenty selective assassinations. When he returned to Córdoba he left behind a paramilitary group that he christened Death to Revolutionaries of the Northeast (*Muerte a Revolucionarios del Noreste*, MRN). Over the decade that followed the MRN would carry out sporadic targeted assassinations of FARC members and their supporters throughout northeastern Antioquia.[34]

Once Fidel Castaño had ensconced himself in southern Córdoba he began his campaign to destroy the EPL. His first step was to host an elegant dinner in Montería in early 1985, to which he invited the department's leading citizens. Castaño spoke at length to his guests, explaining how he would rid the department of law-breakers if given local support. He ended his talk saying, "Look gentlemen, this can be fixed, but only with hammer blows." After a few moments' silence someone was heard to mutter, "Well then, let's do it."[35] Soon the EPL and their allies in the FARC and ELN noticed members of their support network dying throughout the department, especially in its capital Montería. It did not take the guerrillas long to trace the deaths to the Antioquians who had recently bought land on the upper Sinú.

Late in 1985 EPL leaders "Betto," "Cocoliso," "Platón," and "Jairo Chiquito" met with FARC Front 5 commander "Efraín Guzmán" to decide what to do about the Castaños. At length they decided it was best overrun *Las Tangas* with a combined force of 600, killing everyone there, "up to and including the chickens." But before launching the operation they sent a squad of five, led by the wife of an EPL commander, to scout the area and to learn whether ranch approaches were mined and guarded by surveillance cameras. They would also let the main force know when Fidel Castaño arrived for his end-of-year cattle inventory. With the help of a sympathizer working at a nearby ranch the guerrillas masqueraded as recreational fishermen camped on the banks of the Sinú. When Castaño at last arrived at *Las Tangas* on January 26, 1986, the guerrillas approached the ranch on the pretext of selling their catch. But something about them seemed suspicious. One of Fidel Castaño's brothers saw them coming and shouted from a kitchen window, "Look out, here come five sons-of-bitches carrying bags." A gunfight ensued during which one of the guerrillas threw a grenade that failed to explode. They fled leaving two dead, but were quickly captured, taken back to *Las Tangas*, questioned under torture, and then shot. With the names of many EPL and FARC guerrillas and supporters in hand, Fidel Castaño unleashed his men on Turbo, San José de Apartadó, San Pedro, Tierralta, and Montería, where they killed dozens of people.[36]

The Castaños preferred fighting the guerrilla obliquely rather than confronting them in the field. That is, they employed selective assassination of insurgents, of those identified as members of the guerrillas' support network, and of sympathizers of the insurgents as well. The guerrillas had made this strategy easy through their long-standing policy known as "the combination of all forms of struggle," centered on using civilian social and political organizations to help them infiltrate Colombia's political system and progressive social groups, even as they used violence against the government and those whom they identified as "class enemies." Earlier the Colombian Communist party had worked to extend its influence through labor unions, and the FARC and other guerrillas continued that policy from the time of their formation in the mid–1960s. As the FARC and other insurgent groups gained strength during the late 1970s and early 1980s, they intensified their infiltration of left civilian organizations, especially labor unions and allied civil associations. The best known of these was the FARC's political party, the Patriotic Union, or UP, founded in 1985. Members of the UP became the favorite targets of the Castaños' paramilitary army because they were so easy to kill.[37]

Córdoba and the nearby Urabá region of Antioquia and Chocó were turbulent places as Fidel Castaño and his brothers established themselves there in 1984. Both were frontier regions, and Urabá was a place known for its verdant banana plantations and its impoverished, exploited work force. From the earliest days of the Banana Zone's development during the 1960s the guerrillas had successfully established their own labor unions among the workers there. By the 1980s the FARC and EPL controlled the two largest banana workers unions. The FARC's union was Sintrabanano, and the EPL's was called Sintagro. When the FARC launched the UP leftist Colombians rushed to join it, excited that their country at last had a viable social democratic alternative to the traditional Liberal and Conservative parties. Over a brief period of time thousands of Colombians became active in the new party, and a significant number of them lived in the guerrilla strongholds of Córdoba and Urabá. A tragedy of recent Colombian history is that nearly all UP activists, many of them idealistic social democrats opposed to armed revolution, died at the hands of the Castaño brothers and their paramilitary army.[38]

The Castaños viewed UP members as nothing more than FARC operatives disguised as civilians, and therefore fair game in the deadly struggle to dominate the parts of Colombia outside of state control. The same was the case with members of the guerrilla-dominated labor unions and their allied groups in Córdoba and Urabá. By 1986 affiliates of all such groups started falling to men of the paramilitary army headquartered on the upper Sinú, whose members were called the *Tangueros*. One of the first UP leaders to die was the party's candidate for *alcalde* of Tierralta, a town just south of the *Las Tangas,* who was shot in September 1987.[39] Assassinations increased as Colombia prepared for its first-ever local elections of *alcaldes* and *concejales* (city council members). The March 11, 1988, elections were unprecedented in Colombian history because they represented a significant step in the decentralization of political power in the nation. Prior to that time the mayors of municipalities were appointed by departmental governors who themselves were appointed by the national president. So the stakes were higher than ever before, especially for candidates of the *Unión Patriótica.* Violence in Córdoba and Urabá rose to unprecedented levels in the early months of 1988. UP members died everywhere that they stood as candidates. One observer likened Montería to a shooting gallery. And it was not just politicians who died at the hands of the *Tangueros.* Their victims included street vendors and shoemakers, tailors and shopkeepers, doctors and lawyers, school principals and university professors—and their students too. Departmental director of the UP and chief FARC ideologue in Córdoba, Alfonso Cujavante Acevedo, managed to avoid assassination in days preceding the election by surrounding himself with a large bodyguard contingent. He won a seat in Congress in the department's landslide UP victory on March 11. But he made the mistake of dismissing his bodyguard and was gunned down on March 15, shot seven times by a man who then calmly walked across the street, got into a car, and drove away. Cujavante's death was attributed to one of a thirty-strong group of assassins sent to Córdoba from the Magdalena Medio. All members of the group, which was led by Alonso de Jesús Baquero ("El Negro Vladimir"), were graduates of the paramilitary training school bankrolled by the Medellín cartel and located in the Magdalena Medio.[40] The Israeli mercenary who directed the school, Yair Klein, had dubbed the team of assassins "The Magnificent Ones" (*Los Magníficos*).[41]

Violence raged in Córdoba and Urabá through 1988, and not all of it was the responsibility of the Castaños paramilitary army. Between 1985 and 1987 the FARC and EPL unions Sintrabanano and Sintagro had fought one another for membership throughout the Banana Axis (*Eje Bananero*), with many leaders of the respective groups dying as a result. The two guerrilla groups reconciled in 1987, joining forces in the umbrella Símon Bolívar Guerrilla Coordinating Group, or CGSB.[42] That year they called for a "partial insurrection" and in 1988 for a "popular uprising" throughout Colombia. CGSB militancy peaked in its "general insurrection" called for October 26–28, 1988, in which members of the M-19, FARC, ELN, and EPL launched thirty-six simultaneous attacks throughout the central part of the country.[43] Their greatest success came when a combined EPL-FARC force wiped out a tactical military base and a police post in the Serranía de Abibe, east of Turbo. The Battle of Saiza, as CGSB leaders called it, left many soldiers and police dead, along with a number of civilians they described as paramilitaries. Afterward they departed with munitions and fifteen prisoners.[44]

The war for Córdoba raged throughout 1989, with UP activists dying in the cities and the EPL battling *Tangueros* in the mountainous south of the department. Meanwhile paramilitary squads constantly crossed over into Urabá to assassinate Sintagro and Sintrabanano activists along with others belonging to a number of allied civic organizations.[45] Over the years 1986–1991 the Urabá region suffered four times the rate of homicides committed in Colombia at large, with the rate of killings in San José de Apartadó running at the astronomical rate of 500–900 per 100,000 during those years.[46] In September 1989, the EPL complained in its newspaper *En Revolución* that bands of armed paramilitary fighters had free run of the roads of Montería, Tierralta, and Valencia, with local authorities turning a blind eye to their activities. During those years much of Córdoba's violence was of the action-reaction variety, as when

EPL commanders "Beto" and "Gavilín" traveled to *Las Tangas* from Pueblo Bello, a village in Urabá northeast of Turbo. They tortured and then killed ranch manager Umberto Quijano, a friend and confidante of Fidel Castaño, and stole forty-two head of cattle, which they took away to Urabá. Fidel Castaño, who was purchasing paintings in Europe at the time, instructed his men to avenge Quijano's death. A group led by "Cabezón" traveled from the ranch over the mountains to Pueblo Bello, rounded up forty-two men at random, loaded them onto a truck, and drove them back to *Las Tangas*. There they tortured and then executed them, and buried them in shallow graves. News of the Pueblo Bello massacre caused a furor in Colombia. It angered Fidel and Carlos Castaño as well, for neither one condoned random massacres as a means of combating the guerrillas. When the elder Castaño returned from Europe he had "Cabezón" shot for an excessive use of force that had brought unwelcome publicity to the paramilitaries of Córdoba.[47]

By late 1989 leaders of the *Unión Patriótica* despaired over the continued murder of its members. Although the party had elected eighteen *alcaldes* in the 1988 elections, thirteen of them were assassinated shortly afterward. Late that same year UP President Bernardo Jaramillo met personally with Pablo Escobar asking him to have his associate José Gonzalo Rodríguez Gacha stop killing UP members. Late the next year, in December 1989, as Jaramillo prepared to run for President in upcoming elections, the UP leader again asked Pablo Escobar to intervene in the murder of UP members. He sent fellow UP leader Alvaro Salazar to meet with Escobar. Escobar claimed that the UP's real problem lay not so much with Rodríguez Gacha, but rather with Fidel Castaño. He added that there was little he could do to influence the paramilitary leader, whom Escobar had taken to calling "2000" for the number of UP members he estimated Castaño had murdered.[48]

Despite the violence Colombians were in a hopeful frame of mind as the 1990 presidential election approached. Rodríguez Gacha had just been killed, Pablo Escobar was on the run, and the M-19 had demobilized its forces. The M-19 put forward Carlos Pizarro as its candidate for the May 27 presidential election, while the *Unión Patriótica* proclaimed Bernardo Jaramillo as its candidate. Córdoba's paramilitary leaders, however, viewed the M-19 and the UP candidacies as potentially catastrophic for Colombia. They had noted the FARC's January 19 declaration of a "Bolivarian Campaign for a New Colombia," in which the group promised its takeover of the government by 1997. The ELN had announced its "Popular Power, Armed Proselytism" campaign in 1989, and was enjoying an explosive increase in membership.[49] To the Castaños and to others of like mind, rather than presenting Colombia with a social democratic alternative to the traditional Liberal and Conservative parties, the Jaramillo and Pizarro candidacies represented nothing less than threats to put Medellín cartel and FARC puppets in the presidential palace. That is why Carlos Castaño took it upon himself to kill Carlos Pizarro prior to the elections. Accordingly, as he later confessed to journalist Mauricio Aranguren, he had Pizarro assassinated on April 26, 1990. Bernardo Jaramillo was assassinated on March 22, 1990, but Castaño claimed to have opposed that killing.[50]

Meanwhile back in Córdoba the EPL was signaling that it had had enough of war with the Castaños. In a declaration of July 30 Bernardo Gutiérrez expressed concern over the excessive number of human rights violations in Córdoba, observing that the "sea of violence" washing over the department was unlike anything seen before.[51] He entered into peace talks with the government during January 1991. Fidel, Carlos, and Vicente Castaño were ready for peace as well. In July they collaborated in drafting a preliminary version of what in December 1994 became the "Statutes of the Campesino Self-defense Forces of Córdoba and Urabá" (*Estatutos de las Autodefensas Campesinas de Córdoba and Urabá*). Under the heading "Watchword" was the statement "We want peace, we desire peace, because the nation needs peace, and we are a part of the nation."[52]

Demobilization of the EPL took place over the course of 1991 and was carried out amidst a climate of good will that many citizens of Córdoba found shocking. They looked on with astonishment when EPL commander Bernardo Gutiérrez shook hands with Fidel Castaño at the entrance of *Las Tangas* ranch on October 26, and when 600 guerrillas and paramilitary troops handed over weapons to government representatives and returned to civilian life. The former EPL members announced that they had constituted themselves into the Hope, Peace, and Liberty party (*Esperanza, Paz y Libertad*), and that they planned to participate in elections scheduled for the following year. Fidel Castaño deeded *Las Tangas* to the demobilized guerrillas and paramilitaries, an act that his mother laconically described as "Córdoba's agrarian reform of 1991."[53] He also gave them his hacienda *Tanela*, located across the *Serranía de Abibe* in Chocó, bringing the total land grants to 10,000 hectares. Castaño also established a charitable foundation called the Foundation of Peace in Córdoba (*Fundación para la Paz de Córdoba*, or FUNPAZCORD).[54]

* * *

By the end of the 1980s Colombians had shown that if their government failed to protect them from the guerrillas they would do so themselves, although at high cost to national institutions and to the rule of law. The paramilitary organizations ACDEGAM and ACCU had cleared the Middle Magdalena and Córdoba of guerrilla presence through massive killing. And they were far from the only citizen self-defense groups existing in Colombia at the time. Over a hundred similar but less well-known paramilitary forces operated throughout the country, mostly in rural areas, especially in western Santander and around the *Sierra Nevada de Santa Marta*, in the foothills of Meta and Casanare, and in northern Valle.[55]

Sadly the optimism of 1989–1991 proved to be short lived. The FARC and ELN, the country's two remaining guerrilla groups, were preparing to launch their all-out offensive to begin in 1994. Violence soon returned, worse than ever before. Signs of it appeared almost immediately in the Urabá region where in late 1991 the FARC and an EPL faction that had refused to demobilize started executing leaders of the Peace, Justice, and Liberty party.[56] Meanwhile in Córdoba former EPL commander Isidro Antonio Martínez Pastrana ("El Viejo Rafa"), who following his group's demobilization had moved away to Cartagena, continued to direct members of his gang who had also refused to demobilize. But by then the locals knew what to do. During late October 1991, citizens of the upper San Jorge River area collected money to pay for the assassination of El Viejo Rafa, which was effected at his home in Cartagena on November 9, 1991.[57] Thus the problem of renegade EPL members was resolved, at least temporarily.

The Narco-Paramilitary

"Kidnappers will be executed in public: they will be hanged from trees in public places or shot by firing squads. They will be duly marked with a small cross, which is the symbol of our organization Death to Kidnappers."
—From a 1981 leaflet announcing the creation of Death to Kidnappers, or MAS[58]

Illegal drug money has been the common denominator of Colombian violence since the 1970s. Abundant cash generated by illegal drug sales fueled the traffickers' violence against one another, and against the Colombian state and its citizenry. Colombia's guerrillas ceased being innocuous only when illegal drug money started cascading into the country. Their successes from the 1970s onward were, ironically, a function of the most savage form of capitalism: the illegal consumer-producer market dynamic.

It is hardly surprising that illegal drug money played a significant role in the rise of Colombia's exceedingly violent self-defense forces. The nation's first well-known paramilitary group, MAS, sprang up in response to a guerrilla project aimed at separating traffickers from their money via extortionate kidnapping. The year 1981 was marked by a flurry of M-19 kidnappings whose victims included leading trafficker Carlos Lehder and Martha Nieves Ochoa, a sister of Pablo Escobar's associate Jorge Luis Ochoa. Up to that time few in Colombia understood the magnitude of wealth passing into the hands of men like Lehder, Escobar, and Ochoa. But the M-19 did, for during the 1970s the guerrilla group had made use of friends in the illegal drug business to help it purchase weapons with money raised through a series of inventive kidnappings. What the M-19 did not fully appreciate was how dangerous it was to kidnap those connected with the country's burgeoning cocaine cartels. By seizing Martha Nieves Ochoa they set into motion the quick formation of MAS, a group announced in dramatic fashion in early December 1981. MAS immediately went to work seizing, torturing, and killing M-19 members.[59]

The response to the Nieves Ochoa kidnapping surprised and frightened the M-19. It was not used to retaliation by the families of its victims. Nor was it prepared for the savagery of MAS. Within three months the guerrilla group released Martha Nieves Ochoa and collected only a small fraction of the hefty ransom it had initially demanded. By then scores of M-19 members lay dead and several of its leaders had been delivered up to the authorities.

MAS was important in the history of Colombia's paramilitary groups. It showed the nation that a private army operating extra-legally could defeat the guerrillas far more expeditiously than could the nation's police or armed forces. Its success promoted the formation of self-defense groups elsewhere in the country, at a time when pre-existing paramilitary groups such as those headed by Ramón Isaza and Gonzalo Pérez in the Middle Magdalena, and the Castaño brothers in northeastern Antioquia, were unknown outside their immediate areas. MAS-inspired groups appeared over the course of 1982 in Caquetá, Arauca, Casanare, Santander, and Valle, sometimes even adopting the name MAS. That in turn alerted the national government to existence of the paramilitaries. In late 1982, more than four years after the country's first paramilitary organizations appeared, newly elected President Belisario Betancur ordered prosecutors to launch investigations in nine places around the country where paramilitary activity had been reported. On February 20, 1983, Colombia's Solicitor General released his report on Medellín-based MAS. It showed that Pablo Escobar's paramilitary army had consisted of 163 men, 59 of whom were from the army and police, some of them retired from active duty and some not. A number of its active-military members were attached to Battalions Bomboná and Bárbula, both of which were well known to MAS commander Fidel Castaño.[60]

MAS highlighted the divide between the Colombian government and its military establishment. When peace candidate Belisario Betancur took office and immediately released hundreds of jailed guerrillas, members of the military felt betrayed by a civilian leadership not sufficiently sensitive to the danger the guerrillas posed. A month before the Solicitor General released his report on MAS, the armed forces issued a warning to the country. In the January 1983 edition of the *Revista de las Fuerzas Armadas* an article appeared expressing the view that citizen self-defense groups were made up of "that honest part of society" disposed to defend national institutions and their own honor. That in turn, the writer continued, heralded "incalculable and unforeseen consequences that could take our country into a new phase of violence."[61] Those words were prescient. The only thing they did not warn of, because few in Colombia perceived it at the time, was the way illegal drug money would intensify the approaching battle between guerrillas and paramilitaries.

Yet another thing that MAS illustrated was the synergy at work within the paramilitary movement. When Pablo Escobar looked for someone to head his private army he selected fellow *paisa* Fidel Castaño. At the time he knew that Castaño had two years experience hunting down the FARC cadres who had killed his father. His direction of MAS in turn gave the *campesino* Castaño an understanding of how to fight the enemy in an urban setting, knowledge that he would put to use in 1985 when he took the anti-guerrilla struggle into Córdoba's capital Montería.

Fidel Castaño and his paramilitary army were narco-paramilitaries, if indirectly so, in that they owed their establishment in the department to illegal drug money. Fidel Castaño was a man of modest means in 1979 when the FARC abducted his father. He owned a bar in Segovia and a half-share in a dairy farm. Consequently he had limited means to pay his father's ransom. Yet when he and his brothers moved their anti-guerrilla campaign to Córdoba he had a billion pesos in hand, the equivalent of nearly nine million dollars, virtually all of which was derived from cocaine trafficking.[62] Castaño's good fortune was that just when he turned himself into "a money-making machine" to fund his anti-guerrilla fight, Colombia's cocaine boom enjoyed its finest moment. That is, it was earning traffickers fabulous profits at a time when neither the Colombian nor U.S. authorities were doing much to control the cocaine trade. It is instructive also that Fidel Castaño was not so important a trafficker as to ever have been charged with a drug-related crime in either Colombia or the United States.

Money derived from cocaine sales played a decisive role in the rise and fall of the Middle Magdalena paramilitaries. After the mid–1980s drug money became so important to ACDEGAM that its military branch became an outright narco-paramilitary army controlled by the Medellín trafficking group. At first that association, dating from late 1984, seemed benign enough.[63] Thanks to the sudden infusion of money from Rodríguez Gacha and his associate Gilberto Molina, and from Pablo Escobar as well, ACDEGAM's military force quickly swelled to 300 men, their salaries paid via million-peso monthly stipends from the traffickers.[64] Within two years of joining forces with ACDEGAM Rodríguez Gacha was earning as many as $32 million per week through cocaine sales in the United States, and was manufacturing the drug in multi-ton quantities at forty sites scattered throughout the Middle Magdalena, each of them protected by members of the region's paramilitary forces.[65] This happy state of affairs for the Magdalena River paramilitary group changed abruptly in 1987 when ACDEGAM became mired in violence far transcending its war against the FARC. That violence grew out of Rodríguez Gacha's slaughter of UP members, corruption within ACDEGAM's own leadership, the Medellín-Cali cartel war, involvement of ACDEGAM death squads operating in Córdoba and Urabá, and the Medellín cartel's war against the Colombian state.

ACDEGAM's political chief Pablo Guarín soon fell victim to this prolix violence. The Liberal politician had begun criticizing Rodríguez Gacha for his massive attack on the UP, especially following the October 1987 murder of that party's presidential candidate Jaime Pardo Leal. Guarín's end came just a month later when he was murdered by one of his own bodyguards, on order of Rodríguez Gacha.[66]

Somewhat lost in the news of high-level political assassinations during late 1987 was the murder of nineteen merchants who were transporting household appliances and boutique fashions from Cúcuta to Medellín. One of Henry Pérez' paramilitary detachments intercepted their convoy just east of Puerto Boyacá. The paramilitaries, led by Alonso de Jesús Baquero ("El Negro Vladimir") executed and dismembered the merchants and threw their remains into a tributary of the Magdalena River. Two weeks later, when two relatives of the merchants arrived in Puerto Boyacá asking about the missing men, they too were murdered. Not long afterward the wife of Henry Pérez opened a shop selling the stolen merchandise.[67]

The next step in ACDEGAM's downfall came as an outgrowth of the cartel war beginning in late 1987, and it involved the hiring of foreign mercenaries.[68] Medellín led Cali in hiring foreign military instructors thanks to its association with the Castaño brothers, who had well-established contacts with European-based soldiers of fortune. During 1987 Israeli and British mercenaries were hired by the Medellín trafficking group and brought to Colombia. By early 1988 they were busy instructing a group of fifty at several locations in the Middle Magdalena region. Most of their students worked for Rodríguez Gacha and Pablo Escobar, and had links with ACDEGAM as well.[69] Their graduation came just before the March 11, 1988, mid-term elections, a contest marked by left-wing enthusiasm over the prospects of candidates of the FARC-linked UP party. Fidel Castaño immediately pressed them into service in his war against EPL and FARC guerrillas in Córdoba and Urabá. It was thanks to his invitation that Alonso de Jesús Baquero and a group of thirty mercenary-trained paramilitaries rampaged through the region during March and April of 1988. At times they traveled with men from Fidel Castaño's *finca Las Tangas*, lists of names in hand, killing en masse all those pointed out to be guerrilla sympathizers. One of their most infamous attacks took place at the *caserío* (hamlet) called La Mejor Esquina, Córdoba, not far from Buenavista, just off the highway linking Montería and Medellín. There they fell upon the settlement at the high point of its Easter celebration, hoping to find virtuoso EPL kidnapper Antonio Martínez ("El Viejo Rafa") there. The massacre began at 10:30 p.m. with one of the attackers shouting "You're going to die here, guerrilla sons-of-bitches!" Estimates of the dead at La Mejor Esquina ran from twenty-eight to fifty-three.[70]

An immediate effect of the Mejor Esquina massacre was to break the strategic alliance between the EPL and Córdoba's drug traffickers. The slaughter spread panic among the traffickers, many of whom fled the department. One of the first to leave was César de Moya Cura, who had been especially close to El Viejo Rafa. De Moya made his way to Panama and was arrested a year later when the United States invaded the country during its successful pursuit of Manuel Noriega. The Colombian later became a key witness in Noriega's trial. Some months later De Moya was himself indicted, tried, convicted, and jailed in the U.S. for marijuana smuggling and money laundering.[71]

The massacres taking place in Córdoba and Urabá had the effect of speeding demobilization of the M-19 and EPL guerrillas. Carlos Pizarro had alluded to the Mejor Esquina killings when he ordered members of his group to kidnap Conservative politician Álvaro Gómez as a preface to his conversations with the Colombian government. The prospect of cartel-financed paramilitary death squads pursuing his followers yet a second time doubtless gave Pizarro pause. The Gómez kidnapping was Pizarro's way of reminding the Colombian public of the group's continuing existence. It was the opening gambit in the M-19's movement toward demobilization two years later. Similarly, the brutal narco-paramilitary severing of the EPL-trafficker alliance in eastern Córdoba played a significant role in the EPL's own demobilization in 1991.[72]

While the Córdoba and Urabá massacres of early 1988 focused national attention on the Middle Magdalena paramilitaries, it was the investigation of the massacre of the nineteen merchants near Puerto Boyacá in 1987 that eventually brought them unwelcome publicity and clarified their link to the Medellín cartel.

In early 1989 an investigative team was sent to the Magdalena Medio to look into the disappearance of the nineteen merchants from Antioquia. On January 8, the man who had killed them, Alonso de Jesús Baquero, and several of his men intercepted the group, made up mostly of male and female lawyers and police officials sent down from Bogotá. He did so at a place called La Rochela, in the countryside of the department of Santander. There Baquero and his men machine gunned the group, killing eleven of its twelve members. The La Rochela massacre shocked and infuriated Colombians and resulted in the first intensive investigation of the narco-paramilitary phenomenon.[73] Two informants presented themselves to Colombian authorities within days of the La Rochela incident, the first of them Diego Viáfara, an M-19 member who had infiltrated ACDEGAM in 1984. The second was Carlos Castaño Gil.

Viáfara's testimony was jaw-dropping, so much so that he was quickly removed from Colombia to DEA headquarters near Washington, D.C., where between February 28 and March 9, 1989, he gave 500 pages of testimony replete with dates, names, places, and events. That in turn led to many arrests and the destruction of cocaine processing centers across the Middle Magdalena. Within weeks President Virgilio Barco issued a series of decrees striking down the 1965 and 1968 legal provisions permitting the formation of citizen self-defense groups. Barco's decrees also established a specialized police unit charged with the full-time investigation of the narco-paramilitary.[74] Carlos Castaño's cooperation with authorities at DAS was important because it provided inside information on Pablo Escobar and his Medellín-based organization.[75]

By early 1989 Carlos Castaño had come to believe that Pablo Escobar and his personal army of assassins constituted a real threat to the Colombian state. The younger Castaño had disliked Escobar from the moment he first met him in 1984, a feeling that intensified a year later when he witnessed Escobar and M-19 leaders planning the assault on Colombia's Supreme Court building. Castaño was conservative and patriotic, while Pablo Escobar viewed himself as a man of the left and an enemy of the established order. Pablo Escobar stood ever ready to help the guerrilla in its struggle against the Colombian state. Carlos Castaño, on the other hand, perceived traffickers like Escobar to be "godfathers of the guerrilla" and therefore prime targets in his war against revolutionary subversion. That is what led him to have Pablo Escobar's like-minded colleague Gustavo Escobar Fernández assassinated, and M-19 leader Carlos Pizarro as well. About the time of the Pizarro assassination, in early 1990, Carlos Castaño decided that Pablo Escobar needed to die as well. And within a year of this decision Pablo Escobar decided that it was time to have Castaño killed.

After Pablo Escobar entered prison in mid–1991 he correctly perceived that enemies within his own trafficking group, the younger Castaño among them, were conspiring against him.[76] Accordingly he sent six of his *sicarios* to assassinate Carlos Castaño on New Year's Day 1992. The attack failed and later that same day Castaño penned a letter to Escobar, denouncing him for the attack. He forwarded a copy of the letter to his brother Fidel.[77] But Fidel Castaño was not ready to turn against Pablo Escobar. He and the Medellín cartel chief had been friends and associates for many years, and by the early 1990s the elder Castaño was well outside cartel politics and wanted nothing more than to tend his cattle ranches in Córdoba and Urabá and to pursue his passion for art. But his brother's animosity toward Escobar, along with the capo's increasingly erratic behavior, soon drew Fidel Castaño into the battle against his former friend. Escobar's murder of Fernando Galeano, and his subsequent attacks on other members of Galeano's family, were the acts that crystallized Fidel Castaño's opposition to Escobar. The Galeano murder, carried out while Escobar was still housed in the prison referred to as the Cathedral, produced a deadly split within the Medellín cartel.

In 1992 Fidel Castaño was Colombia's dominant paramilitary leader. Sober, ruthless, and brilliant in managing irregular military campaigns, a *paisa* having intimate knowledge of Medellín and its drug underworld, he was the ideal person to lead the battle against Pablo Escobar. Over the latter part of 1992 and through most of 1993 he headed the paramilitary group called the PEPES (Persecuted by Pablo Escobar), made up mostly of Escobar's former associates. Their efficient destruction of Pablo Escobar's trafficking organization broke the drug capo's spirit, convincing him by late 1993 that his own death was nigh. The Colombian government and its U.S. allies would have eventually brought down Pablo Escobar, but without help from the PEPES that would have happened much later and at a much greater expenditure of life.[78]

Colombia's paramilitary movement came full circle during the hunt for Pablo Escobar. In the early 1980s Fidel and Carlos Castaño joined forces with Ramón Isaza to break FARC power in the Middle Magdalena region. By the early 1990s they were working together again to help end Escobar's terrorism. After forming the PEPES the Castaños coordinated with Isaza to close the Medellín-Bogotá highway to Escobar's truck bombs, in that way doubtless saving lives in the nation's capital.[79]

The episode of the PEPES illustrates the difference between narco-paramilitaries and paramilitaries. The mercenary-trained henchmen of Pablo Escobar were narco-paramilitaries. When ACDEGAM was taken over by the Medellín cartel it became part of an entity dedicated to earning money by selling cocaine to foreign consumers. Paramilitary leaders like the Castaños and Ramón Isaza were focused on war against Colombia's guerrilla insurgency. For men like the Castaños earning money through illegal drug sales was simply a means to the end of waging war against the guerrillas and their supporters. As an outlaw dedicated to making and merchandising an illegal product, however, Pablo Escobar happily formed alliances with anyone who opposed the state and its legal regimen. And Escobar helped the guerrillas a great deal. During the years that Escobar fought the Colombian state the FARC and ELN flourished mightily. It was thus posthumous revenge for Pablo Escobar that resurgent guerrillas in Córdoba killed Fidel Castaño in January 1994, only a month after the Medellín drug kingpin met his end on a Medellín rooftop.[80] The death of Fidel Castaño set a regrouping of Colombia's paramilitary forces into motion, one that deepened and intensified armed conflict in the country.

The Paramilitary Offensive of 1994–2002

> "As long as the Colombian guerrillas continue to threaten the lives of their compatriots, ethical reflection leads us to defend ourselves individually or collectively, until such time that the state truly protects us."
>
> —Carlos Castaño, 2001[81]

Public order deteriorated in provincial Colombia during the long struggle against the Medellín cartel. The ELN and the FARC grew as never before, reaching a combined total of

12,000 by 1994, with armed fighters distributed among some fifty fronts spread throughout the nation. Members of the guerrilla groups roamed the countryside almost at will, taking what they wanted at gunpoint with little worry of hindrance by the country's overmatched and under-funded police and military. Public order deteriorated further over the ensuing eight years, during the dysfunctional presidency of Ernesto Samper and the temporizing one of Andrés Pastrana. It was a pleasing state of affairs for the revolutionary insurgents, who became ever more certain that success was at hand. Booming cocaine sales in the United States and Europe financed an influx of high-powered weaponry and new recruits. When he took office President Andrés Pastrana gave the FARC a large expanse of national territory from which to operate and hoped to do the same for the ELN, all in the vain hope that these concessions would help bring about peace. But the concessions only encouraged the guerrillas. By the end of Pastrana's term the FARC was dominant over half of national territory and had driven national law enforcement personnel from scores of municipalities across the nation.

It was within this setting that the nationwide paramilitary coalition AUC, or United Self-defense Forces of Colombia, grew powerful.[82] The AUC expanded to nearly match the guerrillas in numbers by 2001. Many Colombians supported the paramilitary forces even as they were appalled and shamed by their excesses.[83] The paramilitaries relied on selective assassination and massacres to break the hold of the FARC and ELN in key coca growing areas and in important corridors of cocaine export. Levels of violence in such places defied belief during years of the paramilitary offensive. Finally, in mid–2002, the Colombian people took their destiny in hand through democratic means, electing a president committed to driving the guerrillas back and striking at the illegal drug industry that nourished them. As soon as the government of Alvaro Uribe was in place the AUC, whose armed forces then stood at nearly 20,000, entered into a process of demobilization. By late 2005 most AUC members had turned in their weapons.

* * *

As was the case during the Córdoba War of 1985–1991, northwestern Colombia provided the model for citizen self-defense elsewhere in the nation. This was because the region, especially the Urabá zone of Antioquia and Chocó, united a constellation of factors making it valuable territory for the armed left, and a logical starting point for the paramilitary offensive against the guerrillas. It was the *eje bananero*, the Banana Axis, where during the 1980s transnational corporations employed workers who came to be represented by militant unions dominated by the EPL, FARC, and ELN; it was a frontier region with a history of violence; and it offered easy egress of illegal drugs and ingress of weapons and supplies. Once the EPL demobilized in 1991, and the Colombian government became distracted by its war against the Medellín and Cali cartels, the FARC had free reign to consolidate its hold on the Banana Axis. The FARC also moved into Córdoba, where it operated alongside EPL members who had rejected demobilization. The FARC and ELN turned with a vengeance on demobilized EPL members, the *Esperanzados* of the Freedom, Peace, and Liberty party, whom they considered to be traitors to the revolutionary cause. They killed them in an ongoing and intensifying series of attacks reaching a high point in January 1994, when members of FARC Front 5 entered the *finca La Chinita* and machine gunned an *Esperanzado* settlement there killing thirty-six of them.[84]

When FARC and EPL dissidents returned to Córdoba early in the 1990s, resuming their attacks on landowners and merchants, the locals begged officials in the Gaviria administration for help. But the government in Bogotá was busy with its own struggle against Pablo Escobar and could do nothing to help. Nor could citizens of Córdoba turn to Fidel Castaño, because he too was involved in the search for Escobar. The best the government could do was return to the mechanism of legalized citizen self-defense. President César Gaviria did so as one of his last major public acts before leaving office in mid–1994. The paramilitary entity he established was called Convivir, and it allowed citizens to arm themselves under supervision of the armed forces and the Superintendence of Vigilance and Security. Convivir wasn't much, but it was the best the government could do during the dark years of ineffective government and guerrilla resurgence. Formal implementation of Convivir took place early in the administration of President Ernest Samper. By the time Samper left office 414 Convivir units had been chartered throughout the nation.[85]

The disorder spilling over into Córdoba brought a new generation of leaders into ranks of the paramilitary, foremost among them Salvatore Mancuso, a member of the department's upper-middle class and owner with his wife of the farm *Campamento*, on the right bank of the Sinú River south of Montería. The year 1992 found Mancuso fending off three guerrillas who had come to kidnap him. Shortly after that he began guiding army patrols from their base in Montería. He did so on several occasions when they conducted operations against guerrillas living south of his ranch in the Paramillo region of southern Córdoba, and in the Serranía de Abibe extending along the boundary between Córdoba and Urabá. Salvatore Mancuso was one of the first to use radio-telephones to link land owners throughout the department. And he was one of the first to organize a Convivir self-defense group in Córdoba. Still, that did not save him from a near kidnapping by FARC cadres as he and his family drove along the highway linking Tierralta to Montería in May 1995. After his narrow escape Mancuso wrote Minister of Defense Fernando Botero demanding that the government do more to protect the people of his department. Botero never answered his letter. At the moment Colombia's Defense Minister was busy defending himself from the charge that he had accepted money from the Cali cartel while serving as manager of Ernesto Samper's presidential campaign, a crime for which he was later convicted and sent to prison. The government's failure to help his family led Mancuso to join forces with Córdoba's leading anti-guerrilla fighters, those headquartered farther up the Sinú River and led by Carlos Castaño.[86] At the time their alliance was effected, in mid–1995, the Castaños' paramilitary army was preparing to drive the FARC and its allies from Córdoba and Urabá.

Fidel Castaño's death in early 1994, during a skirmish with the EPL near the village of San Pedro de Urabá, had the effect of placing control of his paramilitary force into the hands of his younger brother Carlos. By 1994 it was clear that the lull of the early 1990s had ended and that the FARC and ELN had entered a time of renewed military activity. The middle months of 1994 were marked by guerrilla attacks extending from Putumayo in the south, up through Caquetá and Meta, and northwest through Antioquia and Córdoba. The guerrilla offensive brought about a gathering of paramilitary leaders in the Middle Magdalena town of Cimitarra, Santander, in December 1994. That meeting was designated the First National Conference of an umbrella organization called the United Self-Defense Forces of Córdoba and Urabá (*Autodefensas Unidas de Córdoba and Urabá*, or ACCU). Carlos Castaño was appointed commander of the ACCU, even though he protested that he was too young for the post—he was only twenty-nine at the time. The group created a federation uniting Castaño's own self-defense force with those of Ramón Isaza in the Middle Magdalena region, and of

Héctor Buitrago in Casanare. New faces among those attending were those of Rodrigo Tovar Pupo ("Jorge 40"), a landowner from César, who was named ACCU commander in the departments of Magdalena, César, and the Guajira; and Rodrigo Mercado Peluffo ("Diego Vecino") who was put in charge of ACCU forces in Sucre. Their region of Tovar and Mercado became known as the ACCU Northern Bloc, under the general command of Salvatore Mancuso. The ACCU's first act was to declare war on the FARC in Urabá.[87]

Plans for the Urabá War were still being formulated when Salvatore Mancuso met with Vicente Castaño on the upper Sinú in mid–1995. As Mancuso later recalled it, the meeting was a difficult one. He was uneasy about the Castaño family's reputation for brutality, and the college-educated Mancuso was understandably afraid of being linked to crimes committed by the hard-eyed campesinos from Antioquia. But his mind was made up and at the end of the meeting Mancuso agreed to unite his small anti-guerrilla Convivir group with the ACCU. It was his leadership skills and charisma that soon made him commander of the entire Northern Bloc, a region embracing all Caribbean departments and extending eastward to the Catatumbo region of Norte de Santander.[88]

Carlos Castaño was typically blunt when he announced the events that were about to unfold in Urabá. He did so in a lengthy piece of writing distributed widely across the region. In it he explained that war was coming to the Banana Axis and that all "auxiliaries of the guerrilla" involved in supplying the insurgents, and in receiving their stolen goods, would be targeted. The ACCU operation began in January 1995 in the northernmost Urabá town of Necolí. By March, 130 people had been slain on the spot, with another 122 taken away and killed elsewhere. A general panic ensued and over a thousand families fled the municipality. During April the national government attempted to intervene, and Antioquia's Governor Álvaro Uribe Vélez threatened to halt funding all government-sanctioned Convivir self-defense groups in Urabá unless the killing stopped. But the violence worsened as ACCU forces under the command of Éver Veloza ("H.H."), commander of the Urabá-based ACCU Banana Bloc, moved southward through the towns and villages scattered through the banana plantations along the Gulf of Urabá's eastern shore. On May 18, 1995, the city council of San José de Apartadó asked for a truce, to which Castaño answered that he would not halt his campaign until the FARC ceased its kidnappings, extortion, and attacks on defenseless citizens. A week after that the mayors of towns throughout Urabá met with President Ernesto Samper to ask for his help, but to no avail. During July 1995 Minister of Government Horacio Serpa said the government would not authorize talks between the guerrillas and the ACCU, because that would be tantamount to "partitioning the territory between the FARC and Fidel Castaño." Serpa's remark illustrated how little Bogotá understand the nature of events unfolding in northwestern Colombia. At that moment Fidel Castaño had already been in his grave for eighteen months. Minister Serpa's words were a metaphor for his government's abject ineffectiveness in the face of ghastly civil war.[89]

As the Urabá War unfolded the FARC attempted to match the ACCU, proclaiming its "Guerrilla Dignity" campaign featuring selective assassination of anyone helping paramilitary forces. In August 1995, Antioquia Governor Alvaro Uribe suggested that international peacekeepers be sent into Urabá, an idea that army commander Harold Bedoya later rejected. In late 1995, the army sent General Rito Alejo del Río to take command of the Twenty-second Brigade, headquartered near the city of Turbo. His specific charge was to help protect the *Esperanzados* from attack by the guerrillas and their sympathizers.[90] Del Río was a hard-liner who had known

Carlos Castaño from the time both had studied military tactics in Israel a dozen years before. Del Río had intimate knowledge of his country's paramilitary organizations, having been the officer named to defend fifty-nine soldiers charged with belonging to Pablo Escobar's group MAS in 1982.[91]

Violence in Urabá rose to unprecedented heights during the ACCU offensive. By 1996, homicides throughout the *Eje Bananero* reached an unprecedented 1,200 per 100,000. By June 1996, fifteen elected officials in the FARC bastion San José de Apartadó had been assassinated, and UP and Communist party members were fleeing the town and its surrounding region. Members of the Hope, Peace, and Liberty party were invaluable to the paramilitary effort. Some 600 of them had joined the ACCU during the early 1990s, when it became clear that both the FARC and their former EPL colleagues were bent on exterminating them. As residents of the region, the *Esperanzados* had no trouble identifying FARC and EPL members and sympathizers and helping kill them. During 1996 the European peace organization Pax Christi sent the Bishop of Rotterdam to Urabá, hoping that he might find a way of lessening the bloodshed. The Bishop was not successful. Meanwhile, many citizens were pleased that the guerrillas' hold on Urabá was being broken, and a few said so publicly. Antioquia's Secretary of Government Pedro Juan Moreno referred to that moment in Urabá's history as one of "strong authority." When soft-line members of the military accused Rito Alejo del Río of refusing to interfere with ACCU units, he lashed out at his critics as "defenders of the interests of either the drug traffickers or the subversives."[92] By early 1997, the ACCU had pushed the FARC southward out of Urabá, and was engaging the guerrillas throughout southeast and southwest Antioquia. By that time the ACCU had grown to twenty fronts.[93]

In May 1997, ACCU leaders proclaimed that its offensive was at an end. They said that with the guerrilla presence greatly reduced in Urabá, Convivir chapters would be sufficient to maintain order throughout the region. But they left the Banana Bloc intact, with one of its two constituent fronts charged with monitoring conditions in Turbo, while the second was tasked with policing San José de Apartadó, Carepa, and Chigorodó. Years later, in testimony on the Urabá War, Banana Bloc Commander Éver Veloza said that his men killed 1,500 suspected guerrilla members and sympathizers in that region between 1994 and 1997.[94] By the latter year a million Colombians had been driven from their homes by the fighting in Urabá and the Chocó alone.[95]

Carlos Castaño's relatively quick and relatively easy defeat of the FARC in one of its oldest seats of power galvanized Colombia's other paramilitary leaders, convincing them to accept his leadership in a nation-spanning organization of self-defense forces. It had always been Castaño's dream to knit the country's disparate paramilitary groups into a confederation capable of engaging and defeating the guerrillas everywhere in the country, and then holding the liberated territories and controlling their electoral politics. He had begun laying the groundwork for paramilitary unity in 1990, near the end of the Córdoba War, when, with his friend Carlos Mauricio García Franco ("Doble Cero"), he drafted the "Statutes of the Campesino Self-Defense Forces of Córdoba and Urabá," a fifteen-page set of rules governing associated paramilitary units. The document was published in March 1996, near the end of the Urabá War, and distributed to paramilitary commanders attending the ACCU's Third National Conference, held in Córdoba in November 1996.[96] Five months later, in April 1997, Castaño called yet another meeting of paramilitary leaders at which he launched his nationwide coalition of paramilitary organizations, the United Self-defense Forces of Colombia (*Autodefensas Unidas de Colombia*), or AUC. Commanders from within the ACCU, the largest associated group within the AUC, were named to head five fronts under unified command; these fronts embraced the entire northern portion of the country. Associated structures extended the AUC's reach into the Llanos departments of Meta and Casanare.[97]

The Colombian state was in disarray at the time these events took place. During the mid–1990s rumors circulated that the Samper government would soon be overthrown, and the nation was under sanction by the U.S. for allowing illegal drug monies to permeate the legislative and executive branches of government. All the while the president and armed forces were at swords' points. The Colombian army was in the midst of a humiliating string of defeats by well-armed guerrillas. Armed forces commander Harold Bedoya had shed tears while watching a FARC videotape of the September 1996 attack on the military's premier anti-narcotics base in Putumayo. Several dozen soldiers were killed when a large FARC force overran the Las Delicias base, after which the guerrillas marched seventy survivors away into captivity. The soldiers were released with great fanfare ten months later, in June 1997, after which Samper announced that he would renew peace talks with the FARC. Then Samper further placated the guerrillas by firing hard-line armed forces commander Bedoya. In a widely-reported meeting between the two men Bedoya accused Samper of failure to support the military and blasted him as doing great damage to the nation. Following Bedoya's removal from command junior officers feted him, at one point shouting "Down with the government!"[98] Such division between Colombia's military and civilian leadership was nigh incredible in a country under attack by well-armed revolutionary insurgents. It helps explain the military's complicity in Carlos Castaño's first major action as AUC commander, a massacre carried out during July 1997 at Mapiripán, Meta, in the FARC heartland.

Carlos Castaño and Salvatore Mancuso started planning the Mapiripán attack within days of Ernesto Samper's announcement that he would resume peace talks with the FARC, and that he might grant the insurgents their long-standing demand of a safe haven in southeastern Colombia. The paramilitaries resolved to counter government concessions in the way they knew best, through terror. On July 12, 1997, the last of 200 ACCU troops departed airports in Necolí and San José de Apartadó, in Urabá, and landed at the army-controlled airport at San José de Guaviare. Over the next two days they traveled downstream in launches, stopping at a military base just upriver from Mapiripán. Early on the morning of July 15, they surrounded and cut off the town, and the next day they went from house to house, selecting twenty-seven victims who were summarily executed. Their eviscerated bodies were thrown into the Guaviare River. Following the massacre there was a mass exodus from the town, and not long after that Carlos Castaño warned that there would be many more Mapiripáns.[99]

In mid–1997 the battle lines were drawn for what would prove to be a definitive contest pitting Colombia's paramilitaries against its guerrillas. Crucial municipal elections were approaching in October, and a presidential contest seven months later, in May 1998. Both groups counted on consolidating their hold on territory in order to influence the upcoming elections in their regions of dominance. In March 1997, police commander Rozo José Serrano said that the FARC hoped to win 600 mayoral contests in the municipal elections, which if successful would give them pro-insurgent representation in more than half the country's *municipios.* The contest between the AUC and the guerrillas was unequal at the outset. By 1997 there was in fact a guerrilla presence in half of the country's *municipios.* The paramilitaries were present in just a third of them. The FARC had sixty-four fonts and the ELN thirty, distributed throughout the nation. Meanwhile the AUC counted approximately thirty fronts affiliated with the group's regional blocs. The guerrillas had a clear advantage in troops, with the FARC boasting 10,000 armed fighters along with 5,000 urban militias, and the ELN 2,500 troops. The two groups had nearly 100,000 active supporters and sympathizers across the nation.[100] At the moment of its founding the AUC possessed 4,000 troops, and claimed control of only Córdoba, Urabá, and the Middle Magdalena region. FARC territory included most of the southeastern part of the country, as well as the Catatumbo region of North Santander along the border with Venezuela. The ELN was also present in Catatumbo, and it dominated the southern part of the department of Bolívar. When the AUC launched its nationwide offensive paramilitary groups were soon fighting guerrillas from Caldas northward up through the Coffee Axis, throughout Antioquia and Chocó, and in the departments of César, Sucre, Arauca, Casanare, Caquetá, Santander, Norte de Santander, Boyacá, Cauca, and Nariño.[101]

Colombia's cocaine industry played a key role in the AUC's offensive against the guerrillas, even though in earlier times its leader Carlos Castaño had sought to insulate the paramilitary movement from the trade. Following his brother's death in 1994 Castaño had tried to stop cocaine from being exported through ports along the Caribbean coast of Córdoba and Sucre. At the end of that year when he formally constituted the ACCU, Castaño stressed that no constituent part of the new organization could be involved in drug trafficking, and that ACCU-affiliated groups which did traffic in drugs would be punished for it.[102] Carlos Castaño was a campesino from Antioquia's conservative heartland, and as such he accepted the Church teaching that psychoactive drugs interfered with the exercise of free will and therefore were to be avoided. But like many others he was ultimately forced to embrace drug trafficking as the means to an end. During the Urabá War he turned a blind eye to ACCU taxation of cocaine exports. His brother Vicente, comptroller of the organization, and Banana Bloc commander Éver Veloza ("H.H."), collected the taxes, which came to five million pesos per boatload and from two to three hundred million pesos per month.[103] By 1997 Carlos Castaño had embraced the necessity of funding paramilitary activities through illegal drug revenues. Early that year he traveled to La Cooperativa, Meta, where he met with leading *cocaleros* of the region, among them Héctor Buitrago and his son Germán Darío ("Martín Llanos"), and Castaño's associates and leaders within the Autodefensas of Casanare. Castaño convinced the group that in exchange for paying him just half the taxes that they paid the guerrilla he would take the paramilitary fight into the guerrillas' territory. The Mapiripán massacre, carried out in July of that year, was fruit of the meeting.[104]

Routes of the AUC offensive against the FARC and ELN were determined by the illegal drug industry, because the guerrillas were congregated where coca was grown and cocaine produced. That had been true in Córdoba and Urabá, and it was true in virtually every other place where the AUC sought out the guerrillas between 1997 and 2002. After securing Córdoba and Urabá, AUC commanders moved into contiguous areas to attack the guerrilla: South Bolívar, the Chocó and western Antioquia, the Caribbean coast departments, and the Catatumbo region of Norte de Santander. Three AUC fronts were assigned those tasks. The Central Bolívar Bloc (*Bloque Central Bolívar*, or BCB) became the most powerful component of the AUC precisely because of its seizure of coca and cocaine producing areas. The BCB first drove eastward into the south of Bolívar where the ELN had established a powerful presence in the Serranía de San Lucas, a place replete with coca plantations, cocaine kitchens, and even gold mines. Fierce battles were fought there between 1997 and 1999, with the BCB ending ELN control in the south of Bolívar. As that campaign wound down BCB Commander Rodrigo Pérez Alzate ("Julián Bolívar") sent his forces to wrest the Magdalena River city of Barrancabermeja from ELN control. His men moved block-by-block through neighborhoods of Barancabermeja, expelling the ELN from them during late 2000.[105] As those campaigns went on the BCB also established fronts in the far south of the country, in Putumayo, where with extreme brutality its forces ended FARC domination of the department's 15,000 hectares of coca plantations. That had the effect of driving the guerrillas westward into Nariño, Cauca, and Valle.[106]

During BCB operations Salvatore Mancuso and Rodrigo Tovar Pupo ("Jorge 40") led the AUC Northern Bloc into Magdalena, César, the Guajira, and North Santander. Despite the fact they were enemies, Tovar Pupo joined with long-time paramilitary leader and trafficker Hernán Giraldo of the Santa Marta region to quell the guerrilla threat in northeastern Colombia. Meanwhile, between 1997 and 1999, Salvatore Mancuso directed the Catatumbo Bloc, which was charged with reducing the FARC and ELN presence in the region drained by the Catatumbo River, a premier route of cocaine export through Venezuela. Over 5,000 Colombians, most of them identified as guerrilla sympathizers, were said to have been killed by paramilitary forces during the Catatumbo offensive.[107]

Between 1997 and 2004 the Élmer Cárdenas Bloc attacked FARC strongholds south of Urabá in Chocó. The region extending along the border with Panama was valuable because it held routes of cocaine export to both the Caribbean and the Pacific. Therefore it was an important and historic transit route for every material important to both the drug trade and to armed insurgent groups. Élmer Cárdenas Bloc Commander Freddy Rendón Herrera ("El Alemán") eventually prevailed over the FARC, although with heavy loss of life on both sides and among the civilian population. Especially vicious fighting between AUC and FARC forces took place in the Chocó during the early months of 2002, culminating in the deaths of 112 civilians killed by an errant FARC mortar on May 2 of that year.[108]

The link between drugs and AUC funding was especially clear in AUC operations in the Eastern Llanos and the southwest of the country. During 2001 Vicente Castaño, who by then had already become wealthy through his drug-related activities, sold the command of Centaurs Bloc (*Bloque Centauros*) to his long-time colleague Miguel Arroyave for the sum of two million dollars. Arroyave's cocaine trafficking soon led him into conflict with the Campesino Self-defense Forces of Casanare (*Autodefensas Campesinas de Casanare*, or ACC), led by the Buitrago family. Vicious warfare ensued between the two AUC-affiliated paramilitary Fronts. It culminated in 2004 with victory for the Buitragos, although at the cost of 600 lives on both sides, among them Arroyave's.[109]

The FARC was late in establishing a major presence in the southwestern departments of Valle, Cauca, and Nariño. But it did so after 1997 because of paramilitary and stepped-up army pressure brought against them in their traditional heartland of Meta and Caquetá. When the FARC began arriving in force in Colombia's southwestern departments during 1999, it found itself confronting the troops of recently arrived Calima Bloc commander Éver Veloza ("H.H."). Veloza had been there since 1997, sent to head the newly formed block following successful conclusion of the Urabá War. The Calima Bloc became a significant force in Valle during the spate of mass kidnappings carried out by the ELN between 2000 and 2002.[110] At about that same time Central Bolívar Bloc leader Carlos Mario Jiménez Naranjo ("Javier Montañez") arrived in Valle too. Jiménez was best known by his nickname "Macaco" (ugly), given him by the cocaine traffickers with whom he had worked during the 1980s. Jiménez Naranjo had joined the paramilitaries during in the 1990s, rising to become a BCB commander. A native of Risaralda, in the Coffee Axis, he was able to mediate the war between North Valle cartel leaders Diego Montoya and Wilber Varela that left 1,000 dead between 2003 and 2005. Through that intercession he established an AUC presence in Risaralda, enabling the group to control the corridor used to transport cocaine between that department and locations in the Chocó and Valle.[111]

Illegal drug revenues may have nourished AUC expansion, but the group itself was the child of guerrilla aggressiveness and state ineptitude. The paramilitaries merely balanced this equation. They countered the guerrillas' aggression against state and citizenry with their own savage attacks against the guerrillas and their support base. Thus they gave the state the opportunity to re-establish public order in a legal and democratic way. Colombia's history during the last years of the twentieth century and first years of the twenty-first century reveals the stresses that the struggle to reassert public order had had on the nation's democracy. These stresses became increasingly visible in the waning years of Ernesto Samper's presidency and over the entirety of Andrés Pastrana's term in office. They widened divisions between those demanding strong military action against the guerrillas and those convinced that peace with the guerrillas could be achieved only by negotiations. Those favoring a hard-line approach against the FARC and ELN came to constitute an ever-larger proportion of the Colombian public as the guerrilla offensive intensified. Many Colombians came to tacitly support the paramilitaries as their best alternative to ongoing victimization at hands of the guerrillas. Some were not so tacit. This was manifest in a letter sent to Colombia's Minister of Defense on January 18, 1997, shortly after the Samper government placed a half-billion peso reward on the head of Carlos Castaño. Seventy-five ranchers from Córdoba signed the letter, holding Castaño as a hero, not a villain. "Castaño took away our fear," they wrote, "he taught us how to fight against our enemy."[112] An indication of the way the political winds were blowing in Colombia during Andrés Pastrana's peace initiative with the FARC came shortly after a banquet honoring Rito Alejo del Rio, the army general sacked by Pastrana because of accusations that he had aided the paramilitary during the Urabá War. A national opinion poll taken just after the banquet showed that 82 percent of Colombians did not want the army to fight the paramilitaries. Of those polled 70 percent wanted the army to fight the guerrillas instead.[113]

Andrés Pastrana's willingness to grant the FARC a safe haven in Meta and Caquetá fanned the flames of division between Colombia's civil administration and its military establishment, and it also intensified debate concerning the paramilitaries and their relationship to the nation's armed forces. It brought the historic division between the central government and regional Colombia into sharp relief as well. Part of Pastrana's approach to the FARC involved his striking at the AUC and its allies within the military establishment. That was the reason he had removed Rito Alejo del Río from command of the 17th Brigade in Urabá during 1998, forcing him into retirement early in 1999. Pastrana's act had infuriated many in the military and in Antioquia's political establishment, leading them to organize the protest banquet in Bogotá in April 1999 honoring del Rio. The banquet's theme was "The Country That Does Not Surrender." Retired General Harold Bedoya helped organize the affair, along with Antioquia's former Secretary of Government Pedro Juan Moreno. Another of the organizers was Guillermo Rivera, president of the union representing the demobilized EPL guerrillas whom del Río had been sent to protect from FARC attacks in 1995. All of them wanted to honor the retired general, who they called "The Pacifier of Antioquia."[114] Featured speaker at the banquet was Antioquia's former governor Álvaro Uribe Vélez, recently returned from a European sojourn following FARC threats on his life. Many Colombians viewed Uribe's speech as the beginning of his bid to become Colombia's president in 2002.

The del Río banquet coincided with the Catatumbo campaign of the AUC. Carlos Castaño had announced the operation in April 1999, and what followed was a textbook example of the "Castaño method" in action. Eight hundred members of the AUC Northern Bloc swept into the North Santander *municipio* of La Gabarra in 1999. The town and its surrounding territory had become an ELN stronghold in the 1980s and a center of coca cultivation and cocaine production during the 1990s. The lure of drug revenues led the FARC to go to war with the ELN there during the 1990s, and it drove the ELN out of La Gabarra over the course of the decade. But then between 1999 and 2000 the AUC broke the FARC's hold on the *municipio*. During the first six months of 1999 the AUC massacred scores of people in and around La Gabarra, causing 3,000 of the region's resident to flee. Deserters from guerrilla ranks were especially useful to the AUC in identifying those to be singled out. At its peak one-third of the AUC was made up of former guerrillas who willingly identified their former colleagues and members of the civilian population who had cooperated with them in earlier times. Colombian history of the period is replete with examples such as the one from an AUC massacre carried out in the *municipio* of Yolombó, Antioquia, on August 31, 1999. When a paramilitary unit passed through a village in that municipality an ELN deserter named Rafael pointed out an elderly man who had served a meal to his group years earlier. The man was immediately taken to a nearby school house and executed along with five others from the village.[115] Carlos Castaño's brother Vicente accurately summed up the paramilitary's mode of attack: "The AUC model of fighting was monstrous at first, but then not so much so ... and [it was] extremely rapid."[116]

Vicente Castaño's words explain both the paramilitaries' success in driving the guerrillas out of their traditional strongholds like as Catatumbo and Urabá, and of the link between the extreme violence seen in such places and the illegal drug trade. Colombia's guerrillas had at least a higher political vision that they drew on to justify their illegal acts. The paramilitaries had no such higher ideal. Their intent was simply to kill the guerrillas and their sympathizers quickly and ruthlessly. Because both the guerrillas and the paramilitaries financed their wars with illegal drug money, that intensified their fighting in places of illegal drug export, such as Urabá and Catatumbo. Massacres and other forms of extreme violence characterized the fighting in such places. That was certainly the case in La Gabarra, the last town on the broad Catatumbo River before it sweeps into Venezuela and on to the Gulf of Maracaibo, where ships await the Colombian-produced cocaine so avidly consumed in the greater world. At the height of the Catatumbo War of 1999–2000 a large proportion of the local population fled the region, becoming, by 2001, part of the six percent, or three million Colombians, internally displaced by the paramilitary-guerrilla fighting.[117]

The paramilitary offensive in northwestern Colombia neared its conclusion during 2000–2001. By the latter year the guerrillas had been defeated in territory forming an arc from the Chocó and Urabá, northeastwardly through departments along the Caribbean coast, and down along the Venezuelan border in the Catatumbo region of North Santander. Santander and the Middle Magdalena were cleared of both the FARC and ELN, a process culminating in the Central Bolívar Bloc's driving ELN cadres out of Barrancabermeja. By 2001 the ELN was a disarticulated group severely reduced in size and capable of only sporadic kidnappings and attacks on power lines and oil pipelines. Many of its members had deserted to the AUC.[118] As the paramilitary offensive neared its conclusion in northern Colombia, the AUC turned its attention to attacking the guerrillas' urban militias in provincial cities such as Bucaramanga and the country's second and third cities Medellín and Cali. The most noteworthy of those operations were carried out by the Metro and the Cacique Nutibara Blocs in the *comunas*, or urban slums, of Medellín. The *comunas* of Medellín were occupied by the paramilitaries during bloody block-by-block fighting extending through 2002.[119]

Paramilitary successes had the effect of separating the guerrilla from illegal drug revenue and forcing them back to their original source of income, the Colombian citizenry. Kidnapping skyrocketed to 3,292 in 2000, and 3,078 in 2001, the highest totals ever recorded in Colombia or any other democratic country not engaged in a formally declared war. Many of these kidnappings were carried out through the surprise roadblocks known as *pescas milagrosas*. By mid-2000 the FARC was earning a million dollars per month from ransom payments alone.[120]

As the AUC military project prospered, President Andrés Pastrana's peace process languished. The FARC continued in its fanciful belief that if it could isolate the capital *bogotanos* would rise up against the government and welcome the guerrillas into the city. Hence the guerrilla group continued to carry out wide-ranging military attacks in the hinterlands surrounding Colombia's capital, even as Andrés Pastrana continued to hope he could placate the FARC. In March 1999, two months after he had inaugurated the Cleared Zone, Pastrana acceded to the long-standing FARC demand that Convivir be abolished. Then in April 2000, he sent the army into the South of Bolívar to halt the war to the death that the Central Bolívar Bloc was waging there against the ELN. He did this in an attempt to answer the ELN's demand that it too be awarded its own cleared zone in the coca-rich region in and around the Serranía de San Lucas. The paramilitaries thwarted this effort by withdrawing past the ELN and forcing troops of the national army to confront the guerrillas.[121] There was a similar boomerang effect at the end of 2000 when Pastrana purged 388 members of the armed forces who were accused of having links with the paramilitaries. Fifty of the purged officers and soldiers promptly entered ranks of the AUC.[122] Throughout their negotiations with the government the FARC argued that Pastrana must strike hard at the AUC. This strategy was aimed at helping the guerrillas by both weakening the paramilitaries and diluting the national army's operations being carried out against them beyond borders of the Cleared Zone.[123]

By late 2001 it was clear that Pastrana's peace process with the FARC had failed. Colombians penned inside Bogotá and other cities were reduced to begging the FARC to suspend their kidnapping during the Christmas holiday so they could travel safely to visit relatives. But even when the guerrillas did announce suspension of the *pescas milagrosas* prudent travelers cancelled their holiday travel plans. Meanwhile, Colombians could not help noting that AUC-dominated departments were relatively safe from kidnapping. Steamy Córdoba, at the center of AUC power, had received the improbable nickname "the Switzerland of Colombia" for the civic order that prevailed there. People living in Córdoba reported that the AUC not only did not extort or kidnap, but instead provided them an efficient and popular police force. The paramilitaries were locally famous for trying and executing corrupt public officials, something Colombians had fantasized about from the earliest days of the republic.[124]

Andrés Pastrana had won the presidency in 1998 at the height of a peace movement fanned by the inexorable guerrilla advance and the seeming indifference to the country's plight by the United States, which during the Samper presidency was more interested in punishing Colombia than in understanding the role that illegal drug dollars played in the decline of public morality there. The FARC cleverly played on the anguish of Colombians, to win the amazing concession of an extensive region given to them for their exclusive use by the same government they were dedicated to overthrowing. When the guerrilla group continued its attacks even as the peace talks were ongoing, causing citizens to cry out to them to desist, FARC leader Víctor Suárez ("El Mono Jojoy") cynically remarked that Colombians thought they could have peace at no personal cost.

A great many Colombians opposed Pastrana's ceding control of national territory to the FARC. When it became clear that the decision was a mistake they grew convinced that the country's next chief executive must be one who would take a hard-line approach to the guerrillas. That, not surprisingly, was the AUC's position too. As the 2002 presidential election approached, the AUC leadership committed itself to a political project that would prevent the election of another soft-line president.

Late in the year 2000, the AUC gathered in its Fourth National Conference. It brought together nearly a hundred paramilitary leaders from across Colombia and featured discussion of the need to consolidate their hold on territory freed from the guerrillas. That meant making sure candidates favorable to the AUC were elected in the 2002 local, departmental, and national elections thus insuring that the next president would receive the political support he needed to forcefully address national problems.[125] The clearest expression of the AUC political initiative was a seminar organized by its leaders and held at Santa Fe Ralito, Córdoba, on July 23, 2001. Eleven members of congress, two departmental governors, three *alcaldes*, and numerous lesser public officials and aspiring politicians heard academics and paramilitary chieftains present their analysis of the nation's plight and what to do about it. Conditions in Colombia were especially bleak at the moment. A few days earlier, 100 FARC leaders had escaped from Bogotá's La Picota prison and the guerrilla group had ordered its members to start assassinating *alcaldes* who were not FARC supporters. Dissatisfaction with President Andrés Pastrana was also running high. Three months earlier Pastrana had been nominated for the Nobel Peace Prize; the nomination convinced many Colombians that he had merely used the peace talks for his personal aggrandizement.[126] At the end of the Ralito conference all of those present signed a document pledging to help "re-forge" the republic, to maintain the integrity of national territory, to write a new social contract, and to protect the right of property ownership.[127]

The AUC political project bore abundant fruit in the March 2002 elections. So many hard-line candidates won Senate and Chamber of Representatives seats that Salvatore Mancuso boasted that thirty percent of those serving in the new congress were AUC supporters.[128] His remark dismayed Colombians and was obviously an exaggeration. Rather, the electoral result was evidence that the country's people had shifted to a hard-line position, not that they supported the AUC. Salvatore Mancuso's remark in fact dismayed Colombians and set into motion what became known as the *parapolítica* scandal, which roiled the country's political waters for the next five years, sending to prison dozens of politicians who had conspired with paramilitary leaders to win elective office.[129]

At issue in the *parapolítica* scandal was the presence of illegal paramilitary influence in local and national politics. That interference, running the gamut from promoting the candidacy of paramilitary-approved candidates to the intimidation and even murder of opposing candidates, first became apparent in late 2001 and early 2002 in the AUC heartland of northern

Colombia. In Magdalena, for example, pressure exerted by Northern Bloc Commander Rodrigo Tovar Pupo ("Jorge 40") so terrified members of the opposition that several of them who had not been able to remove their names from ballots in time actually campaigned against themselves.[130] In the Coffee Axis department of Risaralda, Carlos Mario Jiménez Naranjo ("Macaco") simultaneously pursued political, anti-guerrilla and drug trafficking agendas with the help of a gang he recruited and named *Los Macacos*. Local businessman and Senator Habib Merheg was one of several Risaralda politicians accused of being a protégé of Jiménez Naranjo.[131] During the 2002 election paramilitary pressure enabled many candidates to run unopposed, something not seen since times of the *Violencia* a half-century before.

Just as the AUC reached the height of its power in Colombia the question of illegal drugs divided and seriously weakened it. Events external to Colombia hastened that process. The United States declared the AUC a terrorist organization soon after Islamist extremists attacked the country on September 11, 2001, in reaction to the paramilitaries' use of terror and their gross violation of human rights. Then, in September 2002, the U.S. requested the extradition of both Carlos Castaño and Salvatore Mancuso on drug trafficking charges. The U.S. actions shocked Castaño, who took pride in his patriotism and his opposition to AUC reliance on drug money, and who considered himself a friend of the United States.[132] In January 2002, Castaño presided over a meeting of AUC leaders in Cartago, Valle, in which he asked all AUC members and associates to sign a statement promising that they would halt their drug trafficking. AUC associate Diego Montoya and several other traffickers refused to sign. More ominously for the paramilitary group, Diego Murillo ("Don Berna") and Carlos Mario Jiménez Naranjo ("Macaco"), both members of the AUC Directorate, rejected the proposal.[133]

There were other, bloodier examples of how illegal drug trafficking divided the AUC. During October 2001, Carlos Castaño and Salvatore Mancuso ordered 200 of their men to the Sierra Nevada de Santa Marta to do battle against longtime trafficker and AUC associate Hernán Giraldo. On the ninth of that month one of Giraldo's lieutenants had ambushed and killed four members of Colombia's Anti-Drug Police. Castaño and Mancuso ordered their forces to help the government capture the perpetrator, which in turn led to intra-paramilitary warfare that dragged on into mid–2002 and cost the lives of dozens of combatants. When the paramilitary leaders finally agreed to end the fighting in July 2002, Castaño and Mancuso published a statement complaining that the AUC had become "atomized and highly penetrated by drug trafficking."[134] Further proof of this came a month later when Metro Bloc Commander Carlos Mauricio García ("Doble Cero") declared himself in rebellion against the AUC leadership, which he viewed as having been hopelessly corrupted by drug trafficking. That brought him into open conflict with one of the group's leading members, Diego Murillo ("Don Berna"), Commander of the Cacique Nutibara Bloc. September 2003 found Doble Cero and his men engaged in all-out warfare against Don Berna in the mountains of eastern Antioquia. Hundreds of local residents in and around the town of San Roque were driven from their homes by the fighting, and the national army had to be sent in to restore order.[135]

These debates over the place of illegal drugs in AUC operations were far overshadowed by transcendent events having to do with the group's very existence as a military force. By July 2002, it was clear that the AUC had succeeded in blunting the guerrillas' war against the state and in helping elect politicians who supported a militant approach toward the insurgent revolutionaries. And while the paramilitaries did not openly support the presidential campaign of Álvaro Uribe Vélez they were delighted that Uribe had won the election and promised to strike hard at the guerrillas. With these things in mind Carlos Castaño and Salvatore Mancuso moved to demobilize the AUC, so confident were they that Alvaro Uribe would effectively address the guerrilla challenge.

Paramilitary demobilization came dramatically and quickly. It was set into motion on November 29, 2002, when Castaño and Mancuso announced that the AUC would unilaterally cease all offensive operations effective December 1, 2002. That set into motion a flurry of negotiations with the government leading to a pact called the Agreement of Santa Fe de Ralito, signed July 15, 2003.[136] Indicative of the central government's neglect of its outlying regions was the fact that the hamlet in southern Córdoba where the historic document was signed did not appear on any map of Colombia.

Under terms of the Ralito pact, all AUC blocs and their constituent fronts were to demobilize by the end of 2005. Carlos Castaño and Salvatore Mancuso signed the document, along with Vicente Castaño, Diego Murillo, and five other AUC commanders. The signatories' pledge to help create a "Colombia without illegal drugs" was an important part of the agreement, especially given the fact that an estimated half of Colombia's illegal drug industry was in paramilitary hands at the time. Alvaro Uribe sent word from Bogotá that the Ralito accord was "a great relief for the nation." When the document was signed champagne toasts were made all around.[137]

Medellín's Cacique Nutibara Bloc was the first AUC group to demobilize. It did so on November 25, 2003, and was followed by the Self-Defense Forces of Ortega (Tolima) a month later. During 2004 five more fronts demobilized, among them the Catatumbo Bloc. At the ceremony in northwestern Colombia that marked the event, 1,425 combatants surrendered their weapons and returned to civilian life. Eleven more blocs and fronts demobilized during 2005, among them the Heroes of Granada Bloc, presided over by Diego Murillo ("Don Berna"). It was that year's largest demobilization, with 2,033 AUC members laying down their weapons. The most symbolic demobilization of 2004 was that of Córdoba Bloc, founded jointly by Carlos and Vicente Castaño and Salvatore Mancuso. Mancuso and Iván Roberto Duke ("Ernesto Báez") presided over the event, which featured speeches, champagne toasts, and the releasing of thousands of butterflies, all to the accompaniment of Vivaldi's "Four Seasons."[138]

Carlos Castaño did not attend the paramilitary demobilization in Córdoba. He had been assassinated in April 2004 on order of his brother Vicente and with the approval of other AUC Commanders, Diego Murillo among them. Carlos Castaño had considered Murillo one of his best friends within the AUC. "Berna," as the young paramilitary leader called him, was about the age of Castaño's elder brother Fidel and had always been present when important decisions were made, back to the time he and the Castaño brothers joined forces to bring down Pablo Escobar. But Diego Murillo was also one of Colombia's principal cocaine traffickers. When he and his colleagues learned in early 2004 that Carlos Castaño was preparing to surrender to U.S. authorities and would likely give incriminating testimony on drug-dealing within the AUC, his comrades decided to eliminate him. With the moment of his death at hand, Carlos Castaño could hardly have been surprised that his executioners were those he knew so well. He, more than most Colombians, knew the deadly nature of the cocaine trade. Only a few months before his assassination he had nodded in agreement when he heard Diego Murillo utter the words that could well appear on the AUC founder's gravestone: "Traffickers only join forces when it's time to kill or betray one of their friends."[139]

By 2006 all principal AUC blocs and fronts had been demobilized. Only a few renegade groups dedicated to criminal activities remained in scattered parts of the country, hotly pursued by law-enforcement agencies. When it was over some thirty thousand AUC and affiliated forces, and those claiming to have links with them, surrendered to Colombian government officials.[140]

The history of Colombia's paramilitaries stands as a cautionary tale for national governments. It instructs that when states do not enforce their laws citizens are likely to take the law into their own hands. Salvatore Mancuso said as much in a 2003 interview. When asked why he became a paramilitary leader he answered simply "The state did not assume the responsibility that corresponded to it." At that moment the college-educated family man and one-time farmer, who had confronted the guerrillas in Córdoba, stood charged with twenty-one homicides and complicity in three massacres.[141]

CHAPTER 6

Colombia Gets Tough, 2002–2013

The Uribe Phenomenon

"Álvaro is what we need."
—Liberal party politician Alonso Daza,
September 2001[1]

By 2001 the Colombian public had given up on the guerrillas. Three years earlier they had elected peace candidate Andrés Pastrana because he promised to talk with the FARC and ELN and convince them to lay down their arms in exchange for meaningful social reforms. But hopes for peace were dashed when the guerrillas interpreted Pastrana's overtures as a sign of weakness and worked all the harder to topple his government. Fulminating violence was the result, and it grew worse over the course of Pastrana's presidency.

As campaigning for the 2002 presidential election began, Colombians turned increasingly to dissident Liberal Álvaro Uribe Vélez, a ferocious opponent of the FARC, a group that had killed his father in a botched kidnap attempt nineteen years earlier, when the younger Uribe was thirty-one. Uribe had good credentials for dealing with violence. His term as governor of Antioquia from 1995 to 1997 had coincided with the Urabá War, during which paramilitary forces struck hard at the guerrillas, driving violence levels in that region to unprecedented heights.[2] As governor Uribe supported the citizen self-defense program known as Convivir, and worked with both guerrilla and paramilitary groups in an effort to curb the conflict. During his time as governor Uribe worked closely with the army. That boded well for the country in the event he ascended to the presidency. Both Andrés Pastrana and his predecessor Ernesto Samper had poor relations with the Colombian military, a bad state of affairs for a nation under the lash of civil war.

By January 2002, it had become clear that Álvaro Uribe was likely to be Colombia's next president. Late that month the nation's leading news magazine *Semana* featured him on its cover dressed as Superman, over the title "Super Uribe."[3] Colombia's situation at that moment was desperate. Both the FARC and ELN guerrillas were in a triumphal mood and were stepping up their terrorist acts in anticipation of ultimate victory. All save the country's principal highways were subject to guerrilla roadblocks, with many hapless souls caught in them marched away and held until ransomed by their families. Colombians lived as prisoners in their own cities. A national poll taken during February 2002 showed that ninety percent of Colombians perceived their country to be headed in the wrong direction. Álvaro Uribe campaigned on a platform of "Democratic Security," meaning that if elected he would gear his administration to making the Colombian people safe by combating violence and crime. His fellow citizens believed him. In May 2002, he won by a landslide. Voters gave Uribe nearly fifty-three percent of their votes in a contest against three other candidates.

Colombians were filled with high expectations on August 7, the day Uribe was sworn into office. A humorous depiction of the new president appeared in the August 12 edition of *Semana*, showing him dressed as a gung-ho soldier, bandana around his head, holding a machine gun, and with bandoliers crossing his naked chest. It was titled "Born on the Fourth of July," both the title of a Hollywood war movie starring Tom Cruise and Uribe's actual birthday. The depiction of Uribe was all the more humorous because the new president was a slightly built man, boyish in appearance, his wire-rimmed glasses giving him the appearance of an earnest seminarian. Nevertheless, he radiated authority and inspired confidence.

There was nothing humorous about Colombia's condition when Uribe began his term. Guerrilla and paramilitary armies fought for control of territory across rural parts of the nation. Many outlying areas had long since been abandoned by the state, with the mayors of many towns having fled to departmental capitals. Police forces in many remote townships had been annihilated in guerrilla attacks or driven out by the fighting, and had not been replaced. Nor were Colombian cities entirely free of the bloodshed. Over the two years leading up to Uribe's election Carlos Castaño's paramilitary army drove ELN guerrillas from the Magdalena River city of Barrancabermeja through block-by-block fighting that claimed many civilian lives. During 2001 and 2002, Colombians had watched with dismay as paramilitary groups applied the techniques employed in Barrancabermeja in the *comunas* of Medellín, slums in mountains ringing the country's second-largest city. Underscoring the sad state of public order prevailing in Colombia at the time was the FARC rocket attack on Bogotá's Plaza de Bolivar the day of Uribe's inauguration. The rockets missed the plaza and fell in a nearby neighborhood, killing twenty-six of its residents.

Uribe's first act as president was to declare a state of public upset, on August 12, giving him decree-making power. He immediately pushed a wealth tax measure through congress, the proceeds of which would help beef up the armed forces. And he ended the decades-long policy dictating that civilian leaders stay out of military affairs. The workaholic chief executive began each day huddled with commanders of his armed forces plotting a strategy aimed at wresting control of national territory from the numerous illegal groups fighting to dominate it. Uribe effectively became Colombia's commander-in-chief.

The effect of the new president's Democratic Security policy was first seen in Medellín, where the homicide rate had risen to an astronomical 280 per 100,000 people by 2002. On October 15, the national army moved into the city's *comunas* and over the days that followed troops searched houses for weapons, along the way fighting skirmishes with ELN and FARC militias, and with members of paramilitary groups. They arrested anyone implicated in the fighting that had raged there. It was the second time in 2002 that the army had tried to bring peace to the slum neighborhoods. The first attempt failed, but this one did not. Operation Orion, as the offensive was code-named, resulted in the arrest of 243 militants, twenty-nine of whom were identified as militia leaders. Not only did the national police return to Medellín's *comunas*, but a variety of social and educational programs were created to provide help to traumatized residents of the neighborhoods. That had the effect of reintegrating them into the city of five million.[4] Violence levels in Medellín entered into sharp decline from the moment Uribe addressed violence in the *comunas*.[5]

Operation Orion was the first visible sign that Álvaro Uribe would make good on his promise to return state presence to parts of Colombia that had slipped from national control over the preceding twenty-five years. Prior to reform of the national military, which began in the early 1990s, Colombia's armed forces were among the most poorly funded in Latin America, receiving a puny one percent of gross domestic product (GDP). By the end of the 1990s, support for the military had risen to 2.3 percent of GDP, and owing in part to Uribe's emergency spending program it stood at 3.5 percent of GDP by the end of 2002. And in December of that year defense minister Marta Lucía Ramírez promised to push the percentage beyond that. The new wealth tax for military strengthening had brought in $240 million in revenues, which complemented the $253 million for military aid received through the Plan Colombia program during 2002. An additional $430 million of Plan Colombia military spending was budgeted for 2003.[6]

During the presidential campaign Uribe had elaborated a 100-point plan for improving national security. It ran from hiring 10,000 new police and training 10,000 "citizen soldiers" to be deployed throughout the country's 1,120 *municipios*, many bereft of police presence for years, to creating new army units tasked with meeting the insurgent challenge head-on. Two rapid-deployment brigades were being trained to engage FARC fronts in the field beginning in 2003. They would be transported by helicopter to towns under FARC attack, thus remedying the long-standing problem of transporting troops to such places by land, meaning that they arrived hours, or even days, after the guerrillas had withdrawn into the cordillera. Two high mountain brigades were being created to patrol Andean *páramos*, or high-altitude tundras, that historically had provided an unobstructed highway for guerrilla columns marching to attack towns and villages in the valleys below. By taking control of such areas the army would not only deprive the rebels of free passage throughout the country's interior but would disrupt routes of supply to the FARC's many fronts. Other parts of Uribe's 100-point security plan included professionalizing the military and ending the use of draftees in combat situations; creating local vigilance committees and offering cash rewards for information on guerrilla leaders; and creating mechanisms of conflict resolution, particularly in the area of negotiation techniques.[7] Uribe had practical experience in negotiating violent conflicts, dating from the time when he served as governor of Antioquia. During that time Uribe, who held graduate certification in business administration from Harvard University, went so far as to bring in Harvard mediation guru Roger Fisher to train *antioqueños* in negotiation skills.[8]

From his first days in office, Uribe initiated Saturday field trips to towns and villages throughout the country to talk with the people and to hear their concerns. In the course of these *concejos comunitarios* (town meetings) he would frequently turn to one of the cabinet ministers in his entourage and ask, "Why haven't we done anything about this? See that it is taken care of." It was the minister's task to deal with the problem in the days that followed. During his first term Uribe, who slept little and practiced yoga every morning to calm his hyperactive metabolism, conducted 150 of the arduous Saturday *concejos comunitarios*.[9]

Most Colombians agreed that Álvaro Uribe was in fact what the country needed. Four months into his administration *Semana* named him its Man of the Year. An editorial writer remarked on the affection the president had awakened in the people, referring to him as "a kind of Churchill" who "incarnates the national conviction that he is going to win the war against the *violentos*."[10] At the end of Uribe's first year in office *Semana's* director Alejandro Santos published an essay titled "The Year that Hope Returned." "The people are happy," Santos wrote. "Colombians feel they know Uribe. With that air of a campesino that he has he seems close to them." Uribe has imposed a new model of government, Santos continued, taking national territory back from the *violentos* and returning state authority to it. Santos ended his essay by asking a question and then answering it: "How much longer will this romance last? Longer than many people think it will."[11]

The Colombian people's confidence in Álvaro Uribe was based in the fact that he gave them what they demanded. The country became visibly less violent during each succeeding year of his administration. In fact violence levels started falling as soon as it became clear that he would be the country's next president. Much of that trend had to do with the paramilitaries. Their leaders Carlos Castaño and Salvatore Mancuso knew that in Uribe they had a man who would confront the guerrillas with vigor, and who would never hand national territory over to them simply in exchange for their agreement to talk with the government. Uribe drove that point home during the presidential campaign when he alone among presidential candidates refused to meet with FARC leaders in the Cleared Zone (*Zona de Distensión*).

To understand paramilitary attitudes following Uribe's victory it is well to gauge their state of mind in mid–2001, when it appeared that he had little chance of becoming president. July 2001 was when AUC leaders called a meeting of area politicians in southern Córdoba, at a place called Santa Fe de Ralito. Up to that time the paramilitary had proved itself the only group capable of defeating the guerrillas, having brutally pacified Córdoba, Urabá, and numerous other parts of the country through force of arms. Those assembled at Santa Fe de Ralito signed a document in which they agreed to "re-found" the republic by formulating a new social contract, based on protection of the citizenry and the defense of private property, and on preserving the integrity of national territory.[12] The setting in Colombia was grim at the time of the secret meeting in Córdoba: peace talks with the ELN had failed yet again; the Boyajá tragedy had occurred just three months earlier, when a FARC mortar shell crashed through the roof of a crowded church killing over a hundred people cowering inside; and there had been a massive jail break at La Picota prison in which 100 FARC members escaped and returned to their respective fronts. Meanwhile the FARC was acting with near impunity, using the Cleared Zone as a safe haven. At that moment the guerrilla group was tightening its encirclement of Bogotá for what its leaders proclaimed was their final offensive against the national capital.

The Ralito meeting of July 2001 was a continuation of paramilitary political action extending back fifteen years. During the late 1990s, Salvatore Mancuso had explored the idea of forming a new political party to represent national security and anti-guerrilla interests. Ten years before that just such a party had been created in the Middle Magdalena region by paramilitary leader Iván Roberto Duque ("Ernesto Báez"). Called MORENA, or Movimiento de Restauración Nacional, the party fell victim to the takeover of the Middle Magdalena paramilitary movement by the Medellín cartel.[13] Now Duque, along with Mancuso and others, advocated renewed political activism by paramilitary forces, especially their alignment with friendly mainstream politicians everywhere in Colombia, particularly in the country's northern departments where the AUC had already broken the guerrillas' hold over rural areas.[14]

Álvaro Uribe's rise coincided with and benefited from the paramilitaries' desire to work through Colombia's existing political structure to recruit votes for whichever presidential candidate proved to be the most hard-line, and to work for the election of congressional candidates pledged to take the fight to the guerrillas. With Uribe's surge early in 2002, he was guaranteed to receive full support of the paramilitary political apparatus in departments where they had influence. In addition they wanted to give the new chief executive solid working majorities in both houses of congress so that his anti-guerrilla initiatives would enjoy clear sailing at the legislative level. The paramilitary political project was so successful that following the March 2002 congressional elections Salvatore Mancuso could brag that over thirty-five percent of those in the new congress supported the paramilitary cause. Thus on May 26 paramilitaries and their supporters joined with the majority of Colombians to elect Uribe president in a landslide. Paramilitary violence declined in pace with Uribe's rise. With a president they trusted in office, the AUC could end its offensive against the guerrillas and enter into the process of demobilization.

Factors other than Uribe's election figured in the paramilitaries' move to seek accommodation with the Colombian state. As members of an illegal group they were in fact outlaws in the eyes of the government, leaving them in the paradoxical position of fearing prosecution by the same government they had worked hard to put into power. In late 2001, the United States included the AUC among groups that it considered terrorist organizations. Finally, on September 28, 2002, AUC leaders Carlos Castaño and Salvatore Mancuso were indicted in the U.S. for cocaine trafficking, and their extradition requested. All of this, along with Uribe's election, led AUC leaders to enter exploratory talks on demobilization with government peace commissioner Luis Carlos Restrepo. Paramilitary demobilization proceeded quickly after that. In November, Castaño and Mancuso said they were disposed to dismantle the AUC and to aid in the demobilization of their forces. They also pledged to act against drug trafficking by AUC members. Then they issued the surprising communiqué that they would declare a ceasefire effective December 2002 and would continue their negotiations with peace commissioner Restrepo and with members of a peace commission that the new President established that same month.

Colombians greeted these events with amazement. It seemed incredible that an armed group at the height of its power would abruptly agree to end its existence. Yet that seemed to be precisely what the AUC was doing. Talks between paramilitary leaders and government peace commissioners took place during the early months of 2003, producing an agreement at mid-year. The accord between the AUC and the government was signed July 15, 2003, in the *municipio* of Tierralta in southern Córdoba. The negotiations were concluded at Carlos Castaño's general headquarters at Santa Fe de Ralito, a collection of houses on the upper reaches of the Sinú River not far from Córdoba's border with Antioquia.

By the Agreement of Santa Fe de Ralito the entire *municipio* of Tierralta, having an area of over 5,000 square kilometers, was declared a "location zone" (*zona de ubicación*) by the government. In time it would become one of several such places scattered throughout Colombia where paramilitary leaders and their troops gathered to turn in their weapons under the watchful eye of government officials and army officers. It was an expensive undertaking because all who gathered at *zonas de ubicación* prior to their formal demobilization required food and shelter. Luckily for Colombia's cash-strapped government, Plan Colombia funds were available to help defray such expenses.[15]

The Santa Fe de Ralito agreement was unprecedented in Colombian history for its magnitude and sweeping nature. Under its terms the AUC fighting force of 16,000 troops would demobilize over the ensuing seventeen months, and they and all AUC support personnel would submit to government supervision by December 31, 2005. Paramilitary leaders pledged not only to cease their drug trafficking, but they promised to aid in the government's drug eradication program. In exchange the government would pass a law declaring AUC members to be political criminals, as opposed to ordinary ones, thereby entitling them to amnesty for all save their most heinous crimes. AUC leaders were assured that if they faithfully abided by terms of the agreement and ceased illegal activities, especially those connected with drug trafficking, they would not be extradited to the United States.[16]

In August 2003, the government presented legislation to congress that when passed would formalize the promises made at Santa Fe de Ralito. Titled the Law of Justice and Peace, it honored the Colombian tradition of allowing rebels guilty of sedition to lay down their weapons and rejoin civil society under the most generous of terms.[17] Such amnesty was consecrated in the Constitution of 1991, and had also been a fixture in national jurisprudence in one form or another since the birth of the republic. The flaw in the Justice and Peace law was that it applied equally to guerrillas and paramilitary fighters. Under its terms members of both groups were awarded political status, on grounds that by having illegally taken up arms they were guilty of the crime of sedition. This was a major inconsistency in the new law, because while the guerrillas were genuinely seditious the paramilitaries were not. Men like Carlos Castaño and Salvatore Mancuso insisted that they were patriots who took up arms to defend themselves and the country's constitutional order until such time as Colombia's government stepped forward and properly defended its citizens from guerrilla depredations. This inconsistency in Álvaro Uribe's Law of Justice and Peace played a role in allowing the president to renege on his most important promise to the AUC leaders: that if they lay down their arms they would not be extradited to the United States.

Uribe's Justice and Peace law was the subject of intense, often polemical, debate from the moment it was unveiled. At its center was the greater question of whether it was proper to regard members of the paramilitaries as seditious.[18] Crafted for the paramilitaries—no guerrilla group showed interest in accepting its terms—the Law of Justice and Peace was used by the opposition to flog Uribe as a friend of the AUC. Internationally many of those professing interest in Colombia branded the proposed law as little more than the legal sanctioning of impunity. Still, by condoning relatively insignificant prison terms for crimes against humanity, and offering amnesty for other serious crimes, it was squarely in the Colombian tradition of offering generous terms to illegally armed groups in exchange for their laying down their weapons and rejoining civil society.[19]

Final passage of the Law of Justice and Peace occurred on June 21, 2005, nearly two years after it was first presented to congress. Peace commissioner Luis Carlos Restrepo, whose staff had drafted the legislation, expended vast amounts of time and energy seeing the project through to completion. Despite the controversy swirling around the law, the nation's constitutional court declared it valid in November 2006, eleven months after its passage. By that time, debates on the law were, to an extent, moot. As 2006 ended, more than 30,000 of those claiming affiliation with the AUC had turned themselves over to the authorities. Free confession of crimes committed by paramilitary leaders began at the end of that year with a lengthy recounting of misdeeds, the first of the sessions involving Salvatore Mancuso, who detailed his crimes in a PowerPoint presentation. At the time Mancuso was housed at the high-security Itagüí prison near Medellín, along with fifty-eight other top AUC commanders.

There had been countless problems with the paramilitary demobilization as well as with the law that paved the way for it. Many more difficulties were yet to come. Still, these facts do little to dull the luster of a remarkable chapter in Colombia's arduous path back to peaceful civil life. That more than 30,000 members of a fearful paramilitary organization should quickly demobilize and its leaders voluntarily place themselves under government custody, after which they began confessing their crimes in open court, was a phenomenon unique in the annals of modern warfare and a triumph of the rule of law in Colombia.

Colombia was forced to deal with its largest remaining illegal armed group, the communist FARC guerrillas, by military means. The FARC had every reason to fear the hard-line Uribe. Its members had not only killed his father but had attempted to assassinate him on numerous occasions. Thus many were surprised when Uribe adopted a conciliatory tone toward the guerrillas in his victory speech following his 2002 election. In it he pledged to seek international mediation in meetings with the guerrillas, the only precondition being that they cease their hostile acts.[20] While the ELN, severely weakened by the paramilitaries, the FARC, and the Colombian military, did accept Uribe's offer to talk, the FARC rejected it.[21] Instead the group responded to his overture with yet another attempt on his life, on the day of his inauguration. Still, Uribe attempted to draw the guerrilla group into dialogue. On August 12, 2002, he decreed a three-month amnesty for members of illegally armed groups willing to turn themselves in to the authorities. Following that, in a year-end message to the nation, he asked the guerrillas to enter peace talks, lest military operations begin against them. The FARC answered with a series of terrorist acts carried out mostly in urban areas during the early months of 2003. The worst of them was bombing of the El Nogal social club in Bogotá, carried out on February 7. Masterminded by Front 34 commander Aicardo Agudelo ("El Paisa"), it killed 34 people and injured another 168. Another bombing the same week in Neiva left seventeen dead, forty-eight injured, and seventeen houses destroyed. The Neiva bombing was connected to yet another plan to assassinate Uribe. It was one of six FARC attempts to kill Álvaro Uribe over a sixteen month period from November 2001 to February 2003.[22] Other FARC depredations during those months included the execution of two injured pilots and the kidnapping of three U.S. citizens traveling in a plane that had crashed in Caquetá, and the execution of two kidnapped political officials during a failed rescue attempt by the army.[23] These events help explain Álvaro Uribe's frame of mind in early 2003 when FARC commander Manuel Marulanda offered to resume talks with the government if it granted his group a new cleared-out zone in the southern part of the country. Uribe irately refused the request, calling the FARC "a horde of bandits."[24]

The first phase of Colombia's offensive against the FARC began in June 2003. Called Operation Liberty One, it involved the carefully scripted assault on fourteen FARC fronts positioned around Bogotá in the department of Cundinamarca. The fronts in question had been moved into place beginning in 1998, when the guerrilla group was granted its safe haven south of the national capital in the jungles of Meta and Caquetá. Their assignment was to isolate Bogotá and soften up the capital for the FARC final assault. Operation Liberty One ended that dream.

Between June and November 2003, new specialized army units destroyed the FARC cordon around Bogotá. Key to the operation was two new rapid-deployment units that surrounded the FARC fronts one after another. With the FARC fronts' routes of escape blocked commando units were sent in to pinpoint the location of front commanders. By the time the operation ended five notorious FARC commanders lay dead and their fronts dispersed. While Operation

Liberty One unfolded in the lower reaches of the mountains of Cundinamarca, the first of the army's high mountain brigades successfully blocked reinforcements from reaching the war zone via the *páramo* of Sumapaz, lying between the Cleared Zone and the area of fighting. That marked the first time since the emergence of the guerrillas nearly a half-century before that the FARC or any other guerrilla group was denied free passage of the *páramo*.[25] The magnitude of the FARC's defeat in Cundinamarca is suggested in the account of a teenaged guerrilla who survived the army's attack on her front: "The front was defeated, the commanders killed, and the all the comrades fled. The best alternative was to run."[26]

In Colombian military annals the year 2004 was "The Year of the Offensive," when thousands of troops were sent into the FARC's Amazonian fastness to pursue the guerrillas and disrupt their infrastructure. It was the phase of Uribe's Patriot Plan (*Plan Patriota*) that changed the balance of power between the FARC and the Colombian military. Evidence of the shift in strategic balance was visible immediately. During April 2004, army units in Guaviare discovered a FARC camp containing a forty-eight-room hotel, a hospital, a disco, and a munitions factory. Two weeks after that an army unit seized the headquarters of the FARC's military commander Víctor Suárez Rojas ("El Mono Jojoy"). In it were found three restaurants, a bar and media center, a mini-coliseum, and a cultural center.[27] That surpassed the April 2003 feat of an army patrol that stumbled on a FARC cache in Meta containing $16 million, mostly in U.S. currency.[28]

Taking control of the Amazonian river network was an exceedingly important aspect of the anti–FARC offensive. New riverine units of the Colombian navy formed an integral part of the military's 18,000-man Omega Taskforce (*Tarea Conjunta Omega*). The naval patrols worked closely with the air force and army to close the guerrillas' routes of travel and cocaine export along important rivers such as the Caguán, Caquetá, and Putumayo, all part of Colombia's Amazon watershed. Controlling the rivers not only deprived the FARC of its chief source of revenue but led to the exodus of many families whose livelihoods were connected to the cocaine industry. When reporters visited the village of Remolino on the lower Caguán River in July 2004, they found it nearly deserted. Once known as Colombia's "coca capital," Remolino del Caguán had fallen victim to the combined impact of the military offensive and aerial fumigation of coca plantations.[29]

By the end of 2005, the FARC was in strategic retreat from the jungles of southeastern Colombia. Desperate to maintain their revenue stream from cocaine sales the guerrilla group had begun shifting troops from Caquetá westward into the mountainous department of Nariño, which offered convenient routes of export down rivers and streams debouching into the Pacific Ocean. From Nariño and the neighboring department of Putumayo, they could take advantage of similar routes through Ecuador, easily reached across the notoriously porous border with that country. The center of FARC coca cultivation shifted into the Andean massif of southern Colombia, that filled much of Nariño and Cauca and that offered an exceedingly broken terrain ideal for sheltering coca from defoliant-spraying aircraft.[30]

At the end of Alvaro Uribe's first term the Patriot Plan was judged highly successful. While the FARC was not defeated, its fighting force was reduced by half, to 9,000, and its urban cadres were much diminished as well. The group could no longer mobilize its troops in columns but rather was forced to send its fighters out in small groups of five to ten. In June 2006, defense minister Juan Manuel Santos reported that the FARC held no defined territory and that its members were poorly uniformed and provisioned.[31] Meanwhile Colombian military growth was more robust than at any other time in the nation's history. When Álvaro Uribe began his second term—he was re-elected by a landslide in early 2006—military spending comprised 3.3 percent of GDP and the armed forces stood at 380,000. The number of high-mountain battalions had increased to seven and rapid-deployment brigades to seventeen. Thirty-two anti-kidnapping units had contributed to a dramatic reduction in that crime, down from 3,041 in 2001 to 122 in 2006. The nation's police force had grown by 96,000 members. For the first time in years police and military were present in every one of the country's *munici-pios*.[32]

All these things were known by Colombians, who saw their lives objectively improved thanks to Álvaro Uribe's Democratic Security program. But it was the ongoing news of FARC leaders who were apprehended or killed that brought success of the anti-guerrilla campaign into high relief. That was the case in early 2004 when for the first time in history a member of the FARC's executive committee was arrested. The FARC leader in question was Ovidio Palmera ("Simón Trinidad"), scion of a well-to-do Valledupar family with thirty charges pending against him, most of them involving homicide and extortionate kidnapping. Palmera had been arrested in Quito, Ecuador, his apprehension the fruit of a four-month tri-national operation involving police from Ecuador and Colombia, and personnel from U.S. intelligence services.[33]

Ovidio Palmera's arrest in 2004 was merely the first in a succession of blows to FARC leadership. Rapid strides in the area of electronic surveillance had made possible around-the-clock monitoring of guerrilla troop movements and the pinpointing of FARC encampments. The results of these advances became ever clearer over the course of Álvaro Uribe's second term. During 2007, the FARC was badly hurt by two air force strikes. The first, on July 15, severely injured virtuoso kidnapper Carlos Antonio Losada. A laptop computer found at Losada's camp yielded valuable information on FARC plans to assassinate Alvaro Uribe, minister of defense Juan Manuel Santos, and other top government officials. On September 1, air force bombs claimed the life of Tomás Medina ("El Negro Acasio"). Medina was the front leader charged with handling cocaine sales for the FARC. It was believed that over one fourteen-month period during 1998–1999, Medina had presided over massive cocaine exports earning up to $1 billion for the FARC. Magical powers had been attributed to Medina, who had escaped twenty-five previous attempts to apprehend him.[34]

These successes in Colombia's war against the FARC paled in comparison with the killing of the group's second-in-command, Luis Edgar Devia ("Raúl Reyes"), on February 29, 2008. Devia's death created international furor because it occurred at a jungle camp in Ecuador, just a kilometer beyond the border with Colombia. Laptop computers retrieved from the camp yielded an immense amount of data both on FARC operations and on the group's contacts with officials in the governments of Ecuador and Venezuela. Ecuador and Venezuela had become increasingly important to the guerrilla group as the military offensive made its existence on Colombian soil increasingly precarious. Luckily for the FARC, Ecuador's populist president Rafael Correa, who took office in 2007, and Venezuela's Hugo Chávez were enemies of Álvaro Uribe, whom they viewed as a lackey of the United States. This explains why Colombia's sister republics had provided men such as Luis Edgar Devia rest areas (*zonas de descanso*) inside their borders.[35]

Less than a month after Devia's death yet another member of the FARC senior command died, this time at the hands of one of his own men. José Juvenal Velandia ("Iván Ríos") was murdered by a subordinate named Pablo Montoya ("Rojas") in order to collect the $1.5 million reward offered for him, dead or alive. On March 3, 2008, "Rojas," accompanied by two other FARC deserters, turned themselves in to an army unit and handed over Velandia's passport, ID card, right hand, and laptop computer. The computer yielded details on an attack Velandia was planning on Medellín's metro.[36] Six months after Velandia's murder, on September 22, 2008, the most wanted guerrilla leader in Colombia miraculously escaped death when the air force bombed his jungle camp, killing many members of his front. Aicardo de Jesús Agudelo ("El Paisa") was leader of the FARC's elite Teófilo Forero Mobile Column, made up of 600 heavily armed fighters, as well as urban cadres and a non-combatant support staff said to number several thousand. Agudelo and his group had carried out the El Nogal bombing and the killing of Liliana Gaviria, sister of former president César Gaviria. For many years he was the FARC's single most important fund raiser, running a kidnapping-extortion complex centered in Antioquia and bringing in twenty-six million dollars per year.[37] The bombing of his camp seriously injured Agudelo and disrupted the activities of his front.

The drumbeat of bad news for the FARC grew loudest in March 2008, when Colombians received word that the group's founder and supreme leader, Manuel Marulanda, had died of natural causes—though his death may have been hastened by air force bombings near his presumed hideout.[38] This new blow to the guerrilla group, along with the steady flow of news of FARC desertions, had begun convincing even the most skeptical Colombians that the war against the FARC was being won. The passing of Marulanda, Devia, Velandia, and the others served as counterpoints to ongoing protest demonstrations against the FARC, culminating in series of massive marches held throughout Colombia during the first three months of 2008. Those marches demanded the freeing of the guerrillas' several hundred hostages, chief among them former presidential candidate Ingrid Betancourt, who was taken captive in February 2002. Betancourt's photograph, which had appeared on the cover of *Semana* magazine March 31, 2008, showed her as despondent and emaciated. Over the years of her captivity she had become an international symbol of those being held by political extremists. During the latter months of 2007 the FARC had softened its position on the issue. Marulanda Vélez had permitted FARC representatives to meet with those of the Colombian government in Caracas during the latter part of 2007. Those conversations resulted in the release of two other prominent hostages, Clara Rojas and Consuelo González, in early 2008, just six weeks before the death of Manuel Marulanda.

By mid–2008 Colombians found their minds turning ever more to a stanza in their national anthem that goes "The horrible night has ended." Could it be that their long civil war was drawing to a close? Suddenly, on the third day of July, they received news that both amazed and delighted them. Their national army had tricked the FARC into releasing Ingrid Betancourt, three U.S. citizens, and eleven members of the police and military, some of whom had been in the hands of the guerrillas for more than ten years. Not a shot was fired in the operation and no hostage was harmed. To Colombians, traumatized by decades of bloodshed, the rescue seemed a miracle.

The hostage rescue of July 2008, code named Operación Jaque (Operation Checkmate) was the product of years of planning by members of the Colombian and U.S. militaries. The United States had become intensely interested in the subject of hostage extraction after the FARC kidnapped three of its nationals in February of 2003. Consequently the Americans offered full assistance to their Colombian counterparts over the course of the operation. Preparations for the mission gathered momentum during early 2008, after Venezuelan president Hugo Chávez brokered the release in January of Clara Rojas and Consuelo González. That elaborate operation had involved dispatching Venezuelan Red Cross helicopters from the military base at San José de Guaviare to the hostage release site in the Caquetá jungle. Traveling on the helicopters was a group that included physicians, Venezuelan and Colombian political figures, invited dignitaries from Cuba and several other countries, and a camera team from Venezuelan news network Telsur. Those in charge of Operation Checkmate spent many hours studying newsreel footage of the earlier operation, copying it down to the last detail. On the day of the rescue Colombian intelligence broadcast a fake news release to the effect that Hugo Chávez was at that moment meeting with European Union officials in preparation for a pending new release of hostages. Thus FARC Front 1 commander Gerardo Aguilar ("César") was none the wiser when he received a message purporting to be from FARC commanders instructing him to unite three groups of captives in preparation for travel to meet with the FARC's new leader, Guillermo Sáenz ("Alfonso Cano"). But the FARC communication system had been compromised and the message was in fact from Colombian military intelligence. So too were members of the rescue mission that set out early on the morning of July 3. When two red-trimmed white helicopters arrived for the pick-up only one person seemed to suspect that all was not what it seemed. As U.S. hostage Keith Stansell watched the helicopters approach the clearing where it was to land, he shouted to one of the other American captives "Where are the crosses?" It was Stansell, too, who accused the soldier pretending to be an Australian aid worker of having a Colombian accent. The accusation, which was drowned out by the sound of the helicopters' rotating blades, was answered with the words, "Trust me, trust me."[39]

There were theatrical touches in Operation Checkmate worthy of a Hollywood action movie. While all those dealing with the hostages were members of Colombian military intelligence, they played a variety of roles. Two were tall and blond and spoke English, one of them affecting an Australian accent. This was because Australians had been involved in the January 10 rescue mission. Australians had a relatively high profile in Venezuela; arms traders from that country had been selling weapons to the FARC through intermediaries within the Venezuelan government for at least two years.[40] Another of the rescuers pretended to be an Arab of North African origin. His role was to simply gaze with awe at the lush jungle vegetation while a glum Colombian, wearing a Che Guevara T-shirt and pretending to be a FARC guerrilla, stood at his side. It was a dangerous charade, for the guerrillas were heavily armed and the rescuers carried no weapons. Had trouble broken out the 300 soldiers standing by in San José de Guaviare, twenty-five minutes away by helicopter, could not have arrived in time to save the rescuers.[41]

There was a delay in loading the hostages because some resisted being handcuffed prior to lift-off. This caused concern in Bogotá, where war minister Juan Manuel Santos was counting off the minutes on his wristwatch. Twenty-two minutes after the helicopters touched down in the jungle clearing—cleared because coca shrubs were being cultivated there—the passengers, including FARC front commander "César" and a companion called "Gafas," were loaded and the helicopters took off bound for San José de Guaviari. Three minutes into the flight one of the pilots radioed the message "Sistema anti-ice ok," signaling that all had gone as planned and that the hostages were rescued unharmed. That was also the signal to subdue Gerardo Aguilar ("César") and Alexánder Farfán ("Gafas"). To the astonishment of those being rescued, they heard a presumed Red Cross worker shout "We are the National Army of Colombia." The happy hubbub that followed caused the helicopter to perilously lose altitude for several seconds. Minutes later when the passengers climbed down from the helicopters at the departmental capital of Guaviari they were greeted by army commander Mario Montoya. The usually serious Montoya was leaping up and down with joy.

After a quick lunch the fifteen boarded a Fokker jet for the flight over the Eastern Cordillera to Tolemaida military base in Cundinamarca. There they were met by Armed Forces Minister Santos, Commander of the Armed Forces Freddy Padilla, and U.S. Ambassador William Wood, who accompanied them on to Bogotá. The flight took longer than normal because the Fokker had to circle Tolemaida for a time until a U.S. Air Force C-130 arrived to transport the three Americans separately on to Bogotá. The delay was of little concern to the former captives. The jubilant Colombians in the rear of the aircraft spent the extra time alternately in prayer and in singing spirited renditions of their national anthem.[42]

Plan Colombia

"With the help of Plan Colombia the Nation has increased control of its territory and has improved public security. Hence it has helped bring about a sense of public tranquility."

—Security analyst Alfredo Rangel[43]

The world was charmed on July 2, 2008, when it received word that the Colombian military had neatly plucked fifteen hostages from hands of the FARC, and had done so by duping the guerrillas. Colombians were ecstatic when they heard the news. Operation Checkmate was very much made in Colombia. Never before had the old adage "In Colombia civilians make war and the military brings peace" been more apt. Even the military's U.S. allies were kept in the dark about the daring rescue. As one Colombian put it, "the gringos knew that something was cooking in the jungle" when their spy planes reported unusual movement of hostage groups a few days before the rescue. But it was not until the day before the hostage extraction that any high U.S. official learned what was afoot. Hours before the mission Juan Manuel Santos briefed U.S. presidential candidate John McCain on the matter. McCain, on an official visit to Bogotá at the time, could only respond, "My God! Good luck!"[44]

For the FARC, Operation Checkmate was the humiliating climax of a disastrous six months. The year 2008 had begun with massive marches in Bogotá and elsewhere protesting its long-term holding of hostages. Then in quick succession the guerrilla group witnessed the deaths of three members of its directorate, chief among them the group's founder, Manuel Marulanda Vélez.

These events put Colombians into an extraordinarily happy frame of mind, and no one benefited more from this than Álvaro Uribe Vélez. First elected president six years earlier, at a time when academics were labeling Colombia a failed state, and when FARC leaders fantasized about a triumphal march into the national capital, Uribe had won election on the promise that he would make the country a safe place for the average Colombian. That by 2008 the two-term president had indeed done so drove his popularity rating to heights never before seen in the country. Following the hostage rescue Uribe's approval rating reached ninety-two percent, likely a record in the annals of democratic governance. Uribe's popularity and level of administrative success were certainly unparalleled in Colombian history.

Álvaro Uribe's popularity at the end of two presidential terms set him apart from his most notable peers. It was almost a given that famous public figures in Colombia should suffer slings and arrows as their term in office neared its end. The country's first president, Simón Bolívar, died a broken, embittered man. Rafael Núñez, known as the country's "Regenerator," gave the nation a new constitution and a national anthem, but not peace. Early-twentieth-century President Rafael Reyes set Colombia on the path to economic modernization but was forced into exile. Alfonso López Pumarejo, who governed in the mid–twentieth century, brought important reforms to Colombia but was driven from office because of scandals surrounding his administration and involving members of his immediate family. Only the slight, bespectacled, youthful-appearing Alvaro Uribe, among Colombia's leading political figures, had the luxury of preparing to leave office at the end of his term in office with his popularity intact and to the accolades of a substantial majority of his fellow citizens. The only possible exception to this generalization was Simón Bolívar's successor Francisco de Paula Santander, known to Colombian history as the "Man of the Laws." Yet even Santander's historical legacy is tarnished by his implication in an assassination attempt against then-president Simón Bolívar in 1828.

In fairness to the luminaries of Colombian political history mentioned here, it must be pointed out that Alvaro Uribe took up leadership of the country with a level of popular support, and with substantial attending benefits, that no previous chief executive had ever enjoyed. As the most hard-line candidate in the 2002 presidential contest it was clear *a priori* that he would vigorously address the massive violence and kidnapping that afflicted Colombia at the time. Uribe had campaigned on the concept of "Democratic Security," vowing to attack these problems. Colombians put their faith in Uribe and were gratified to see sharp declines in violence even before he took office. Bound up in the new president's early successes and inextricable from them was a program of military reform and strengthening that had been under way for at least four years prior to his election. Alvaro Uribe thus had the advantage of coming into office with a much-improved military. The United States-backed program known as Plan Colombia was important in this, and in Uribe's success in reducing the power of the FARC and other illegal armed groups.

* * *

Plan Colombia was the brainchild of Alvaro Uribe's predecessor Andrés Pastrana, who formulated it as a complement to his peace talks with FARC and ELN guerrillas. This was suggested in Pastrana's original name for the program, the "Plan for Peace, Prosperity, and Strengthening of the State" (*Plan para la paz, prosperidad y fortalecimiento del Estado*). As initially presented, the program was not overtly military. Civilians in the country's planning ministry had drafted it, with help from soldiers and civilians working in the ministry of defense. Released to the public in September 1999, it was presented as a kind of Marshall Plan for Colombia, to be underwritten chiefly by the United States and countries of the European Union. It was to complement Pastrana's peace plan, which featured granting the FARC the Cleared Zone in the southeastern part of the country as an inducement to their entering into peace talks with the government. Widely discussed abroad, Pastrana's program was debated very little in Colombia.[45]

Soon renamed "Plan Colombia," the program was embraced by the United States, which by the end of the 1990s had become concerned over the escalating violence in Colombia and its potential for spreading internationally. Both the Clinton administration and congressional Republicans rushed to endorse Pastrana's aid proposal, but initially only as part of a two-year Andean anti-drug package heavily military in nature. Colombia was allotted $860 million of the $1.6 billion designated for the Andean Regional Initiative. Enabling legislation for the program was passed in the United States during mid–2000, and the assistance, mostly in the form of Blackhawk and Huey helicopters, and training and support for two anti-narcotics army brigades, started showing up in Colombia during early 2001. The aid, and the increased contact with the U.S. military that came with it, were viewed as godsends in Colombian military and national security circles. Plan Colombia was formulated at a crucial moment in a "silent revolution" in military reorganization that had been going on in Colombia for nearly a decade. With the active collaboration of the U.S. military, and the infusion of sophisticated new weaponry, the impact of Colombia's military reform soon became apparent to all.

Feeble and ineffective attempts at military reform in Colombia had begun during the administration of César Gaviria (1990–1994) after peace talks with the FARC and the ELN broke down late in 1991.[46] Continuation of the reform effort became impossible during the administration of Ernesto Samper (1994–1998), a time of very bad relations between the government and the military establishment. Flaws in military organization and security policy were placed in sharp relief by the shocking series of defeats of the military at the hands of FARC guerrillas during the mid–1990s.

Civilian-military relations improved with the election of Andrés Pastrana, but only to an extent. The theme of military reform returned with vigor when the new president's minister of defense, Rodrigo Lloreda, helped formulate what became known as the military's New Form of Operation (NFO, or *Nueva Forma de Operar*), featuring professionalization of the military, the creation of rapid-response mobile combat units, and technological modernization. But it was also Lloreda's task to assist in Pastrana's creation of the Cleared Zone for the FARC. This angered the military and also gave impetus to the paramilitary AUC.[47] Still, thanks to Lloreda's reform effort, and despite problems created by establishment of the Cleared Zone, needed change began taking place in Colombia's military. And those changes involved the United States. Colombia's relations with its powerful ally warmed when Andrés Pastrana pledged in November 1998 to vigorously attack the illegal drug trade in his country. The U.S. was anxious to improve its relations with Colombia following the gloomy span of the Samper administration, when relations were strained and officials in the Clinton administration openly called Colombia a "narcodemocracy." By the end of Samper's term in office it was clear in the United States that the strained relations had played a significant role in both the deterioration of public order in Colombia and the increase in cocaine production there.

The United States began positioning itself to help Colombia militarily before Ernesto Samper left office. Deteriorating conditions in Colombia had led to ongoing meetings between military and civilian defense specialists in the two countries during the latter 1990s, one of the most important of which took place in Houston, Texas, early in 1998. The seminar produced a plan for stabilizing the country, published in a pamphlet titled "Project Houston." Other meetings followed and by the end of 1998, with Pastrana's administration in place, and with long-awaited military reform under way, the stage was set for progress. The positive results of these reform efforts were quickly apparent. On November 1, 1998, the FARC attacked Mitú, the departmental capital of Vaupés. Although the guerrillas inflicted heavy casualties, especially among police stationed in the town, they were quickly driven from Mitú by troops flown in on U.S.-supplied combat helicopters. FARC cadres were surprised by this quick response and suffered heavy losses during their withdrawal from the town.[48]

Colombia's security situation was complex in mid–2002 at the end of Pastrana's presidential term. Despite the fact that military reform had gained momentum on his watch, and that Plan Colombia had procured badly needed hardware for the armed forces, Andrés Pastrana failed to craft an integrated national security policy.[49] And how could he have done so, with the FARC attacking and kidnapping with near impunity out of the Cleared Zone, which lay distressingly close to the national capital? That impossible situation had led Pastrana to send the armed forces to reclaim the 42,000-square-kilometer area in February 2002.

The resounding failure of his peace policy left Pastrana's successor Álvaro Uribe with a nearly free hand to use Plan Colombia military aid in the struggle against illegal armed groups. The dispensation to use U.S. military aid against the insurgents, rather than exclusively in the war against illegal drugs, was granted to Uribe by the U.S. in October 2002, three months after he had entered office. After the terrorist attacks in the U.S. on September 11, 2001, the Americans had placed the FARC and ELN on its list of terrorist organizations. By then the link between illegal drugs and violence in Colombia was clear to U.S. officials. Thus it was that Alvaro Uribe was uniquely prepared to send his armed forces into action against the *violentos* at the onset of his presidency. That meant he would be giving full attention to the FARC, for during 2003 both the ELN and the AUC had entered into negotiations with the government.

The story of the FARC's decline and Colombia's return to relative peace is bound up in Álvaro Uribe's vigorous attack on the guerrilla group through his Patriot Plan (*Plan Patriota*), the military component of his umbrella Democratic Security program. In early 2003, Uribe started informing the public of his military plan to retake control of national territory lost to insurgent groups from the late 1970s onward. When the FARC responded with a series of terrorist attacks, including the deadly bombing of Bogotá's El Nogal social club in February 2003, a furious Uribe sent a message to the FARC: "Wait there patiently, because no matter how dense the jungle or how difficult the topography, we will get there to defeat you."[50] Backing his words was the promise of U.S. military collaboration at the level of training and technical support, and of consultation on strategy. While it is true that Colombia could have defeated the FARC without U.S. aid, the support contributed greatly to Uribe's achievement. One of Colombia's top security analysts set Plan Colombia's contribution to the military success of Alvaro Uribe and his armed forces at forty percent. Others set the figure much higher.[51]

Once the Patriot Plan was set into motion in June 2003, the FARC's days as a significant force in Colombian national life were numbered. Following the scheme outlined five years before in the military's New Form of Operation, army mobile units supported by specialized battalions rather quickly and easily ended the guerrillas' encirclement of Bogotá. During 2004, code named "The Year of the Offensive," the 17,000-man Omega Taskforce swept into Colombia's southeastern jungles, seizing FARC supplies and occupying villages that the guerrillas had held for decades. The offensive continued over the ensuing years, driving the FARC ever deeper into the Amazonian jungle and toward the boundaries of neighboring countries. These successes won Alvaro Uribe a second four-year term in 2006. He reached the peak of his popularity in July 2008, following the memorable rescue of FARC hostages.

The U.S. component of Plan Colombia was a five-year program that ended on December 31, 2005. Over its funding period the program received $4.5 billion, 76 percent of it devoted to military matters and 24 percent to humanitarian concerns. Through the U.S. Department of Defense, Plan Colombia funding was channeled into training and equipment for specialized units, such as anti-narcotics, commando, and high mountain battalions, as well as for the naval riverine patrols that helped Colombia establish control over its rivers for the first time in the nation's history.[52] The program's military component allowed Colombia's air force to quadruple its rotary and fixed-wing fleet of combat and transport aircraft. That buildup was launched in 2001 with the delivery of sixty-three Blackhawk and Huey helicopters to the army and police. The aid also led to the creation of elite anti-kidnapping units and to the establishment of a "mini–Pentagon" in Bogotá where logistical standardization and control and supply acquisition were systematized within a high-tech setting. Military communications were modernized through creation of an air intelligence strategic communication network.[53] All the while Colombia steadily increased its defense spending, pushing it from an average of 1.5 to 2 percent of GDP during the 1980s to 4.6 percent of GDP by 2006. By the latter year its armed forces, including police, numbered 380,000, bringing them to the Latin American average.[54]

A substantial portion of Plan Colombia's non-military funding was devoted to judicial reform and improvement. At U.S. suggestion Colombia's penal system shifted from the case, or Napoleonic, method, to the oral accusatory method used in trying cases in the United States. This brought a streamlining of criminal procedure which reduced procedural time from an average of three years per case, to between 25 and 163 days. Personnel from the U.S. Department of Justice established thirty-five Oral Trial Courtrooms where they supervised the training of judges in oral trial procedure and legal evidence.[55] Other significant justice-related programs included the establishment of forty-two Justice Houses (*Casas de Justicia*) in parts of the country where the citizenry had been traditionally poorly served by the nation's justice system. Specializing in civil and domestic matters, the popular new courts processed more than four million cases between January 2002 and December 2006.[56] Other public-order reforms involved the establishment of a witness protection program, the adoption of an "early-warning system" to protect human rights in zones of ongoing conflict—which included armoring the offices of human rights workers, and the teaching of courses in crime scene management and forensic technology.[57]

Plan Colombia funding was also devoted to paramilitary demobilization, an activity taking place over a significant portion of Álvaro Uribe's first and second terms. Throughout the process, during which over 31,000 men, women, and children laid down their weapons and returned to civil life, monies from the U.S. program helped pay for things such as the provision of food and shelter at demobilization sites, and, subsequent to that, the administration of thirty-seven service centers across the nation providing aid to the former combatants, most of whom were young men. Demobilization of the paramilitaries was guided by provisions of the Law of Justice and Peace, passed in 2005. U.S. Department of Justice personnel worked closely with Colombians involved in the Justice and Peace program to help improve their prosecutorial, investigative, and forensic capabilities. Those who received this training included prosecutors, public defenders, police, and judges. Plan Colombia funds were also designated to help monitor the demobilized and support their efforts to reenter civil society. Former child soldiers of both the paramilitaries and the guerrillas received Plan Colombia aid through yet another program. Still another component of Justice and Peace-related aid through Plan Colombia helped facilitate reparations and reconciliation among those who had been victimized by the paramilitaries. All of these activities were carried out in cooperation with allied programs administered through agencies within the Colombian government and armed forces. Many of the activities mentioned here continued after Plan Colombia ended in 2005. Post-Plan Colombia non-military aid for Justice and Peace-related activities, for example, received $11,442,000 during 2008.[58]

Plan Colombia contributed meaningfully to the restoration of peace in Colombia. During the five years it was in effect homicide rates fell by forty-nine percent. It helped return police to 170 *municipios*. It also bolstered policing in all of Colombia's thousand *municipios* through the Campesino Soldiers (*Soldados Campesinos*) program. Through this initiative 10,000 citizen soldiers were recruited throughout the country and charged with patrolling their own neighborhoods and reporting suspicious activities to their uniformed supervisors. This program, inspired by a similar one in Peru that had been effective in combating that country's *Sendero Luminoso* (Shining Path) guerrillas, freed up soldiers of the regular army to pursue the enemy in the field.[59]

During 2006, Colombia's national planning office began work on a document summarizing the positive results of foreign aid during the years 1999–2005, and projecting "follow-on" activities through 2013. Sometimes referred to as Plan Colombia II, it invited foreign governments and non-governmental organizations to remain involved in the country's task of strengthening democracy and promoting social development.[60] Armed with this document Álvaro Uribe visited George W. Bush at his Texas ranch during March 2007, where he won the U.S. president's commitment to budget $750 million in aid for Colombia that year. Congressional Democrats subsequently trimmed the aid package by fifteen percent and requested that more of the funding be devoted to social, as opposed to military, programs, in order to achieve a 45 percent social/55 percent military division.[61] By 2009 the total U.S. aid appropriation to Colombia, from the time Plan Colombia was launched, stood at $6.8 billion, with more than $2 billion having been contributed since 2005. From 2009 onward the 45/55 percent social/military program formula was used as a standard for future distribution of funds.[62]

With peace returning to Colombia, increasing energy was devoted to consolidate previous gains, particularly in areas that had witnessed heavy FARC and AUC activity. The Colombian government's plan for 2007–2013 detailed a range of anti-poverty, aid to ethnic minorities, and refugee resettlement programs that foreign aid monies were to help promote. In 2007 the U.S. House of Representatives directed the Departments of State and Defense to draft a multi-year scheme of U.S. aid to Colombia. The resulting document became the counterpart of Colombia's plan for 2007–2013. The U.S. document projected aid to Colombia over the same period, with funding earmarked for the following six areas: (1) improving national security; (2) alternative development; (3) social services; (4) enhancing justice and protecting human rights; (5) strengthening the economy; (6) winning the peace—demobilization and reintegration. Total U.S. aid to Colombia was, by that projection, to decline from the $626,220,000 budgeted for 2007, to $449,661,000 designated for fiscal year 2013. The "improving national security" category, covering many military-related programs, remained constant throughout the projected outlay, running from between 70 and 75 percent of allocated funds.[63] Of course the document did not reflect the 2009 decision to reduce the proportion of aid devoted to Colombian military programs to no more than 55 percent of total aid. The formula mandating a lower proportion of U.S. aid to military funding was applied from 2009 onward.

Implicit and explicit in all U.S. aid programs to Colombia was the effort to meet the Andean nation's historic challenge of extending the presence of the state into all corners of national territory. It was the lack of state presence in the country's many remote regions that allowed the guerrillas to gain a foothold and later grow prosperous by taxing coca and later trafficking in cocaine. Álvaro Uribe's Democratic Security program was founded in two interconnected promises: that he would make Colombia's people safe by defeating the illegal armed groups that preyed on them, and that he would then keep them safe by integrating the *violentos'* former safe havens into the greater nation.

As of 2009 Colombia's most ambitious program of territorial integration involved the Macarena area of southern Meta. Dominated by the Macarena Mountains (Serranía de la Macarena), not only is it one of the world's richest sites in terms of biodiversity, but it was also the seat of FARC power and its center of coca cultivation and cocaine manufacture until 2004. With the guerrillas in retreat it became the task of the Colombian government and a host of foreign government and non-government organizations to make La Macarena effectively part of Colombia. The epicenter of development activity became the town of Vista Hermosa and its surrounding *municipio*, on the eastern edge of the Macarena range. Key to drawing the formerly remote spot into national life became the improvement of the highway putting Vista Hermosa within easy reach of Meta's capital Villavicencio—and from there, Bogotá. It is this highway that allows campesinos of the region to earn their livelihoods through the sale of legal plant and animal products that abound there.

A civilian agency called the Center for Coordinated Integral Action was put in place to manage programs re-establishing civilian government in all six municipios of the Macarena region, including the valley of the Río Duda, on the western side of the mountain range, the original heartland of the FARC. Development of this extensive zone became part of a sequenced framework for stabilizing conflict zones once at the center of guerrilla and paramilitary activity and of illegal drug production. La Macarena was the principal one of ten other similarly remote, traditionally forgotten parts of Colombia targeted to experience a sequenced framework of development aimed at drawing them into the greater nation.[64]

The reintegration of La Macarena into national life had been crucial to Colombia's government from the moment it began its offensive against the FARC in 2004. Just 150 kilometers south of Bogotá, La Macarena was immensely valuable to the FARC not only because it had been their headquarters since the 1960s, and because it was so close to Bogotá, but because it was the center of the guerrilla group's illegal drug industry. Thousands of hectares of coca grew in the mountains of La Macarena and scores of cocaine kitchens dotted its valleys. This explains why the FARC fought hard to defend the region after 2004. But the Uribe government, bolstered by Plan Colombia and the U.S. government's commitment to attack the cocaine industry at its source, was equally determined to drive both the FARC and the illegal drugs from the strategically important region.

The drive to reclaim La Macarena, the third phase of the Patriot Plan, and designated Operation Green Colombia, began poorly for the army. On December 27, 2005, 300 members of the FARC, commanded by Gener García Molina ("Jhon 40"), attacked a company of soldiers camped near Vista Hermosa, killing twenty-nine of them. It was an especially bitter blow to the armed forces, as a year earlier it had sent thirteen battalions, numbering 3,200 men, to comb the mountains of southwestern Meta in search of the guerrilla leader, called "the capo of the FARC" by the U.S. Drug Enforcement Agency. The operation of early 2005, code named "The Emperor," failed in its objective. Despite the fact that a half-million dollar bounty was being offered for his arrest, "Jhon 40" remained at large somewhere in La Macarena.[65]

January 16, 2006, marked the formal beginning of Operation Green Colombia. It consisted of two parts. The first involved army penetration of the valley of the Río Duda, and the second sent 930 campesinos, who were paid 27,000 pesos per day (about ten dollars) in Plan Colombia funds, to manually destroy coca fields. It was slow and dangerous work. On February 6, a bomb planted by the FARC killed six police and wounded seven others guarding the coca eradicators. A week later FARC snipers killed six police agents who were guarding the campesinos. In March a campesino was killed and two others injured by a FARC mine wired to a coca bush. On April 4, an army platoon was ambushed by the FARC and twelve of its members killed. Meanwhile, army occupation of villages along the Río Duda moved apace. On May 28, as Colombians were voting Alvaro Uribe a second presidential term, the army was in heavy combat with the FARC in the region of La Uribe, the guerrilla group's former headquarters on the upper Río Duda. By month's end they had established military and police presence in the town of La Uribe for the first time in Colombia's history.[66]

Operation Green Colombia moved to its conclusion during early August 2006. By that time 155 cocaine manufacturing laboratories had been destroyed, five thousand gallons and over three tons of liquid and solid cocaine precursor chemicals seized, and nearly 3,000 hectares of coca manually uprooted. But, on August 1, a bomb planted five meters beneath a coca field was detonated by the FARC, killing five campesinos uprooting shrubs above it.[67] That act changed the character of the attack on coca in La Macarena. Following the incident the government resumed aerial fumigation of coca, despite the defoliant's harmful effect on surrounding vegetation and wildlife. U.S. ambassador William Wood defended the decision, pointing out that over the previous six months thirty-five lives had been lost in manual eradication of coca in La Macarena while in just ten days of aerial fumigation 1,769 hectares of coca had been sprayed, with no loss of life.[68]

Shortly after the decision was made to fumigate coca fields in La Macarena in early August 2006, the *New York Times* published an article stating that Plan Colombia's promise to reduce cocaine flows to the United States had not been kept. It pointed out that to date 300,000 hectares of coca had been fumigated in Colombia, yet there was no appreciable decline in either the quantity or the purity of cocaine being sold on U.S. streets.[69] Colombia's interior minister Sabas Pretelt responded that instead of criticizing Colombia the international community should be thankful for the dedication and sacrifice of all those who fought the illegal drug trade in his country. Meanwhile, U.S. anti-drug czar John Walters defended Plan Colombia, pointing out that both coca cultivation and cocaine production had been compromised in Colombia and that those involved in drug-related activities were coming under intense pressure.[70]

Plan Colombia was controversial from the moment it was introduced. The program's coca eradication component was just one target of the overall criticism that despite the billions of dollars spent on fumigation, and the millions of gallons of pesticides sprayed over Colombia's verdant countryside, there has been little decline in either total hectares of the shrub planted in Colombia or tons of cocaine exported. Hence, the critics concluded, Plan Colombia, and U.S. policy throughout the area of illegal drug supply in Latin America, was irrevocably "addicted to failure."[71] Colombian scholars blasted their own military's uncritical acceptance of U.S. aid, arguing that it would militarize the conflict in a way that did not necessarily lead to solution of Colombia's security problem.[72] At the moment Plan Colombia was being launched a prominent journalist opined that the funding would change little and that Colombia's violence would likely never cease.[73]

By 2010, five years after the conclusion of Plan Colombia, it was safe to say that the program fulfilled its military goal, even if it failed in its intent to eliminate cocaine exports from the country. Plan Colombia played a significant role in reducing violence levels in Colombia, while in its extended form, as Plan Colombia II, it had helped return levels of violence and crime to roughly those of the country's relatively peaceful 1965–1975 period.[74] The U.S. aid program played a vital role in helping Colombia develop a national security program appropriate to a country with extraordinary public order challenges springing from broken terrain, numerous frontier regions, and an armed insurgency receiving significant foreign support across poorly defended national borders. It is true that Plan Colombia was a marriage of unequals. Colombia's vice president, Francisco Santos, complained of bad treatment in Washington, D.C. in the wake of a 2008 scandal involving the Colombian army. A tongue-in-cheek article in *Semana* suggested that Colombia seemed to have become the gringos' fifty-first state. The piece listed a dozen examples of significant U.S. influence in the country, running from the move to the accusatory trial system with virtually no national debate on the matter, to the modification of strike legislation in response to pressure exerted by U.S. labor leaders.[75]

The final verdict on Plan Colombia must be that the aid program was necessary and proper. Colombia's illegal drug industry sprang up in response to demand for marijuana, and then cocaine, originating in the United States. Thus the United States owed Plan Colombia to the Andean nation. It was the Nixon administration's aerial fumigation of Mexican marijuana which drove large-scale marijuana cultivation into Colombia during the early 1970s. Fumigation of marijuana was counter-productive then—certainly for Colombia—and critics of coca fumigation argue that it is counter-productive now. But this argument ignores the point of why Colombian presidents extending back to César Gaviria endorsed coca eradication. The illegal drug trade financed Colombia's New Violence, which manifested itself most significantly in the FARC insurgency. To break the FARC it was necessary to attack its main source of revenue, the cocaine industry. Colombia had no choice other than to pursue the eradication of coca by every means available. That included embracing the United States and its military assistance provided through Plan Colombia.

States that participate in global commerce cannot control markets, but they can influence the way demand is satisfied. Thanks in part to Plan Colombia much of Colombia's national territory was, by 2010, reclaimed from those who not so long before presided over the coca plantations and cocaine kitchens that dotted the landscape. Colombia still produces cocaine, but not as it did before. The trade is no longer dominated by FARC fronts operating with impunity throughout the country's Amazon jungles. Plan Colombia is in considerable part to be thanked for this.

Slogging Toward Peace

"Now we must consolidate the achievements arrived at.... Nothing could be more harmful at this crucial juncture than to ease up the pressure placed on the activities of the illegal armed groups and other violence generating factors."
—Government of Colombia, Strategy for the period 2007–2013[76]

Many problems remain to be solved or otherwise dealt with before peace reigns in Colombia. The country's illegal-drug-related violence, which grew progressively worse from the 1970s to the first years of the 2000s, vastly aggravated other deep-seated problems that had existed over the life of Colombia as an independent state. Principal among them can be called the "two nations problem." For at least a hundred years Colombia has been two countries, one modern and the other premodern. It has been a place of city and countryside. The former is where progress has taken place over a century's time and at an ever accelerating pace, where health care, education, and all other social amenities are available, and where social ascent, though difficult, takes place. The other, problematic, Colombia, is the countryside, often remote from the cities and premodern in many respects. Time moves slowly in rural Colombia. Personal advancement is possible there, but usually only in a rough pioneering sort of way. Much of the outlying countryside retains the character of frontier land. All of eastern Colombia remains a frontier zone stretching from the Llanos in the north to jungles of the Amazon watershed in the south. Much of the Pacific littoral is also in the nature of frontier. It is a place of mangrove swamps and the world's heaviest rainfall, and most of its people are descended from African slaves. They are poor, and for most Colombians out of sight and mind. People of the Pacific littoral live in places poorly supplied with state services. They are hard to reach, bereft of opportunity, and in many cases outside the reach of the nation's legal protections.

The premodern character of much of rural Colombia aggravates problems connected to peacemaking. It is precisely these poor and distant regions, making up two-thirds of national territory, where illegal drugs and guerrillas remain. Nor are trans–Andean Colombia and the country's Pacific littoral the only places remote and ill-served by the state. Along with them must be counted the massif of the southern Andes, the lower Cauca River area, most of Urabá and Chocó, southern Magdalena and Cesar, and the northwestern border of Santander del Norte—the Catatumbo region. Though not quite frontier zones, these places have much in common with Colombia's eastern llanos, Amazonian jungles, and Pacific littoral. They are the crux of the country's ongoing problems of public order. Until they have better public infrastructure, better highways, and greater economic opportunities for the citizens who live there they will be prone to involvement in the illegal drug industry. And where drug trafficking exists so too do crime and violence, drug mafias and guerrillas. Local power structures in many such places are compromised, when not dominated, by the lucrative trade in illegal drugs and those who manage and profit from it.[77] Linking such places to the greater, modern nation is at once Colombia's greatest contemporary challenge and the heart of its struggle to achieve peace.[78]

* * *

Colombia's three recent decades of violence and bloodshed have taught the country's leaders what must be done to restore peace. And that does not mean returning the country to the status quo ante of 1965–1975, that interval of relative calm sandwiched between the end of *La Violencia* and beginnings of the country's drug-inspired New Violence. It is clear today that if Colombia is to achieve true peace the *campo* must be made a more humane and just place than it was during the late 1970s, when growing drug-related violence was aggravated by self-styled social reformers carrying guns.

Some say that Colombia will never achieve real peace. That was the opinion of former United Nations special envoy to Colombia Jan Egland, who visited the country in 2007. In Egland's view Colombia will always possess armed insurgents because its people are incapable of solving the problem of rural poverty.[79] FARC guerrillas, most of whom were *campesinos*, believed the same.

These gloomy facts notwithstanding, Colombians are trying to address the complex of problems afflicting rural areas. They are attacking the ills of places most hard-hit by the recent violence. The task is daunting, as the case of the *municipio* of Becerril, Cesar, illustrates. Becerril is strategically important in the sense that it is the gateway to the Serranía de Perijá, running along the border with Venezuela and lying mid-way between Lake Maracaibo and the Sierra Nevada de Santa Marta. When FARC leader Ovidio Palmera ("Simón Trinidad") established himself there in 1987 the town was the center of a dairy zone producing 70,000 liters of milk daily. When Pineda became part of the FARC general command, he was replaced as Front 41 commander by Willington Vargas ("Caraquemada"), whose cruelty to people of the region led to his execution by his own guerrilla colleagues. During the latter 1990s, paramilitary leader Rodrigo Tovar Pupo ("Jorge 40") arrived in Becerril to do battle with and drive out the FARC. He and his men branded inhabitants of the region "auxiliaries of the guerrillas" and killed some five hundred of them. By the first decade of the twenty-first century the town lay in ruins and most of its former residents had long since fled. A particularly Kafkaesque touch was that because the residents of Becerril failed to pay their electric bills before fleeing the paramilitary the electric company refused to restore power to the town. As of mid–2007 the main effort at civic improvement in Becerril had been to purchase fifty burros for use by school children in the *municipio*, some of whom had to walk up to two hours to reach the town's school.[80] It may be of some comfort to the few people left in Becerril that both Rodrigo Tovar Pupo and Ovidio Pineda ended their violent careers serving long prison terms in the United States following their conviction on drug trafficking charges.

As part of its attempt to revive places like Becerril, the Colombian government has targeted 332 villages in 53 priority *municipios* across the country for what it calls "social recovery." The stated goal of this action is "to increase governability, legitimacy, credibility, and citizens' confidence in the State, and in themselves as a community." The selected villages and *municipios* are in northeastern Colombia in the departments of Cesar, Norte de Santander and La Guajira, and in the northwestern departments of Chocó, Antioquia, and Córdoba. Other priority sites are in Cauca and Nariño, in the southwest, and most departments in the country's sparsely populated Eastern Llanos and Amazon regions. All selected sites were once seats of guerrilla or paramilitary strength, or were battlegrounds of the two groups. And they were invariably sites of coca cultivation and manufacture, with several of them being important sites of cocaine export.[81]

Colombia's planning department has been tasked with coordinating state, international, and NGO development aid and programs in these violence-ravaged places. In so doing it directs some 200 programs to rebuild infrastructure in targeted municipalities, and attempts to redirect local economies from illegal into legal directions. An example of this effort is the alternative development "jagua project" in the village of Napipí, Chocó. Currently the people of Napipí are cultivating a local fruit called the jagua, whose deep blue pulp yields a safe organic dye prized by the tattoo industry. Billed as "a blue way to fight the war on drugs," the project is funded in part through a $300,000 grant from USAID. Part of the U.S. commitment to development in the Chocó springs from a U.S. congressional directive to emphasize aid to Colombia's Afro-Colombian and indigenous communities, both of which are heavily represented in Chocó.[82] Numerous non-governmental humanitarian agencies, multinational organizations, most importantly the United Nations and the European Union, participate in similar development projects across Colombia.[83]

The greatest of all consolidation projects initiated under Álvaro Uribe's Democratic

Security regimen is taking place in the department of Meta. Its focus is the department's southwestern portion, where Andrés Pastrana had removed all government presence between November 1998 and February 2002, when he created the Cleared Zone for the FARC. By early 2002 the folly of this decision had become clear. The country's largest guerrilla group had used the region as a staging point for its assault on Bogotá. In the process they made life insupportable for the residents of Meta's twenty-five *municipios* lying beyond the designated Cleared Zone. During late January 2002, some 200,000 Meta residents staged their noisy "saucepan protest" (*cacerolazo*) against FARC destruction of the department's electric grid. The guerrilla group had blown up twenty electric transmission towers, thereby plunging the department into darkness. Further complicating Meta's situation during 2002 and 2003 was warfare between paramilitary factions vying for dominance of cocaine trafficking in the central part of the department. As well as fighting one another, the paramilitary armies of Germán Buitrago Parra ("Martín Llanos") and Miguel Arroyave had long staged incursions against the FARC across the Ariari River in the direction of the Serranía de la Macarena.[84]

With Alvaro Uribe's election, and subsequent paramilitary demobilization, intra–AUC warfare fell to a low level in Meta. During the years of paramilitary demobilization phases two and three of the Patriot Plan offensive broke FARC strength in Meta, most importantly in the region of La Macarena, and particularly in the valley of the Río Duda, lying between the La Macarena mountain range and the Eastern Cordillera of the Andes. Reclamation of the La Macarena region is considered the third and final phase of the Patriot Plan.

Not only is the La Macarena project the Colombian government's first and most ambitious scheme of integrated territorial reintegration, it is its most difficult. Throughout the decades of FARC domination of the region the only authority known by people in places such as the valley of the Río Duda was that of the FARC. Their only personal identification documents were those issued by the guerrilla group. Because they lived outside the reach of the state many farm families of the region never received title to the land they worked, thus reducing them to the condition of squatters and making them prey to others better prepared to take possession of the land legally. And the greatest single complicating factor for the people living throughout the extensive region is their decades-long association with the illegal drug industry. The government's reclamation project has required serious effort in reorienting La Macarena's agriculture to legal production. That effort has been judged a success, however, with coca planting down 75 percent by 2008, with no replanting of crops.[85]

Despite these and many other problems La Macarena's incorporation into greater Colombia has moved apace. The project has become a model for similar ones around the country. Foreign governments and international human rights organizations work with a range of Colombian agencies to provide social services for those living in the targeted regions. Vista Hermosa, the principal town of La Macarena, now possesses all state services. Plan Colombia funds have helped build a meeting hall, complete with dormitories where visiting technical teams from Bogotá and elsewhere are housed during extended visits to the region. Some 191 billion pesos (about $90 million) have been appropriated for a paved highway linking the town of La Uribe, former headquarters of the FARC, with San Juan de Arma, which already possesses a highway linking it with Villavicencio, the capital of Meta. That project is being assisted by soldiers attached to the Armed Forces Omega Taskforce, as it is considered part of the Patriot Plan strategy to deny the guerrillas safe haven through road building.[86]

Highway building represents a gauge of Colombia's seriousness in responding to the needs of its frontier settlers. The linking of Uribe to Villavicencio and thence to Bogotá is the first step in tying the entire La Macarena region into the nation's highway grid. Completing the task will cost hundreds of billions of pesos more and will result in extending the highway down the Río Duda valley to the town of La Macarena, and thence northward along the east side of the mountains to Vista Hermosa. Once completed, the costly highway will need to be maintained, and travelers on it protected. This, and similar projects across Colombia, form the consolidation phase of Álvaro Uribe's Democratic Security policy whose stated goal is "to strengthen social policy so as to improve the lives of the Colombian people as a whole."[87] The degree of its success will depend, though, not on Uribe but on the will of presidents who follow him, and of all others working to make good on the country's development blueprint.

Infrastructure-building projects such as the one described here inject the Colombian state into the lives of its most marginal citizens as never before. Ambitious anti-poverty programs figure prominently in the social development plan addressing the period 2007–2013. The frightening breakdown of public safety of the late 1990s and first years of the twenty-first century convinced wealthy Colombians of the wisdom of paying the special tax on wealth that was voted into effect early in Alvaro Uribe's presidency. It paid for improvements in the nation's armed forces. Over the years since its passage there has been talk of making the tax permanent and also of making it more regressive, so that less affluent Colombians can share the cost of Democratic Security. There is logic in the proposal, though it moved one journalist to suggest that if the well-to-do want national security burdens to be shared more fairly across society then the draft should be re-instituted so their children might join those of poor families on the fields of battle.[88]

Thanks to Colombians' willingness to pay for improved security through tax increases the armed forces budget came to total 3.9 percent of GDP—4.6 percent when adjusted to reflect retirement benefits by the end of the first decade of the twenty-first century. For the first time in history the nation's armed forces, totaling 460,000 men and women in 2009, exceeded the average for Latin America. Given Colombia's extraordinary and ongoing challenges in the area of internal security it seems likely that further security-related taxation may be in store for Colombians. When Juan Manuel Santos announced his intention to succeed Alvaro Uribe in 2010, he announced his intention to promote a "strategic leap" in the area of security. Santos was in fact elected to succeed Uribe during mid–2010.[89]

Even though Colombians began saying their country was in its post-conflict phase after 2008, it was still not at peace at the end of the first decade of the twenty-first century. As the year 2010 began the war against the FARC, and against ELN remnants, gave little sign that either group was ready to lay down its weapons. Its new leader Guillermo Sáenz Vargas ("Alfonso Cano") spoke of adapting his group's strategy to cope with improvements in his country's national army. Although FARC troop strength had fallen to 8,500 by 2009, with several thousand of the guerrillas operating from camps located across borders with Ecuador and Venezuela, tactical improvements had enabled the FARC to rebound from the setbacks of 2003–2008 and to move to a virtual one-to-one kill ratio with the Colombian military. During the first six months of 2009 the FARC lost 259 men in 7,000 engagements with Colombia's military forces while killing 295 of their enemy. The guerrilla group achieved that degree of success through the use of trailside bombs, snipers, and landmines. Sáenz and his military chief Víctor Suárez Rojas ("El Mono Jojoy") heavily mined the perimeters of camps located in particularly inaccessible parts of Meta, Cauca, northern Antioquia, and Tolima. On the other hand, by 2010

FARC guerrillas were present in only twenty-six percent of national territory, and they exercised direct influence on just nine percent of the population. Thus they had been pushed away from most populated areas and into lightly-populated and remote parts of the nation.[90]

The emergence of populist, anti–U.S., and socialist regimes in Venezuela and Ecuador helped the FARC maintain its integrity as a fighting force. Members of the governments and militaries of both countries, fearful that the United States military presence in Colombia threatened their national interests, provided varying degrees of sympathy for the FARC, even at the level of military supply. During early 2009 several shoulder-held rocket launchers and rockets capable of bringing down helicopters and sinking river patrol boats were seized at a camp of FARC commander Gener García ("Jhon 40") in La Macarena. They were discovered to have been originally purchased by the Venezuelan army.[91] Ecuadorian officials in the government of Rafael Correa were proved to have had ongoing contact with the FARC's second-in-command Luis Edgar Devia in the months prior to his death in the March 2008 bombing of his camp. Devia's death led to the breaking of relations between Ecuador and Colombia, as the camp was located on Ecuadorian soil. Relations between Colombia and Ecuador deteriorated further during 2009 when a video was discovered showing Víctor Suárez describing the FARC's support of Correa's 2007 presidential campaign.[92] By late 2009, Ecuadorian leaders acknowledged that the guerrilla group from neighboring Colombia and its drug trafficking arm had "managed to penetrate various levels of political, juridical, and social institutions" in their country.[93]

Cocaine trafficking figured into the mix of FARC support in Ecuador and Venezuela. Just as occurred in Colombia when drug trafficking began yielding great profits in the 1970s, officials in both countries were implicated in aiding the FARC's cocaine exports. A former advisor to Ecuador's interior minister and a vocal FARC supporter was arrested in 2008 on cocaine trafficking charges. He was an associate of Ecuadorian traffickers Miguel and Jefferson Ostariza.[94] Venezuelan security chief Hugo Carvajal had long and close relations with both the FARC and Colombian drug traffickers. Since the 1970s weapons had reached illegal groups in Colombia across the country's poorly-patrolled borders with Ecuador and Venezuela. But what became clear during 2008 and afterward was that high-level officials in both neighboring countries were assisting the FARC in weapons purchase and drug smuggling. During July 2009 Colombian officials named Venezuelan General Cliver Alcalá as the officer who provided the rockets and rocket launchers to FARC Front 43 commander Gener García.[95] Much of this information has been obtained from FARC computers seized in police and military operations conducted during 2008 and 2009. The computers of Luis Edgar Devia and a FARC organizer known as "Camila" yielded 1,136 gigabytes of information. At that time Colombia FARC Front 48 operated openly in the town of Puerto Nuevo, Ecuador. That village lies across the San Miguel River, which forms part of the border between Ecuador and Colombia's department of Putumayo. It is not far from the Colombian town of Puerto Asís. Five other FARC camps operated in the same border region. FARC Fronts 32 and 29 also operated on Ecuadorian soil.[96] From these camps the Colombian guerrillas moved shipments of cocaine through Ecuador. Some of these shipments were from Ecuadorian-grown coca processed into cocaine in "kitchens" located in that country's Amazonian region. FARC camps in Ecuador even house victims of extortionate kidnappings carried out in Colombia.[97]

Colombia's FARC guerrillas clearly benefited from their ideological affinity with the presidents of Ecuador and Venezuela, Rafael Correa and Hugo Chávez. Both populist leaders were critical of Colombia's alliance with the United States and fearful of it as well. Political fashions change, however, and Colombia's neighbors will probably come to regret letting the international drug trade become established within their national territory. The leaders of Ecuador and Venezuela would be wise to study Colombia's example of what happens when political leaders wink at illegal drug trading and allow its monies to corrupt those in high government circles.

FARC movement into Ecuador and Venezuela was a function of the success of the Colombian military's attack on cocaine production in Colombia's east—in places like La Macarena. Disruption of the guerrilla group's river and air transport of cocaine in the Amazon region had a profound impact on the FARC insurgency.

Since the year 2002 Colombia has made significant progress in reducing illegal drug production and in combatting the violence attending it. Thanks to the country's multi-faceted attack on cocaine production, manufacture of that drug had fallen to 295 metric tons by 2008. That represented a 58 percent drop from Colombia's peak cocaine production of 695 metric tons in 2000. Coca plantings likewise fell sharply, to 81,000 hectares, down from more than 160,000 hectares in 2000. Whereas Colombia exported 96 percent of the world's cocaine at the dawn of the twenty-first century, by 2010 it supplied about 51 percent of world supply. Colombia's improved law enforcement, dating from the year 2002, had the effect of pushing coca growing and cocaine processing into Venezuela, Ecuador, and Central America, and also led to a resurgence of coca growing in Bolivia and Peru—and to cocaine production there as well. By 2008 Bolivia satisfied about 13 percent of world cocaine demand and Peru about 36 percent.[98] By 2012 Colombia's cocaine production had declined 72 percent from its level of ten years earlier (620 metric tons in 2002), to slightly more than 173 metric tons.[99]

Despite these notable advances in its battle against the illegal drug industry Colombia remains a significant exporter of cocaine. Today the zones of cocaine export in Colombia are places of extreme violence, where drug gangs battle for dominance, in the process killing significant numbers of innocent bystanders. This stands in tragic contrast to the country as a whole, where rates of violence approach the average for all of Latin America.[100] The Pacific coast towns of Tumaco and Buenaventura, at the center of cocaine export from that region, are among the world's most violent places. Tumaco, which is Nariño's major port on the Pacific Ocean, registered a homicide rate of 157.5 per 100,000 residents in 2008, while Buenaventura's rate in 2006 was 121.[101] It is worth remembering that homicide rates in major cocaine-consuming countries are in single digits. Such is the burden that Colombians continue to bear in supplying recreational drugs to consumers in wealthy countries.

Despite the violence flowing from Colombia's illegal drug industry, two things have worked to lessen the industry's negative impact there. First, the cocaine trade no longer generates the profits it once did. Control of end-product marketing has passed into the hands of foreign trafficking organizations, most notable among them the Mexican drug cartels. They, along with trafficking groups in Brazil, Russia, and elsewhere, have reduced Colombian cocaine profits by approximately fifty percent. By one estimate Colombian producers earned just twenty-five percent of the amount received in cocaine sales on the streets of U.S. and European cities.[102] This reliance on non–Colombians to deliver the commodity to consumers has externalized a major part of the violence previously suffered mostly by Colombians. Thousands of Latin Americans continue to die each year in battles between drug gangs vying to supply the U.S. market, but today most of them are Mexicans. And there are signs that such violence is moving into the United States itself. As of 2010 Mexican drug cartels were operating out of U.S. cities and perpetrating drug-related killings on U.S. soil.[103]

The dramatic fall in profits derived from cocaine exports has badly hurt the FARC's money-raising capability. Whereas the guerrilla group's drug-related revenues were in the range of $600 million annually during the latter 1990s, its drug revenues had shrunk to something approaching $100 million annually a decade later.[104] The FARC is cash-strapped for the first time in recent memory. In 2008 the guerrilla group was forced to solicit a $300 million loan from Venezuelan President Hugo Chávez.[105]

The FARC's decline was directly related to the way Colombia's government removed illegal drugs as the *sine qua non* of national disorder, set into motion by Álvaro Uribe's war against the traffickers. Throughout his eight years as President Uribe extradited traffickers to the United States with abandon. By early 2006, he had sent 784 Colombians away to be tried and then jailed in the United States.[106] In so doing he enjoyed the support of an expanded police force. Specialized anti-narcotics police units, foremost among them the Dijín, doggedly pursued those shown to be significant in the country's illegal drug industry. The highlight of Colombia's pursuit of traffickers came on July 4, 2008, with the arrest of Oscar Varela García ("Capachivo"), head of the North Valle cartel, which had been the most violent of the country's several cartels. Successor to the Medellín and Cali cartels, the North Valle cartel had exported 300 tons of cocaine annually during the 1990s, half of Colombia's total production. "Capachivo" was the last leader of the North Valle cartel. The group's previous leaders had been captured or killed, with many of the former group extradited to stand trial in the United States. So effective was the campaign to bring down the country's last cartel that some of those named in U.S. extradition warrants surrendered voluntarily in order to enter into plea bargaining with U.S. authorities. And it was not just the cartel's top figures who were arrested. Careful police work led to the arrest of cartel accountants, financial agents, front men, and even those connected with the group's several "collection offices" (*oficinas de cobro*), the places where orders to "settle accounts" were handed out to cartel gunmen, at one point numbering some 1,000. The best part of the North Valle cartel's destruction was that it was an all–Colombian operation. Unlike the case with the Cali cartel, the U.S. Drug Enforcement Agency was not a part of destruction of the North Valle trafficking group.[107]

Colombia's success in destroying the country's major trafficking groups was the fruit of an effort extending back to the 1980s, during the time of the redoubtable Colonel Jaime Ramírez Gómez, commander of police anti-narcotics operations from 1982 until his murder by Medellín cartel gunmen in 1986. The work of Ramírez and many thousand other police officers killed in the course of anti-narcotics work eventually, painfully, forced Colombia's illegal drug industry to change in a fundamental way. That constant pressure at the level of law enforcement reduced drug trafficking to a matter handled through police work. Drug trafficking in Colombia will never again produce traffickers like Pablo Escobar, who fought the Colombian state with a high degree of success for nineteen long and bloody years.

Colombia's illegal drug industry was forced to come to terms with the State during the first decade of the twenty-first century. The nation's leaders had set that process into motion years earlier, during the 1980s and '90s, when they broke up the Medellín and Cali cartels. But it fell to Alvaro Uribe, and his successor in the presidency, Juan Manuel Santos, and all of those working with them in public capacities to subdue the narcoguerrilla and the narcoparamilitaries, and, finally, the last of the country's drug cartels. The Colombian government's increasingly effective police work against the country's trafficking community, coupled with declining revenues from cocaine export, drove traffickers into rationalization of their activities. That is, they started entering into strategic alliances to obtain the best possible advantages from their manufacture and sale of their commodity. In the face of their growing problems members of the drug mafia, leaders of beleaguered FARC fronts, and demobilized remnants of the AUC did not hesitate to join forces in the pursuit of drug dollars. The best example of a drug capo who prospered through trafficker-FARC-paramilitary cooperation at the level of cocaine manufacture and export is that of Daniel "El Loco" Barrera. Barrera was a trafficker who had long helped FARC fronts move cocaine from eastern and northeastern Colombia to and through Venezuela. With the North Valle cartel's decline and ultimate demise in 2008, Barrera briefly managed the greater part of Colombia's illegal drug exports. Still early 2008 found him contemplating surrender to U.S. authorities in hopes that he might serve less time in an American prison than in a Colombian one. He ended not turning himself in but, rather, fleeing to Venezuela.[108]

Colombia may have tamed its illegal drug industry but it has not yet extinguished it. Former members of the demobilized paramilitary army AUC contribute to ongoing lawlessness in parts of Colombia. Significant numbers of them turned to illegal pursuits following AUC demobilization. In mid–2008 analysts put the numbers of such groups, often calling themselves *Águilas Negras* (Black Eagles), at between 6,000 and 8,000.[109] Colombian law enforcement agencies coined their own term to describe these groups: BACRIM (criminal gangs). As most paramilitary activity was financed through the illegal drug trade it is impossible to determine the degree to which these groups sprang from the AUC or from outright trafficking organizations. The distinction is immaterial to an extent because both were armed illegal groups. Yet the state is prevailing over these BACRIM through active prosecution of what some are calling Colombia's "Fourth War."[110] One such success involved the surrender of 108 members of "Los Rastrojos," the once–800-strong private army of North Valle cartel leader Wilber Varela ("Jabón"), who was killed during 2008.[111] Another blow against emergent criminal groups involved operations against a key trafficker of northwestern Colombia, Daniel Rendón ("Don Mario"). Rendón seized control of trafficking operations in northwestern Colombia following the extradition to the United States of his chief rival Diego Murillo ("Don Berna") in 2008. Rendón's arrest in San José de Apartadó in April 2009 was especially sweet to Colombia's law enforcement community, as the trafficker had offered $1,000 bounties for each police officer killed by his men.

Detail on the arrest of Daniel Rendón suggests the extent to which Colombia had progressed since the days when major traffickers could hire foreign mercenaries to train assassins, who, in turn, were unleashed upon anyone who dared oppose them. The pursuit of Rendón over a year's time was unremitting. All told, the police staged eighty operations within the capo's sphere of operations in Córdoba, Urabá, and Chocó. More than three hundred men from the National Police and Dijín participated in the operation leading to his capture. Among them was the commando group called the Police Anti-drug Jungle Unit, which had participated in the bombing of FARC leader Luis Edgar Dévia's camp a year earlier. By the end of the year-long pursuit of Daniel Rendón, 910 members of his trafficking organization had been arrested. Incredibly, during the year of hot pursuit by police, Rendón's BACRIM continued to ship multi-ton shipments of cocaine out of the country while at the same time conducting a bloody war with rival drug gangs during which more than a thousand died.[112]

What these vignettes from the annals of Colombian law enforcement suggest is that the country's struggle against the illegal drug trade is arduous and unending. They also reveal that the careers of drug capos in Colombia are growing increasingly brief. Nine bloody years passed from the time Pablo Escobar declared war on the Colombian state and his death on a Medellín rooftop. It took Colombian police just eighteen months to put an end to Daniel Rendón's career as the country's leading trafficker. Successes such as the one described here explain the continued downward trend seen in Colombian cocaine exports projected for the year 2009 and for future years as well.[113]

* * *

Colombia has been a victim of the globalized trade in illegal drugs. But the Andean nation has demonstrated that victimization can be ended through aggressive action. Colombia has taken arms against its illegal drug industry and put it on the defensive. In the process the state has grown stronger. But it has also grown weaker in terms of loss of national sovereignty. This, we are told, is the fate of all countries in today's interconnected world, but in Colombia's case its struggle against the illegal drug industry has led it to sacrifice its sovereignty to a rather extreme degree. The onslaught of drug-related violence during the late 1990s forced Colombia and the United States into cooperation unprecedented over the long span during which the two countries had enjoyed cordial relations. Mutual national security concerns lay behind the two nations' collaboration through Plan Colombia. At the end of the twentieth century, Colombia seemed close to being overwhelmed by violence financed by and rising from the illegal drug trade, and the United States was frightened by the ever-increasing flows of cocaine and heroin reaching U.S. streets from Colombia. It also it feared that the drug-related upset might destabilize the entire region of northern South America.

Over ten years' time U.S. aid was invaluable to Colombia in terms of strengthening its national security apparatus. On the other hand the aid forced Colombia to accede to U.S. wishes more than is usual in bilateral international relations, even in highly asymmetrical relationships. A few examples serve to illustrate. Alvaro Uribe's government did not hesitate to support the U.S. invasion of Iraq in March 2003 despite overwhelming opposition to the attack throughout Colombia. Under other circumstances Uribe's decision might have been different. But at that moment the Colombian President was huddled with his military and members of the U.S. Southern Command preparing to launch the operation that would end FARC encirclement of Bogotá. Uribe had no option other than to support the Bush administration's unpopular action.

There were similar though more complex issues involved in Uribe's decision to extradite the paramilitary leaders, despite his initial promise not to do so. During May 2008, Uribe did extradite the AUC leaders—to the applause of most Colombians. At one level the decision was in response to the *parapolítica* scandal that had raged over much of Uribe's second presidential term and which had sent thirty-three members of the national Congress to jail. The scandal raised fears that the politicians' links to paramilitary leaders had delegitimized the democratic process in the country.[114] Still none of this might have prompted Uribe's action in contradiction to his early assurances to AUC leaders were it not for U.S. insistence in early 2008 that the men be sent to stand trial on drug trafficking charges. At that moment there was serious need in Colombia for a continuation of Plan Colombia II funding from the U.S. The fact that the paramilitary leaders' extradition took place six or more years after their indictment in the United States had much to do with a debate among agencies within the American government. The Department of Justice and Drug Enforcement Agency had demanded immediate extradition of the AUC leaders, while the CIA and Department of State asked for postponement of extradition until such time that paramilitary demobilization was complete.[115] The latter two U.S. agencies obviously won the debate. Thus paramilitary extradition was inevitable regardless of any commitment made to them by Colombia's President. This places future peacemaking with Colombia's insurgent groups in some degree of jeopardy. *Violentos* having prior involvement with drug trafficking, which means most of them, will think twice before accepting Colombian government pledges to shield them from suffering the exemplary punishment mandated under harsh U.S. anti-drug laws.

The most recent complication arising from Colombia's marriage of convenience with the United States involves its relations with other South American nations, especially Venezuela and Ecuador. When Ecuador failed to renew the U.S. lease of its Pacific coast Manta military base, from which U.S. anti-drug surveillance flights had long originated, Colombia offered to let the Americans' AWAC and Orion surveillance aircraft make use of its principal air force base, Palanquero, northwest of Bogotá, and six other military bases scattered throughout the country. It was an eminently logical decision for Colombia, given its ongoing war against illegal drugs and drug-financed FARC insurgents. Members of Colombia's military were especially happy with the agreement because through it they gained exposure to advanced U.S. airborne surveillance technology. But the agreement raised loud objections from Venezuelan President Hugo Chávez, who accused Colombia of letting the U.S. establish a beachhead on its soil for a planned U.S. invasion of his country. Never mind that Colombian law permits the stationing of only 800 U.S. military personnel in the country, that the U.S. had been making use of Colombian air force bases since at least 1999, and that command of all bases involved remained in Colombian hands.

The agreement, signed in July 2009, strained Colombia's relations with other South American states as well, particularly Brazil and Chile, whose leaders also criticized the agreement.[116] The reaction of Brazil and Chile angered some in Colombia because it revealed the relative unconcern of those countries' leaders over Venezuela's aid to FARC guerrillas—the same organization that was bent on the violent overthrow of the democratically elected government of a sister republic.[117] However, Brazil and Chile's response was understandable at the level of ideology. A left-right dynamic was at work in the flap over U.S. use of Colombian military bases. Even though Alvaro Uribe was a member of the Liberal party he was widely seen as a man of the right. Brazil's Luiz Inácio Lula da Silva and Chile's President Michelle Bachelet, not to mention the presidents of Venezuela and Ecuador, all in office in 2009, were associated with the political left. Thus they were inclined to sympathize with the FARC's claim to be social reformers opposing an unjust state, a state that was furthermore was a lackey of the United States.

If the democratically elected leaders of some Latin American states showed little sympathy for Colombia's government in its struggle against the armed insurgency, other foreign politicians were actively involved in helping Colombia's communist insurgency. In 2007, for example, Swiss Senator Pierre Gontard was implicated in helping the FARC launder a half-million dollars that the group had extorted through a kidnapping. The money, which had been laundered through a Costa Rican bank, was later recovered through Interpol analysis of data contained on a computer of former FARC leader Luis Edgar Devia.[118]

Influential groups within Colombia also oppose their national government as presently constituted, and share the FARC's loathing of the Colombo-U.S. alliance. In some cases this leads them to collaborate with the FARC and the ELN. During 2009 several members of Colombia's congress were placed under investigation on charges of working within the political system to promote FARC interests. The matter was referred to as the FARC-*política* scandal.[119] Left-wing labor unions also have a long tradition of supporting guerrilla groups in Colombia and of welcoming their cadres as members. A director of the agrarian union Fensuagro was apprehended at a FARC camp during June 2009. Two years earlier representatives from three Colombian unions attended an international congress held in Quito, Ecuador, in which members of the FARC and ELN also participated. At the end of the meeting the Colombian union officials signed a final document endorsing the guerrillas' "all forms of struggle" doctrine justifying the pursuit of social change through both legal and illegal means.[120] This linking of democratic process and armed struggle has muddied the waters of political reform in Colombia since the country's guerrillas embraced it as a route to seizing power during the 1960s. It has consistently generated violence against left politicians, as seen in the annihilation of the FARC's Unión Patriótica party by narco-paramilitary leaders during the 1980s. The "combination of all forms of struggle" has been an anchor around the necks of Colombia's democratic left up to the present moment. Endorsement of the doctrine within Colombia has also helped create uncertainties in the minds of foreigners regarding how they should perceive the guerrillas within the setting of the nation's reform efforts.

Negative impressions of Colombia have long been conveyed by influential Colombian academics and journalists. Their negativism springs from the class-analysis paradigm through which they indict Colombia's unequal society. Because such criticism has dominated public discourse in the country for six decades, it has contributed to the difficulties foreigners have in grasping Colombia's complex realities. All of this predisposes foreigners to approach Colombia with little understanding or sympathy. The country's close relationship with the United States has merely heightened the negative impression of Colombia in many quarters.

At a fundamental level it does not matter what the world thinks of Colombia. The important thing is that on election day of 2002, people of the country resolved to set things right. With their votes they made Álvaro Uribe their agent of change. Uribe justified their decision, and with the help of a great many people saw his program of Democratic Security through to a successful conclusion. Colombians signaled their desire to continue Uribe's pro-security initiatives when they elected his former Minister of Defense Juan Manuel Santos to succeed him in the presidency during 2010. From this perspective it is perhaps best to view both Uribe and Santos as symbols of the Colombian public's ability to act when sufficiently provoked.

Conclusion

Victim of Globalization

"*Kings of Cocaine* traces America's drug epidemic back to its chief source—the
murderous Colombian drug-smuggling group known as the Medellín cartel."
—Dust jacket of *Kings of Cocaine*, Guy Gugliotta and Jeff Leen, 1989[1]

Words like "jaw-dropping" and "astonishing" are commonly used to describe events of
the illegal drug trade between Colombia and the United States. When cocaine became the
recreational drug of choice among the U.S. glitterati around 1980, and crack cocaine swept
through urban ghettos a few years later, Colombians were cast as the villains in the illegal drug
drama. Who can forget the scene in the 1983 film *Scarface* when hard-faced Colombian traffickers in Miami use a chain saw to execute a young Cuban-American rival? Viewers are informed
somewhat unnecessarily that "the Colombians are the worst of all."

Americans were aware that their illegal drug use generated violence in Colombia, but
were not especially concerned about it. High school students were admonished that when they
smoked marijuana they killed a Colombian; as a result they began using "killing a Colombian"
as a euphemism for lighting up a joint.

Colombia's illegal drug trade, the violence and crime flowing from it, and the country's
successful struggle to quell the disorder, stand at the center of this study. Colombia and its
people paid a fearful price for their involvement in the illegal enterprise. The story told here
is of a South American nation having no prior history of illegal drug exportation becoming
the chief supplier to U.S. consumers, first of marijuana, then of cocaine. This extraordinary
development in Colombian economic history took place at lightning speed. When the United
States government poisoned Mexican marijuana through aerial fumigation during 1970 and
1971, U.S. traffickers responded by flying a bit farther south, to Colombia, cash in hand, drawing
citizens of that country into a fateful economic relationship. The outcome is well known.
Soon Colombians were satisfying U.S. demand not only for marijuana but for vastly more
lucrative cocaine. Thousands of Colombians involved in the illegal drug trade paid with their
lives, and many innocent victims of the drug-related violence died as well. Colombia ended
by becoming the American nation most affected by the international trade in illegal drugs.

The inability of states to control markets, revealed here in the United States' inability
to halt its own citizens' use of cocaine, also victimized Colombia. During the golden age of

Colombian cocaine export, 1978–1984, the alkaloid poured into the U.S. largely undetected and unchecked. When the governments of both countries at last began moving against Colombian traffickers in 1983, the cocaine industry was entrenched in both places. By that time Colombia's leading traffickers were wealthy and powerful. They reacted to the attempt to shut down their business by declaring war on the Colombian state. The cartel war lasted ten bloody years, ending symbolically with Pablo Escobar's death at the hands of Colombian security forces on December 2, 1993. The latter years of Colombia's struggle against illegal drugs, 1994–2002, were complicated by a civil war pitting Marxist guerrilla insurgents against paramilitary armies. Finally, between 2002 and 2008, an energized Colombian State took on both the guerrillas and the paramilitary forces, bringing the civil war to an end. Throughout Colombia's "New Violence," the forces of disorder depended on revenues generated by illegal drug sales. That was the case throughout the entire period of disorder, 1975–2008. Ultimately some 300,000 Colombians died in the course of the country's drug-suffused New Violence.

Important to this work is the didactic quality of the Colombian experience. It tells of a mid-sized developing nation laboriously learning how to dominate its illegal narcotics industry and the violence flowing from it. Colombia's achievement is all the more notable because it was the first Western Hemisphere state to confront the massive disruptions in public life rising from illegal drug production and supply. Notably, Colombia addressed this problem through democratic means. Even as violence spiraled to unprecedented levels elections were held at regular four-year intervals. That was the case even at the height of the violence in 1998, when peace candidate Andrés Pastrana was elected in the hope that FARC guerrillas would enter into meaningful peace negotiations with his government. Four years later, when it was clear that the FARC would not lay down their weapons, Colombians elected law-and-order President Alvaro Uribe. Uribe's subsequent attack on the FARC and all other law-breakers proved so effective that Colombians awarded him an unprecedented second presidential term in 2006. When Uribe left office in 2010 voters chose his former Minister of Defense, Juan Manuel Santos, to succeed him. Santos pledged to continue Uribe's hard line against law breakers. By then the FARC were defeated and close to initiating legitimate peace talks.

Illegal Drugs and Colombia's New Violence

"The great massacres in this country have been closely linked to drug trafficking."
—Historian Toño Sánchez, Jr., 2003[2]

By 1965 Colombia's ugly low-level civil war known as the *Violencia* had ended. That conflict, beginning in 1947, pitted members of the country's Liberal and Conservative parties against one another. The *Violencia* ended besmirching Colombia's image. Before that diffuse civil war Colombia was known as Latin America's foremost democracy and economic success story. By the 1950s it was viewed as a violent place where citizens slaughtered one another for little apparent reason. In 1958, however, the country's political leaders came together to restore political stability and end the *Violencia* by the year 1965. Colombia went on to enjoy a decade of civil peace, lasting from the latter 1960s through the first years of the 1970s. How sad, then, that precisely during that span of time foreign narcotics traffickers, most of them from the United States, descended on the country in search of merchandise. Once they found Colombians willing to supply it to them, the country's window of peace closed. Colombia's involvement in the international narcotics trade opened a Pandora's box of evils, the most damaging of which was extreme civil violence.

Colombia's new drug-money-inspired violence had a devastating impact on the national psyche. Because the source of the New Violence was imperfectly perceived, following the end of the *Violencia* by just ten years, many Colombians incorrectly concluded that violence had been continuous in their country since 1947. Flowing from that misconception was the assumption that they might simply be violent by nature. As violence levels rose during the cartel war of the 1980s and early 1990s, becoming a full-fledged civil war between the mid–1990s and the first years of the twenty-first century, opinion-makers in Colombia and elsewhere reported that the country was condemned to never-ending war. They did this in a swelling stream of newspaper op-ed pieces, academic presentations, and book-length studies bearing titles like *A Country of Barbarians* and *Hot Lead Nation*.[3] Analysts of the New Violence came to be known as *violentólogos*. Their gloomy assessment of the new disorder, and its relationship to what they perceived as national character flaws, overlay the long-standing critique among academics that Colombia was an inequitable place given over to ongoing social violence. Sober and restrained by nature, Colombians grew depressed about their country, its prospects, and about themselves as well.[4] At the dawn of the twenty-first century, when their civil war was at its worst, half of Colombia's forty-three million people contemplated emigration. In 1999 alone a quarter-million of them purchased one-way tickets out of the country. When questioned about their decision to emigrate, half of them responded that Colombia had become "unlivable." Meanwhile another three million citizens living in the countryside were internally displaced by warfare raging between guerrilla and paramilitary armies.[5]

Only toward the end of their New Violence of 1975–2008 did Colombians come to understand that illegal drug money was the real source of the conflict. That understanding allowed them to be persuaded that they were neither barbarous by nature nor condemned to endless wars of social retribution. It also made clear to them what they needed to do to end the bloodletting.

Making sense of Colombia's New Violence has been the aim of this history. Previous works on Colombia's New Violence focus on one or another of its component parts. In this work each source of disorder—traffickers, guerrilla insurgents, and paramilitary forces—is examined independently while taking care to show their interconnection with other causative factors. The end result is to recount the same history from different perspectives. What emerges is a nuanced though sometimes contradictory view of events all the while keeping before them their linkage to the common coin of Colombia's recent bloodshed, the illegal drug trade.

Post-Conflict Colombia

"We are inspired and greatly admiring of all Colombia has accomplished."

* * *

"Over the last eight years of our Democratic Security Policy we have been able to move forward toward democratic prosperity and to think about issues that go beyond the internal security situation."
—Remarks exchanged by U.S. Secretary of State Hillary Rodham Clinton and Colombian Foreign Minister María Ángela Holguín, May 31, 2011[6]

Colombians are among the world's happiest people.[7] And why shouldn't they be? They are confident and hard-working as a group, they are pacific and law-abiding in general, and

Table 1. Homicides in Colombia per 100,000 population, 1965–2010

1965: 28	1975: 24	1984: 32	1993: 72	2002: 66
1966: 27	1976: 25	1985: 39	1994: 68	2003: 53
1967: 27	1977: 26	1986: 48	1995: 65	2004: 44
1968: 28	1978: 25	1987: 50	1996: 67	2005: 39
1970: 21	1979: 28	1988: 64	1997: 64	2006: 40
1971: 22	1980: 31	1989: 66	1998: 63	2007: 39
1972: 22	1981: 35	1990: 68	1999: NA	2008: 36
1973: 21	1982: 34	1991: 75	2000: 63	2009: 35
1974: 23	1983: 33	1992: 74	2001: 65	2010: 36

SOURCES: Juan Carlos Echeverry, Natalia Salazar, Verónica Navas, "El conflicto colombiano en el contexto internacional," in Astrid Martínez Ortiz, ec., *Economía, crímen y conflicto* (Bogotá: Universidad Nacional de Colombia, 2001) 97; Colombian National Police.

they live in one of Latin America's most economically dynamic and politically stable nations, one that over the past century rarely experienced the painful economic fluctuations of a Brazil, a Mexico, or an Argentina. Colombia averages three percent GDP growth or better decade after decade, even in times of social upset.[8] How strange, then, that even as the country prospered it lived simultaneously through three decades of crime and violence that ending placing its judicial and armed forces in check. These apparent contradictions make Colombia a difficult subject of study.

By 2012 Colombia had emerged from its time of troubles and was involved in post-conflict activity aimed at addressing all the sources of social disruption. Its success in so doing instructs other Latin American nations, particularly those troubled by narcotics trafficking. Mexico, for example, recently found itself fighting the same war against drug cartels that Colombia successfully waged twenty years earlier. But the Mexican experience differs from Colombia's. Colombia was the first American state to be attacked from within by unimaginably wealthy drug traffickers capable of challenging a weak national state and willing to stop at nothing to protect their illegal enterprise and themselves. The way Colombian traffickers formed strategic alliances with other anti-state actors—the guerrillas and the paramilitaries—set the Andean nation apart from her sister republics. For these reasons Colombia's drug-related violence was particularly virulent and difficult to control. It progressively corrupted, broke down, and nearly overwhelmed the state's judicial and law enforcement systems.

Post-conflict Colombia is marked by a concerted effort to integrate violence and drug-trafficking parts of the country into the greater nation. Doing so is difficult because Colombia has been historically neglectful of its rural population, today making up a quarter of its forty-five million inhabitants. Yet the recent ordeal has strengthened the Colombian state and positioned it to meet the needs of its rural-dwelling citizens. This is because the country is close to ending the armed guerrilla insurgency that has plagued it for the past fifty years.

Little more than a month after the 2010 presidential inauguration of former Defense Minister Juan Manuel Santos, Colombians received word that the armed forces had killed FARC military chief Víctor Suárez ("El Mono Jojoy") in a massive attack on his camp in La Macarena, Meta. Suárez was one of a dozen commanders of FARC fronts killed over the course of 2010.

Table 2. Extortionate Kidnappings in Colombia, 1965–2010			
1965: negligible	1977: negligible	1989: 917	2001: 3,078
1966: negligible	1978: negligible	1990: 1,017	2002: 2,986
1967: negligible	1979: negligible	1991: 1,616	2003: 2,121
1968: negligible	1980: 25	1992: 1,078	2004: 1,440
1969: negligible	1981: 73	1993: 1,001	2005: 800
1970: negligible	1982: 89	1994: 1,497	2006: 687
1971: negligible	1983: 150	1995: 1,260	2007: 521
1972: negligible	1984: 299	1996: 1,250	2008: 437
1973: negligible	1985: 257	1997: 1,986	2009: 213
1974: negligible	1986: 215	1998: 2,216	2010: 282
1975: negligible	1987: 387	1999: 2,945	
1976: negligible	1988: 751	2000: 3,706	

SOURCES: Jorge A. Restrepo, Michael Spagat, Juan F. Vargas, "The Dynamics of the Colombian Civil Conflict: A New Data Set."

Three months after Suárez' death commandos of the police Anti-Drug Jungle Unit killed Pedro Oliverio Guerrero ("Cuchillo"), the principal trafficker of illegal drugs in the eastern part of the country. Known as "the assassin of assassins," Guerrero died December 24, 2010, at a site near Mapiripán, Meta.[9]

Actions leading to killing or imprisoning perpetrators of violence such as these explain the sharp declines in Colombian homicide rates following implementation of the Democratic Security program crafted by Álvaro Uribe, and continued under his successor Santos. Table 1, left, reveals the parabola of violent deaths in Colombia from the country's relatively benign decade of peace, 1965–1975, through its rise during the "golden moment" of cocaine export to the United States, 1975–1985. It indicates the steep increase in homicides during the Medellín cartel's war against the Colombian state between 1984 and the first years of the 1990s. And it reveals the skyrocketing of killings in Colombia from the mid–1990s to Uribe's presidency, a time when guerrilla and paramilitary groups fought for precedence in Colombia's rural areas. Finally, Table 1 reveals the sharp drop in homicides occurring when Alvaro Uribe took office and launched his Democratic Security program.

Table 2, above, showing extortionate kidnappings in Colombia, tracks both the increase in strength of Colombia's guerrilla insurgents and their turn to kidnapping as a means to finance their revolutionary project. The sharp drop in kidnapping in Colombia after 2002 likewise reflects the success of Uribe's Democratic Security program, and, particularly, the Colombian army's Patriot Plan offensive against the FARC between 2004 and 2008. It was guerrillas of the FARC and the ELN who turned Colombia into the "kidnapping capital of the world" during the late 1990s.

The improvements in public order in Colombia described here correspond closely to and are the product of reforms in the nation's armed forces, particularly its army and related forces, extending back to the early 1990s. Increases in military spending were integral to improvements in public safety in Colombia during the first decade of the twenty-first century. Table 3, below, reveals the increased revenue devoted to Colombia's armed forces during years between the country's post–*Violencia* years to the time of Uribe's Democratic Security program. The country's parsimony in armed forces funding during 1975–2002 is striking when considered along-

Table 3. Armed Forces Funding as a Percentage of GDP, 1965–present

1965–1988: 1.5 percent	2000–2002: 2.3 percent	2006–present: 4.6 percent
1988–2000: 2 percent	2002–2006: 3.5 percent	

Sources: Camilo Granada, "La evolución del gasto en seguridad y defensa en Colombia, 1950–1994," in Malcolm Deas and María Victoria Llorente, comps., *Reconocer la guerra para construir la paz* (Bogotá: Editorial Norma, 1999), 539–597; Republic of Colombia, Nacional Planning Department and Department of Justice and Security, "Plan Colombia Progress Report, 1999–2005 (Bogotá: Departamento Nacional de Planeación, September 2006), 17; *Semana*, "El precio de la seguridad," May 25, 2009, 42–43.

side data contained in tables 1 and 2, above, reflecting the country's descent into civil warfare and generalized lawlessness.

Table 4, below, showing cocaine production in Colombia between 1965 and the present day, is key to understanding Colombia's New Violence. Export of this commodity to the global market tracks perfectly with the deterioration of public order in the country between 1975 and 2002. The sharp and ongoing decline in cocaine production in Colombia after 2002 severely weakened criminal and anti-state forces in the country.

Thanks to the pacification of its national territory Colombian leaders began devoting increased attention to international affairs. This brought improved relations with the country's neighboring states, particularly with Venezuela. Over the first seven months of the administration of Juan Manuel Santos, Colombia signed seventeen accords with the government of Hugo Chávez, one of which addressed the cross-border flow of illegal drugs. At the regional level Latin America's third most populous nation gave signs that it was emerging as a significant force in regional diplomacy thus leaving behind decades of relative isolation from international

Table 4. Estimated Cocaine Manufacture in Colombia in Metric Tons, 1965–2010

1965: negligible	1975: 20	1985: 145	1995: 230	2005: 545
1966: negligible	1976: 30	1986: 185	1996: 300	2006: 540
1967: negligible	1977: 50	1987: 230	1997: 350	2007: 395
1968: negligible	1978: 79	1988: 270	1998: 435	2008: 295
1969: negligible	1979: 90	1989: 250	1999: 550	2009: 270
1970: negligible	1980: 135	1990: 240	2000: 577	2010: 290
1971: negligible	1981: 153	1991: 230	2001: 694	
1972: 1	1982: 191	1992: 250	2002: 623	
1973: 2	1983: 206	1993: 290	2003: 510	
1974: 13	1984: 110	1994: 300	2004: 484	

SOURCES: These figures represent estimated maximum cocaine production capacity, and are derived from numerous sources. Useful sources on Colombian cocaine production for the 1970s are Antonil, *Mama Coca*, and Fabio Castillo, *Los jinetes*. For the 1980s see Sewell Menzel, *Cocaine Quagmire*, and Francisco Thoumy, *Political Economy*. For the 1990s see Eduardo Pizarro, *Una democracia asediada*, and Dominic Streatfield, *Cocaine*. Sources for further research on these decades are contained in Bruce M. Bagley, ed., *Drug Trafficking Research in the Americas: An Annotated Bibliography* (Boulder: Lynne Rienner Publishers, 1996). Official estimates for cocaine production in recent years are published on-line by the United Nations Office on Drugs and Crime, by the U.S. Government in its *International Narcotics Control Strategy Reports*, and by the Colombian Government, especially *Presidencia de la República* and National Police of Colombia.

forums. Over the first months of the Santos administration the new president played significant roles in meetings of the United Nations and the Organization of American States. Santos also moved Colombia toward membership in the Organization of Economic Cooperation and Development (OECD).[10]

The notable inequality among Colombians was addressed in May 2011 when the country's Congress approved a complex piece of legislation called the Law of Victims, authorizing monetary compensation for the thousands of victims of the New Colombian Violence. The new law also addressed the problem of the many citizens who lost their land during the conflict, land estimated at 6.6 million hectares (16.3 million acres). Under provisions of the Law of Victims the estimated four million Colombians who fled the countryside during the civil war could reclaim what they lost.[11] The law played a role in the decision of the FARC to enter into peace talks with the government in October 2012.

Defeat in the field was the overriding factor forcing FARC guerrillas into peace talks. Thanks to improvements at every level of the Colombian military, FARC guerrillas were no longer safe from death in military engagements, especially through air strikes. That was how the group's leader Guillermo Sáenz ("Alfonso Cano") met his end in eastern Cauca in November 2011.[12] Early in 2012, thirty-six mid-level FARC commanders were killed by Air Force bombs while attending a training course in Arauca.[13] And even as FARC Secretariat member Jorge Torres ("Pablo Catatumbo") talked peace with government representatives in Havana, Cuba, the man Torres left to replace him in the field, Jorge Eliécer Zambrano ("Caliche") and seven other FARC members were killed in an Air Force bombing in western Cauca.[14]

Those ongoing reverses led the FARC's closest allies at the international level to join the chorus asking them to demobilize. In one of his last public remarks prior to his death in early 2013 Hugo Chávez said he hoped that the FARC would "jump into politics without firearms."[15] It was a sentiment echoed by Ecuador's Rafael Correa, Bolivia's Evo Morales, and other left-leaning Latin American Presidents. FARC leaders dragged out peace negotiations with the Santos administration chiefly because of the government's demand that they stand trial for crimes they were charged with, and to serve jail time if convicted. FARC leaders especially feared extradition to the United States to face narcotics trafficking charges following their reentry into Colombian civil society. This fear was based on the fate of paramilitary leaders who had agreed to serve jail time for their crimes following their demobilization in 2008. Shortly after that date Álvaro Uribe surprisingly had them extradited them to the U.S. to stand trial on drug trafficking charges. They were quickly sentenced to lengthy terms in U.S. federal prisons.[16] The FARC's fear of extradition to the United States played a role in their renunciation of cocaine trafficking in late 2013. The previous year the group had announced that it would cease extortionate kidnapping.[17]

Unlike the paramilitary leaders, FARC and ELN commanders hoped to escape imprisonment when they at last demobilized.[18] Colombians have a long history of granting amnesty to revolutionaries. It was that forgiving attitude that led Colombians to re-elect Juan Manuel Santos to a second presidential term in June 2014, in preference over a hardline candidate supported by Álvaro Uribe. During his campaign Santos assured Colombians that he would sign a peace agreement with the FARC by the end of 2014. should that occur santos would find himself in the company of earlier generations of Colombian leaders who ended episodes of civil violence through democratic political means.

Questions remained for Colombia as they always do when assessing this complex nation.

Would Colombians act to make good on the promises contained in the country's progressive 1991 constitution? Would their leaders create a democratic and non-violent movement capable of channeling the pent-up desire for social reform that runs deep in the country? Would Colombia continue to lead Latin America in democratic governance and consistent economic growth? Those who know the country believe that the answer to these questions is "Yes."

Glossary

ACCU: United Self-Defense Forces of Córdoba and Urabá (*Autodefensas Unidas de Córdoba y Urabá*).

ACDEGAM: Farmers and Cattleman's Association of the Middle Magdalena (*Asociación Campesina de Agricultores y Ganaderos del Magdalena Medio*).

Alcalde: Mayor of a town.

Alkaloids: A family of more than 900 organic compounds found in many plants. When consumed they produce physiological effects involving the brain. Morphine, codeine, and cocaine are alkaloids.

Apuntería: The system of buying shares in cocaine shipments.

Armed clientelism: The process of increasing political influence at the local level through coercion and violence.

AUC: United Self-Defense Forces of Colombia (*Autodefensas Unidas de Colombia*).

BACRIM: Acronym for criminal bands that emerged following paramilitary demobilization; many of them are involved in drug trafficking.

Bajo Cauca: The lower reaches of the Cauca River, extending from northeastern Antioquia into southern parts of the departments of Sucre and Bolívar.

Banana Axis: The region around the Gulf of Urabá where Colombia's banana industry is located.

BCB: Central Bolívar Block (*Bloque Central Bolívar*) of the AUC.

BNDD: U.S. Bureau of Narcotics and Dangerous Drugs.

Bonanza marimbera **(Marijuana Bonanza):** The peak of the marijuana trade in Colombia extending from the mid–1970s into the early 1980s.

Cabecera: Equivalent to county seat in the U.S.

Campesino: A country person, a farmer.

Caserío: Hamlet, or group of houses located in the countryside.

Cleared Zone: See *Zona de Despeje.*

Cocaine base: The substance resulting from the refining of the paste (*pasta*) derived from coca leaves. In the mid–1980s it sold in Colombia at $1,800 per kilo, while a kilo of cocaine sold for $6,000.

Cocaleros: Traffickers dealing in coca growing and cocaine production.

Coffee Axis: The region in Colombia's Andean Central Cordillera running from Quindío northward into Antioquia, where most of Colombia's coffee is grown.

Comandos populares: "People's commandos." Militias formed in Urabá by demobilized EPL members during the early 1990s, to resist attacks by FARC guerrillas.

Comunas: Slums ringing Medellín.

Concejales: City council members.

Concejo: City council.

Costeño: Person from the Caribbean coastal region of Colombia.

Creole: A person of European descent.

DAS: National Office of Security; Colombia's FBI (*Departamento Nacional de Seguridad*).

Department: The largest administrative subdivision in Colombia; equivalent to a state in the United States.

Dijín: Dirección Central de Policía Judicial e Investigación. Anti-drug unit of the Colombian police.

Eastern Llanos: A plains area shared by Colombia and Venezuela, lying east of the Eastern Cordillera of the Andes Mountains and bound on the east by the Orinoco River.

Eje bananaro: See Banana Axis.

Eje cafetero: See Coffee Axis.

ELN: National Liberation Army (*Ejército de Liberación Nacional*).

EPL: Popular Liberation Army (*Ejército Popular de Liberación*).

Esperanzados: "Hopeful ones." The name given to demobilized members of the EPL guerrilla group who demobilized in 1991, going on to form the Peace, Justice, and Liberty Party (*Esperanza, Paz y Libertad*).

FARC: Colombian Revolutionary Armed Forces (*Fuerza Revolucionaria Armada Colombiana*).

Finca: A farm or ranch.

Foco **theory:** The revolutionary strategy of Ernesto "Che" Guevara, based in forming armed rural enclaves.

Fronts: Operational units of guerrilla groups; a fighting force ideally running from 30 to 300 soldiers.

Fronts, paramilitary: Operational units of indeterminate size affiliated with regional blocks.

FUNPAZCORD: Foundation for Peace in Córdoba (*Fundación para la paz en Córdoba*). Established in 1991 when paramilitary forces of Fidel Castaño reached a peace accord with EPL guerrillas.

Gringo: Term commonly used in Colombia to describe a person from the United States.

Iron triangle of violence: Term used to describe Colombia's stubborn crime and violence as a function of the country's broken terrain, its weak government, and its lawbreakers' ability to take advantage of both thereby acting with a high degree of impunity.

Justice Minister (*Ministro de Justicia*): Equivalent to the U.S. Attorney General.

Law of Metal: Accept a bribe or be shot. Also known as *plata o plomo* (money or lead).

M-19: The populist revolutionary guerrilla group originating in the ANAPO movement of Gustavo Rojas Pinilla.

MAS: Death to Kidnappers (*Muerte a Secuestradores*): The paramilitary group organized in 1981 by Colombian cocaine traffickers.

Mona: Blond; a variety of Colombian marijuana known in the U.S. as Colombia Gold.

Mules: Those who smuggle drugs, often in their stomachs or body cavities.

Municipio: Equivalent to a county in the United States. It's administrative center is called the *cabecera*, where administrative offices are located.

Office, or collection office (*oficina*, or *oficina de cobro*): The place from which trafficking organizations exercised discipline on employees and competitors.

Padrino: Literally "godfather." In Colombian criminal parlance, the one who gives the orders.

Paisa: A person from the department of Antioquia.

Páramo: Treeless and cold regions of the Andes found at elevations of more than 10,000 feet.

Parapolítica: The name given to a political scandal during the administration of Álvaro Uribe Vélez, concerning links between paramilitary leaders and elected officials.

Pasta **(paste):** The grayish substance derived from coca leaves, at the first stage of cocaine production. During the mid–1980s it sold in Colombia for $600 (U.S.) per kilo, one-tenth the price of one kilo of cocaine.

PEPES: *Persiguidos por Pablo Escobar* (Persecuted by Pablo Escobar). A group established by Fidel Castaño in 1993 dedicated to killing Escobar.

Pesca milagrosa: Miraculous fishing trips. The guerrilla practice of stopping Colombians at surprise roadblocks and kidnapping for ransom those judged to be the most affluent.

Psychoactive drug: Drugs that affect the mind or behavior.

Punta roja: Red-tip, a variety of Colombian marijuana.

Raspachín: One who harvests coca leaves.

Rubia: Blond; a variety of Colombian marijuana known in the U.S. as Colombia gold.

SAC: Society of Colombian Farmers (Sociedad de Agricultores de Colombia).

Sicario: Assassin. A person hired specifically to carry out a murder.

Suplente: A stand-in for an elected senator or representative. Abolished in the Constitution of 1991.

Tangueros: Members of Fidel Castaño's paramilitary army headquartered in his ranch *Las Tangas*, 1985–1991.

Traquetos: Lower-level traffickers. From the word *traficar*, to traffic. Also said to be An onomatopoeic term derived from the noise made by a machine gun.

Vacuna: Protection money paid to guerrilla groups as insurance against kidnapping or other crimes.

Ventanilla siniestra: Tellers' window in Colombia's central bank during the late 1970s and early 1980s where money earned through illegal drug sales could be deposited.

Violencia: A low-level civil war between Liberal and Conservative party members beginning in 1947 and ending in 1965.

Violentólogos: Coined during the late 1980s to describe academics and journalists in Colombia and elsewhere specialized in study of Colombian violence.

Zona de Despeje **(also *Zona de Distensión*):** The "Cleared Zone." The 42,000 kilometer square area in Caquetá and Meta granted to the FARC between late 1998 and February 2002 in exchange for entering into peace talks with the Colombian government.

Zonas de ubicación: Areas set aside for paramilitary demobilization during 2003–2006.

Chapter Notes

Introduction

1. Saúl Franco states that 338,378 Colombians were victims of homicide between 1975 and 1995. See: *El quinto: No matar. Contextos explicativos de la violencia en Colombia* (Bogotá: Editorial Tercer Mundo, 1999), 1, 31–39. Franco sees the rise of the illegal drug trade as central to Colombia's rising homicide rate after 1975.

2. Robert Sabbag, *Loaded. A Misadventure on the Marijuana Trail* (Boston: Little, Brown, 2002), 45.

3. There are a great many works on *La Violencia*, among them the present writer's *When Colombia Bled: A History of the Violencia in Tolima* (Tuscaloosa: University of Alabama Press, 1985).

4. Herman Schwartz, *States versus Markets. The Emergence of a Global Economy*, 2nd ed. (New York: St. Martin's Press, 2000), xii.

5. This is demonstrated in John M. Walsh, "Connecting the Dots. ONDCP's (Reluctant) Update on Cocaine Price and Purity" (Washington, D.C.: Washington Office on Latin America, April 23, 2007).

6. José R. Fuentes, "Life of a Cell: Managerial Practice and Strategy in Colombian Cocaine Distribution in the United States" (Ph.D. dissertation, City University of New York, 1998), 276.

7. David Bushnell, *The Making of Modern Colombia. A Nation in Spite of Itself* (Berkley: The University of California Press, 1993), vii.

8. For example in one much-read volume Mario Arrubla dismissed previous generations of national historians as apologists whose works contained "equal measures of ingenuousness and hypocrisy." *Colombia hoy*, 6th ed. (Bogotá: Siglo Veintiuno Editores, 1980), 7.

9. Notable collections of these writings appeared during the 1970s and '80s. Chief among them were Jaime Jaramillo Uribe, ed., *Manual de historia de Colombia*, 3 vols. (Bogotá: Instituto Colombiano de Cultura, 1978–80), and Alvaro Tirado Mejía, ed., *La Nueva Historia de Colombia*, 6 vols. (Bogotá: Editorial Planeta, 1989).

10. Gonzalo Sánchez, ed. *Colombia: Violencia y democracia. Informe presentado al Ministerio de Gobierno* (Bogotá: Universidad Nacional de Colombia, Instituto de Estudios Políticos y Relaciones Internacionales, 1987).

11. William Ospina's assessment of his country and its people, found in a 2003 essay, is that "the case of Colombian society over the past fifty years is that of a criminal State that has criminalized the entire country." See Eduardo Posada Carbó, *La nación que soñamos* (Bogotá: Editorial Norma, 2006), 230.

12. Exemplary of this new approach to violence scholarship in Colombia are the essays collected in Astrid Martínez Ortiz, ed., *Economía, crímen y conflicto* (Bogotá: Universidad Nacional de Colombia, Facultad de Ciencia Económica, 2001).

13. The best example of this new Colombian optimism is Eduardo Posada Carbó's *La nación soñada. Violencia, liberalismo y democracia en Colombia* (Bogotá: Editorial Norma, 2006).

Chapter 1

1. Russell Ramsey, *Guerrilleros y soldado* (Bogotá: Editorial Tercer Mundo, 1981), 318.

2. On this point see James D. Henderson, "Progreso económico y cambio social: de Ospina Pérez al Frente Nacional," *La modernización en Colombia. Los años de Laureano Gómez, 1889–1965* (Medellín: Editorial Universidad de Antioquia, 2006), 475–509.

3. Deaths for each year of the *Violencia* are found in James D. Henderson, *La modernización en Colombia*, 618.

4. The best study of the Bogotá riot is Herbert Braun, *The Assassination of Gaitán: Public Life and Urban Violence in Colombia* (Madison: University of Wisconsin Press, 1985).

5. James D. Henderson, *La modernización en Colombia*, 618.

6. Carlos Lleras Restrepo, the third president under the National Front accord, was not related to Alberto Lleras Camargo, the first National Front president.

7. Details of these events are found in James Henderson, *Modernization in Colombia*, 348–379.

8. ANAPO stands for National Popular Alliance (*Alianza Nacional Popular*).

9. A play on words in Spanish, it was called "la ventanilla siniestra." In that context the word "siniestra" can mean either "on the left" or "sinister."

10. Two histories of the ELN are Carlos Medina Gallego, *ELN: Una historia contada dos veces* (Bogotá: Roberto Quito Editores, 1996), and Alejo Vargas, *Guerra o solución negociada. ELN: Origen, evolución y procesos de paz* (Bogotá: Circulo de Lectores, 2006).

11. A fact recently established in Harvard University's study of the degree of "geographic fragmentation" in 155 nations.

12. The connection between coffee and the war are explored in Charles Bergquist, *Coffee and Conflict in Colombia, 1886–1910* (Durham: Duke University Press, 1978).

13. This is calculated on the basis of 70,000 dead over three years, in a country of five million people.

14. Political power-sharing did not end fully until the administration of Virgilio Barco, 1986–1990. While López Michelsen's was the last of the four power-sharing presidencies stipulated in the National Front agreement, the country's two succeeding chief executives honored the agreement's power-sharing ideal in cabinet-level and lesser appointments.

15. Events surrounding the Medellín Massacre are recounted in Guy Gugliotta and Jeff Leen, *Kings of Cocaine. Inside the Medellín Cartel—an Astonishing True Story of Murder, Money, and International Corruption* (New York: Simon and Schuster, 1989), 22.

16. David F. Musto, *The American Disease: Origins of Narcotic Control* (New Haven: Yale University Press, 1973).

17. Both were sold for nasal congestion. Agnew's Powder was 99 percent cocaine. Julia Buxton, *The Political Economy of Narcotics: Production, Consumption and Global Markets* (New York: Palgrave, 2006), 15.

18. Useful sketches on early drug use in the U.S. are found in David Musto, *The American Disease*, 1–5, and James P. Gray, *Why Our Drug Laws Have Failed and What We Can Do About It* (Philadelphia: Temple University Press, 2001), 20–21. The history of cocaine is told in Paul Gootenberg, *Andean Cocaine: The Making of a Global Drug* (Chapel Hill: University of North Carolina Press, 2009).

19. By David Musto's estimate, in *The American Disease*, 5, there were 250,000 drug addicts in the United States in the year 1900.

20. James Gray, *Why Our Drug Laws Have Failed*, 23, 28.

21. James Gray, *Why Our Drug Laws Have Failed*, 25.

22. Good accounts of Anslinger's anti-marijuana campaign are found in David Musto, *The American Disease*, 192–221; James Gray, *Why Our Drug Laws Have Failed*, 20–28; and Ron Mann, director, *Grass*, narrated by Woody Harrelson (Sphinx Productions, 2000), 80 minutes.

23. Described in Tom Wolfe, *The Electric Kool-Aid Acid Test* (New York: Farrar, Straus & Giroux, 1968).

24. Dominic Streatfield, *Cocaine: An Unauthorized Biography* (New York: Thomas Dunne Books, 2001), 199.

25. The term "mythic status" is that of Robert Sabbag, who wrote the history of marijuana smuggler Gary Long, in *Loaded: A Misadventure on the Marijuana Trail* (Boston: Little, Brown and Company, 2002).

26. Robert Sabbag, *Loaded*.

27. Dominic Streatfield, *Cocaine*, 232.

28. Adler, Lou. *Up in Smoke*, starring Cheech Marin and Tommy Chong. 1978. 85 minutes.

29. Patricia A. Adler, *Wheeling and Dealing: An Ethnography of an Upper-Level Drug Dealing and Smuggling Community* (New York: Columbia University Press, 1985), 6; Enrique Cirueles, *The Mafia in Havana: A Caribbean Mob Story* (New York: Ocean Press, 2004), 96.

30. The figures for cocaine seizures are from Dominic Streatfield, *Cocaine*, 204, and from Bruce Porter, *Blow: How a Small-Town Boy Made $100 Million with the Medellín Cocaine Cartel and Lost it All* (New York: St. Martin's Press, 2001), 11.

31. *Semana*, November 7, 2005, 74.

32. In David F. Musto, *La enfermedad americana. Orígenes del control antinarcóticos en EU*, expanded edition (Bogotá: Tercer Mundo Editores, 1993), 297.

33. Dominic Streatfield, *Cocaine*, 233.

34. David Musto, *La enfermedad americana*, 285.

35. For greater detail see Lawrence A. Gooberman, *Operation Intercept: The Multiple Consequences of Public Policy* (New York: Pergamon Press, 1974).

36. United Status of America. Domestic Council on Drug Abuse Task Force. "White Paper on Drug Abuse, September 1975—a Report From the Domestic Council Drug Abuse Task Force (Washington, D.C.: Government Printing Office, 1975).

37. Robert Sabbag, *Loaded*, passim.

38. Bourne was a user of both cocaine and marijuana. David Musto, *La enfermedad americana*, 296–301.

39. One suspects, for example, that officials in Santa Marta were bribed to allow the turning off of lights at the city's airport when planes loaded with marijuana took off there. Fabio Castillo, in *Los jinetes de la cocaína* (Bogotá: Editorial Documentos Periodísticos, 1987), 106–110, suggests the linkages between politicians and those working in the drug industry on the Atlantic Coast of Colombia during the late 1970s and early 1980s.

40. Fabio Castillo, *Los jinetes*, 180.

41. Hernando Ruiz Hernández, "Implicaciones sociales y económicas de la producción de la marihuana." In Asociación Nacional de Instituciones Financieras (ANIF), *Marihuana. Legalización o represión* (Bogotá: ANIF, 1979), 116.

42. John D. Martz, *The Politics of Clientelism: Democracy and the State in Colombia* (New Brunswick, New Jersey: Transaction Publishers, 1997), 166–167.

43. *Sábado*, October 23, 1976.

Chapter 2

1. Robert Sabbag, *Loaded*, 211.

2. In the words of Dominick Streatfield, they "soon grew sick of substandard Tijuana grass and the Mexi-

cans' coma-like business acumen." See his *Cocaine: An Unauthorized Biography* (New York: Thomas Dunne Books, 2001), 207.

3. Information on of the early history of cannabis in Colombia can be found in Darío Betancourt Echeverry, *Mediadores, rebuscadores, traquetos y narcos* (Bogotá: Ediciones Antropos, 1998); Francisco E. Thoumi, "Trayectoria del narcotráfico en Colombia," in Alvaro Tirado Mejía, ed., *Nueva Historia de Colombia*, vol. 8 (Bogotá: Planeta Colombia, 1998); Hernando Ruiz, "Implicaciones sociales y económicas."

4. Bertha Hernández de Ospina, *El tábano* (Bogotá: Instituto de Estudios Socio-Políticos del Conservatismo, 1970), 66.

5. Lawrence Gooberman, *Operation Intercept*, 182.

6. Darío Betancourt, *Mediadores*, 48; Mario Arango, *Narcotráfico*, 182–183; Germán Castro Caicedo, *Colombia amarga* (Bogotá: Carlos Valencia Editores, 1979), 108.

7. Accounts of the Medellín rock concert are found in Rafael Ortegón Páez, *Vorágine alucinante en la historia de las drogas* (Bogotá: Ediciones Tercer Mundo, 1983), 235–237; Simon Strong, *Whitewash: Pablo Escobar and the Cocaine Wars* (London: Macmillan, 1995), 23–25; Geoff Simons, *Colombia: A Brutal History* (London: Saqi Books, 2004), 58.

8. Lawrence Gooberman, *Operation Intercept*, 184; Hank Messick, *Of Grass and Snow: The Secret Criminal Elite* (Englewood Cliffs, N.J.: Prentice-Hall, 1979), 173.

9. On October 20, 1969, the *New York Times* published a piece titled "How the Middle Class Turns On."

10. In 1975 per-capita GDP in Colombia was approximately $300, while in the U.S. it was $3,119 in 1970.

11. Fabio Castillo, *Los jinetes*, 21.

12. Francisco E. Thoumi, *Political Economy and Illegal Drugs in Colombia* (Boulder, Colorado: Lynne Rienner, 1995), 126.

13. As told to Robert Sabbag by former big-time smuggler Alan Long. See Sabbag's *Loaded*, 211.

14. Patricia Adler, *Wheeling and Dealing*, 44.

15. Fabio Castillo, *Los jinetes*, 21; Hernando Ruiz, "Implicaciones sociales y económicas," 170–179.

16. Hank Messick, *Of Grass and Snow*, 169.

17. James Mills, *The Underground Empire: Where Crime and Governments Embrace* (New York: Doubleday, 1986), 1039.

18. Saul Franco, *El quinto*, 32; Hernando Ruiz, "Implicaciones," 207.

19. According to Darío Betancourt and Martha Luz García, *Contrabandistas, marimberos y mafiosos. Historia social de la mafia colombiana, 1965–1992* (Bogotá: Tercer Mundo Editores, 1994), 107–108, the cocaine belonged to Darío Mejía, president of Barranquilla's Club de Caza y Tiro, and the marijuana to Pablo Lafaurie.

20. Fabio Castillo, *Los jinetes*, 20. According to Rafael Ortegón, *Vorágine alucinante*, 288–289, two American pilots attempted to repeat Retat's feat a year later but were caught and arrested.

21. Robert Sabbag, *Loaded*, 130.

22. Paul Eddy, with Hugo Sabogal and Sara Walken, *The Cocaine Wars* (New York: Norton, 1988), 122–124.

23. Dominick Streatfield, *Cocaine*, 207.

24. Peter Dale Scott, and Jonathan Marshall, *Cocaine Politics: Drugs, Armies, and the CIA in Central America*, 2nd ed. (Berkeley: University of California Press, 1998), 66.

25. Daniel Pécaut, *Crónica de dos décadas de política colombiana, 1968–1988* (Bogotá: Siglo Veintiuno Editores, 1989), 248; Rafael Ortegón, *Vorágine alucinante*, 291; Andrés López Restrepo, "Narcotráfico, ilegalidad y conflicto en Colombia," in María Emma Willis and Gonzalo Sánchez, eds., *Nuestra guerra sin nombre. Transformaciones del conflicto en Colombia* (Bogotá: Editorial Norma, 2006), 415.

26. USA, "White Paper."

27. Andrés López Restrepo, "Costos del combate a la producción, comercialización y consumo de drogas y a la violencia generada por el narcotráfico," in Francisco E. Thoumi, ed., *Drogas ilícitas en Colombia. Su impacto económico, político y social* (Bogotá: Planeta Colombiana, 1997), 427; Sewall Menzel, *Cocaine Quagmire. Implementing the U.S. Anti-Drug Policy in the North Andes* (New York: University Press of America, 1997), 20; Gabriel Murillo Castaño, "Narcotráfico y política en la década de los ochenta. Entre la represión y el diálogo," in Carlos Gustavo Arrieta, Luis Javier Orjuela, Eduardo Sarmiento Palacios, and Juan Gabriel Tokatlian, eds., *Narcotráfico en Colombia. Dimensiones políticas, económicas, jurídicas e internacionales* (Bogotá: Tercer Mundo Editores, 1990), 294; Juan Gabriel Tokatlian, *Drogas, dilemas y dogmas: Estados Unidos y la narcocriminalidad organizada en Colombia* (Bogotá: Tercer Mundo Editores, 1995), 37; Rafael Ortegón, *Vorágine alucinante*, 307–308.

28. Saul Franco, *El quinto*, 32; Juan Tokatlian, *Drogas*, 77; Fabio Castillo, *Los jinetes*, 23–26.

29. He did so in his capacity as President of the National Association of Financial Institutions, ANIF (Asociación Nacional de Instituciones Financieras), in a symposium held in March of that year. Papers presented at the meeting dealt with marijuana and issues surrounding its legalization in Colombia. See note 30, below.

30. Rensslaer W. Lee, III, *The White Labyrinth* (New Brunswick, New Jersey: Transaction Publishers, 1989), 38. Congressional debates on the question of marijuana earnings are contained in Gabriel Murillo, "Narcotráfico," 215–222. Ernesto Samper Pizano's views on marijuana legalization are found in "Marihuana: entre la represion y la legalización," in Asociación Nacional de Instituciones Financieras (ANIF), *Marihuana. Legalización o represión* (Bogotá: Fotolito Calidad, 1979), 1–8.

31. For discussion of the Parents' Movement against drugs see David Musto, *La enfermedad americana*, 302–306.

32. According to Robert Sabbag, Operation Stopgap, which involved the DEA, the U.S. Coast Guard and Office of Customs, "virtually shut down" marijuana shipping between Colombia and the U.S. East Coast. See: *Loaded*, 294.

33. A graph showing marijuana's decline between 1982 and 1999 is found in Ricardo Rocha García, *La*

economía colombiana tras 25 años de narcotráfico (Bogotá: Siglo de Hombre Editores, 2000), 78.

34. Gabriel Murillo, "Narcotráfico," 222.

35. Gustavo Duncan, *Los Señores de la Guerra. De paramilitares, mafiosos y autodefensas en Colombia* (Bogotá: Planeta Editores, 2006), 215.

36. This process is described in greater detail below.

37. Julia Buxton, *The Political Economy of Narcotics*, 41.

38. Enrique Cirules, *The Mafia in Havana. A Caribbean Mob Story* (New York: Ocean Press, 2004), 96.

39. Dominick Streatfield, *Cocaine*, 208.

40. Dominick Streatfield, *Cocaine*, 205.

41. Antonil. *Mama coca* (London: Hassle Free Press, 1978), 88. Antonil claims to have visited a cocaine laboratory operating in 1969 outside the southern Colombian city of Popayán.

42. Mario Arango Jaramillo and Jorge Child, *Narcotráfico. Imperio de la cocaína* (Medellín: Editorial Vieco, 1984), 166–167; Eduardo Sáenz Rovner, *La conexión cubana. Narcotráfico, contrabando y juego en Cuba entre los años 20 y comienzos de la Revolución* (Bogotá: Universidad Nacional de Colombia, 2005), 17–18.

43. Arango and Child, *Narcotráfico*, 181, 281 n. 6. The authors' informant was one of the contrabandists.

44. Arango and Child, *Narcotráfico*, 179–180.

45. Arango and Child, *Narcotráfico*, 182.

46. Robert Sabbag, *Snowblind. A Brief Career in the Cocaine Trade* (New York: Bobbs-Merrill, 1976), 90–92.

47. Alonso Salazar, and Ana María Jaramillo, *Medellín: Las subculturas del narcotráfico, 1975–1990* (Bogotá: CINEP, 1992).

48. Dominick Streatfield, *Cocaine*, 206.

49. Alonso Salazar, *Pablo Escobar. Auge y caída de un narcotraficante* (Barcelona: Planeta, 2001), 49.

50. Abdón Espinosa Valdarrama, "Vivencias y estragos del narcotráfico," *El Tiempo*, August 3, 2006; Alonso Salazar, *Pablo Escobar*, 51; Fabio Castillo, *Jinetes*, 30. A metric ton of paste yields approximately 300 kilos of cocaine.

51. Círculo de Lectores, *Confesiones de un narco* (Bogotá: Cargraphics, 2003), 107.

52. Salazar and Jaramillo, *Medellín*, 41–41.

53. Robert Sabbag, *Snowblind*, 265.

54. Guy Gugliotta and Jeff Leen, *Kings of Cocaine. Inside the Medellín Cartel. An Astonishing True Story of Murder, Money, and International Corruption* (New York: Simon and Schuster, 1989), 19–20.

55. Alonso Salazar, *Pablo Escobar*, 73–75; Gugliotta and Leen, *Cocaine Cowboys*, 25–27.

56. In his anonymously published book *Un narco se confiesa y acusa* (Editorial Colombia Nuestra), page 13, Fabio Ochoa describes his chance meeting, in Miami, with a gringo pilot in search of cocaine, which led to his becoming a major trafficker.

57. Alonso Salazar, *Pablo Escobar*, 49; Arango and Child, *Narcotráfico*, 183–184; Robert Sabbag, *Loaded*, 275–275; Bruce Porter, *Blow. How a Small-town Boy Made $100 Million and Lost it All* (New York: St. Martin's, 2001), 152.

58. Alonso Salazar, *Pablo Escobar*, 75.

59. Antonil, *Mama Coca*, 93.

60. Antonil, *Mama Coca*, 87; Rafael Otorgón, *Vorágine alucinante*, 307; Ricardo Vargas Meza, *Drogas, máscaras y juegos. Narcotráfico y conflicto armado en Colombia* (Bogotá: Tercer Mundo, 1999), 86.

61. Gugliotta and Leen, *Cocaine Cowboys*, 121–122.

62. Arango and Child, *Narcotráfico*, 194–196.

63. Fabio Castillo, *Jinetes*, 52–53; Alonso Salazar, *Pablo Escobar*, 51–55.

64. Bruce Porter, *Blow*, 20.

65. Paul Eddy, Hugo Sabogal, and Sara Walden, *The Cocaine Wars* (New York: W.W. Norton, 1988), 148.

66. Eddy, Sabogal, and Walden, *The Cocaine Wars*, 47.

67. Antonil, *Mama Coca*, 113, cites "Latin American Commodities Report" for September 2, 1977, which estimated coffee revenues that year at around $2 billion and those from cocaine at about $3 billion.

68. It must be noted that estimates on Colombian cocaine production vary greatly. The figure for 1975, supplied by the U.S. government, was twelve to eighteen tons. A Swedish estimate for 1977 set Colombia's cocaine exports at a much higher level: sixty-eight tons (and export tonnage for 1975 at 53 tons). See *Semana*, November 7, 2005, 74–75; Fabio Castillo, *Jinetes*, 150.

69. Gary Web, *Dark Alliance: The CIA, the Contras and the Crack Explosion* (New York: Seven Stories Press, 1998), 88–89; Simon Strong, *Whitewash*, 59–60.

70. Bruce Porter, *Blow*, 171; Keven Jack Riley, *Snow Job: The War against International Drug Trafficking* (New Brunswick, NJ: Transaction Publishers, 1996), 188.

71. Betancourt and García, *Contrabandistas*, 109–110.

72. Fabio Castillo, one of the closest students of Colombia's illegal drug trade during the 1960s and '70s, makes this observation in *Jinetes*, 35.

73. Simon Strong, *Whitewash*, 33; Alonso Salazar, *Medellín*, 44.

74. Events surrounding the deaths remained murky. See Arango and Child, *Narcotráfico*, 223–224; John Martz, *The Politics of Clientelism*, 171.

75. Graciela Uribe Ramón, *Veníamos con una manotada de ambiciones. Un aporte a la historia de la colonización del Caquetá*, 2nd ed. (Bogotá: Universidad Nacional de Colombia, 1998), 205.

76. David McClintick, *Swordfish: A True Story of Ambition, Savagery, and Betrayal.* (New York: Pantheon Books, 1993), 439.

77. Mauricio Rubio, *Del rapto a la pesca milagrosa. Breve historia del secuestro en Colombia* (Bogotá: Universidad de los Andes, Centro de Estudios sobre Desarrollo Económico [CEDE], Facultad de Economía, Documento 35, December 2003). Table 2, Conclusion, illustrates the appalling, unprecedented rise of kidnapping in the country during the 1980s and 1990s.

78. *Semana*. March 29, 2004: 56–57.

79. Manuel Marulanda Vélez is the name of a labor leader killed during the 1950s while in police custody. The communist leader took it as a memorial to the slain labor leader. His birth name was Pedro Antonio Marín.

80. Mauricio Rubio, *Del rapto a la pesca milagrosa. Breve historia del secuestro en Colombia* (Bogotá: Universidad de los Andes, Centro de Estudios sobre Desarrollo Económico [CEDE], Facultad de Economía, Documento 35, December 2003), 6–7.

81. Alvaro Villarraga S., and Nelson R. Plazas N., *Para reconstruir sueños. Una historia del EPL*, 2nd ed. (Bogotá: Gente Nueva Editorial, 1995), 91.

82. Castaño describes how he killed one such person in Mauricio Aranguren Molina, *Mi confesión. Carlos Castaño revela sus secretos* (Bogotá: Editorial Oveja Negra, 2001), 111–115.

83. Fabio Castillo, *Jinetes*, 41–42.

84. Mark Bowden, *Killing Pablo* (New York: Atlantic Monthly Press, 2001), 35–36.

85. Malcolm Deas, "Seguridad e inseguridad en el último cuarto del siglo XX," in Alvaro Tirado Mejía, ed., *Nueva Historia de Colombia*, 7: *Historia política desde 1989* (Bogotá: Planeta, 1998), 249–250.

86. This point is made by Alfredo Rangel in *Guerra insurgente y Colombia: Guerra en el fin del siglo* (Bogotá: D'vinni Ltda., 2001), 360–361.

87. Mauricio Rubio, "M-19, secuestro y narcotráfico" (unpublished typescript, October 2004), 25.

88. A point made by Fabio Castillo, in *Jinetes*, 54.

89. Fabio Castillo, *Jinetes*, Alonso Salazar, *Medellín*, 43.

90. Círculo, *Confesión*, 105; Betancourt and García. *Contrabandistas*, 63–66.

91. Ciro Krauthausen, *Crímen organizado en Italia y Colombia* (Bogotá: Editorial Planeta, 1998), 408.

92. Eduardo Pizarro Leongómez, *Una democracia asediada. Balance y perspectivas del conflicto armado en Colombia* (Bogotá: Editorial Norma, 2004), 218; John Martz, *The Politics of Clientelism*, 224.

93. Discussions of Escobar's use of violence to avoid prosecution are found in Fabio Castillo, *Jinetes*, 54–63, and Gugliotta and Leen, *Kings of Cocaine*, 24–25, 241–250, 301–305.

94. Mauricio Rubio, "M-19, secuestro," 23–24.

95. Mauricio Rubio, "M-19, secuestro," 11–12.

96. Penny Lernoux, *In Banks We Trust* (New York: Penguin Books, 1986), 149; Fabio Castillo, *Jinetes*, 113; Fabio Castillo, *La coca nostra* (Bogotá: Documentos Periodísticos, 1991), 127; Mauricio Rubio, "M-19, secuestro," 17; U.S. Senate. Committee on Foreign Relations, Subcommittee on Terrorism, Narcotics and Internacional Operations. "Drugs, Law Enforcement and Foreign Policy." [The Kerry Report] (Washington: U.S. Government Printing Office, 1989), 495–496.

97. Germán Castro Caycedo, *El Karina* (Bogotá: Plaza & Janés, 1985); Vera Grabe, *Razones de vida* (Bogotá: Editorial Planeta, 2000), 152–153.

98. Alonso Salazar, *Pablo Escobar*, 83–86; Gugliotta and Leen, *Kigas of Cocaine*, 91–92.

99. Alonso Salazar, *Pablo Escobar*, 82.

100. "El huevo del serpiente," *Malpensante*, October 31, 2006, 40–41.

101. Alonso Salazar, *Pablo Escobar*, 87–88; Gugliotta and Leen, *Kings of Cocaine*, 88.

102. Details of the Jader Alvarez children's kidnapping and murder are contained in David McClintick, *Swordfish*, 79–83, 113–121, 356–358, 367–370, 417–419, 439.

103. Eddy, Sabogal, and Walden, *The Cocaine Wars*, 291.

104. John Martz, *The Politics of Clientelism*, 193. Fabio Castillo, *Jinetes*, 102, describes Pereira, in Colombia's coffee-growing area, as one of the world's centers of illegal Quaalude production, specializing in the manufacture of a "jumbo" variety of the pill.

105. David Musto, *La enfermedad*, 306–307.

106. Bruce Porter, *Blow*, 203; Gugliotta and Leen, *Kings of Cocaine*, after page 90, contains a photo of U.S. customs agents examining the cargo seized in Miami.

107. The *suplente* is elected on the ticket of a better-known candidate, and serves in the event that representative or senator cannot, for whatever reason, assume his or her seat.

108. On July 17, 1980, General Gabriel García Meza took control of the Bolivian government in what came to be called the "cocaine coup." García Meza was expelled and exiled by the military on August 4, 1981.

109. Círculo de Lectores, *Confesiones*, 59.

110. For discussion of these families of traffickers see Fabio Castillo, *Jinetes*, 41–110.

111. Gugliotti and Leen, *Kings of Cocaine*, 145–157; Eddy, Sabogal, and Walden, *The Cocaine Wars*, 303–321; Gary Webb, *Dark Alliance*, 115.

112. For detail on their activities see Billy Corbin, ed., *Cocaine Cowboys* (Magnolia Films, 2005). The documentary features extensive interviews with both Roberts and Munday.

113. Gary Webb, *Dark Alliance*, 61.

114. U.S. Senate. *Drugs, Law Enforcement*, 117–118.

115. The U.S. government made much of a photograph taken during June 1984 that showed Nicaraguan official Federico Vaughan and Barry Seal off-loading cocaine at the César Sandino International Airport in Managua. The photo is found in Gugliotta and Leen, *Kings of Cocaine*, after page 420.

116. U.S. Senate. *Drugs, Law Enforcement*, 41, 61. According to this source neither offer was accepted.

117. A good discussion of the World Finance Corporation, "a spectacular scam with a pin-stripe name," is found in Penny Lernoux, *In Banks We Trust*, 146–168.

118. Penny Lernoux, *In Banks We Trust*, 149; U.S. Senate. *Drugs, Law Enforcement,* 63–65; Fabio Castillo, *La coca nostra*, 127–128.

119. Fabio Castillo, *Jinetes*, 145; Rensselaer Lee, *The White Labyrinth*, 3.

120. Alonso Salazar, *Pablo Escobar*, 93–96; Simon Strong; *Whitewash*, 70–71.

121. Gustavo Salazar Pineda, *El confidante de la mafia se confiesa. El narcotráfico colombiano al descubierto* (Madrid: Editorial el Tercer Nombre, 2006), 15–16, 73–74; Max Mermelstein, *The Man Who Made it Snow* (New York: Simon and Schuster, 1990), 105; Gugliotta and Leen, *Kings of Cocaine*, 95–96.

122. Max Mermelstein, *The Man Who Made it Snow*, 177; Fabio Castillo, *Jinetes*, 93–95; Alonso Salazar, *Pablo Escobar*, 111–112.

123. Frank Safford and Marco Palacios, *Colombia: Fragmented Land, Divided Society* (New York: Oxford University Press, 2002), 315; James Mills, *The Underground Empire*, 1124.

124. Jorge Eliécer Orozco, *Lehder ... el hombre* (Bogotá: Plaza Janes, 1987), passim; Fabio Castillo, *Jinetes*, 93–99; Gugliotta and Leen, *Kings of Cocaine*, 85–86, 113–114; Hedí, Sabogal, and Walden, *The Cocaine Wars*, 186–189; Simon Strong, *Whitewash*, 87–89.

125. Alonso Salazar, *Pablo Escobar*, 88–90.

126. Alonso Salazar, *Pablo Escobar*, 98–100.

127. Alonso Salazar, *Pablo Escobar*, 104–105.

128. Mark Bowden, *Killing Pablo*, 35–36.

Chapter 3

1. Mark Bowden, *Killing Pablo*, 51.

2. Gabriel Murillo, "Narcotráfico," 223; Stephen Dudley, *Walking Ghosts: Murder and Guerrilla Politics in Colombia* (New York: Routledge, 2004), 98.

3. Sewall Menzel, *Cocaine Quagmire*, 33, puts Colombia's cocaine production in 1984 at an estimated 110 metric tons.

4. A photograph of a wide-eyed customs agent standing over the shipment is contained in Gugliotta and Leen, *Kings of Cocaine*, after page 90.

5. Lehder had been fighting the U.S. indictment for at least a year. During 1982 he had offered to cooperate with the DEA in exchange for dropping the indictment. Gugliotta and Leen, *Kings of Cocaine*, 114–115, 118, 329.

6. *El Espectador* had located news of the arrest in a DAS document of 1976. The document, complete with photographs of Escobar and the others, is reproduced in Gugliotta and Leen, *Kings of Cocaine*, after page 90.

7. Fabio Castillo, *Los jinetes*, 60–63; Gugliotta and Leen, *Kinas of Cocaine*, 117–118.

8. He did so following a brief stop-over in Bogotá of U.S. president Ronald Reagan. John Martz, *The Politics of Clientelism*, 215.

9. The cartel's chief accountant in Miami, Max Mermelstein, was also present. He recalled the tent as the largest he had ever seen.

10. El Chopo (The Rifle) was not related to paramilitary leader Fidel Castaño.

11. Details of the Medellín summit of early February 1984 are found in Gustavo Salazar, *El Confidante de la mafia*, 140–143; Gugliotta and Leen, *Kings of Cocaine*, 119; Max Mermelstein, *El hombre*, 175–189.

12. An account of the "ether trail" to Tranquilandia is contained in Gugliotta and Leen, *Kings of Cocaine*, 119–128. Detail on ether transactions in Colombia is found in Fabio Castillo, *Los jinetes*, 145–149.

13. On March 11, the day after the Tranquilandia raid, a second bribe was offered to Ramírez through another of his brothers, by men who identified themselves as representatives of Pablo Escobar. Eddy, Sabogal, and Walden, *The Cocaine Wars*, 299–300.

14. Accounts of the Tranquilandia raid are found in Eddy, Sabogal, and Walden, *The Cocaine Wars*, 296–

300; Gugliotta and Leen, *Kings of Cocaine 129–137*; Rensselaer Lee, *The White Labyrinth*, 170–172. A map showing Tranquilandia, its supply routes, and routes of cocaine export extending from Tranquilandia to the United States and Europe, is contained in Fabio Castillo, *Los jinetes*, 149.

15. Tambs and his Colombian ambassadorship are discussed in Gugliotta and Leen, *Kings of Cocaine*, 103–107, 177–178.

16. Gugliotta and Leen, *Kings of Cocaine*, 138.

17. *Time*, April 16, 1984: 35.

18. Many Colombians believed the cartel paid for the Florencia attack, something army commander Rafael Forero asserted. Gabriel Murillo, "Narcotráfico," 223–224.

19. The trafficker's memorandum is contained in Eddy, Sabogal, and Walden, *The Cocaine Wars*, 299–300. The account of López' meeting with Escobar and Ochoa is from Gugliotta and Leen, *Kings of Cocaine*, 173–174, based on the authors' 1987 interview with López.

20. The photo of Borge assistant Fredrico Vaughan off-loading cocaine with Escobar and Seal is shown in Gugliotta and Leen, *Kings of Cocaine*, after page 240.

21. Gugliotta and Leen, *Kings of Cocaine*, 174–175.

22. Gugliotta and Leen, *Kings of Cocaine*, 178–179; *Semana*, July 9, 2007: 80.

23. Between 1982 and 1995 there was no requirement that CIA agents report allegations of drug trafficking by its agents, assets, and non-staff employees, this through a 1982 secret agreement between the CIA and U.S. Attorney General William French Smith. Gary Webb, *Dark Alliance*, 468.

24. Ron Chepesiuk, *The Bullet or the Bribe: Taking Down Colombia's Cali Drug Cartel* (Westport, CT: Praeger, 2003), 64–65.

25. Gugliotta and Leen, *Kings of Cocaine*, 187–198.

26. Gugliotta and Leen, *Kinas of Cocaine*, 183.

27. Gustavo Salazar, a lawyer who worked for Escobar and other traffickers, named Medellín lawyer Vladimir Mosquera as the cartel's principal attorney in charge of bribery. The Ochoa brothers, Salazar explains, consistently urged Escobar to employ bribery rather than violence. Gustavo Salazar, *El confidante de la mafia*, 145.

28. Gustavo Salazar, *El confidante de la mafia*, 146.

29. Gugliotta and Leen, *Kings of Cocaine*, 185–188.

30. John Martz, *The Politics of Clientelism*, 255.

31. Gugliotta and Leen, *Kings of Cocaine*, 215, 245–246; Alonso Salazar, *Pablo Escobar*, 134.

32. Details of the Reagan administration's financing of Nicaragua's Contra rebels first came to light in U.S. Senate hearings presided over by John Kerry in 1988. See U.S. Senate, *Drugs, Law Enforcement*. Two of the best discussions of this sordid episode in U.S. international relations are Peter Scott, *Cocaine Politics*, and Gary Webb, *Dark Alliance*. For further information on Matta Ballesteros and the "Mexican trampoline" see James Mills, *The Underground Empire*, 1150–1151; Ron Chepesiuk, *The Bullet or the Bribe*, 112; Simon Strong, *Whitewash*, 142; Fabio Castillo, *La coca nostra*, 14, 20, 25, 71, 76, 94, 142, 256, 257; Gugliotta and Leen, *Kings of Cocaine*, 245.

33. Details on the struggle of the U.S. to extradite Ochoa and Rodríguez from Spain are contained in Simon Strong, *Whitewash*, 302–321; and in Gugliotta and Leen, *Kings of Cocaine*, 196–199, 255–259.

34. James Mills, *The Underground Empire*, 1146–1155.

35. James Mills, *The Underground Empire*, 1152.

36. Leaders of the M-19's war faction were Iván Marino Ospina, Alvaro Fayad, Carlos Pizarro, and Luis Otero. Leaders of the peace, or political faction, were Andrés Amarales and Antonio Navarro Wolf. Ana Carrigan, *The Palace of Justice: A Colombian Tragedy* (New York: Four Walls Eight Windows, 1993), 82. The moment Fayad conceived the scheme of seizing the Palacio is described in Olga Behar, *Noches de humo. Cómo se planeó y ejecutó la toma del Palacio de Justicia* (Bogotá: Editorial Planeta, 1988), 43–46.

37. Astrid Legarda, *El verdadero Pablo. Sangre, traición y muerte...* (Bogotá: Ediciones Gato Azul, 2005), 41.

38. Marino was killed in Cali late the following month. An M-19 operative named Alejo attended at least one of the planning meetings of Escobar and guerrilla leader Iván Marino Ospina. Alejo's account of the meeting is contained in Alonso Salazar, *Pablo Escobar*, 143–144.

39. Ana Carrigan, *The Palace of Justice*, 175. Eyewitness to the May 1985 meeting of Carlos Pizarro and Esobar at Estación Cocorná, Antioquia, was Carlos Castaño, whose account is found in Mauricio Aranguren, *Mi confesión*, 41–42. Witness to the July 1985 meeting between Iván Marino, Alvaro Fayad, and Pablo Escobar, was Escobar *sicario* and confidant Jhon Jairo Velásquez ("Popeye"), whose account appears in Astrid Legarda, *El verdadero Pablo*, 35–47. The weapons purchased in Panama had been sent there from Nicaragua. Both Cuba and Nicaragua were eager for the M-19 to remain in the field, because they feared a U.S. military invasion of Colombia. According to Carlos Castaño, Escobar charged his brother, Fidel Castaño, with helping arm the guerrillas with weapons owned by the cartel.

40. Ana Carrigan, *The Palace of Justice*, 108–111.

41. Eddy, Sabogal, and Walden, *The Cocaine Wars*, 323. Eyewitnesses reported that M-19 leader Andrés Amarales carried out the executions.

42. Jhon Jairo Velásquez watched the event unfold with the happy Escobar. Astrid Legarda, *El verdadero Pablo*, 46.

43. Astrid Legarda, *El verdadero Pablo*, 47.

44. Twenty years after the incident Colombians continued to demand punishment of military commanders who ordered the interrogation and murder of the Palace of Justice survivors. See, for example, "¿Crimen de Estado?," *Semana*, July 19, 2007, 28–33. In 2010 an army colonel was sentenced to thirty years in prison for the murders. But details of the incident remained in doubt. See *Semana*, "Alguien miente," June 20, 2011, 36–37.

45. Gugliotta and Leen, *Kings of Cocaine*, 282–284.

46. Attributed to *El Tiempo* columnist Germán Santamaría. *Semana*, July 9, 2007, 190.

47. Mexico's drug violence of the first decade of the twenty-first century, though costly in terms of lives lost, did not involve a concerted attack on that nation's democratic institutions and elected officials.

48. Fabio Castillo, *La coca nostra*, 13.

49. Darío Betancourt, *Mediadores*, 165.

50. Simon Strong, *Whitewash*, 63. An anthropological study that compares Colombia's drug mafia and the Italian Mafia is Ciro Krauthausen, *Crímen organizado en Italia y Colombia*. A sociological approach to the same subject is taken in Gustavo Duncan, *Los Señores de la Guerra*. David McClintick, *Swordfish*, 532, 594, discusses DEA "Operation Green Ice," which established links between the Colombian drug cartels and the Sicilian Mafia. Paramilitary leader of Italian descent Salvatore Mancuso was accused of exporting $400 million worth of cocaine to Europe with the help of the Italian Mafia during 2003–2006. *Semana*, November 27, 2006, 47–48.

51. Correa Arroyave was one of the two brothers-in-law who died. The other was Rodrigo Pardo Murillo.

52. Gugliotta and Leen, *Kings of Cocaine*, 254.

53. Gugliotta and Leen, *Kings of Cocaine*, 255.

54. *Semana*, October 20, 2003, 88–91; January 4, 2005, 36–38; March 7, 2005, 22–26; August 13, 2007. Patiño's chief enemy in the war was Juan Carlos Ramírez Abadía ("Chupeta"), who was captured by Brazilian authorities in August 2007.

55. In October 1987 they sent a 2,000 kilogram shipment to Atlanta, Georgia. Fabio Castillo, *La coca nostra*, 186.

56. Cali made use of the help of Ochoa's associate and former friend Rafael Cardona, who gave them his travel plans. Ochoa was traveling with Cardona's mistress and Cardona wanted revenge. Fabio Castillo, *La coca nostra*, 20–25.

57. The best account of the November 1987 cartel summit is Fabio Castillo, *La coca nostra*, 19–30. Others include Gugliotta and Leen, *Kings of Cocaine*, 309–317, 338; Ron Chepesiuk, *The Bullet or the Bribe*, 123–129; Alonso Salazar, *Pablo Escobar*, 181–190; Simon Strong, *Whitewash*, 163–182; Betancourt and García, *Contrabandistas*, 72.

58. The mercenary attack took place on June 3, 1989. The machine gun assault on soccer fans occurred on September 25, 1990. Further detail on the Medellín-Cali cartel war is found in Gugliotta and Leen, *Kings of Cocaine*, 336–338; Alonso Salazar, *Pablo Escobar*, 178–179, 338; Simon Strong, *Whitewash*, 181–182; Círculo de Lectores, *Confesión*, 130–131.

59. Little is known about the mediation efforts of Rodríguez Gacha. He is believed to have attended a meeting with members of José Santacruz Londoño's organization near New York City. Fabio Castillo, *La coca nostra*, 251; Gugliotta and Leen, *Kings of Cocaine*, 337–338.

60. Fabio Castillo, *Los jinetes*, 193–194.

61. *Semana*, June 19, 2003, 50–51, treats police raids on *oficinas de cobro*.

62. The best historical studies of violence in Valle del Cauca are Darío Betancourt, *Matones y cuadrilleros. Origen y evolución de la violencia en el occidente colombiano* (Bogotá: Tercer Mundo Editores, 1990), and his

Mediadores, rebuscadores, traquetos y narcos. Valle del Cauca 1890–1997 (Bogotá: Ediciones Antropos, 1998).

63. For more on this aspect of Colombian history see James D. Henderson, *Modernization in Colombia: The Laureano Gómez Years, 1889–1965* (Gainesville: University Press of Florida, 2001), 357, 374–375.

64. Círculo de Lectores, *Confesiónes*; Simon Strong, *Whitewash*, 295–302. Urdinola was arrested in 1991, convicted of five murders, and sent to prison where he died of a heart attack in 2004. Witnesses testified that he may have killed as many as 5,000 people. Ron Chepesiuk, *The Bullet*, 88–89; José Fuentes, "The Life of a Cell," 44.

65. Detail on these events can be found in CINEP, *Deuda con la humanidad. Paramilitarismo de Estado, 1988–2003* (Bogotá: CINEP [Centro de Investigación Popular], 2004, 29–74. A monograph on the Trujillo massacre is A. Atehortúa Cruz, *El poder de la sangre. Las historias de Trujillo, Valle* (Cali: Imprenta Departamental del Valle, 1995). See also Daniel Pécaut, *Guerra contra la sociedad* (Bogotá: Editorial Planeta, 2001), 220–222; Darío Betancourt, *Mediadores*, 133–134. The most recent study of the Trujillo Massacre is Grupo de Memoria Histórica, *Trujillo: Una tragedia que no cesa* (Bogotá: Editorial Taurus, 2009).

66. CINEP, *Deuda*, 66. Executed with Arcila was a demobilized former member of the Ejército Popular de Liberacion (EPL), Mauricio Castañeda Giraldo. Growth of the North Valle cartel is treated in Gustavo Duncan, *Señores de la Guerra*, 325–332.

67. One group formed for the purpose of "social cleansing" was called the Chirimoyos. Formed by a person having connections with the police, and with a major political party, its members dedicated themselves to eliminating beggars, petty thieves, vagrants, homosexuals, and prostitutes from the streets of Cali and other cities and towns in Valle. Darío Betancourt, *Mediadores*, 165.

68. John Martz, *The Politics of Clientelism*, 229.

69. Alvaro Camacho Guizado and Alvaro Guzmán Barney, *Colombia: Ciudad y violencia* (Bogotá: Ediciones Foro Nacional, 1990), 188–189.

70. Darío Betancourt, *Mediadores*, 165.

71. The best discussion of Rodríguez Gacha's jungle conflict against the FARC is contained in Fabio Castillo, *Jinetes*, 334–336.

72. Stephen Dudley, *Walking Ghosts*, 101.

73. Rodríguez Gacha was called "the Mexican" because he loved all things Mexican.

74. Stephen Dudley, *Walking Ghosts*, 102.

75. That took place in October 2002, when the UP failed to muster the minimum number of votes needed to achieve political representation.

76. Gustavo Salazar, *El confidante de la mafia*, 88–101.

77. Fabio Rincón, *Leyenda y verdad de El Mejicano* (Bogotá: Aquí y Ahora Editores, 1990).

78. A photograph of the sign is found in Toño Sánchez Jr., *Crónicas que da miedo contar* (Bogotá: Editorial A. Sánchez S., 2003), 223.

79. This is the assessment of Toño Sánchez Jr., whose *Crónicas* is a study of the alliance of the two men.

80. This development is described in greater detail below in chapter 5, "The Paramilitary Offensive, 1994–2004."

81. Detail on these bases is contained in Fabio Castillo, *La coca nostra*, 226–250. Castillo bases his information on the exhaustive testimony of Diego Viáfara, a former member of both the guerrillas and the paramilitary, who gave himself up to Colombian authorities in 1989.

82. The call came from Córdoba, probably from Fidel Castaño, who supported the mercenary-taught classes. Toño Sánchez Jr., *Crónicas*, 132.

83. Toño Sánchez Jr., *Crónicas*, 132–133.

84. The best account of the Segovia Massacre is found in Stephen Dudley, *Walking Ghosts*, 65–76.

85. Robin Kirk, *More Terrible Than Death: Massacres, Drugs, and America's War in Colombia* (New York: Public Affairs, 2003), 128–129. The best account of Alonso Baquero's career is found in Stephen Dudley, *Walking Ghosts*, 65–75, 117–126.

86. Mauricio Rubio, *Crimen e impunidad. Precisiones sobre la violencia* (Bogotá: Editorial Tercer Mundo, 1999), 139. Rubio dwells on the subject of homicide and impunity, pointing out not surprisingly that the quadrupling of homicides in Colombia between the 1970s and the 1990s had to do with proliferation of armed groups in the country.

87. Pax Christi Netherlands, *Impunity in Colombia* (The Hague, Netherlands: Pax Christi Netherlands, 1989).

88. John Martz, *The Politics of Clientelism*, 249.

89. David Bushnell, *Colombia*, 252.

90. Saúl Franco, *El quinto*, 26. Tripling of the 1972 average would occur in 1988. Its quadrupling would occur during 1993.

91. Jaime Arocha R., Alvaro Camacho G., Darío Fajardo M., Alvaro Guzmán B., Luis Alberto Andrade A., Carlos Eduardo Jaramillo, Carlos Miguel Ortiz S., Santiago Peláez V., Eduardo Pizarro L., Gonzalo Sánchez G., *Colombia: Violencia y democracia* (Bogotá: Universidad Nacional de Colombia, 1987), 27.

92. Jorge Orlando Melo and Jaime Bermúdez, "La lucha contra el narcotráfico: éxitos y limitaciones," in Malcolm Deas and Carlos Ossa, comps., *El gobierno Barco. Política, economía y desarrollo social en Colombia 1986–1990* (Bogotá: Editorial Nomos, 1994), 125.

93. Stephen Dudley, *Walking Ghosts*, 103.

94. Andrés López, "Narcotráfico," 420–426.

95. Eddy, Sabogal, and Walden, *The Cocaine Wars*, 329–330; Gugliotta and Leen, *Kings of Cocaine*, 307–317.

96. Alvaro Tirado Mejía, "Política exterior colombiana. La última década," in Alvaro Tirado Mejía, ed., *Nueva Historia de Colombia*, vol. 7, *Historia política desde 1986* (Bogotá: Editorial Planeta, 1998), 220–221.

97. U.S. Senate, *Drugs, Law Enforcement*.

98. Gugliotta and Leen, *Kings of Cocaine*, 326–328; references to articles on the racist character of this legislation is found in James P. Gray, *Why Our Drug Laws Have Failed and What We Can Do About It* (Philadelphia: Temple University Press, 2001), 138, note 1.

99. Gugliotta and Leen, *Kings of Cocaine*, 307–308, 337; Fabio Castillo, *La coca nostra*, 261–262; Stephen Dudley, *Walking Ghosts*, 142.

100. Daniel Pécaut, *Guerra contra la sociedad*, 175.

101. Simon Strong, *Whitewash*, 222.

102. Simon Strong, *Whitewash*, 217–220; Mark Bowden, *Killing Pablo*, 72.

103. Andrés López, "Narcotráfico," 420–426; Simon Strong, *Whitewash*, 222–223; Mark Bowden, *Killing Pablo*, 72–74.

104. The best account of the Mexican's final days is found in Mark Bowden, *Killing Pablo*, 78–84. See also Ron Chepesiuk, *The Bullet*, 131.

105. This point is made in Fabio Castillo, *La coca nostra*, 279.

106. The process of Colombia's caving in to Escobar's demands is traced in Fabio Castillo, *La coca nostra*, 273–294; Simon Strong, *Whitewash*, 241–248. Escobar's kidnappings of Diana Turbay and others is discussed in Gabriel García Márquez, *News of a Kidnapping* (New York: Alfred A. Knopf, 1997).

107. Ron Chepesiuk, *The Bullet*, 134.

108. Toño Sánchez Jr., *Crónicas*, 174.

109. Escobar's court statement is in Luis Cañón M., *El Patrón. Vida y muerte de Pablo Escobar* (Bogotá: Editorial Planeta, 1994), 307–309.

110. Miguel Silva, "César Gaviria: los años del revolcón (1990–1994)." In Alvaro Tirado Mejía, ed., *Nueva Historia de Colombia*, vol. 7 (Bogotá: Editorial Planeta, 1998), 83.

111. Antonio Navarro Wolff was the co-chair for the M-19. César Gaviria was the Liberal party co-chair, and the Conservative party was represented by Álvaro Gómez Hurtado.

112. Simon Strong, *Whitewash*, 254.

113. Luis Cañón, *El Patrón*, 319.

114. Alonso Salazar, *Pablo Escobar*, 281–286; Luis Cañón, *El Patrón*, 311–320.

115. Alonso Salazar, *Pablo Escobar*, 294–295.

116. Luis Cañón, *El Patrón*, 311.

117. Details on the Henry Pérez assassination are found in Toño Sánchez Jr., *Crónicas*, 167–181.

118. Simon Strong, *Whitewash*, 372–373.

119. Details on the Moncado and Galeano murders are found in Luis Cañón, *El Patrón*, 329–336; Alonso Salazar, *Pablo Escobar*, 299–301; Toño Sánchez Jr., *Crónicas*, 229–233; Simon Strong, *Whitewash*, 273–274.

120. Toño Sánchez, *Crónicas*, 248; Luis Cañón, *El Patrón*, 345–351.

121. Mauricio Aranguren, *Mi confesión*, 142; Simon Strong, *Whitewash*, 68–70.

122. Mark Bowden, *Killing Pablo*, 167–168.

123. Alonso Salazar, *Pablo Escobar*, 197.

124. From an interview published in *Semana*, May 31, 1994, 38–45. While purporting to be by Fidel Castaño, the information it contained was by Castaño's younger brother Carlos.

125. Mauricio Aranguren, *Mi confesión*, 148–149.

126. Alonso Salazar, *Pablo Escobar*, 316–318.

127. Mark Bowden, *Killing Pablo*, 197, 269–271.

128. These estimates of cocaine reaching the U.S.

from Colombia during 1994 are from Joseph Toft, who at the time was DEA chief in the country, as cited in Mark Bowden, *Killing Pablo*, 271. Darío Betancourt, *Mediadores*, 113, finds that the "Cali cartel" was made up of several trafficking networks operating in geographic regions that overlapped. They fell into the Northern region, the Central (Cali) region, and the Pacific (Buenaventura) region. His map on page 116 shows that there was also a "central sub-region" with the city of Buga at its center.

129. Both the 243–340 ton and the 500 ton estimates are from DEA sources cited in Mark Bowden, *Killing Pablo*, 271; and Simon Strong, *Whitewash*, 327.

130. Ron Chepesiuk, *The Bullet*, 89, 177–178.

131. Alejandro Santos Rubiano, "Vicisitudes del gobierno de Ernesto Samper," in Alvaro Tirado Mejía, ed., *Nueva Historia de Colombia*, vol. 7 (Bogotá: Editorial Planeta, 1998), 162–163.

132. Alejandro Santos, "Vicisitudes," 157–187; Ron Chepesiuk, *The Bullet*, 191–196; Simon Strong, *Whitewash*, 307–312. The five to six million dollars given by Cali traffickers to the Samper campaign were dwarfed by the forty million dollars that they gave to the successful 1995 campaign of Mexico's Ernesto Zedillo. Luis Astorga, "Mexico," in Menno Vellinga, ed., *The Political Economy of the Drug Industry: Latin America and the International System* (Gainesville: University Press of Florida, 2005), 95–102. See also Luis Astorga, *El siglo de las drogas. El narcotráfico, del Porfiriato al nuevo milenio* (Mexico City: Plaza y Janes, 2005).

Chapter 4

1. Álvaro Villarraga, *Para reconstruir sueños*, 212.

2. José F. Ocampo, "The Present Stage of the Colombian Revolution," *Latin American Perspectives*, Issue 6, Vol. 2, No. 3 (Fall 1975), 14.

3. FARC strategist Luis Morantes ("Jacobo Arenas") recalled the words of Manuel Marulanda Vélez at the group's 1974 Fifth Conference: "At last we've repaired the damage that almost destroyed us" (*Por fin nos hemos repuesto del mal que casi nos liquida*). Jacobo Arenas, *Cese el fuego. Una historia política de las FARC* (Bogotá: Editorial Oveja Negra, 1985), 90.

4. Arturo Alape, *El bogotazo, memorias del olvido* (Bogotá: Publicaciones Universidad Central, 1983), 192, 293–297, 510. The riot, known as the *bogotazo*, quickly fizzled out. Castro, in Bogotá for a meeting of socialist youth, was able to return home on April 12 thanks to the intercession of Cuba's ambassador to Colombia.

5. Gaitán's action is described in Ignacio Torres Giraldo, *Los inconformes, historia de la rebeldía de las masas en Colombia*, vol. 6 (Bogotá: Editorial Latina, 1978), 1069; and Terrance Horgan, "The Liberals Come to Power. *Por debajo de la ruana*" (Ph.D. thesis, Nashville, Tennessee: Vanderbilt University, 1983), 565. Conservative actions in 1939, and Liberal guerrilla formation during the 1950s, are discussed in James D. Henderson, *Modernization in Colombia*, 268–269, 321–323.

6. The national police struck against everyone on the left, particularly members of the labor movement,

many of whose leaders were Communist party members. Among its leaders killed by Conservative police during the 1950s were Manuel Marulanda Vélez, Aurelino Rodríguze, and Angel María Cano. Eduardo Pizarro Leongómez, *Los FARC* (Bogotá: Editorial Tercer Mundo, 1991), 63; interview with Jorge Regueros Peralta, Bogotá, June 15 and 26, 1993.

7. Eduardo Pizarro, *Las FARC*, 41; Eduardo Pizarro Leongómez, "Las FARC-EP: ¿repliegue estratégico, debilitamiento o punto de inflexión?" In María Emma Willis and Gonzalo Sánchez, eds., *Nuestra guerra sin nombre. Transformaciones del conflicto en Colomba* (Bogotá: Editorial Norma, 2006), 177.

8. The final phases of the *Violencia* are described in James D. Henderson, *When Colombia Bled: A History of the Violencia in Tolima* (Tuscaloosa: University of Alabama Press, 1985), 203–229, and in the same author's *Modernization in Colombia*, 395–405.

9. Eduardo Pizarro, "Las FARC-EP," 176.

10. Robert H. Dix, *Colombia: The Political Dimensions of Change* (New Haven: Yale University Press, 1967), 279–280; Eduardo Pizarro Leongómez, "Revolutionary guerrilla Groups in Colombia," in Charles Bergquist, ed., *Violence in Colombia: The Contemporary Crisis in Historical Perspective* (Wilmington, Delaware: Scholarly Resources, 1992), 176.

11. The most extensive account of this attempt to form a guerrilla force in the Eastern Llanos is found in Alfonso Moncada Abello, "El caso de Vichada," in *Un aspecto de la Violencia* (Bogotá: Promotora Colombiana de Ediciones, 1963), 391–430.

12. Colombian-Cuban relations during 1961 are discussed in Germán Cavellier, *Política internacional de Colombia*, vol. 4 (Bogotá: Universidad Externado de Colombia, 1997), 377–382.

13. Carlos Arango Z., ed., *FARC. Veinte años: De Marquetalia a La Uribe* (Bogotá: Ediciones Aurora, 1984), 188; Gonzalo Sánchez, *Ensayos de historia social y política del siglo XX* (Bogotá: El Ancora Editores, 1985), 266.

14. Further detail on these events is contained in James D. Henderson, *Modernization in Colombia* 399–404; and in *When Colombia Bled*, 221–223, 318.

15. Part of the Amazon River watershed, it was a vast and largely unpopulated place where the hand of the Colombian state rested but lightly.

16. Carlos Arango, *FARC: Veinte años*, 90.

17. Eduardo Pizarro, "Revolutionary Guerrilla Groups in Colombia," 177; James D. Henderson, *Modernization in Colombia*, 411–412.

18. Early history of the ELN is contained in Carlos Medina, *ELN*, 27–187, and Eduardo Pizarro Leongómez, *Insurgencia sin revolución. La guerrilla en perspective comparada* (Bogotá: Editorial Tercer Mundo, 1996), 95–101. The Anorí campaign told from the military perspectiva is recounted in Luis Alberto Villamarín Pulido, *Cóndor en el aire* (Bogotá: Ediciones Luis Alberto Villamaría Pulido, 1999).

19. The early days of the EPL are discussed in Alvaro Villarraga, *Para reconstruir sueños*, 13–113; Eduardo Pizarro, "Revolutionary Groups in Colombia," 178–180; Toño Sánchez, *Crónicas*, 14–16, 52–53.

20. Román D. Ortiz, "La guerrilla mutante," in Francisco Leal Buitrago, ed., *En la encrucijada. Colombia en el siglo XXI* (Bogotá: Editorial Norma, 2006), 331.

21. These estimates of guerrilla strength are drawn from Eduardo Pizarro, *"Las FARC-EP,"* 182–183; Juan Gabriel Tokatlian and Ana Mercedes Botero, "La política exterior de Colombia hacia Estados Unidos, 1978–1990. El asunto de las drogas y su lugar en las relaciones entre Bogotá y Washington," in Carlos Gustavo Arrieta, Luis Carlos Orjuela, Eduardo Sarmiento Palacio and Juan Gabriel Tokatlian, eds., *Narcotráfico en Colombia. Dimensiones políticas, económicas, jurídicas e internacionales* (Bogotá: Tercer Mundo Editores, 1990), 371; Román D. Ortiz, "La guerrilla mutante," in Francisco Leal Buitrago, ed., *En la encrucijada. Colombia en el siglo XXI* (Bogotá: Editorial Norma, 2006), 326–326.

22. Residents of Puerto Boyacá quoted in *Semana*, February 6, 2006, page 46, recalled that during the early days of FARC recruitment in the 1970s many of them were sympathetic to the FARC's reform message. They recalled that many sang the Socialist International and that the hammer and sickle was frequently seen. See also Toño Sánchez, *Crónicas*, 103–104; Mauricio Archila and Ingrid Bolívar, eds., *Conflictos, poderes e identidades en el Magdalena Medio, 1990–2001* (Bogotá: Ediciones Antropos, 2006), 322–330.

23. Five months later the army captured those who carried out the Rincón assassination, dealing yet another severe blow to the ELN. See Alvaro Valencia Tovar, *Historia de las fuerzas militares de Colombia*, vol. 3 (Bogotá: Editorial Planeta, 1993), 154.

24. Mauricio García Durán, *De La Uribe a Tlaxcala. Procesos de paz* (Bogotá: Ediciones Antropos, 1992), 85.

25. Alvaro Villarraga, *Para reconstruir los sueños*, 131–143.

26. Fabio Castillo, *Los jinetes*, 32–35.

27. The announcement is contained in Darío Villamizar Herrera, *Aquel 19. Una historia del M-19, de sus hombres y sus gestas. Un relato entre la guerra, la negociación y la paz* (Bogotá: Editorial Planeta, 1995), 585–586.

28. Daniel Pécaut, *Crónica*, 347; Román D. Ortiz and Gerson Arias, "La apuesta de la Novena Conferencia de las FARC," *Unidad de Análisis 48* [March 2007] (Bogotá: Fundación Ideas Para la Paz, www.ideaspaz.org/publicaciones), 3.

29. Whether Turbay's National Security Statute was akin to the National Security Doctrines of Southern Cone countries has been debated by scholars. Political scientist Francisco Leal Buitrago argues that it did, and historian Malcolm Deas that it did not. See Leal's *La inseguridad de la seguridad. Colombia, 1958–2005* (Bogotá: Editorial Planeta, 2006), 25–82, and Deas' "Seguridad," 250.

30. Darío Villamizar, *Aquel 19*, 170–182.

31. The FARC's change of strategy during 1980, along with description of their defeat of the army detachment, are described in Arturo Alape, *Tirofijo: Los sueños y las montañas. El mar, la ciudad, la muerte natural, la búsqueda insaciable de un sueño como ideal* (Bogotá: Editorial Planeta, 1994), 153–170.

32. Mauricio Rubio, "M-19, secuestro," 15. Jaime Guillot Lara, an affluent marijuana smuggler and close friend of M-19 founder Jaime Bateman, had surely instructed the guerrilla group in techniques of money laundering through banks such as the World Finance Corporation. See notes 53 and 54, below. For detail on the *Karina* incident, see chapter 2.

33. Daniel Pécaut, *Crónica*, 350.

34. Daniel Pécaut, *Crónica*, 351.

35. Socorro Ramírez V., and Luis Alberto Restrepo M., *Actores en conflicto por la paz. El proceso de paz durnate el gobierno de Belisario Betancur, 1983–1986* (Bogotá: Siglo Veintuno Editores, 1988), 51; John Martz, *The Politics of Clientelism,*

36. Accounts of peace negotiations taking place under Betancur are contained in Laura Restrepo, *Historia de un entusiasmo*, 2nd ed. (Bogotá: Editorial Aguilar, 2006); Enrique Santos Calderon, *La Guerra por la paz* (Bogotá: Fondo Editorial CEREC, 1985); Otto Morales Benítez, *Papeles para la paz* (Bogotá: Editorial Arbol Que Piensa, 1991); Alvaro Leyva Durán, ed., *¿Paz? ¡Paz! Testimonios y reflexiones sobre un proceso* (Bogotá: Editorial La Oveja Negra, 1987); Mauricio García Durán, *Movimiento por la paz en Colombia* (Bogotá: Ediciones Antropos, 2006); Jacobo Arenas, *Cese el fuego;* S. Ramírez and L.A. Restrepo, *Actores en conflicto;* Daniel Pécaut, *Crónica de dos décadas*, 349–395; John Martz, *The Politics of Clientelism*, 204–229.

37. See chapter 2.

38. Daniel Pécaut, *Crónica de dos décadas*, 323–324.

39. Malcolm Deas, "Seguridad," 252.

40. J. Mark Ruhl, "Colombia: Armed Forces and Society" (Syracuse, N.Y.: Maxwell School of Citizenship and Public Affairs, Syracuse University, 1980); Juan Salcedo Lora, "Respuestas personalísimas de un General de la república sobre cosas que casi todo el mundo sabe," in Malcom Deas and María Victoria Llorente, comps., *Reconocer la Guerra para construir la Paz* (Bogotá: Editorial Norma, 1999), 355–359; Camilo Granada, "La evolución del gasto en seguridad y defensa en Colombia, 1950–1994," in Deas and Llorente, *Reconocer la Guerra*, 539–597; Brian Loveman, *For "la patria." Politics and Armed Forces in Latin America* (Wilmington, Delaware: Scholarly Resources), 1999.

41. Juanita León, *País de plomo. Crónicas de guerra* (Bogotá: Editorial Aguilar, 2005), 246–250.

42. Eduardo Pizarro, "Las FARC-EP," 183.

43. Eduardo Pizarro, *Una democracia asediada*, 87.

44. See chapter 3, on the dire consequences of this decisión for the FARC's political party the Unión Patriótica, UP, formed in 1985.

45. German Santamaría, *Colombia y otras sangres* (Bogotá: Editorial Planeta, 1987), 153–158.

46. Mauricio García Durán, *De La Uribe*, 86.

47. *Semana*, June 14, 1999, 30–33.

48. Fabio Sánchez Torres, and Mario Chacón, "Conflicto, Estado y descentralización: del progreso social a la disputa armada por el control local, 1974–2002," in María Emma Willis and Gonzalo Sánchez, eds., *Nuestra guerra sin nombre. Transformaciones del conflicto en Colombia* (Bogotá: Grupo Editorial Norma, 2006), 362; *Semana*, February 28, 2000, 31–32.

49. Víctor Negrete Barrera, "El conflicto armado y la 'parapolítica en Córdoba," *Revista Foro*, No. 61 (May 2007), 58.

50. Mauricio García Durán, *De La Uribe*, 89–90; Marco Palacios, "La solución política al conflicto armado," in Alvaro Camacho Guizado and Francisco Leal Buitrago, comps., *Armar la paz es desarmar la guerra* (Bogotá: Giro Editores, 1999), 539; S. Ramírez and L.A. Restrepo, *Actores en conflicto*, 172–173.

51. Alvaro Villarraga, *Para reconstruir los sueños*, 91.

52. Toño Sánchez, Jr., "Las cuentas de 'El Viejo Rafa,' in *Cuentos que dan miedo*, 17–19.

53. This is the conclusion drawn by Jesuit scholar Fernán González, in his introduction of Socorro Ramírez and Luis Alberto Restrepo's history of the peace process under Belisario Betancur, *Actores en conflicto*.

54. Among the discussions of Barco's peace program are Eduardo Pizarro Leongómez, "Política de paz, y aperture democrática," in Alvaro Tirado Mejía, ed. *Nueva História de Colombia*, vol. 7 (Bogotá: Editorial Planeta, 1998), 261–288; Ana María Bejarano, "Estrategias de paz"; and Mauricio García Durán, *De La Uribe*.

55. Stephen Dudley, *Walking Ghosts*, 102.

56. Alvaro Villarraga, "La Batalla de Saiza," *Para reconstruir los sueños*, 231–236; Francisco Leal, *La inseguridad*, 109 n 28.

57. Following his release Gómez told of hearing airplanes taking off overhead.

58. Pizarro's directive is found in Rodrigo Marín Bernal, *Itinerario politico de un secuestro* (Bogotá: Editorial Tercer Mundo, 1988), 53–54.

59. Barco's Peace Plan and the CGSB response to it are found in Rodrigo Marín, *Itinerario*, 159–177.

60. Up to that time mayors had been appointed by departmental governors, who in turn were appointed by the national president.

61. Ricardo Santa María Salamanca, "Aspectos políticos del gobierno de Barco (1986–1990)." In Alvaro Tirado Mejía, ed., *Nueva Historia de Colombia*, vol. 7, 75.

62. Ricardo Santa María, "Aspectos," 78.

63. John Martz, *The Politics of Clientelism*, 260.

64. Mauricio Aranguren, "Pizarro tenía que morir," *Mi confesión*, 39–51.

65. The somewhat benign image that Colombians have of the M-19 is owed in part to the fact that the group did not finance operations through massive extortion and kidnapping. While former members of the M-19 have been reluctant to admit it, the group's chief source of funds was in fact monies derived from illegal drug sales. One of the group's leaders, Alvaro Jiménez, admitted that almost all of his colleagues in Medellín knew Pablo Escobar. That was because the guerrilla group and the drug trafficker had a common enemy, the Colombian state. They logically shared their talents and resources in advancing their common struggle. The Alvaro Jiménez remark, and a discussion of the M-19-drug link, are found in Mauricio Rubio, "M-19, secuestro, y narcotráfico," 8–24.

66. The actions of both the M-19 and the EPL accord with analyst Alfredo Rangel's observation that the

first lesson learned from Colombia's long history of peace negotiations with insurgent groups is that "exhaustion of the military option precipitates political negotiations." *Guerra insurgente*, 414.

67. Toño Sánchez, Jr., *Crónicas*, 14.

68. Toño Sánchez, Jr., *Crónicas*, 13.

69. The Honduran CIA asset Juan Ramón Mata Ballesteros did not buy land but rather opened an auto dealership in Montería early in the 1980s, which he used as an office for his cocaine smuggling operation northward to Central America and thence to southern California. When locals would ask about buying one of his cars they were told the vehicles were not for sale. Toño Sánchez, *Crónicas*, 16.

70. Toño Sánchez, *Crónicas*, 53.

71. Mauricio García Durán, *De la Uribe*, 211.

72. Alvaro Valencia Tovar, *Historia*, 202–203.

73. Mauricio García Durán, *De la Uribe*, 171–249.

74. Carlos Medina, *ELN*, 233.

75. Alfredo Rangel, *Guerra insurgente*, 398.

76. See discussions of armed clientelism in Francisco Leal, *La inseguridad*, 243–244; Gustavo Duncan, *Los Señores*, 280–283; and Fabio Sánchez and Mario Chacón, "Conflicto, Estado y descentralización: del progreso social a la disputa armada por el control local, 1974–2002," in María Emma Willis and Gonzalo Sánchez, eds., *Nuestra guerra sin nombre. Transformaciones del conflicto en Colombia* (Bogotá: Editorial Norma, 2006), 399.

77. Colombia's rate of homicides per 100,000 population rose to 80 over the period 1985–95. And the country registered 255,000 homicides during 1980–1994, as opposed to 179,000 between 1948 and 1966. Mauricio Rubio, *Homicidios, justicia, mafias y capital social* (Bogotá: Universidad de los Andes, Centro de Estudios Sobre Desarrollo Económico [Documento CEDE 96–06], 1966: 67; Juan Tokatlian, *Drogas*, 130–131 n 9.

78. Eduardo Posada Carbó, *La nación soñada*, 243–245.

79. *Semana*, September 27, 1994: 28. These figures are calculated on a peso-dollar exchange rate of 836 to 1 in 1993.

80. Román Ortiz, "La guerrilla mutante," 325–326; Eduardo Pizarro, "Las FARC-EP," 189–190. The figure for FARC supporters within the civilian population is calculated on Pizarro's estimate that the guerrilla group had four such sympathizers for each armed member.

81. Mauricio García Durán, *De la Uribe*, 185.

82. Stephen Dudley, *Walking Ghosts*, 180.

83. Mandato Ciudadano Por la Paz, la Vida y la Libertad. *Conversaciones de Paz: Redefinición del Estado*. Bogotá: Mandato Ciudadano, 1999, "Plataforma para un gobierno de reconstrucción y reconciliación nacional, Fuerzas Armadas Revolucionarias de Colombia, FARC-EP," 40–42.

84. Eduardo Pizarro, "Las FARC-UP," 187–189.

85. In formulating this unrealistic plan FARC leaders may have been misled by left pundits who for thirty years had stressed the irredeemable character of the country's political system and institutional framework. For more on this see Eduardo Posada-Carbó, "Language and Politics: On the Colombian 'Establishment.'" *Latin American Research Review*. 42:2 (2007): 111–135.

86. Patricia Madariaga, *Matan y matan y uno sigue ahí. Control paramilitar y vida cotidiana en un pueblo de Urabá* (Bogotá: Universidad de los Andes, 2006), 25.

87. Patricia Madariaga, *Matan y matan*, 26.

88. CINEP, *Deuda*, 359–361.

89. *Semana*, December 6, 1994, 50.

90. *Semana*, December 6, 1994, 40.

91. See chapter 3.

92. The Narco-cassette scandal and Joe Toft's role in it are discussed in Ron Chepesiuk, *The Bullet or the Bribe*, 190–196.

93. Among works dealing with the Narco-cassette scandal and the turbulent Samper administration are Ernesto Samper, *Apuí estoy y aquí me quedo. Testimonio de un gobierno* (Bogotá: El Ancora Editores, 2000); Santiago Medina Serna, *La verdad sobre las mentiras* (Bogotá: Editorial Planeta, 1997); Ingrid Betancourt Pulecio, *Si sabía. Viaje a través del expediente de Ernesto Samper* (Bogotá: Ediciones Temas de Hoy, 1996); Claudia Mora Pineda, ed., *Poder, justicia e indignidad. El juicio al Presidente de la República Ernesto Samper Pizano* (Bogotá: Utopia Ediciones, 1996); Ernesto Rojas Morales, *Colombia a la deriva. Una mirada ética a la política y un juicio moral a la campaña "Samper Presidente"* (Bogotá: Litho Copias Calidad, 1997); Manuel Vicente Peña, *El narcofiscal* (Bogotá: Fundación Deberes Humanos, 2000).

94. An army colonel was ultimately jailed for the crime, while North Valle cartel leader Hernando Gómez Bustamante ("Rasguño") admitted his organization paid to have the Conservative party leader killed. See Juan Carlos Giraldo, *De Rasguño, y otros secretos del bajo mundo* (Bogotá: Icono Editorial, 2007); Gustavo Duncan, *Los Señores de la Guerra*, 231; *Semana*, July 23, 2007, 37; *La Otra Verdad* (Bogotá), 1:2:29–37.

95. By 1994 Colombia was proclaimed to be the world's most violent country, with a homicide rate of 77 per 100,000 population, or 23,000 during that year. During the latter 1990s the number of homicides in Colombia ran 25,000 per year. *Latin American Update*, April 1994, 18; Alvaro Tirado, "Política exterior," 227.

96. These episodes are recorded in Samper's *Aquí estoy*, 288–295.

97. Alejandro Santos, "Vicisitudes," 173; Luis Alberto Restrepo, "Los arduos dilemas de la deocracia en Colombia," in María Emma Willis and Gonzalo Sánchez, eds., *Nuestra guerra sin nombre. Transformaciones del conflicto en Colombia* (Bogotá: Editorial Norma, 2006), 337–338.

98. A history of the Miraflores battle is Luis Alberto Villamarín Pulido, *Drama, pesadilla y ... espectáculo* (Bogotá: Ediciones Luis Alberto Villamaría Pusido, 1997). See also *Semana*, June 23, 1997, 34–37; *Semana*, January 12, 1998, 18–23; Robin Kirk, *More Terrible Than Death*, 242–245.

99. *Semana*, March 9, 1998, 57.

100. Luis Alberto Restrepo, "Los arduos dilemmas"; *Semana*, July 28, 1997, 26–32.

101. *Semana*, March 9, 1998, 52–25; Francisco Leal, *La inseguridad*, 203–216.

102. Douglas Farah and Stephen Braun, *Merchant of Death: Money, Guns, Planes and the Man Who Makes War Possible* (Hoboken, N.J.: John Wiley and Sons, 2007), 160.

103. His elder brother Fidel had died fighting the guerrillas in 1994.

104. Details of the Mitú attack are found in *Semana*, November 9, 1998, 50–53; July 19, 1999, 25–26; September 6, 1999, 26–27.

105. *Semana Special Edition*, January 11, 1999. *Semana*, February 11, 2008, 30. A history of the Cleared Zone is Luis Alberto Villamarín Pulido, *La silla vacía* (Bogotá: Talleres de TM Editores, 2002).

106. *Semana*, June 7, 1999, 23; *Semana* June 21, 1999, 28.

107. Strong U.S. reaction against these murders led Suárez to later refer to his order as "The mistake from hell." The incident is described in Burt Ruiz, *The Colombian Civil War* (Jefferson, North Carolina: McFarland, 2001), 30.

108. *Semana*, May 31, 1999, 47.

109. *Semana*'s lead article in its edition of June 28, 1999, was "Exodus," and featured the plight of these hapless victims of the growing violence.

110. *Semana*, May 5, 2003, 62.

111. *Semana*, March 1, 1999, 37; *Semana*, August 23, 2999, 35.

112. *The Economist*, April 21, 2001, "Colombia Survey," 7; Mauricio Cabrera Gálvis, "Los dineros ilícitos en la economía colombiana," *Revista Javeriana*, vol. 143, no. 739 (October 2007), 35. It is estimated that in 1992 some 40,000 hectares were devoted to coca cultivated. By 2000 an estimated 135,000 to 150,000 hectares were.

113. Tokatlian writing in Alvaro Camacho Guizado, Andrés López, and Francisco Thoumi, *Las drogas: Una Guerra fallida. Visiones críticas* (Bogotá: Tercer Mundo, 1999), xvi.

114. Elva María Restrepo, Fabio Sánchez Torres, and Mariana Martínez, *¿Impunidad o castigo? Análisis e implicaciones de la investigación penal en secuestro, terrorismo y peculado* (Bogotá: Universidad de los Andes, CEDE Document 9 [February 2004]), *passim*, especially 9, "Evolución del Secuestro, 1962–2002."

115. Francisco Gutiérrez Sanín, "Criminal Rebels? A Discusión of Civil War and Criminality from the Colombian Experience," *Politics and Society*, vol. 32, n. 2 (June 2004), 266; Mauricio Rubio, *Del rapto a la pesca milagrosa*, 25–33; *Semana*, November 12, 2001.

116. *Semana*, November 22, 1999, 42–44.

117. *Semana*, May 1, 1999, 23–24.

118. From an interview with FARC deserter "Rafael Quintana," *Semana*, February 24, 2008, 25.

119. Norwegian diplomat Jan Egland brokered the trip, featuring stops in Stockholm, Brussels, Bern, Paris, Rome, and Madrid. *Semana*, February 7, 2000, 20–24.

120. In April 1999 the Bishop of Ariari, headquartered in Villavicencio, Meta, denounced these kidnappings. A year later U.S. journalist Alma Guillermoprieto wrote on this subject in a piece titled "The Children's War," *The New York Review of Books*, May 11, 2000, 37–40. See also *Semana*, April 19, 1999, 46.

121. Jaime Zuloaga Nieto, "El incierto camino de la solución negociada," *Síntesis 2001. Anuario social, político y económico de Colombia* (Bogotá: Tercer Mundo Editores, 2001), 70.

122. The ERG was the Ejército Revolucionario Guevarista. *Semana*, October 22, 2000, 26.

123. *Semana*, November 19, 2001, 44–46.

124. *Semana*, October 1, 2007, 88; *Síntesis 2001. Anuario social, político y económico de Colombia* (Bogotá: Tercer Mundo Editores, 2002), 187.

125. Jaime Zuloaga, "El incierto camino," 89–93; *Semana*, January 28, 2002, 22–25, 32–33; *The Economist*, February 9, 2002, 32.

126. Jaime Zuloaga, "El incierto camino," 89.

127. Six years later the Assemblymen were executed by their captors just before an army patrol arrived to free them. Events surrounding the Betancourt kidnapping are reported in *Semana*, March 4, 2002, 26–30. A photo of the armored car in which Uribe was riding on April 4, 2002, can be seen in *Semana*, December 16, 2002, 79.

Chapter 5

1. Toño Sánchez, Jr., *Crónicas*, 100.

2. One of the many places these events are discussed is James D. Henderson, *When Colombia Bled*.

3. Mauricio Rubio, *Del rapto a la pesca milagrosa*, 6–7. For further detail on the Marquetalia attack see chapter 4.

4. Early history of the FARC is contained in Jacobo Arenas, *Cese el fuego*; Eduardo Pizarro, "Revolutionary Guerrilla Groups"; and Patricia Lara, *Siembra vientos y recogerás tempestades* (Bogotá: Editorial Planeta, 1982), 89–117.

5. For other information on Eder's kidnapping see chapter 2.

6. Details on Eder's kidnapping, and others carried out by the FARC during the latter 1960s, are contained in Alejo Vargas Velásquez, *Política y armas al inicio del Frente National* (Bogotá: Imprenta Universidad Nacional, 1996), 119–151; and in Mauricio Rubio, *Del rapto a la pesca milagrosa*, 6–7.

7. Mario Iván Ureña Sánchez, "Evolución histórica e ideológica del paramilitarismo contemporáneo en Colombia" (Unpublished typescript. Bogotá, Colombia, 2007. Universidad La Grán Colombia), 24.

8. Toño Sánchez, Jr., *Crónicas*, 100.

9. Mauricio Aranguren, *Mi confesión*, 63.

10. See chapter 4.

11. *Semana*, July 9, 2007, 187; María Alejandra Vélez, *FARC-ELN: Evolución y expansion territorial* (Bogotá: Universidad de los Andes, 2000 [CEDE Document 08]).

12. *Semana*, February 6, 2006, 46; *Semana*, April 30, 2007, 51.

13. *Semana*, April 30, 2007, 51–52; *Semana*, May 7, 2007, 80; Fabio Castillo, *La coca nostra*, 200–201.

14. Otty Patiño Hormaza and Alvaro Jiménez Mil-

lán, eds., *Las verdaderas intenciones de los paramilitares* (Bogotá: Intermedio Editores, 2002), 68–73.

15. *Semana*, February 6, 2006, 46.

16. Otty Patiño, ed., *Las verdaderas intenciones*, 68–73; Toño Sánchez, Jr., *Crónicas*, 107–108, 223.

17. The best discussion of ACDEGAM is found in Carlos Medina Gallego, *Autodefensas, paramilitares y narcotráfico en Colombia. Origen, desarrolloy consolidación. El caso de "Puerto Boyacá"* (Bogotá: Editorial Documentos Periodísticos, 1990), 219–242. See also Toño Sánchez, *Crónicas*, 107–112.

18. Carlos Medina, *Autodefensas*, 233.

19. Mauricio Aranguren, *Mi confesión*, 58–60.

20. Mauricio Aranguren, *Mi confesión*, 64.

21. Mauricio Aranguren, *Mi confesión*, 66–67.

22. Mauricio Aranguren, *Mi confesión*, 67, 83–84.

23. For further detail on MAS see chapter 2.

24. Mauricio Aranguren, *Mi confesión*, 87.

25. Mauricio Aranguren, *Mi confesión*, 89.

26. Mauricio Aranguren, *Mi confesión*, 88, 103.

27. Toño Sánchez, Jr., *Crónicas*; 15; Stephen Dudley, *Walking Ghosts*, 147.

28. Mauricio Romero, *Paramilitares y autodefensas, 1982–2003* (Bogotá: Editorial Planeta, 2003), 130–135.

29. Alfonso Aranguren, *Mi confesión*, 184–185.

30. Toño Sánchez, Jr., *Crónicas*, 12–15, 53.

31. See Mauricio Aranguren, *Mi confesión*, 107–111, for Castaño's account of his experience in Israel.

32. Toño Sánchez, Jr., *Crónicas*, 50.

33. Mauricio Aranguren, *Mi confesión*, 111–115.

34. Mauricio Romero, *Paramilitares*, 198.

35. Toño Sánchez, *Crónicas*, 52–53.

36. Toño Sánchez, *Crónicas*, 53–55.

37. For detail on the UP, and the killing of its members, see chapters 3 and 4.

38. The history of the *Unión Patriótica* is told in Stephen Dudley's *Walking Ghosts*.

39. Mauricio Romero, *Paramilitares*, 126–127.

40. For more detail on the schools see chapter 3.

41. Toño Sánchez, *Crónicas*, 55–57.

42. For more on the CGSB see chapter 4.

43. A map showing the locations of the attacks are found in Clara Inés García, *Urabá: Region, actors y conflicto, 1960–1990* (Bogotá: Gente Nueva Editorial, 1996), 160.

44. The Battle of Saiza is discussed in Villarraga and Plazas, *Para Reconstruir los Sueños*, 231–236.

45. José Gutiérrez, *Vértigo en el jardín del mal* (Bogotá: La Buena Semilla, 2007), 92–94.

46. Mauricio Romero, *Paramilitares*, 181.

47. Glenda Martínez, *Salvatore Mancuso: Su vida* (Bogotá: Editorial Norma, 2004), 96–97; José Gutiérrez, *Vértigo*; Mauricio Aranguren, *Mi confesión*, 137. Virgilio Barco established a presidential human rights commission following the Pueblo Bello massacre. The Inter-American Court of Human Rights handed down its finding on the massacre January 31, 2006. During April 1990 officials searched *Las Tangas*, retrieving the 42 victims of the massacre, and other cadavers as well. CINEP, *Deuda*, 52.

48. Stephen Dudley, *Walking Ghosts*, 143–144.

49. Mario Aguilera Peña, "ELN: Entre las armas y la política," In María Emma Willis and Gonzalo Sánchez Gómez, eds. *Nuestra Guerra sin nombre. Transformaciones del conflicto en Colombia* (Bogotá: Editorial Norma, 2006), 223; García Durán, *De la Uribe*, 185.

50. Mauricio Aranguren, *Mi confesión*, 39–51. Officially the Pizarro assassination remains unresolved. Many reject the claim of Carlos Castaño that he acted alone in having the former M-19 leader killed. See, for example, *Semana*, April 26, 2010, 18, "Veinte años sin Pizarro."

51. Villarraga and Plazas, *Para Reconstruir los Sueños*, 311.

52. Carlos Castaño Gil, *Compendio de entrevistas*, 2nd ed. (Colombia: Talleres Colombia Libre, 1997), 10. Approved by ACCU leaders July 1990, the Statutes of the ACCU were rewritten in March 1996.

53. Mauricio Aranguren, *Mi confesión*, 82; Glenda Martínez, *Salvatore Mancuso*, 97–98.

54. Carlos Miguel Ortiz Sarmiento, *Urabá: Pulsiones de vida y desafíos de muerte* (Medellín: La Carreta Ediciones, 2007), 157.

55. Paramilitary activity for the years 1988 through 2003 is tracked in CINEP, *Deuda*.

56. CINEP, *Deuda*, 72.

57. Toño Sánchez, *Crónicas*, 91.

58. Eddy, Sabogal, and Walden, *The Cocaine Wars*, 285.

59. See chapter 2.

60. CINEP, *Deuda*, 69–70.

61. CINEP, *Deuda*, 70.

62. One billion pesos were worth $8,868,000 in 1984.

63. For further detail on the Medellín cartel–Middle Magdalena paramilitary relationship see chapter 3.

64. Fabio Castillo, *La coca nostra*, 228.

65. Stephen Dudley, *Walking Ghosts*, 101.

66. Toño Sánchez, *Crónicas*, 126–129.

67. Toño Sánchez, *Crónicas*, 134–135. Sixteen years later, in 2004, the Inter-American Court of Justice condemned the Colombian government for its part in the massacre, citing the complicity of army officers in ACDEGAM's military activities. *Semana*, July 26, 2004, 52.

68. Detail on the Cartel War is contained in chapter 3.

69. For more detail see chapter 3.

70. The Mejor Esquina massacre is described in detail in Toño Sánchez, *Crónicas*, 58–77. Martínez was not at the Easter celebration.

71. Toño Sánchez, *Crónicas*, 79.

72. Investigation of the Córdoba and Urabá massacres of March and April 1988 led to the issuing of arrest warrants for Pablo Escobar, José Gonzalo Rodríguez Gacha, and Fidel Castaño. For further information on M-19 demobilization see chapter 4.

73. For further information on Alonso de Jesús Baquero see chapter 3.

74. The most exhaustive account of Viáfara's testimony is contained in Fabio Castillo, *La coca nostra*, 197–250.

75. For his account of this collaboration with DAS during the pursuit of Pablo Escobar, under the assumed name of "Alekos," see Mauricio Aranguren, *Mi confesión*, 128–141.

76. For detail on Escobar's year of voluntary confinement see chapter 3.

77. The letter is contained in Mauricio Aranguren, *Mi confesión*, 125.

78. The PEPES and the hunt for Pablo Escobar are discussed in chapter 3.

79. Toño Sánchez, *Crónicas*, 247, 273.

80. Fidel Castaño was killed by a lucky shot fired from a group of EPL guerrillas he was pursuing at the time. See Mauricio Aranguren, *Mi confesión*, 21–37, for the account of his death by Castaño's brother Carlos.

81. Mauricio Aranguren, *Mi confesión*, 322.

82. See below for information of formation of the AUC.

83. As the guerrilla offensive of 1994–2002 reached its high point, and as guerrilla kidnapping made highways of the country unsafe, average Colombians saw the paramilitaries as fighting to protect them.

84. Detail on the killing of *Esperanzados* can be found in CINEP, *Deuda*, 72–106, and on the *La Chinita* massacre in Glenda Martínez, *Salvatore*, 122–123; Patricia Madariaga, *Matan y matan*, 25–26; *Semana*, May 26, 2008, 38.

85. Discussions of Convivir are contained in Gonzalo de Franco, "La fuerza pública y la estrategia para enfrentar el fenómeno guerrillero," in Malcolm Deas and María Victoria Llorente, comps., *Reconocer la guerra para construir la paz* (Bogotá: Cartographics, 1999), 504–509; CINEP, *Deuda*, 359–361; *Semana*, February 25, 1995, 22–24, and March 22, 1999, 33–34.

86. Glenda Martínez, *Salvatore*, 108–111.

87. Glenda Martínez, *Salvatore*, 111.

88. Glenda Martínez, *Salvatore*, 109–110.

89. Mauricio Romero, *Paramilitares*, 206–209.

90. The UP mayor of Apartadó, Nelson Campo, elected in 1992, had planned the *La Chinita* massacre of January 1994. He was convicted of the crime and served a prison sentence for it. Mauricio Romero, *Paramilitares*, 212.

91. CINEP, *Deuda*, 311–326.

92. *El Espectador*, June 27, 1996.

93. Rafael Pardo Rueda, *Fin del paramilitarismo. ¿Es posible su desmonte?* (Bogotá: Ediciones B, 2007), 27; Carlos Miguel Ortiz, *Urabá*, 158; *Semana*, July 9, 1996, 32–38, 40–41.

94. Mauricio Romero, *Paramilitares*; *Semana*, July 14, 2008, 32.

95. Alejandro Santos, "Vicisitudes," 186–187.

96. Carlos Castaño, *Compendio de entrevistas*, 9–26; *Semana*, March 31, 1997, 30. See also José Jairo González, "Los paramilitares y el colapso estatal en Meta y Casanare," in Leonardo A. Archila R., ed., *Parapolítica. La ruta de la expansión paramilitar y los acuerdos políticos*, 2nd expanded edition (Bogotá: Intermedio Editores, November 2007): 318–319.

97. Gloria Martínez, *Salvatore*, 124–125. The 52 AUC Fronts, as they existed in 2003, and the geographic areas in which they operated, are listed in Juan Carlos Garzón, "La complejidad paramilitar: una aproximación estratégica," in Alfredo Rangel, ed., *El poder paramilitar* (Bogotá: Editorial Planeta, 2005), 118.

98. *Semana*, July 28, 1997, 26–32.

99. CINEP, *Deuda*, 283–284; *Semana*, January 31, 2005, 36–39.

100. This figure is based on a four-to-one ratio of civilian supporters for each armed guerrilla in the field.

101. *Semana*, March 31, 1997, 26–32.

102. Eduardo Pizarro, *Una democracia asediada*, 122.

103. *Semana*, August 6, 2007, 34–38.

104. José Jairo González, "Los paramilitares," 319.

105. An analysis of the fighting in Barrancabermeja is Andrés R. Vargas, "Guerra civil en Colombia: el caso de Barrancabermeja," in Jorge A. Restrepo and David Aponte, eds., *Guerra y violencias en Colombia. Herramientas e interpretaciones* (Bogotá: Pontificia Universitaria Javeriana, 2009) 423–466.

106. Mauricio Aranguren, *Mi confesión*, 208; *Semana*, November 7, 2005, 41–42.

107. *Semana*, December 6, 2004, 58–59; *Semana*, February 12, 2007, 34; *Semana*, May 19, 2008, 38.

108. Carlos Miguel Ortiz, *Urabá*, 165.

109. Juan Carlos Vargas, *Cuando la Guerra es el único camino. Memorias de un ex combatiente* (Bogotá: Norma, 2007), 146–179; *Semana*, March 19, 2007, 27–32.

110. Alvaro Guzmán B., and Renata Moreno Q., "Autodefensas, narcotráfico y comportamiento estatal en Valle del Cauca, 1997–2005," in Leonardo A. Archila R., ed., *Parapolítica. La ruta de la expansión paramilitar y los acuerdos políticos*, 2nd expanded ed. (Bogotá: Intermedio Editores, 2007), 267–273.

111. *Semana*, November 7, 2005, 42–44.

112. Mauricio Romero, *Paramilitaries*, 152.

113. *Semana*, July 19, 1999, 111.

114. Mauricio Romero, *Paramilitaries*, 192–194.

115. CINEP, *Deuda*, 273.

116. *Semana*, October 9, 2006, 36. For a short history of the AUC Catatumbo offensive see Salud Hernández-Mora, "El negocio del terror. Coca y violencia en el Catatumbo," in Leonardo Archila Ruiz, ed., *El poder, para ¿Qué?* (Bogotá: Intermedio Editores, 2007): 59–133.

117. Massacres in Colombia are treated in María Victoria Uribe and Teófilo Vásquez, *Enterrar y callar. Las massacres en Colombia, 1980–1993*, 2 vols. (Bogotá: Editorial Presencia, 1995). Studies of Colombia's displaced population during the late 1990s and first years of the twenty-first century include Clara Marcela Barona de Ayerbe and Sara Lucía Franky Calvo, eds., *Un país que huye. Desplazamiento y violencia* (Bogotá: Editora Guadalupe, 1999); Ana María Ibáñez and Carlos Eduardo Vélez, *Instrumentos de atención de la población desplazada en Colombia: Una distribución desigual de las responsabilidades municipales* (Bogotá: University of the Andes, December 2003 [CEDE Document 37]); Ana María Ibáñez and Pablo Querubín, *Acceso a tierras y desplazamiento forzoso en Colombia* (Bogotá: University of the Andes, May 2004 [CEDE Document 23]).

118. Román Ortiz, "La guerrilla mutante," 341.

119. The best account of this process is Ricardo Aricapa, *Comuna 13: Crónica de una Guerra urbana* (Medellín: Editorial Universidad de Antioqia, 2005). A documentary film source is Scott Dalton and Margarita Martínez, *La Sierra*, 2005.

120. Eduardo Pizarro Leongómez, *Una democracía asediada. Balance y perspectivas del conflicto en Colombia* (Bogotá: Editorial Norma, 2004), 334, n. 4.

121. Mauricio Aranguren, *Mi confesión*, 283–284.

122. Mauricio Romero, *Paramilitares*, 256.

123. Román Ortiz, "La guerrilla mutante," 338.

124. *Semana*, July 12, 1999, 40–44.

125. Mauricio Aranguren, *Mi confesión*, 327–329.

126. Carlos Castaño was indignant when he learned of Pastrana's nomination for the world's most prestigious award. See Mauricio Aranguren, *Mi confesión*, 262.

127. *Semana*, January 22, 2007, 24–29.

128. *Semana*, August 18, 2003, 32.

129. Mauricio Romero, ed., *Paramilitaries*, contains abundant detail on paramilitary involvement in elections taking place between 2000 and 2007. The *parapolítica* scandal has been reported on extensively in Colombia since 2002. See chapter 6, for further detail on this matter.

130. Priscila Zúñiga, "Ilegalidad, control local y paramilitaries en Magdalena," in Leonardo A. Archila R., ed., *Parapolítica. La ruta de la expansión paramilitar y las acuerdos políticos*, 2nd expanded edition (Bogotá: Intermedio Editores, 2007), 252.

131. Édgar Artunduaga, *H.P. Historias particulares de los Honorables Parlamentarios* (Bogotá: Editorial Oveja Negra, 2006), 286; *Semana*, November 7, 2005, 42–44; *Semana*, February 12, 2007, 32; *Semana*, September 3, 2007, 58.

132. Mauricio Aranguren, *Mi confesión*, 205–210.

133. Alfredo Serrano Zabala, *La batalla final de Carlos Castaño* (Bogotá: Editorial Oveja Negra, 2007), 39–40; *Semana*, July 29, 2002, 24–26.

134. *Semana*, July 22, 2002, 40–41.

135. *Semana*, September 29, 2003, 50–51.

136. Detail on the Uribe government's negotiations with the paramilitaries is container in chapter 6.

137. Glenda Martínez, *Salvatore*, 137, 141–145; *Semana*, July 21, 2003, 32–35.

138. Detail on the nineteen demobilizations taking place between November 25, 2003 and September 11, 2005, are contained in Natalia Springer, *Desactivar la Guerra. Alternativas audaces para consolidar la paz* (Bogotá: Aguilar, 2005), 327. Other detail is contained in chapter 6.

139. Mauricio Aranguren, *Mi confesión*, 155. Detail on Castaño's death are contained in Alfredo Serrano Zabala, *La batalla final de Carlos Castaño* (Bogotá: Editorial Oveja Negra, 2007).

140. *The Economist*, June 3, 2006, 14.

141. *Semana*, August 11, 2003, 25; Glenda Martínez, *Mancuso*, 126 n. 12.

Chapter 6

1. Silvana Paternostro, *My Colombian War: A Journey Through the Country I Left Behind*. New York: Henry Holt, 2007, 248.

2. See chapter 5.

3. *Semana*, January 28, 2002.

4. *Los Angeles Times*, March 25, 2002; *Semana*, April 2, 2007, 32; Harvey F. Kline, *Showing Teeth to the Dragons: State Building by Colombian President Alvaro Uribe Vélez* (Tuscaloosa: University of Alabama Press, 2009), 184–187; Ricardo Aricapa, *Comuna 13*, 212–236; *Semana*, October 21, 2002, 22–28.

5. Michael Spagat, "Colombia's Paramilitary DDR [Demobilization, Disarmament, and Reintegration]: Quiet and Tentative Success" (Bogotá: Centro de Recursos para el Analisis de Conflictos [CERAC], 2006), 6.

6. U.S. Department of State. "United States Policy Towards Colombia" (Washington, D.C., December 2002), 15.

7. Armando Borrero Mansilla, "Cómo se va a ganar la Guerra," *Semana*, December 23, 2002, 38–40.

8. *Semana*, May 27, 2002, 42.

9. Harvey Kline, *Showing Teeth to the Dragons*, 42–43; Alexandra Samper, "Doce horas con Uribe," *Semana*, July 28, 2003, 30–32.

10. *Semana*, December 16, 2002, 68–70.

11. Alejandro Santos, "El año que volvió la esperanza. Análisis del primer año de gobierno de Alvaro Uribe," *Semana*, July 28, 2003, 24–28.

12. *Semana*, January 22, 2007, 24–29.

13. See chapter 5.

14. The best work on this process is Leonardo Archila, ed., *Parapolítica*; see also *Semana*, February 12, 2007, 31–32.

15. Details on early stages of the paramilitary-government negotiations are contained in CINEP, *Deuda*, 395; *Semana*, November 25, 2002, 40–44; *Semana*, December 2, 2002, 38–39.

16. *Semana*, June 2, 2003, 28–34; *Semana*, July 21, 2003, 32–35; Glenda Martínez, *Salvatore Mancuso*, 137–167.

17. An exploration of Colombia's tradition of granting amnesty for political crimes is Sven Schuster, "'Progresar es perdonar': algunas reflexiones sobre las amnistías en Colombia, siglos XIX a XXI" (Universidad Católica de Eichstätt, Alemania, 2009) *sven-schuster@gmx.de* Accessed September 2009.

18. See the compilation of positions taken regarding the law's sedition clause as related to the paramilitaries in Gerson Iván Arias and Joanna Rojas, "La 'sedición paramilitary': Principales momentos y posturas del Debate" (Bogotá: Fundación Ideas Para la Paz, August 2007), 1–29.

19. Detail on the law is found in Harvey Kline, *Showing Teeth to the Dragons*, 49–73.

20. *Semana*, June 3, 2002, 38–40.

21. See Harvey Kline, *Showing Teeth to the Dragons*, 101–129, for detail on the unproductive peace talks with the ELN during Uribe's first term.

22. *Semana*, February 17, 2003, 32–37.

23. *Semana*, February 17, 2003, 30–31; *Semana*, May 18, 2003, 36–42. Details on the crash, and a photo of the plane, are found in Mark Bowden, "Flight Risk," *The Atlantic*, July/August 2009: 21–24. After a U.S. company ignored pilot warnings that the Cesna Caravans

were insufficient, one of them crashed. Three uninjured Americans were taken captive by the FARC. The airplane's passengers were contract workers involved in anti-drug and anti-FARC activities, and were paid by the U.S. government through Plan Colombia.

24. *Semana*, April 21, 2003, 14–21; *Semana*, April 28, 2003, 19.

25. For a description of High Mountain Battalion Number 1 see Jineth Bedoya Lima, *Diario de un combate, y otras crónicas de Guerra* (Bogotá: Círculo de Lectores, 2005), 85–88.

26. *Semana*, November 10, 2003, 44.

27. Harvey Kline, *Showing Teeth to the Dragons*, 47.

28. The soldiers spirited the money away and spent most of it in the red light districts of nearby towns. A Colombian film, *Soñar no cuesta nada* (Dreams are Free), released in 2007, dramatized the event.

29. *Semana*, July 19, 2004, 62–69.

30. *Semana*, August 1, 2005, 40–42; *Semana*, October 17, 2005, 48–54.

31. Harvey Kline, *Showing Teeth to the Dragons*, 48.

32. Harvey Kline, *Showing Teeth to the Dragons*, 41, 195–196; *Semana*, May 2, 2002, 32; *The Economist*, September 8, 2007, 39.

33. *Semana*, January 5, 2004, 20–23; *Semana*, December 6, 2004, 40–44; Silvana Paternostro, *My Colombian War*, 84.

34. *El Tiempo*, September 23, 2007; *Semana*, September 10, 2007, 36–38.

35. *Semana*, March 17, 24–39.

36. *The Economist*, March 15, 2008, 47; *Semana*, March 17, 2008; Myrtle Beach, South Carolina, *Sun News*, March 8, 2008.

37. *Semana*, May 8, 2006, 47; *Semana*, March 10, 2008; *Semana*, September 29, 2008, 52–53.

38. *Semana*, May 26, 2008, 24; Camden, New Jersey, *Courier-Post*, May 24, 2008; Myrtle Beach , South Carolina, *Sun News*, May 24, 2008.

39. Marc Gonsalves, Keith Stansell, and Tom Hughes, *Out of Captivity: Surviving 1967 Days in the Colombian Jungle* (New York: Harper Collins, 2009), 418, 420.

40. *Semana*, May 19, 2008, 24–32.

41. *Semana*, July 7, 2008, 40–44.

42. Accounts of Operation Checkmate are contained in Marc Goncalves, et. al., *Out of Captivity*; J.G. Ortiz Abella, ed., *Operación Jaque. Secretos no revelados* (Bogotá: Editorial Oveja Negra, 2008); Juan Carlos Torres, *Operación Jaque. La verdadora historia* (Bogotá: Editorial Planeta, 2008); *Semana*, July 7, 2008, 40–44; *Semana*, September 29, 2008, 32–36.

43. *Cambio*, September 4, 2007, 42.

44. Juan Carlos Torres, *Operación Jaque*, 126, 194–195.

45. Francisco Leal, *La inseguridad*, 217–218.

46. This reform effort is discussed in Eduardo Pizarro Leongómez, "La reforma militar en un contexto de la democratización política," in Francisco Leal Buitrago, comp., *En busca de la estabilidad perdida. Actores políticos y sociales en los años noventa* (Bogotá: Tercer Mundo Editores, 1995), 196–208.

47. Eduardo Pizarro, *Una democracia*, 99, note 20; 343.

48. *Semana*, November 9, 1998, 50–53.

49. Francisco Leal, "Políticas de seguridad: De improvisación en improvisación," in Francisco Leal Buitrago, ed., *En la encrucijada*, 225–231.

50. Harvey Kline, *Showing Teeth to the Dragons*, 46.

51. Alfredo Rangel Suárez. Personal interview, October 11, 2007.

52. Connie Veillette, "Plan Colombia: A Progress Report" (Washington, D.C.: Congressional Research Service, Library of Congress, June 22, 2005).

53. U.S. Department of State, "Report to Congress: U.S. Assistance Programs in Colombia and Plans to Transfer Responsibilities to Colombia" (Washington, D.C.: U.S. Department of State, March 2006).

54. Colombia, National Planning Department and Department of Justice and Security, "Plan Colombia Progress Report, 1999–2005" (Bogotá: Departamento Nacional de Planeación, September 2006), 17; Harvey Kline, *Showing Teeth to the Dragons*, 195–196.

55. Colombia, National Planning Department and Department of Justice and Security, "Colombia's Strategy for Strengthening Democracy and Promoting Social Development, 2007–1013" (Bogotá: Departamento Nacional de Planeación, February 2007), 58–59; Connie Veillette, "Plan Colombia," 12.

56. Colombia, National Planning, "Colombia's Strategy," 34–35.

57. Robert B. Charles, "U.S. Policy in Colombia," in Analisa DeGrave, ed., *Taking Sides. Clashing Views on Latin American Issues* (Dubuque, Iowa: McGraw-Hill, 2007), 53–60 [excerpted from June 17, 2004 testimony before the U.S. House Committee on Government Reform]; United States of America, USAID, "Colombia Quarterly Results/ACI" (Washington, D.C.: USAID, September 30, 2006).

58. United States of America, Department of State, "Memorandum of Justification Concerning Conditions for Assistance for the Demobilization, Disarmament and Reintegration of Former Members of Foreign Terrorist Organizations in Colombia" (Washington, D.C.: Department of State, 2008).

59. Connie Veillette, "Plan Colombia"; Alfredo Rangel, "El éxito de Plan Colombia," *Cambio*, September 4, 2006, 24; *Semana*, March 10, 2003, 27.

60. Colombia, National Planning, "Colombia's Strategy."

61. U.S. Department of State, "Report on the Multiyear Strategy for U.S. Assistance Programs in Colombia" (Washington, D.C.: Department of State, April 2009); BBCMundo.com., May 2, 2007, "Plan Colombia: ¿en qué se gasta el dinero?"

62. U.S. Department of State, "Report on the Multiyear Strategy."

63. U.S. Department of State, "Report on U.S. Assistance Programs in Colombia" (Washington, D.C.: Department of State, 2007).

64. The complex reintegration and anti-drug program is detailed in U.S. Department of State, "Memorandum of Justification," 34–35.

65. *Semana*, February 6, 2006, 38–40.

66. *El Tiempo*, July 31 and August 3, 2006.

67. *El Tiempo*, August 3, 2006.

68. *El Tiempo*, August 14, 2006.

69. The article, under the byline of Juan Forero, was reprinted in *El Tiempo* August 27, 2006.

70. *El Tiempo*, August 21, 2006.

71. Cogent statements of these criticisms are Joy Olson, "Addicted to Failure. Statement of Joy Olson Before the Subcommittee of the Western Hemisphere House International Relations Committee, March 30, 2006" (Washington, D.C.: Washington Office on Latin America, 2006); Russell Crandall, *Driven by Drugs: U.S. Policy toward Colombia*, 2nd ed. (Boulder: Lynne Rienner, 2008); Brian Loveman, ed., *Addicted to Failure: U.S. Security Policy in Latin America and the Andean Region* (New York: Rowman and Littlefield, 2006).

72. Francisco Leal, *La inseguridad*, 226–227.

73. Alma Guillermoprieto, "Colombia: War Without End?" *New York Review of Books*, April 27, 2000, 31–39.

74. See chapter 1.

75. *Semana*, March 23, 2009, 36–37.

76. Colombia, National Planning, "Colombia Strategy," 82.

77. Sociological aspects of these matters are treated in Gustavo Duncan, *Los Señores*, and in the same author's "El dinero no es todo: acerca del narcotráfico en la persistencia del conflicto colombiano" (Bogotá: Ediciones Uniandes, 2008), Departamento de Ciencias Políticas, Documento #152, 40 pages.

78. This is the conclusion drawn in Soledad Granada, Jorge A. Restrepo, and Andrés R. Vargas, "El agotamiento de la política de seguridad: evolución y transformaciones recientes en el conflicto armado colombiano," in Jorge A. Restrepo and David Aponte, eds., *Guerra y violencias en Colombia* (Bogotá: Pontificia Universidad Javeriana, 2009) 27–124.

79. *Semana*, November 26, 2007, 66–67.

80. *Semana*, August 13, 2007, 56–60.

81. Colombia, National Planning, "Colombia Strategy," 68–75.

82. Steve Curwood, "Living on Earth," National Public Radio, June 21, 2009; United States, Department of State, "Report on U.S. Assistance," 26; Colombia, National Planning, "Colombia Strategy," 68–75.

83. Colombia, Presidencia, Agencia Presidencial para la Acción Social y Cooperación Internacional, "Desembolsos Asistencia Oficial al Desarrollo [AOD] en Colombia, 1998–2007" (Bogotá, June 2008).

84. For information on these intra–AUC battles see Juan Carlos Vargas, *Cuando la Guerra*, 146–179; *El Tiempo*, March 9, 2007 and September 23, 2007; *Semana*, March 19, 2007, 27–31.

85. *Semana*, May 25, 2009, 52.

86. *Semana*, May 25, 2009, 52–54.

87. Colombia, National Planning, "Colombia Strategy," 69.

88. *Semana*, July 21, 2008, 23; *Semana*, May 18, 2009, 54–55; *Semana*, May 25, 2009, 42–43; *Semana*, July 20, 2009, 48.

89. The idea was proposed by then-former defense minister Juan Manuel Santos—who went on to be elected President for the 2010–2014 term. *Semana*, May 25, 2009, 42–43.

90. *Semana*, July 27, 2009, 36–37.

91. *Semana*, July 27, 2009, 28–31. See especially "Las mentiras de Chávez," *Semana*, August 17, 2009, 24–28.

92. *Semana*, July 20, 2009, 22–28. Ecuador restored relations with Colombia in August 2009.

93. The quote is from an official report on FARC activities in Ecuador compiled over the course of 2009, discussed in *Semana*, December 14, 2009, 34–39.

94. *The Economist*, July 25, 2009, 35–36; *Semana*, July 20, 2009, 24–25.

95. *Semana*, February 4, 2008, 30–34; *Semana*, May 19, 2008, 24–32; *The Economist*, May 24, 2008, 50–54; Connie Viellette, "Plan Colombia," 13; *Semana*, July 27, 2009, 28–31; *Semana*, August 3, 2009, 24–28, 56.

96. *Semana*, December 14, 2009, 38.

97. *Washington Post*, May 20, 2009; *The Economist*, July 25, 2009, 35–36.

98. Alfredo Rangel, "La caída del narcotráfico," *Semana*, March 8, 2010, 78.

99. From a United Nations report cited in *Time* magazine, August 13, 2012: 9.

100. Colombia's homicide rate stood at 61 per 100,000 when Uribe took office in 2002. It declined to 39 in 2007 and 34 in 2008. *Semana*, June 15, 2009, 13.

101. *Semana*, February 23, 2009, 39; *Semana*, December 11, 2006, 88.

102. Darío González Posso, "Armas químicas y biológicos," in Jairo Estrada Alvarez, comp., *El Plan Colombia y la intensificación de la guerra* (Bogotá: Universidad Nacional de Colombia, 2002), 438.

103. Among the many assessments of drug-related violence in Mexico and the U.S. see *The Economist*, January 27, 2007, 33; National Public Radio, *On Point*, August 23, 2009; Alfredo Curtido interview; *Time*, August 25, 2008, 37; National Public Radio, "Mexican Drug Deaths," June 25, 2009.

104. Harvey Kline, *Showing Teeth to the Dragons*, 196.

105. *Semana*, May 19, 2008, 24–32.

106. *Semana*, May 19, 2008, 40.

107. "Cómo se acabó un cartel," *Semana*, July 21, 2008, 46–47.

108. *El Tiempo*, September 27, 2007; *Semana*, July 28, 2008, 36–37; *Semana*, April 20, 2009, 28–29.

109. *Semana*, June 2, 2008, 52–53.

110. A recent study of the BACRIM is Soledad Granada, Jorge A. Restrepo, and Alonso Tobón García, "Narcoparamilitarismo en Colombia: una herramienta conceptual para la interpretación de dinámicas recientes del conflicto armado colombiano," in Jorge A. Restrepo and David Aponte, eds., *Guerra y violencias en Colombia. Herramientas e interpretaciones* (Bogotá: Pontificia Universitaria Javeriana, 2009) 467–499.

111. *Semana*, June 1, 2009, 37.

112. More than 300 members of Colombia's police forces were involved in Daniel Rendón's arrest. *El Universal*, April 15, 2009.

113. Stuart Lippe, U.S. Department of State (Email of May 25, 2010); U.S. Department of State, "Colombia (from International Narcotics Control Strategy Report-INSCR March 2010)," 13 pages.

114. *Semana*, March 3, 2008, 42–44; *Semana*, April 14, 2008.

115. Harvey Kline, *Showing Teeth to the Dragons*, 99.

116. Analyses of the Colombo-U.S. agreement, and of the way it subsequently distanced Colombia from other South American nations, are found in *Semana*, June 20, 2009, 30; *Semana*, August 31, 2009, and *The Economist*, December 5, 2009, 44.

117. *The Economist*, August 8, 2009, 32.

118. *Semana*, July 21, 2008, 52.

119. *Semana*, June 15, 2009, 28–29.

120. Rachel Godfrey-Wood, "Moving beyond Taboos: Colombia's Trade Unions," *Colombia News*, March 11, 2009 www.Colombiareports.com. Accessed March 2009.

Conclusion

1. Guy Gugliotta and Jeff Leen, *Kings of Cocaine. Inside the Medellín Cartel: An Astonishing True Story of Murder, Money, and International Corruption* (New York: Simon and Schuster, 1989).

2. Toño Sánchez, *Crónicas*, 301.

3. Gonzalo Guillén, *Un país de cafres. Antología de la corrupción contemporánea en Colombia* (Bogotá: Planeta, 1995); Juanita León, *País de plomo*.

4. See introduction, "The Left and the Right of Violence Scholarship in Colombia."

5. *Semana*, June 28, 1999, 22–23; *Semana*, November 6, 2000, 58–60; U.S. Department of State, "Colombia: Report on Reform Activities," December 2006. See also Jorge Camacho Velásquez, ed., *Un país que huye. Desplazamiento y violencia en una nación fragmentada* (Bogotá: Editora Guadalupe, 1999).

6. U.S. Department of State, "Remarks: Secretary of State Hillary Rodham Clinton and Colombian Foreign Minister María Angela Holguín" (Washington, D.C: Department of State, May 31, 2011).

7. "A mal tiempo ... los colombianos son felices," *Semana*, September 11, 2006, 134–138; "Los colombianos son felices," *Semana*, July 27, 2009, 31.

8. For a sketch of Colombia's economic stability during years of *La Violencia*, 1947–1965, see James D. Henderson, "The False Paradox of Economic Progress amid Violence," *Modernization*, 325–347.

9. *Myrtle Beach Sun News*, September 24, 2010; *Semana*, December 27, 2010: 37; *Semana*, January 24, 2011: 34–35.

10. *Semana*, "Líder regional?," April 18, 2011: 24–27.

11. *The Economist*, June 4, 2011: 46; *Semana*, December 20, 2010: 34–35; *Semana*, May 30, 2011, 52–74, gives a detailed analysis of the new law and its implications.

12. Details on the death of Sáenz are contained in *Semana*, November 7, 2011: 1–14.

13. *Semana*, April 2, 2012: 24–27.

14. *Semana*, May 13, 2013: 52.

15. María Jimena Duzán, "Por qué creo que la paz va a resultar," *Semana*, March 4, 2013, 24.

16. For example the United States offered a reward of up to $5 million for information leading to the arrest and/or conviction of FARC Commander Luciano Marín ("Iván Márquez"). U.S. Department of State. Bureau of International Narcotics and Law Enforcement Affairs-Narcotics Reward Program, "Luciano Marín Arango."

17. *The Economist*, March 3, 2012: 48.

18. During the 2014 Presidential campaign Juan Manuel Santos revealed that his government was in preliminary talks with the ELN leadership. *The Economist*, June 21, 2014: 37.

Bibliography

Aguilera Peña, Mario. "ELN: Entre las armas y la política." In María Emma Willis and Gonzalo Sánchez Gómez, eds., *Nuestra Guerra sin nombre. Transformaciones del conflicto en Colombia*. Bogotá: Editorial Norma, 2006: 211–266.

Alape, Arturo. *El bogotazo, memorias del olvido*. Bogotá: Publicaciones Universidad Central, 1983.

_____. *Tirofijo: Los sueños y las montañas. El mar, la ciudad, la muerte Natural, la búsqueda insaciable de un sueño como ideal*. Bogotá: Editorial Planeta, 1994.

Antonil. *Mama Coca*. London: Hassle Free Press, 1978.

Arango Jaramillo, Mario, and Jorge Child. *Narcotráfico. Imperio de la Cocaína*. Medellín: Editorial Vieco, 1984.

Arango Z., Carlos, ed. *FARC. Veinte años: De Marquetalia a La Uribe*. Bogotá: Ediciones Aurora, 1984.

Aranguren Molina, Mauricio. *Mi confesión. Carlos Castaño revela sus secretos*. Bogotá: Editorial Oveja Negra, 2001.

Archila, Mauricio, and Ingrid Bolívar, eds. *Conflictos, poderes e identidades en el Magdalena Medio, 1990–2001*. Bogotá: CINEP, 2006.

Archila Ruiz, Leonardo A., ed. *El Poder, para ¿qué?* Bogotá: Intermedio Editores, 2007.

_____, _____. *Parapolítica. La ruta de la expansión paramilitar y los acuerdos políticos*, 2nd ed. Bogotá: Intermedio Editores, November 2007.

Arenas, Jacobo. *Cese el fuego. Una historia política de las FARC*. Bogotá: Editorial Oveja Negra, 1985.

Arias, Gerson Iván, and Joanna Rojas. "La 'sedición paramilitar': Principales momentos y posturas del Debate." Bogotá: Fundación Ideas Para la Paz, August 2007: 1–29.

Aricapa, Ricardo. *Comuna 13: Crónica de una guerra urbana*. Medellín: Editorial Universidad de Antioquia, 2005.

Arocha R., Jaime, et al. *Colombia: Violencia y democracia*. Bogotá: Universidad Nacional de Colombia, 1987.

Artunduaga, Edgar. *H.P. Historias particulares de los Honorables Parlamentarios*. Bogotá: Editorial Oveja Negra, 2006.

Asociación Nacional de Instituciones Financieras (ANIF). *Marihuana. Legalización o represión*. Bogota: ANIF, 1978.

Astorga, Luis. *El siglo de las drogas. El narcotráfico, del Porfiriato al nuevo milenio*. Mexico City: Plaza y Janes, 2005.

Atehortúa Cruz, A. *El poder de la sangre. Las historias de Trujillo, Valle*. Cali: Imprenta Departamental del Valle, 1995.

Bagley, Bruce M., ed. *Drug Trafficking Research in the Americas: An Annotated Bibliography*. Boulder: Lynne Rienner Publishers, 1996.

Bartola de Eyerbe, Clara Marcela, and Sara Lucía Franky Calvo, eds. *Un País que huye. Desplazamiento y violencia*. Bogotá: Editora Guadalupe, 1999.

Bedoya Lima, Jineth. *Diario de un combate, y otras crónicas de guerra*. Bogotá: Círculo de Lectores, 2005.

Bejarano, Ana María. "Estrategias de paz y apertura democrática: Un balance de las administraciones Betancur y Barco." In Francisco Leal Buitrago and León Zamoc, eds., *Al filo del caos. Crisis política en la Colombia de los años 80*. Bogotá: Tercer Mundo Editores, 1990: 57–124.

Bejarano Avila, Jesús Antonio. "La política de paz durante la administración Barco." In Malcolm Deas and Carlos Ossa, comps., *El gobierno Barco. Política, economía y desarrollo social*. Bogotá: Fondo Cultural Cafetero, 1994: 79–98.

Betancourt Echeverry, Darío, and Martha Luz García. *Contrabandistas, marimberos y mafiosos. Historia social de la mafia colombiana, 1965–1992*. Bogotá: Tercer Mundo Editores, 1994.

_____, and _____. *Matones y cuadrilleros. Origen y Evolución de la violencia en el occidente colombiano*. Bogotá: Tercer Mundo Editores, 1990.

Betancourt Echeverri, Darío. *Mediadores, rebuscadores, traquetos y narcos*. Bogotá: Ediciones Antropos, 1998.

Betancourt Pulecio, Ingrid. *Sí sabía. Viaje a través del expediente de Ernesto Samper*. Bogotá: Ediciones Temas de Hoy, 1996.

Borrero Mansilla, Armando. "Cómo se va a ganar la guerra." *Semana*. December 23, 2002: 38–40.

216

Bowden, Mark. "Flight Risk. When a U.S. Company Ignored Pilot Warnings in Colombia, Four Americans Died, and Three were Taken Captive." *The Atlantic*. July/August, 2009: 21–24.

_____. *Killing Pablo*. New York: Atlantic Monthly Press, 2001.

Bushnell, David. *Colombia: A Nation in Spite of Itself*. Berkeley: University of California Press, 1993.

Buxton, Julia. *The Political Economy of Narcotics: Production, Consumption and Global Markets*. New York: Palgrave, 2006.

Cabrera Galvis, Mauricio. "Los dineros ilícitos en la economía colombiana." *Revista Javeriana*. Vol. 143, no. 739 (October 2007): 33–39.

Camacho Guizado, Álvaro, and Francisco Leal Buitrago, comps. *Armar la paz es Desarmar la guerra. Herramientas para lograr la paz*. Bogotá: CEREC, 1999.

_____, and Alvaro Guzmán Barney. *Colombia: Ciudad y violencia*. Bogotá: Ediciones Foro Nacional, 1990.

_____, Andrés López Restrepo, and Francisco Thoumi. *Las drogas: Una guerra fallida. Visiones críticas*. Bogotá: Ediciones Tercer Mundo, 1999.

Camacho Velásquez, Jorge, ed. *Un país que huye. Desplazamiento y violencia en una Nación fragmentada*. Bogotá: Editora Guadalupe, 1999.

Cañón M., Luis. *El Patrón. Vida y muerte de Pablo Escobar*. Bogotá: Editorial Planeta, 1994.

Carrigan, Ana. *The Palace of Justice: A Colombian Tragedy*. New York: Four Walls Eight Windows, 1993.

Castillo, Fabio. *La coca nostra*. Bogotá: Documentos Periodísticos, 1991.

_____. *Los jinetes de la cocaina*. Bogotá: Editorial Documentos Periodísticos, 1987.

Castro Caicedo, Germán. *Colombia amarga*. Bogotá: Carlos Valencia Editores, 1979.

_____. *El Karina*. Bogotá: Plaza and Janes, 1995.

Cavelier, Germán. *Política Internacional de Colombia*, 4 vols., revised edition. Bogotá: Universidad Externado de Colombia, 1997.

Charles, Robert B. "U.S. Policy in Colombia." In Analisa De Grave, ed., *Taking Sides: Clashing Views on Latin American Issues*. Dubuque, Iowa: McGraw-Hill, 2007: 53–60 (excerpted from June 17, 2004 testimony before the U.S. House Committee on Government Reform).

Chepesiuk, Ron. *The Bullet or the Bribe: Taking Down Colombia's Cali Drug Cartel*. Westport, Connecticut: Praeger, 2003.

Centro de Investigación Popular (CINEP). *Deuda con la Humanidad. Paramilitarismo De Estado, 1988–2003*. Bogotá: CINEP, 2003.

Circulo de Lectores. *Confesiones de un Narco*. Bogotá: Cartographics, SA, 2003.

Cirules, Enrique. *The Mafia in Havana: A Caribbean Mob Story*. New York: Ocean Press, 2004.

Colombia. National Planning Department and Department of Justice and Security. "Colombia's Strategy for Strengthening Democracy and Promoting Social Development, 2007–1013." Bogotá: Departmento Nacional de Planeación, February 2007. 88 pages.

Colombia. Nacional Planning Department and Depart-

ment of Justice and Security. "Plan Colombia Progress Report, 1999–2005." Bogotá: Departamento Nacional De Planeación, September 2006. 21 pages.

Colombia. Presidencia. Agencia Presidencial para la Acción Social y Cooperación. Dirección de Cooperación Internacional. "Desembolsos Asistencia Oficial al Desarrollo AOD en Colombia, 1998–2007." Bogotá, June 2008.

Corben, Billy, ed. *Cocaine Cowboys*. Magnolia Films, 2005.

Crandall, Russell. *Driven by Drugs: U.S. Policy toward Colombia*, 2nd. Ed. Boulder: Lynne Rienner, 2008.

Curwood, Steve. "Living on Earth." Washington, D.C.: National Public Radio, June 21, 2009.

Dalton, Scott, and Margarita Martínez. *La Sierra*. DVD, 2004.

Deas, Malcolm, and Carlos Ossa, comps. *El gobierno Barco. Política, economía y desarrollo social*. Bogotá: Fondo Cultural Cafetero, 1994.

Deas, Malcolm. "Seguridad e inseguridad en el último cuarto del siglo XX." In *Nueva Historia de Colombia*, vol. 7: *Historia política desde 1989*. Bogotá: Editorial Planeta, 1998: 249–259.

Dix, Robert H. *Colombia: The Political Dimensions of Change*. New Haven: Yale University Press, 1967.

Dudley, Stephen. *Walking Ghosts: Murder and Guerrilla Politics in Colombia*. New York: Routledge, 2004.

Duncan, Gustavo. "El dinero no es todo: Acerca del narcotráfico en la persistencia del Conflicto colombiano." Bogotá: Legis, 2008. Universidad de los Andes Documento CESO 153: 40 pages.

_____. *Los Señores de la Guerra. De paramilitares, mafiosos y autodefensas en Colombia*. Bogotá: Editorial Planeta, 2006.

_____. "Narcotraficantes, mafiosos y guerreros. Historia de una subordinación." In Alfredo Rangel, comp., *Narcotráfico en Colombia. Economía y violencia*. Bogotá: Editorial Kimpers, 2005: 19–86.

Duzán, María Jimena. "Por qué creo que la paz va a resultar." *Semana*, March 4, 2013: 22–25.

Echeverry, Juan Carlos, Natalia Salazar, Verónica Navas, "El conflicto colombiano en el Contexto internacional," in Astrid Martínez Ortiz, ed., *Economía, crimen y Conflicto* (Bogotá: Universidad Nacional de Colombia, 2001): 77–128.

Eddy, Paul, Hugo Sabogal, and Sara Walden. *The Cocaine Wars*. New York: W.W. Norton, 1988.

Espinosa Valderrama, Abdón. "Vivencias y estragos del narcotráfico." *El Tiempo*. August 3, 2006.

Farah, Douglas, and Stephen Braun. *Merchant of Death: Money, Guns, Planes and the Man Who Makes War Possible*. Hoboken, New Jersey: John Wiley and Sons, 2007.

Franco, Gonzalo de. "La fuerza pública y la estrategia para enfrentar el fenómeno Guerrillero." In Malcolm Deas and María Victoria Llorente, comps., *Reconocer La guerra para construir la paz*. Bogotá: Cartographics, 1999: 477–536.

Franco, Saúl. *El quinto: No matar. Contextos explicativos de la violencia en Colombia*. Bogotá: Editorial Tercer Mundo, 1999.

Fuentes, José R. "Life of a Cell: Managerial Practice and Strategy in Colombian Cocaine Distribution in the United States." Ph.D. dissertation, City University of New York, 1998.

Fuerzas Armadas Revolucionarias de Colombia, FARC-EP. "Plataforma para un Gobierno de reconstrucción y reconciliación nacional." In *Mandato Ciudadano Por la Paz, la Vida y la Libertad*. Bogotá: Fundación País Libre, 1999: 40–42.

García, Clara Inés. *Urabá: Region, actors y conflicto, 1960–1990*. Bogotá: Gente Nueva Editorial, 1996.

García Durán, Mauricio. *De La Uribe a Tlaxcala. Procesos de Paz*. Bogotá: CINEP, 1992.

_____. "De Turbay a Uribe: Sin política de paz pero con conflicto Armado." In Francisco Leal Buitrago, ed., *En la encrucijada. Colombia en el Siglo XXI*. Bogotá: Editorial Norma, 2006: 479–511.

_____. *Movimiento por la paz en Colombia*. Bogotá: CINEP/Ediciones Antropos, 2006.

Garzón, Juan Carlos. "La complejidad paramilitar: una aproximación estratégica." In Alfredo Rangel, ed., *El poder paramilitar*. Bogotá: Editorial Planeta, 2005: 47–135.

Giraldo, Juan Carlos. *De Rasguño, y otros secretos del bajo mundo*. Bogotá: Icono Editorial, 2007.

Godfrey-Wood, Rachel. "Moving Beyond Taboos: Colombia's Trade Unions." Colombia News, March 11, 2009. www.colombiareports.com

Gonsalves, Marc, Keith Stansell, and Tom Howes, with Gary Brozek. *Out of Captivity: Surviving 1967 Days in the Colombian Jungle*. New York: Harper Collins, 2009.

González, José Jairo. "Los paramilitares y el colapso estatal en Meta y Casanare." In Leonardo A. Archila R., ed., *Parapolítica. La ruta de la expansión Paramilitar y los acuerdos políticos*, 2nd. Ed., expanded. Bogotá: Intermedio Editores, November 2007): 309–339.

González-Plazas, Santiago. "La erradicación manual de cultivos ilícitos en la sierra de La Macarena: un ejercicio sobre la futilidad de las políticas." Bogotá: Universidad del Rosario, Facultad de Economía y Centro de Estudios y Observatorio de Drogas y Delito (CEODD), July 2007.

González Posso, Darío. "Armas químicas y biológicas en el Plan Colombia. Interrogantes sobre la 'estrategia antinarcóticos.'" In Jairo Estrada Alvarez, comp., *El Plan Colombia y la intensificación de la guerra*. Bogotá: Universidad Nacional de Colombia, 2002: 421–447.

Gooberman, Lawrence A. *Operation Intercept: The Multiple Consequences of Public Policy*. New York: Pargamon Press, 1974.

Gootenberg, Paul. *Andean Cocaine: The Making of a Global Drug*. Chapel Hill: University of North Carolina Press, 2009.

Grabe, Vera. *Razones de Vida*. Bogotá: Editorial Planeta, 2000.

Granada, Camilo. "La evolución del gasto en seguridad y defensa en Colombia, 1950- 1994." In Malcolm Deas and María Victoria Llorente, comps., *Reconocer la guerra para construer la paz*. Bogotá: Editorial Norma, 1999: 539–597.

Granada, Soledad, Jorge A. Restrepo, and Andrés R. Vargas. "El agotamiento de la política de seguridad: evolución y transformaciones recientes en el conflicto armado colombiano." In Jorge A. Restrepo and David Aponte, eds., *Guerra y violencias en Colombia*. Bogotá: Pontificia Universidad Javeriana, 2009: 27–124.

_____, _____, and Alonso Tobón García. "Neoparamilitarismo en Colombia: una herramienta conceptual para la interpretación de dinámicas recientes del conflicto armado colombiano." In Jorge A. Restrepo and David Aponte, eds., *Guerra y violencias en Colombia. Herramientas e interpretaciones*. Bogotá: Pontificia Universitaria Javeriana, 2009: 467–499.

Gray, James P. *Why Our Drug Laws Have Failed and What We Can Do About It: A Judicial Indictment on the War On Drugs*. Philadelphia: Temple University Press, 2001.

Gugliotta, Guy, and Jeff Leen. *Kings of Cocaine: Inside the Medellín Cartel—An Astonishing True Story of Murder, Money, and International Corruption*. New York: Simon and Schuster, 1989.

Guillén, Gonzalo. *Un país de cafres. Antología de la corrupción contemporánez en Colombia*. Bogotá: Editorial Planeta, 1995.

Guillermoprieto, Alma. "The Children's War." *New York Times Magazine*. May 11, 2000.

_____. "Colombia: Violence Without End?" *New York Times Magazine*. April 27, 2000.

_____. "Our New War in Colombia." *New York Times Magazine*. April 13, 2000: 34–39.

Gutiérrez, José. *Vertigo en el jardín del mal*. Bogotá: La Buena Semilla, 2007.

Gutiérrez Sanín, Francisco. "Criminal Rebels? A Discusión of Civil War and Criminality from the Colombian Experience." *Politics and Society*. Vol. 32, No. 2 (June 2004): 257–285.

Guzmán B., Álvaro, and Renata Moreno Q. "Autodefensas, narcotráfico, y comportamiento estatal en Valle del Cauca, 1997–2005." In Leonardo A. Archila, ed., *Parapolítica. La ruta de la expansión paramilitar y los acuerdos políticos*, 2nd expanded edition. Bogotá: Intermedio Editores, 2007: 258–308.

Henderson, James D. *Modernization in Colombia. The Laureano Gómez Years,* Gainesville: The University Press of Florida, 2001.

_____. *When Colombia Bled. A History of the Violencia in Tolima* Tuscaloosa: University of Alabama Press, 1985.

Hernández-Mora, Salud. "El negocio del terror. Coca y violencia en el Catatumbo." In Leonardo Archila Ruiz, ed., *El poder, para ¿Qué?* Bogotá: Intermedio Editores, 2007: 59–133.

Horgan, Terrance. "The Liberals Come to Power. *Por debajo de la ruana*." Unpublished Ph.D. thesis. Vanderbilt University, 1983.

Ibáñez, Ana María, and Pablo Querubín. *Acceso a tierras y desplazamiento forzoso en Colombia*. Universidad of the Andes (CEDE Document 23), May 2004.

_____, and Carlos Eduardo Vélez. *Instrumentos de atención de la población Desplazada en Colombia: Una distribución desigual de las responsabilidades Munic-*

ipales. Bogotá: Universidad of the Andes (CEDE Document 37), December 2003.

Isaacson, Adam. Personal interview. Charlottesville, Virginia. August 6, 2009.

Jaramillo, Jaime Eduardo, Leonidas Mora, and Fernando Cubides. *Colonización, coca, y guerrilla*. Bogotá: Universidad Nacional de Colombia, 1986.

Kirk, Robin. *More Terrible Than Death: Massacres, Drugs, and America's War in Colombia*. New York: Public Affairs, 2003.

Kline, Harvey F. *Showing Teeth to the Dragons: State Building by Colombia's President Alvaro Uribe Vélez*. Tuscaloosa: University of Alabama Press, 2009.

Krauthausen, Ciro. *Padrinos y Mercaderos. Crimen organizado en Italia y Colombia*. Bogotá: Editorial Planeta, 1998.

Lara, Patricia. *Siembra vientos y recogerás tempestades*. Bogotá: Editorial Planeta, 1982.

Leal Buitrago, Francisco, ed. *En la encrucijada*. Bogotá: Editorial Norma, 2006.

_____. *La inseguridad de la seguridad. Colombia, 1958–2005*. Bogotá: Editorial Planeta, 2006.

_____. "Políticas de seguridad: De improvisión en improvisión." In Francisco Leal Buitrago, ed., *En la encrucijada. Colombia en el siglo XXI*. Bogotá: Editorial Norma, 2006: 513–544.

Lee, Rensslaer W., III. *The White Labyrinth*. New Brunswick, N.J.: Transaction Publishers, 1989.

Legarda, Astrid. *El verdadero Pablo. Sangre, traición y muerte....* Bogotá: Ediciones Gato Azul, 2005.

León, Juanita. *País de plomo. Crónicas de Guerra*. Bogotá: Editorial Aguilar, 2005.

Lernoux, Penny. *In Banks We Trust*. New York: Penguin Books, 1984.

Leyva Durán, Alvaro, ed. *¿Paz? ¡Paz! Testimonios y reflexiones sobre un proceso*. Bogotá: Editorial La Oveja Negra, 1987.

López Restrepo, Andrés. "Costos del combate a la producción, comercialización y Consumo de drogas y a la violencia generada por el narcotráfico," in Francisco E. Thoumi, ed., *Drogas ilícitas en Colombia. Su impacto económico político y Social*. Bogotá: Editorial Planeta, 1997: 409–460.

_____. "Narcotráfico, ilegalidad y conflicto en Colombia." In María Emma Willis and Gonzalo Sánchez Gómez, eds., *Nuestra Guerra sin nombre. Transformaciones del conflicto en Colombia*. Bogotá: Editorial Norma, 2006: 407–439.

Loveman, Brian, ed. *Addicted to Failure: U.S. Security Policy in Latin America and the Andean Region*. New York: Rowman and Littlefield, 2006.

_____. *For the Patria: Politics and the Armed Forces in Latin America*. Wilmington, Delaware: Scholarly Resources, 1999.

Madariaga, Patricia. *Matan y matan y uno sigue ahí. Control paramilitar y vida Cotidiana en un pueblo de Urabá*. Bogotá: University of the Andes, 2006.

Mando Ciudadano por la Paz, la Vida y la Libertad. *Conversaciones de Paz: Redefinición del Estado*. Bogotá: Mandato Ciudadano, 1999.

Marín Bernal, Rodrigo. *Itinerario político de un secuestro*. Bogotá: Editorial Tercer Mundo, 1988.

Martínez, Glenda. *Salvatore Mancuso: Su vida*. Bogotá: Editorial Norma, 2004.

Martínez Ortiz, Astrid, ed. *Economía, crímen y conflicto*. Bogotá: Universidad Nacional de Colombia, 2001.

Martz, John D. *The Politics of Clientelism: Democracy and the State in Colombia*. New Brunswick, New Jersey: Transaction Publishers, 1997.

McClintick, David. *Swordfish: A True Story of Ambition, Savagery, and Betrayal*. New York: Pantheon Books, 1993.

Medina Gallego, Carlos. *Autodefensas, paramilitaries y narcotráfico en Colombia. Origen, desarrollo y consolidación. El caso de "Puerto Boyacá."* Bogotá: Editorial Documentos Periodísticos, 1990.

_____. *ELN: Una historia contada a dos veces. Entrevista con "el cura" Manuel Pérez y Nicolás Rodríguez Bautista, "Gabino."* Bogotá: Rodríguez Quito Editores, 1996.

Medina Serna, Santiago. *La verdad sobre las mentiras*. Bogotá: Editorial Planeta, 1997.

Melo, Jorge Orlando, and Jaime Bermúdez. "La lucha contra el narcotráfico: éxitos y Limitaciones." In Malcolm Deas and Carlos Ossa, comps., *El gobierno de Barco. política, economía y desarrollo social en Colombia, 1986–1990*. Bogotá: Editorial Norma, 1994.

Menzel, Sewall. *Cocaine Quagmire: Implementing the U.S. Anti-Drug Policy in the North Andes-Colombia*. New York: University Press of America, 1997.

Mermelstein, Max. *The Man Who Made it Snow*. New York: Simon and Schuster, 1990.

Mills, James. *The Underground Empire: Where Crime and Governments Embrace*. New York: Doubleday, 1986.

Messick, Hank. *Of Grass and Snow: The Secret Criminal Elite*. Englewood Cliffs, New Jersey: Prentice-Hall, 1979.

Mora Pineda, Claudia, ed. *Poder, justicia e indignidad. El juicio al Presidente de la República Ernesto Samper Pizano*. Bogotá: Utopios Ediciones, 1996.

Morales Benítez, Otto. *Papeles para la paz*. Bogotá: Editorial Arbol Que Piensa, 1991.

Murillo Castaño, Gabriel. "Narcotráfico y política en la década de los ochenta. Entre la Represión y el diálogo." In Carlos Gustavo Arrieta, Luis Javier Orjuela, Eduardo Sarmiento Palacio, and Juan Gabriel Tokatlian, eds., *Narcotráfico en Colombia. Dimensiones políticas, económicas, jurídicas e internacionales*. Bogotá: Tercer Mundo Editores, 1990: 199–276.

Negrete Barrera, Víctor. "El conflicto armado y la 'parapolítica en Córdoba." *Revista Foro*, No. 61 (May 2007), 56–65.

Olson, Joy. "Addicted to Failure." Statement of Joy Olson Before the Subcommittee of The Western Hemisphere House International Relations Committee, March 30, 2006. Washington, D.C.: Washington Office on Latin America, 2006.

Orozco, Jorge Eliécer. *Lehder ... el hombre*. Bogotá: Plaza y Janes, 1987.

Ortegón Páez, Rafael. *Vorágine alucinante en la historia de las drogas*. Bogotá: Tercer Mundo Editores, 1983.

Ortiz, Román D., and Gerson Arias. "La apuesta de la Novena Conferencia de las FARC." *Unidad de análisis 48.* Bogotá: Fundación Ideas Para la Paz. www.ideaspaz.org/publicaciones Pages 1–7.

_____. "La guerrilla mutante." In Francisco Leal Buitrago, ed. *En la Encrucijada. Colombia en el siglo XXI.* Bogotá: Editorial Norma, 2006: 323–356.

Ortiz Abella, J.G., ed. *Operación Jaque. Secretos no revelados.* Bogotá: Editorial Oveja Negra, 2008.

Ortiz Sarmiento, Carlos Miguel. *Urabá: Pulsiones de vida y desafíos de muerte.* Medellín: La Carreta Ediciones, 2007.

Palacios, Marco. "La solución política al conflicto armado." In Alvaro Camacho Guizado and Francisco Leal Buitrago, comps., *Armar la paz es desarmar la Guerra.* Bogotá: Gira Editores, 1999.

Pardo Rueda, Rafael. *Fin del paramilitarismo. ¿Es posible su desmonte?* Bogotá: Ediciones B, 2007.

Patiño Hormaza, Otty, and Alvaro Jiménez Millán, eds. *Las verdaderas intenciones de los paramilitares.* Bogotá: Intermedio Editores, 2002.

Pécaut, Daniel. *Crónica de dos décadas de política colombiana, 1968–1988.* Bogotá: Siglo Veintiuno Editores, 1989.

_____. *Guerra contra la sociedad.* Bogotá: Editorial Planeta, 2001.

Pizarro Leongómez, Eduardo. *Insurgencia sin revolución. La guerrilla en perspectiva comparada.* Bogotá: Tercer Mundo Editores, 1996.

_____. "La reforma militar en un contexto de la democratización política." In Francisco Leal Buitrago, comp., *En busca de la estabilidad perdida. Actores políticos y sociales en los años noventa.* Bogotá: Tercer Mundo Editores, 1995. 159–208.

_____. *Las FARC.* Bogotá: Tercer Mundo Editores, 1991.

_____. "Las FARC-EP: ¿repliegue estratégico, debilitamiento o punto de inflexión?" In María Emma Willis and Gonzalo Sánchez Gómez, eds., *Nuestra Guerra sin nombre. Transformaciones del conflicto en Colombia.*

_____. "Política de paz y apertura democrática." In Alvaro Tirado Mejía, ed., *Nueva Historia de Colombia,* vol. 7, *Historia política desde 1986.* Bogotá: Editorial Planeta, 1998: 261–288.

_____. "Revolutionary Guerrilla Groups in Colombia." In Charles Bergquist, ed., *Violence in Colombia: The Contemporary Crisis in Historical Perspective.* Wilmington, Delaware: Scholarly Resources, 1992. 169–193.

_____. *Una democracia asediada. Balance y perspectivas del Conflicto en Colombia.* Bogotá: Editorial Norma, 2004.

Porter, Bruce. *Blow: How a Small-Town Boy Made $100 Million with the Medellín Cartel and Lost it All.* New York: St. Martin's Press, 2001.

Posada Carbó, Eduardo. *La nación soñada. Violencia, liberalismo y democracia en Colombia.* Bogotá: Editorial Norma, 2006.

_____. "Language and Politics: On the Colombian 'Establishment.'" *Latin American Research Review* 42:2 (2007): 111–135.

Ramírez V., Socorro, and Luis Alberto Restrepo. *Actores en conflicto por la paz. El proceso de paz durante el go-bierno de Belisario Betancur, 1982–1986.* Bogotá: Siglo Veintuno Editores, 1988.

Rangel Suárez, Alfredo. *Guerra insurgente y Colombia: Guerra en el fin del siglo.* Bogotá: D'vinni Ltda. Editores, 2001.

_____, ed. *La batalla perdida contra las drogas: ¿Legalizar es la opción?* Bogotá: Intermedio Editores, 2008.

Regueros Peralta, Jorge. Personal interview. Bogotá. June 16 and 26, 1993.

Restrepo, Elvira María, Fabio Sánchez Torres, and Mariana Martínez. *¿Impunidad o Castigo? Análisis e implicaciones de la investigación penal en secuestro, Terrorismo y peculado.* Bogotá: Universidad de los Andes, CEDE Document 9 (February 2004).

Restrepo, Jorge A., and David Aponte, eds. *Guerra y violencias en Colombia. Herramientas e interpretaciones.* Bogotá: Pontificia Universidad Javeriana, 2009.

_____, Michael Spagat, Juan F. Vargas, "The Dynamics of the Colombian Civil Conflict: A New Data Set." *Homo Oeconomicus* 21(2): 396–423.

Restrepo, Lara. *Historia de un entusiasmo.* Bogotá: Editorial Aguilar, 2nd ed., 2006 (1995).

Restrepo, Luis Alberto. "Las arduos dilemmas de la democracia en Colombia." In María Emma Willis and Gonzalo Sánchez, eds., *Nuestra guerra sin nombre. transformaciones del conflicto en Colombia.* Bogotá: Editorial Norma, 2006: 315–346.

Reyes Posada, Alejandro. "Compra de tierras por narcotraficantes." In Francisco Thoumi, ed. *Drogas ilícitas en Colombia. Su impacto económico, político y social.* Bogotá: Editorial Ariel, 1997.

Riley, Jack. *Snow Job: The War against Internacional Drug Trafficking.* New Brunswick, New Jersey: Transaction Publishers, 1996.

Rincón, Fabio. *Leyenda y verdad de El Mejicano.* Bogotá: Aquí y Ahora Editores, 1990.

Rocha García, Ricardo. "Sobre las magnitudes del narcotráfico." In Alfredo Rangel Suárez, comp., *Narcotráfico en Colombia: Economía y violencias.* Bogotá: Fundación Seguridad y Democrácia, 2005. 145–182.

Rojas Morales, Ernesto. *Colombia a la deriva. Una mirada ética a la política y un juicio Moral a la campaña "Samper Presidente."* Bogotá: Litho Copias Calidad, 1997.

Romero, Mauricio. *Paramilitares y autodefensas, 1982–2003.* Bogotá: Editorial Planeta, 2003.

Rubio, Mauricio. *Crimen e impunidad. Precisones sobre la violencia.* Bogotá: Tercer Mundo Editores, 1999.

_____. *Del rapto a la pesca milagrosa. Breve historia del secuestro en Colombia.* Bogotá: University of the Andes, Centro de Estudios sobre el Desarrollo (CEDE), Facultad de Economía, Documento 35 (December 2003).

_____. *Homicidios, justicia, mafias y capital social.* Bogotá: University of the Andes, Centro de Estudios sobre el Desarrollo (CEDE), Facultad de Economía, Documento 96–06, 1996.

_____. "M-19, secuestro y narcotráfico." Unpublished typescript. October 2004. 34 pages.

Ruhl, J. Mark. "Colombia: Armed Forces and Society." Syracuse, New York: Syracuse University, Maxwell

School of Citizenship and Public Affairs Occasional Paper, 1980.

Ruiz, Bert. *The Colombian Civil War*. Jefferson, North Carolina: McFarland, 2001.

Ruiz Hernández, Hernando. "Implicaciones sociales y económicos de la producción de la Marihuana." In Asociación Nacional de Instituciones Financieras (ANIF): Bogotá: ANIF, 1979. 111–228.

Sabbag, Robert. *Loaded: A Misadventure on the Marijuana Trail*. Boston: Little Brown, 2002.

_____. *Snowblind: A Brief Career in the Cocaine Trade*. New York: Bobbs-Merrill, 1976.

Sáenz Rovner, Eduardo. *La conexión cubana. Narcotráfico, contrabando y juego en Cuba entre los años 20 y comienzos de la Revolución*. Bogotá: Universidad Nacional de Colombia, 2005.

Safford, Frank, and Marco Palacios. *Colombia: Fragmented Land, Divided Society*. New York: Oxford University Press, 2002.

Salazar J., Alonso, and Ana María Jaramillo. *Medellín: Las subculturas del narcotráfico, 1975–1990*. Bogotá: Centro de Investigación Popular (CINEP), 1992.

_____. *Pablo Escobar. Auge y caída de un narcotraficante*. Barcelona: Editorial Planeta, 2001.

Salazar Pineda, Gustavo. *El confidente de la mafia se confiesa. El narcotráfico colombiano al descubierto*. Madrid: Editorial el Tercer Nombre, 2006.

Salcedo Lora, Juan. "Respuestas personalísimas de un General de la república sobre Cosas que casi todo el mundo sabe." In Malcolm Deas and María Victoria Llorente, comps., *Reconocer la Guerra para construer la paz*. Bogotá: Editorial Norma, 1999. 347–388.

Samper, Alexandra. "Doce horas con Uribe." *Semana*. July 28, 2003. 30–32.

Samper Pizano, Ernesto. *Aquí estoy y aquí me quedo. Testimonio de un gobierno*. Bogotá: El Ancora Editores, 2000.

_____. "Marihuana: entre la represión y la legalización." In Asociación Nacional de Instituciones Financieras (ANIF), *Marihuana: Legalización o represión*. Bogotá: ANIF, 1979. 1–8.

Sánchez, Fabio, and Mario Chacón. "Conflicto, Estado y descentralización: del progreso social a la disputa armada por el control local, 1974–2002." In Emma Willis and Gonzalo Sánchez, eds., *Nuestra Guerra sin nombre. Transformaciones del conflicto en Colombia*. Bogotá: Editorial Norma, 2005. 347–403.

Sánchez, Gonzalo. *Ensayos de historia social y política del siglo XX*. Bogotá: El Ancora Editores, 1985.

Sánchez, Toño, Jr. *Crónicas que da miedo contar*. Bogotá: Editorial A. Sánchez S., 2003.

Santamaría, Germán. *Colombia y otros sangres*. Bogotá: Editorial Planeta, 1987.

Santamaría Salamanca, Ricardo. "Aspectos políticos del gobierno de Barco (1986–1990). In Alvaro Tirado Mejía, ed., *Nueva Historia de Colombia*, vol. 7: *Historia política desde 1986*. Bogotá: Editorial Planeta, 1998. 61–81.

Santos Calderón, Enrique. *La guerra por la paz*. Bogotá: Fondo Editorial CEREC, 1985.

Santos Pubiano, Alejandro. "Vicisitudes del gobierno de Ernesto Samper." In Alvaro Tirado Mejía, ed., *Nueva Historia de Colombia*, vol. 7: *Historia política desde 1986*. Bogotá: Editorial Planeta, 1998.

Schuster, Sven. "'Progresar es perdonar': algunas reflexiones sobre las amnistías en Colombia, siglos XIX a XXI." Universidad Católica de Eichstätt, Germany. sven-schuster@gmx.de

Schwartz, Herman M. *States versus Markets: The Emergence of a Global Market*, 2nd ed. New York: St. Martin's Press, 2000.

Scott, Peter Dale, and Jonathan Marshall. *Cocaine Politics: Drugs, Armies, and the CIA in Central America*. Berkeley: University of California Press, 1998.

Serrano Zabala, Alfredo. *La batalla final de Carlos Castaño*. Bogotá: Editorial Oveja Negra, 2007.

Silva, Miguel. "César Gaviria: los años del revolcón (1990–1994)." In Alvaro Tirado Mejía, ed., *Nueva Historia de Colombia*, vol. 7: *Historia política desde 1986*. Bogotá: Editorial Planeta, 1998. 83–106.

Simons, Geoff. *Colombia: A Brutal History*. New York: Saqi Books, 2004.

Spagat, Michael. "Colombia's Paramilitary DDR: Quiet and Tentative Success." Bogotá: Centro de Recursos para el Analisis de Conflictos (CERAC), 2006. 7 pages.

Springer, Natalia. *Desactivar la guerra. Alternativas audaces para consolidar la Paz*. Bogotá: Editorial Aguilar, 2005.

Streatfield, Dominic. *Cocaine: An Unauthorized Biography*. New York: Thomas Dunne Books, 2001.

Strong, Simon. *Whitewash: Pablo Escobar and the Cocaine Wars*. London: Macmillan, 1995.

Thoumi, Francisco E., ed. *Drogas Ilícitas en Colombia. Su impacto económico, político y social*. Bogotá: Editorial Ariel, 1997.

_____. *Political Economy and Illegal Drugs in Colombia*. Boulder, Colorado: Lyne Rienner, 1995.

_____. "Trayectoria del narcotráfico en Colombia." In *Nueva Historia de Colombia*, vol. 8. Camilo Calderón Schraeder, ed. Bogotá: Planeta Colombiana Editorial, 1998: 9–22.

Tirado Mejía, Alvaro. "Política exterior colombiana. La última década." In Alvaro Tirado Mejía, ed., *Nueva Historia de Colombia*, vol. 7: *Historia política desde 1986*. Bogotá: Editorial Planeta, 1998. 193–229.

Tokatlian, Juan Gabriel. *Drogas, dilemas y dogmas: Estados Unidos y la narcocriminalidad organizada en Colombia*. Bogotá: Tercer Mundo Editores, 1995.

_____, and Ana Mercedes Botero. "La política exterior de Colombia hacia Estados Unidos, 1978–1990. El asunto de las drogas y su lugar en las relaciones entre Bogotá y Washington." In Carlos Gustavo Arrieta, Luis Carlos Orejuela, Eduardo Sarmiento Palacio, and Juan Gabriel Tokatlian, eds., *Narcotráfico en Colombia. Dimensiones políticas, económicas, jurídicas e internacionales*. Bogotá: Tercer Mundo Editores, 1990.

Torres, Juan Carlos. *Operación Jaque. La verdadera historia*. Bogotá: Editorial Planeta, 2008.

Torres Giraldo, Ignacio. *Los inconformes, historia de la rebeldía de las masas en Colombia*. 5 vols. Bogotá: Editorial Latina, 1978.

United States Department of State. Bureau of International Narcotics and Law Enforcement Affairs Reward Program. "Luciano Marín Arango."

United States Department of State. "Colombia" (From International Narcotics Control Strategy Report-INSCR March 2010).

United States Department of State. "Memorandum of Justification Concerning Conditions for the Assistance for the Demobilization, Disarmament, And Reintegration of Former Members of Foreign Terrorist Organizations in Colombia." 2008. 41 pages.

United States Department of State. "Remarks: Secretary of State Hillary Rodham Clinton and Colombian Foreign Minister María Ángela Holguín." Washington, D.C.: Department of State, May 31, 2011.

United States Department of State. "Report on the Multiyear Strategy for U.S. Assistance Programs in Colombia." April 2009. 14 pages.

United States Department of State. "Report on U.S. Assistance Programs in Colombia." 2007. 37 pages.

United States Department of State. "Report to Congress: U.S. Assistance Programs in Colombia and Plans to Transfer Responsibilities to Colombia." March 2006. 32 pages.

United States Department of State. "United States Policy Towards Colombia." December 2002. 24 pages.

United States Domestic Council Drug Abuse Task Force. "White Paper on Drug Abuse, September 1975—A Report From the Domestic Council Drug Abuse Task Force." Washington, D.C.: Government Printing Office, 1975.

United States Senate. Committee on Foreign Relations, Subcommittee on Terrorism, Narcotics and International Operations. *Drugs, Law Enforcement and Foreign Policy*. Washington, D.C.: U.S. Government Printing Office, 1982.

United States of America. USAID. "Colombia Quarterly Results/ACI." September 30, 2004. 14 pages.

Ureña Sánchez, Mario Iván. "Evolución histórica e ideológica del paramilitarismo contemporáneo en Colombia." Unpublished typescript. Bogotá, 2007. Universidad La Gran Colombia.

Uribe, Juan Gabriel. "El proceso de la liberación." In Álvaro Gómez Hurtado, *Soy Libre*. Bogotá: Ediciones Gama, 1989. 233–273.

Uribe, María, and Teófilo Vásquez. *Enterrar y callar. Las masacres en Colombia, 1980–1993*, 2 vols. Bogotá: Editorial Presencia, 1995.

Uribe Ramón, Gabriela. *Veníamos con una manotada de ambicones. Un aporte a la Historia de la colonización del Caquetá*, 2nd ed. Bogotá: Universidad Nacional, 1998 (1992).

Valencia Tovar, Álvaro, ed. *Historia de las fuerzas militares de Colombia*, 6 vols. Bogotá: Editorial Planeta, 1993.

Vargas, Alejo. *Guerra o solución negociada. ELN: Origen, evolución y procesos de paz*. Bogotá: Intermedio Editores, 2006.

Vargas, Andrés R. "Guerra civil en Colombia: el caso de Barrancabermeja." In Jorge A. Restrepo and David Aponte, eds., *Guerra y violencias en Colombia. Herramientas e interpretaciones*. Bogotá: Pontificia Universitaria Javeriana, 2009: 423–466.

Vargas, Juan Carlos. *Cuando la guerra es el único camino. Memorias de un ex combatiente*. Bogotá: Editorial Norma, 2007.

Vargas Meza, Ricardo. *Drogas, masacres y juegos. Narcotráfico y conflicto armado en Colombia*. Bogotá: Tercer Mundo Editores, 1999.

Vargas Velásquez, Alejo. *Política y armas al inicio del Frente Nacional*. Bogotá: Imprenta Nacional, 1996.

Veillette, Connie. "Plan Colombia: A Progress Report." Washington, D.C.: Library of Congress, 2005, June 22.

Vélez, María Alejandra. *FARC-ELN: Evolución y expansión territorial*. Bogotá: Universidad de los Andes, 2000 (CEDE document 08).

Vellinga, Menno, ed. *The Political Economy of the Drug Industry: Latin America and The International System*. Gainesville: University Press of Florida, 2005.

Villamarín Pulido, Luis Alberto. *Cóndor en el aire*. Bogotá: Ediciones Luis Alberto Villamarín Pulido, 1999.

_____. *Drama, pesadilla y ... espectáculo*. Bogotá: Ediciones Luis Alberto Villamarín Pulido, 1997.

_____. *La silla vacía*. Bogotá: Tallares de TM Editores, 2002.

Villamizar Herrera, Darío. *Aquel 19. Una historia del M-19, de sus hombres y sus Gestos. Un relato entre la guerra, la negociación y la paz*. Bogotá: Editorial Planeta, 1995.

Villarraga S., Álvaro, and Nelson R. Plazas N. *Para reconstruír sueños. Una historia Del EPL*, 2nd ed. Bogotá: Gente Nueva Editorial, 1995 (1994).

Webb, Gary. *Dark Alliance: The CIA, the Contras, and the Crack Explosion*. New York: Seven Stories Press, 1998.

Youngers, Coletta A., and Eileen Rosin, eds. *Drugs and Democracy in Latin America: The Impact of U.S. Policy*. Boulder, Colorado: Lynne Rienner, 2004.

Zuluaga Nieto, Jaime. "El incierto camino de la solución negociada." *Síntesis 2000. Anuario social, político y económico de Colombia*. Bogotá: Tercer Mundo Editores, 2001.

Zúñiga, Priscila. "Ilegalidad, control local y paramilitares en Magdalena." In Leonardo A. Archila R., ed., *Parapolítica. La ruta de la expansión paramilitar y los acuerdos políticos*. Bogotá: Intermedio Editores, November 2007. 233–258.

Index

ACCU (*Autodefensas Campesinas de Córdoba y Urabá* [United Self-defense Forces of Córdoba and Urabá]) 141–144, 210*n*52; fronts 143, 144, 145, 211*n*97; *see also* paramilitary groups
ACDEGAM (*Asociación Campesina de Agricultores y Ganaderos de Magdalena Medio* [Farmers and and Cattleman's Association of the Middle Magdalena]) *see* paramilitary groups
ADO (*Organización Autodefensa Obrera* [Workers' Self-defense Organization]) 99, 103
Afro-Colombians *see* Colombia
agrarian reform *see* land reform
Agudelo, Aicardo de Jesús ("El Paisa") 160, 163
Aguilar, Gerardo ("César") 164
Aguilar, Gilberto 128
Águilas Negras (Black Eagles; criminal gang) 181
Aguirre, Adán de Jesús ("El Águila") 95
Air Force of Colombia 96, 123; Plan Colombia 169; strikes against FARC guerrillas 162, 191
Alcalá, Cliver 178–179
Alliance for Progress 3
Amarales, Andrés 203*n*36
amnesty 75, 94, 101, 102, 106, 154, 159, 191, 212*n*17
Amnesty International 100
ANAPO (*Alianza Nacional Popular*) *see* political parties
Anslinger, Harry J. 20, 23
Antioquia 35; contraband 36
ANUC (*Asociación Nacional de Usuarios Campesinos* [National Association of Campesino Service Users]) 97
Aranguren, Mauricio 133
Arcila Cardona, Daniel 70
Arenas, Jacobo *see* Mornates, Luis
Armed Forces of Colombia 97, 99–100, 102, 103, 114–115, 118–119, 125, 135–136, 144–147, 149, 155, 156, 167, 177, 189–190; budget 103, 156, 162, 169, 177, 189–190; citizen self-defense groups 135–136; communication network 169; growth 161–162; illegal drug reduction 179; Lleras Doctrine 103; New Form of Operation (NFO; *Nueva Forma de Operar*) 167; offensive against FARC (2003–2005) 160–161, 189; Omega Taskforce 176; Operation Checkmate (*Operación Jaque*) hostage rescue (2008) 163–165; paramilitary and 149; professionalization 156; reform and reorganization 167, 189–190; riverine units 161, 169; special forces 116; troop level 169; Year of the Offensive (2004) 161, 168
Armero tragedy (1985) 65
arms trafficking 164; *see also* Bout, Viktor
Army of Colombia 65, 96, 99, 102–103, 115, 124–125, 126, 144, 203*n*44; anti-kidnapping units 162, 169; Citizen Soldiers (*Soldados Campesinos*) 156, 170; commando units 160; corruption 76; high-mountain brigades 156, 161, 162; negotiation techniques 156; paramilitary 135; rapid-deployment brigades 156, 160, 162; vigilance committees 156
Arroyave, Miguel 146, 176
AUC (*Autodefensas Unidas de Colombia* [United Self-defense Forces of Colombia]), 140, 143–153, 158, 168; Armed Forces of Colombia and 149; demobilization 140, 152–153; drugs, illegal 145–146, 151, 152, 181, 182; fronts 152; massacres 140; political project 150–151 (*see also* paramilitary groups, political project); "Statutes of the Campesino Self-defense Forces of Córdoba and Urabá" 143; troop strength 145; *see also* Castaño Gil, Carlos
Australia 164

Bachelet, Michelle 183
BACRIM (criminal gangs) 181
Bahamas 40, 48, 51–52
Banana Axis (*eje bananero*) 132, 140, 142, 143
banana zone 131, 142
Baquero, Alonso de Jesús ("El Negro Vladimir") 73–74, 132, 137, 138
Baquero Borda, Hernando 64
Barco, Virgilio 75, 76–77, 78, 79, 80, 106–108, 138, 198*n*14
Barrera, Daniel ("El Loco") 181
Bateman, Jaime 45, 52, 102, 106
Battle of Saiza (1988) *see* guerrillas; Simón Bolívar Guerrilla Coordinating Group (CGSB)
Bayer, Tulio 95

Bedoya, Harold 115, 144, 147
Betancourt, Ingrid 163–165
Betancur, Belisario 32, 48, 50,
    55–56, 58, 59–60, 62, 102–
    104, 126–127, 129, 135; para-
    military and 135
Blanco, Griselda 38, 39, 43, 52
bogotazo (1948) 93, 205n4
Bolívar, Simón 166
Bolivia 39, 48, 50; "cocaine coup"
    (1980) 201n108
Borge, Thomas 60
Botero, Fernando 113–114, 141
Botero Moreno, Hernán 62
Bourne, Peter G. 22, 24, 31,
    198n38
Bout, Viktor 115, 117
Brazil 183
Buitrago, Héctor 141–142, 145,
    146
Buitrago Parra, Germán Darío
    ("Martín Llanos") 145, 146
Burroughs, William 20, 35
Bush, George H.W. 77
Bush, George W. 170, 182

Caballero, Francisco 98
Cali cartel 5–6, 48, 53, 67–68,
    82, 86, 87, 113, 141, 180,
    205n128
Camacho, Luis Roberto 76
Camacho Leyva, Luis Carlos
    100
Camarena, Enrique 63
Campo, Nelson 211n90
Cano, Alfonso see Sáenz Vargas,
    Guillermo
Cano, Ángel María 206n6
Cano, Guillermo 64–65, 76
Cardona, Rafael 56
Cardona Vargas, Jaime 52
Carranza, Víctor 72, 78
cartel war (1987–1988) 67–68,
    110, 137
cartels 53; terrorist acts 79, 80,
    84–85
Carter, Jimmy 24, 31
Carvajal, Hugo 178
Castañeda, Carlos 21, 203n39
Castañeda Giraldo, Mauricio
    204n66
Castaño, Carlos Mario ("El
    Chopo") 56
Castaño, Jesús 121, 127–128
Castaño Gil, Carlos 73, 85, 108,
    110, 116, 127–134, 138, 139, 141,
    144, 147, 148, 151–152, 155, 157,
    158–159; "godfathers of the
    guerrillas" 130
Castaño Gil, Fidel 46, 52, 73, 84,
    85, 110, 127–134, 135, 136,

138–139, 141, 210n74; MAS
    128; Pablo Escobar 128
Castaño Gil, Vicente 129, 145,
    146, 148, 152
Castellanos, Manuel 123
Castro, Fidel 3, 7, 35–36, 46, 60,
    93, 94, 95, 100, 122, 205n4
Castro Gil, Tulio 61
Catatumbo War (1999–2000) see
    paramilitary groups
Central America 60–62
CGSB (Simón Bolívar Coordi-
    nating Group) see guerrillas
Chávez, Hugo 162, 164, 178–179,
    180, 183, 190, 191
Chile 183
CIA (Central Intelligence
    Agency): illegal drugs and 61,
    62, 202n23
Cleared Zone (*Zona de Disten-
    sión*) 115–116, 119, 120, 140,
    147, 149, 157, 160, 161, 166,
    167, 168, 176, 209n115
clientelism, armed 111, 208n76
Clinton, William J. 116, 167
coca 39, 104, 117–118, 171, 176,
    209n112; cultivation, decline in
    179; fumigation 118, 161, 172,
    173; manual eradication 172
cocaine 3, 15, 18–19, 20, 32–41,
    51, 53, 82, 83, 179; Chile 22,
    27; cocaine wars (*see* cartel war
    [1987–1988]; cocaine wars);
    crack cocaine 51, 61; earnings
    200n67; export 22, 25, 40, 181;
    export, decline in 182; export
    to United States 86, 180,
    205n129; export to world 179;
    export via rivers 161; "golden
    moment" of Colombian
    cocaine export (1978–1983)
    47–52, 189; industry 33–34, 87
    (*see also* Tranquilandia); Mafia
    22; manufacture 33–34, 39, 57,
    200n50; Medellín Massacre
    (1975) 18–19; production,
    Bolivia 179; production,
    Colombia 41, 53, 118, 171, 179,
    190, 200n68, 202n3 (*see also*
    Medellín cartel); production,
    Latin America 87; production,
    Peru 179; profits, decline 179;
    Tranquilandia see Tranquilan-
    dia, Medellín cartel; *see also*
    drugs, illegal
coffee 17, 40, 198n12
Coffee Axis 147
Cold War 122–123
Colmenares, Rosendo 95
Colombia: Afro-Colombians
    174; anti-drug operations 31;

Anti-drug Police see Dijín;
    anti-poverty programs 177;
    Armed Forces see Armed Forces
    of Colombia; Army of Colom-
    bia see Army of Colombia;
    Center for Coordinated Inte-
    gral Action 171; coca fumiga-
    tion see coca, fumigation;
    cocaine export see cocaine,
    export; cocaine production see
    cocaine, production; defense
    spending 169; democratic gov-
    ernance 192; democratic
    process 186; economy 188, 192;
    emigration 187; frontier zones
    124, 176–177; geographic frag-
    mentation 17, 198n11; heroin
    35–36; human rights violations
    3, 4; illegal drug earnings 32;
    inequality 184, 187, 191; infra-
    structure 174–177; interna-
    tional relations 190–191; iron
    triangle of violence see Colom-
    bia, violence: iron triangle of
    violence; judicial reform 169,
    173; judiciary 76, 77, 78–79 (*see
    also* Supreme Court of Colom-
    bia); land reform see land
    reform; Law of Justice and
    Peace (2005) 169; Law of Vic-
    tims (2011) 191; Marijuana
    Bonanza (*Bonanza Marimbera*)
    29, 32–33; marijuana export
    23, 26–33 (*see also* marijuana);
    modernization 1, 3, 11; mortal-
    ity and illegal drugs 1, 197n1;
    National Front see National
    Front; negative perception of
    184; neoliberalism 110; New
    History 6–8; Organization of
    Economic Cooperation and
    Development (OECD) 191;
    planning 170, 175, 177;
    poverty, rural 174–175, 177;
    rule of law 66; rural areas see
    rural Colombia; state-
    strengthening 166, 182; state
    weakness 16–18, 42, 56, 78,
    93–94, 121–122 (*see also* iron
    triangle of violence); Superin-
    tendence of Vigilance and
    Security 141; Supreme Court
    see Supreme Court of Colom-
    bia; taxation 155, 177; "two
    nations" problem 174; United
    States and 2, 24, 116, 167, 182–
    183 (*see also* Plan Colombia);
    violence 5, 15–18, 208n95; vio-
    lence levels 3, 4, 8
Colombians, character of, 7–8,
    187–188, 197n11, 208n85

Communist Party of Colombia, labor unions and 131; *see also* political parties

Conservative Party *see* political parties

Constitution of 1991 77, 80–81, 82, 108, 110–111, 192

contra rebels, cocaine trafficking 61

contraband *see* crime

Convivir *see* paramilitary groups, citizen militias

Cooper, Donald 98

Córdoba, J.A. 24

Córdoba War (1985–1991) *see* paramilitary groups

Correa, Rafael 162, 178, 191

Correa Arroyave, Pablo 52, 67, 203*n*51

Correa Ramos, Pablo 67

crime: contraband 36 (*see also* Antioquia); corruption 25, 30, 31, 53–54, 75–76, 81, 91, 113–114; criminal gangs 181 (*see also* Águilas Negras; BACRIM); homicide rates 41, 74–75, 111, 179, 188, 189, 204*n*90, 208*n*77, 208*n*95, 214*n*100; homicides 44, 119, 174, 204*n*86; impunity *see* impunity; kidnapping, extortionate 34, 41, 42–43, 118, 119, 123–125, 149, 189 (*see also* ELN; EPL; FARC; guerrillas, communist; M-19; *pescas milagrosas*); money laundering 15, 32, 36, 39, 45 (*see also* money laundering); reduction in 162

Cuba 35, 49, 95, 96, 98, 100, 101, 122, 206*n*12

Cuban Revolution 7

Cujavante Acevedo, Alfonso 132

DAS (*Departamento Administrativo de Seguridad* [Administrative Security Department]) 67, 76, 78, 83, 138

Da Silva, Luiz Inácio Lula 183

DEA (Drug Enforcement Agency) *see* United States

De Greiff, Monica 78–79

Del Rio, Rito Alejo 117, 130, 142–143, 147

Democratic Alliance M-19 *see* political parties

De Moya Cura, César 109–110, 187

desplazados (displaced citizens) *see* violence, displaced citizens

Devia, Luis ("Raul Reyes") 119, 162, 178, 181

Dijín (*Dirección Central de Policía*

e Investigación [Police Central Investigative Unit]) 54, 57–58, 62, 65, 76, 151, 180, 181

displaced citizens (*desplazados*) *see* violence

drug cartels *see* Cali cartel; Medellín cartel; North Valle cartel

drug traffickers, amnesty 32

drugs, illegal 174; *bazuco* 51; cartels *see* cartels; coca *see* coca; cocaine *see* cocaine; corruption, political *see* crime, corruption; crack cocaine 51; economic impact 51; extradition of traffickers *see* extradition; globalization 19; guerrillas 34, 89–90, 97; heroin 87; LSD 21, 22; Mafia 30, 35; marijuana 3, 12–13, 15, 19, 20, 21–22, 26–33, 51 (*see also* marijuana); market forces 185–186; massacres *see* massacres; Medellín Massacre (1975) 17–18; Mexican trampoline 62, 202*n*32; mortality from drug trade 186; Panama *see* Panama; reduction 179; traffickers 21, 24, 31, 36–37, 181, 186–188; Tranquilandia *see* Tranquilandia; Venezuela 146, 148; *see also* AUC, ELN; EPL; FARC; guerrillas; guerrillas, communist; M-19; paramilitary groups

Duarte, Gentil 124

Duque, Iván Roberto ("Ernesto Báez") 152, 157

Echavarría, Diego 43, 57

Ecuador 36, 161, 162, 164, 177–179, 183; FARC and 178–179

Eder, Howard 123

Egland, Jan 174, 209*n*119

ELN (Ejército de Liberación Nacional [National Liberation Army]) 6, 15, 82, 84–85, 87, 91–93, 96–97, 98, 103, 104–105, 107, 110–111, 117, 133, 134, 139–141, 145–149, 154–155, 160, 168, 177, 306*n*18; Eagle Flight Offensive (1992) 112; fronts 144; illegal drugs 145–146; kidnapping, extortionate 42, 91, 97, 105, 112, 117, 118, 120, 154; peace talks 215*n*16; "Popular Power, Armed Proselytism" campaign (1989) 133; Simocota Manifesto (1965) 96; Simón Bolívar Guerrilla Coordinating Group (CGSB) *see* guerrillas; triumphalism 154;

troop strength 145; *see also* guerrillas, communist

El Salvador 83, 102

Emerald Mafia 36, 41, 66–67, 72, 78

Emerald War (1973) 67

emerald zone 78

EPL (*Ejército Popular de Liberación* [Popular Liberation Army]), 15, 80, 93, 97, 105–106, 107, 109–110, 129–134, 137, 140, 141, 143; demobilization 82, 110, 113, 134, 137; illegal drugs 91, 105–106, 129; kidnapping, extortionate 105–106, 110, 112, 117, 129; Simón Bolívar Guerrilla Coordinating Group (CGSB) *see* guerrillas; Sintagro (labor unión) 131, 132; *see also* guerrillas, communist

ERG (*Ejército Revolucionario Guevarista* [Guevarrist Revolutionary Army]) 119, 209*n*122; *see also* guerrillas, communist

Escobar Fernández, Gustavo 130, 138

Escobar Gaviria, Pablo 40, 43, 44, 46, 48, 49, 50–69, 76, 77, 78, 79–80, 82–88, 135, 136, 138–139, 180, 203*n*39, 210*n*74; guerrillas 138; M-19 63–65, 138; terrorist acts 79, 80, 84–85, 108–109, 107*n*65

extradition 191; Colombo–U.S. extradition treaty 51, 75, 76, 77; demobilized FARC guerrillas 186; illegal drug traffickers 4, 37, 38, 48, 51, 52, 53–54, 59–60, 62–63, 64, 75, 77, 79, 81, 82, 180, 201*n*5; "Indictables" 80; paramilitary leaders 182, 191

FARC (*Fuerzas Armadas Revolucionarias Colombianas* [Revolutionary Armed Forces of Colombia]), 6, 15, 42, 45, 58, 82, 87, 90, 96, 97–104, 108, 110–120, 123, 124–129, 131, 133, 134, 139–151, 154–157, 160–168, 170–184, 186, 191; Bolivarian Campaign for a New Colombia 133; child soldiers 119; Cleared Zone (*Zona de Distensión*) *see* Cleared Zone; coca cultivation 161, 171, 172; cocaine 34, 57–58, 91, 104, 112, 117, 161, 162, 171, 172, 178, 180; decline 168, 176, 177–178, 180; defeat 186, 191;

desertions 163; drug trafficking renunciation 191; drugs, illegal 6, 71, 91, 104, 112, 117, 118, 145–146, 149, 181; female members 119; fronts 97–98, 99, 104, 112, 124, 140, 144, 156; "Guerrilla Dignity" campaign (1995) 142; hostages 163–165; illegal drug earnings 117; kidnapping, extortionate 34, 42, 72, 104, 118, 123, 124–126, 149, 154, 163, 168, 178, 191; Medellín cartel 70–71, 91; mortar attacks 119, 157; New Form of Operation (NFO, *Nueva Forma de Operar*) 104, 112; peace talks 186, 191; political project 150; protests against 163, 165; recruitment, forced 90, 119; revenue, illegal drug sales 180; Simón Bolívar Coordinating Group (CGSB) *see* guerrillas; Sintrabanano (labor union) 131, 132; Strategic Military Plan 104; surveillance of 162; terrorist acts 160, 158, 176; triumphalism 112, 114, 119, 120, 133, 149, 154, 165, 176; troop strength 145; *Union Patriótica* (UP; Patriotic Union Party) *see* Patriotic Union Party; *see also* FARC-EP (*Ejército Popular* [Popular Army]; guerrillas, communist
FARC-EP (*Fuerzas Armadas Revolucionarias de Colombia-Ejército Popular* [Revolutionary Armed Forces of Colombia-Popular Army]) 104
FARC-*política* scandal 184
Farfán, Alexander ("Gafas") 164
Fayad, Álvaro 63, 64, 203*n*39
Fiocconi, Laurent 99
Fisher, Roger 156
Ford, Gerald 23–24, 31
Forero, Juan 214
Franco, Irma 65
Franco, Ricardo 124

Gaitán, Jorge Eliécer 13, 93, 94
Galán, Luis Carlos 41, 48, 50, 55, 79, 102
Galeano, Fernando 83–84, 139
García, Daniel 125
García, Luis 31
García, Nicolás 117
García Franco, Carlos Mauricio ("Doble Cero") 130, 143, 151
García Márquez 11, 111–112
García Molina, Gener ("Jhon 40") 171, 178

Gaviria, César 83, 110, 113, 140–141, 163, 167, 205*n*111
Gaviria, Gustavo 50, 52, 55
Gaviria, Liliana 163
Gechem Turbay, Jorge 120
Gil, Rosa 127, 134
Ginsberg, Allen 20, 21
Giraldo, Hernán 146, 151
Gómez, Alfonso ("El Padrino") 37, 39–40, 43, 50
Gómez Bustamente, Hernando ("Rasguño") 208*n*94
Gómez Castro, Laureano 13, 14
Gómez Hurtado, Álvaro 25, 95, 107–108, 114, 122–123, 137, 205*n*111
Gómez Martínez, Juan 80
Gontard, Pierre 183
González, Consuelo 163, 164
González, Efraín 11
González, Felipe 52
González, Octavio 39, 41
González Videla, Edgardo 56, 59
Guarín, Pablo Emilio 126, 127, 136
Guerrero, Pedro Oliverio ("Cuchillo") 189
guerrillas 122, 135, 188; criticism of 111–112; "godfathers" of 130, 138; illegal drugs 89–90, 97, 117, 135, 136; kidnapping, extortionate 189; Simón Bolívar Guerrilla Coordinating Group (CGSB) 107, 111, 132; *see also* M-19
guerrillas, communist 3, 7, 12, 15, 16, 24, 31, 76, 87–88, 89–120, 122, 155, 186; amnesty 75; cocaine 34, 89–90, 117; "combination of all forms of struggle" strategy 131, 184; "independent republics" 95–96, 123; kidnapping, extortionate 42–43, 46, 89–90, 116, 117, 140, 149; Montoneros (Argentina) 45; offensive of 1994–2002 140, 144; paramilitary groups and 121; Tupamaros (Uruguay) 45; *see also* ADO; CGSB; ELN; EPL; FARC
guerrillas, liberal 94, 95, 205*n*5
guerrillas, populist *see* M-19
Guevara, Ernesto "Che" 95
Guillot Lara, Jaime 45, 50, 207*n*32
Gutiérrez, Bernardo 130, 132
Guttman, Isaac 69

Hendrix, Jimi 22
Hernández de Ospina, Bertha 27

heroin 35–36
hippies: Colombia 28; United States 21, 28
Honduras 61
Hope, Peace, and Liberty Party *see* political parties
Hopper, Dennis 35
Hoxha, Enver 98
Hoyos Jiménez, Carlos Mauro 77
human rights violations *see* Colombia

illegal drugs *see* drugs, illegal
impunity 16, 42, 44, 47, 57, 70, 74, 76, 77, 78, 118, 121, 153, 157, 204*n*86; DAS and 76; Dijín and 76; *see also* crime
Ingersoll, John 28
Inter-American Court of Justice 210*n*67
Irish Republican Army 119
iron triangle of violence 16–18, 42, 56, 78, 93–94, 121–122
Isaza, Ramón 124–125, 128, 139, 141
Israel 129–130, 143

Jader, Yadid 41
Jader, Zuleika 41
Jader Álvarez, Carlos 41, 46–47, 201*n*102
Jamarillo, Bernardo 133
Jiménez Gómez, Carlos 59, 70
Jiménez Naranjo, Carlos Mario ("Macaco," "Javier Montañez") 146–147, 151
Joplin, Janice 22
Jung, Jorge 38, 40

Karina (ship) 45, 101
Kennedy, John F. 3, 23
Kerouac, Jack 20
Kerry, John 77, 202*n*32
kidnapping, extortionate: MAS (Muerte a Secuestradores [Death to Kidnappers]) 46–47; *see also* crime
Klein, Yair 132
Korean War 93

labor unions: Communist Party (of Colombia) 131; Fensuagro, (labor union) 184; guerrillas 131, 184
Lafaurie, Pablo 199*n*19
land reform 122, 134
Landazábl, Fernando 103
Lansky, Meyer 30
Lara Bonilla, Rodrigo 48, 51, 55, 56, 58–59, 68, 77
Larrota, Antonio 94–95

Larrota, Ramón 95
Leary, Tomothy 21
Lehder, Carlos 40, 46–47, 48–49, 51, 53, 54, 58, 59, 62, 63, 77, 135
Liberal Party *see* political parties
Lleras Camargo, Alberto 2, 13, 94, 95
Lleras Restrepo, Carlos 14, 24, 77, 97, 101
Lloreda, Rodrigo 167
Loaiza, Gerardo 95
Loaiza, Henry 69–70
Long, Alan 21, 24, 31, 199n13
López Michelsen, Alfonso 14–15, 17, 25, 31, 32, 43, 50, 59, 80, 102, 113, 123, 198n14
López Pumarejo, Alfonso 166
Losada, Carlos Antonio 162
Los Rastrojos (criminal gang) 181
Low Murta, Enrique 78, 81

M-19 15, 41, 44–47, 50, 52, 58, 63, 69–70, 80, 81, 93, 98–103, 106, 107, 125, 135, 137, 207n65; demobilization 82, 107–109, 137; drugs, illegal 91, 106, 135; kidnapping, extortionate 41, 45–47, 50, 135; Pablo Escobar and 63–65; Simón Bolívar Guerrilla Coordinating Group (CGSB) 132
Mafia 50, 67; Italian 203n50
Mancuso, Salvatore 141, 142, 144, 146, 150–153, 157, 158–158, 203n50
Manessman Corporation 105
marijuana 44, 47; Colombia Gold 21, 26–33; Cuna Indians 28; fumigation 185; Jamaica 26, 27, 28, 29; Mexico 26, 29, 185, 198n2; United States 47; *see also* drugs, illegal
Marín, Luciano ("Iván Márquez") 215n18
Marín, Pedro Antonio *see* Marulanda Vélez, Manuel
Marino Ospina, Iván 63, 64, 203n38, 39
Martínez Pastrana, Antonio ("El Viejo Rafa") 105–106, 109, 134, 137
Martínez Poveda, Hugo 86
Marulanda Vélez, Manuel (labor leader) 206n6
Marulanda Vélez, Manuel ("Tiro Fijo") 42, 95–96, 114, 116, 117, 123, 160, 163, 165, 200n79
Marxist-Leninist Communist Party *see* political parties
MAS (*Muerte a Secuestradores*

[Death to Kidnappers]) 46–47, 128, 134–136, 143; *see also* kidnapping; M-19; paramilitary groups
massacres 74, 107–108, 137–138, 148, 186, 211n117; Bojayá, Choco (2001) 120, 157; Gilberto Molina birthday party, Cundinamarca (1989) 78; illegal drugs and 148, 186; La Chinita, Antioquia (1994) 113, 140, 142, 211n90; La Gabarra, North Santander (1999) 148; La Mejor Esquina, Córdoba (1988) 137; La Rochela, Santander (1989) 74, 138; Mapiripán, Meta (1997) 144, 145, 211n117; Medellín, Antioquia (1975) 17–18, 41; Puerto Bello, Antioquia (1989) 132–133, 210n47; Puerto Boyacá, Boyacá (1987) 137, 138; Segovia, Antioquia 73, 78; Trujillo, Valle (1989–1991) 69–70; Turbo, Córdoba (1988) 78; Yolombó, Antioquia (1999) 148
Mata Ballesteros, Juan Ramón 62, 63, 208n69
Maza Márquez, Miguel 78, 83, 86
McCain, John 165
Medellín cartel 5–6, 53, 57, 67–68, 82, 83, 85, 113, 139, 198; cocaine export to U.S. (1980–1985) 65; FARC and 61, 70–71; Mexico 71–72; offices (*oficinas de cobro*) 69–70, 180; paramilitary groups 136, 138 (*see also* MAS); Tranquilandia *see* Tranquilandia
Medellín Massacre (November 1975) *see* drugs, illegal; violence
Medina Caracas, Tomás ("El Negro Acacio") 117, 162
Mejía, Darío 199n19
Meneses, Norwin 49
Mercado, José Raquel 45, 98–99
Mercado Peluffo, Rodrigo ("Diego Vecino") 142
mercenaries, foreign 68, 73, 79, 83, 137, 203n58
Merheg, Habib 151
Mermelstein, Max 202 9
Mexico 188, 203n47; drug cartels 179–180; marijuana 21, 37, 40
Milian Rodríguez, Ramón 49
Millán, Fernando 117
MOEC (*Movimiento Obrero Estudiantil Campesino* [Worker,

Student, Campesino Movement]) 94
Molina, Gilberto 72, 78, 136
Moncada, William 83–84
money laundering 50, 62, 207n32; Panama 49; *see also* crime
Montoya, Diego 69–70, 147
Montoya, María 81
Montoya, Mario 165
Montoya, Pablo ("Rojas") 163
Montoya Vélez, Diego 80
Morales, Evo 191
Morantes, Luis ("Jacobo Arenas") 58, 71, 107, 205n3
Moreno, Pedro Juan 143, 147
Mosquera, Vladimir 202n27
MRL Party *see* political parties
Munday, Mickey 49
Muñoz, "Tyson" 68, 84
Murillo, Diego ("Don Berna") 85, 151, 152, 181

Nadaístas 11
narcotics, illegal *see* drugs, illegal
National Front (1958–1974) 3, 6–7, 11, 12–14, 24, 34, 122
National Latin Movement *see* Lehder, Carlos
National Restoration Movement *see* political parties
Navarro Wolf, Antonio 108, 203n36, 205n111
neoliberalism *see* Colombia
Nicaragua 49–50, 60, 102; Contra rebels *see* Contra rebels; Contra War 49, 61; Sandinistas 58, 60, 102
Nieves Ochoa, Marta 46–47, 52, 135
Nixon, Richard 23, 28–29
Noguera, Juan 31
non-governmental organizations (NGOs) 175, 176
Noriega, Manuel 31, 47, 59, 60, 102
North Valle cartel 67, 69, 87, 147, 180, 181, 208n94; cocaine export 180
Núñez, Rafael 166

Ocampo, Santiago 56
Ochoa, Fabio 38, 49, 51, 56, 60, 63, 67–68, 81, 200n56, 202n27
Ochoa, Jorge Luis 38, 39, 46, 48, 49, 51, 52, 56, 59, 60, 61, 62, 63, 67–68, 77, 81, 135, 202n27
Ochoa, Juan 81
Olózaga, Hernán 35–36
Olózaga, Tomás 35–36

Organization of American States
    2
Ortega, Daniel 102, 116–117
Ortega, Jairo 50, 52, 55
Ospina, Alfonso 129
Ospina, William 197n11
Ospina Pérez, Mariano 13, 93,
    122
Ostaiza, Jefferson 178
Ostaiza, Miguel 178
Otero, Luis 203n36

Padilla, Freddy 165
Palace of Justice (*Palacio de Justi-
    cia*) attack (1985) 63–65, 106,
    138, 203n44
Palmera, Ovidio ("Simón
    Trinidad") 162, 175
Panama 27, 36, 47, 48, 49, 146
Panamanian Defense Forces 49
paramilitary groups 4, 6, 42, 46–
    47, 72, 73, 83, 87–88, 108, 110,
    113, 116, 120, 120–153, 154,
    155, 157–160; ACCU *see*
    ACCU; ACDEGAM (*Aso-
    ciación Campesina de Agricul-
    tores y Ganaderos de Magdalena
    Medio* [Farmers and Cattle-
    man's Association of the Mid-
    dle Magdalena]) 126–127,
    136–137, 139; Anti-Subversive
    Alcalde's Front (*Frente de
    Alcaldes Antisubversivos*) 126;
    AUC *see* AUC; *Autodefensas
    Campesinas de Casanare*
    (Campesino Self-defense
    Forces of Casanare) 145, 146;
    Catatumbo War (1999–2000)
    148–149; citizen militias 121,
    122, 123, 138, 140, 141; civil
    defense 121, 123; Common
    Front (*Frente Común*) 126;
    Córdoba War (1985–1991)
    129–134, 136, 140; demobiliza-
    tion 4, 6, 121, 140, 152–153,
    157–160, 183; drugs, illegal 117,
    121, 128, 134–139, 147, 151,
    152, 158–159, 176, 181; extradi-
    tion of leaders 182, 191; Foun-
    dation for Peace in Córdoba
    (*Fundación para la Paz de Cór-
    doba*; FUNPAZCORD) 134;
    geographic distribution 121;
    guerrillas and 121, 135; illegal
    groups 121, 158; impunity 121;
    Justice and Peace Law (2005)
    159; MAS (*Muerte a
    Secuestradores* [Death to Kid-
    nappers]) *see* MAS; MRN
    (*Muerte a Revolucionarios del
    Noreste* [Death to Revolu-

cionaries of the Northeast])
    130; narco-paramilitaries 136,
    138, 139; *parapolítica* scandal
    see paramilitary groups, politi-
    cal project; Patriotic Union
    Party (UP) 131, 133; PEPES
    (*Perseguidos por Pablo Escobar*
    [Persecuted by Pablo Escobar])
    85–88, 139; political project
    150–151, 157–158, 182; Santa
    Fe de Ralito, Córdoba, Agree-
    ment (2002) 152, 158; Santa Fe
    de Ralito, Córdoba, meeting
    (2001) 150, 157; Self-defense
    Forces of Ortega, Tolima 152;
    Statutes of the Campesino
    Self-defense Forces of Córdoba
    and Urabá (*Estatutos de las
    Autodefensas Campesinas de
    Córdoba y Urabá*) 133–134;
    Urabá War (1995–1997) 142–
    143, 154
Pardo Buelvas, Rafael 99
Pardo Leal, Jaime 136
Pardo Murillo, Rodrigo 203n51
Parra, Guido 85
parties, political *see* political par-
    ties
Pastrana, Andrés 4, 90, 115–120,
    140, 147, 149, 150, 154, 166–
    167, 168, 176, 186; Plan for
    Peace, Prosperity and Strength-
    ening of the State (*Plan para la
    paz, prosperidad y Fortalec-
    imiento del Estado*) 166
Pastrana, Misael 14, 24–25, 28,
    97
Patiño Fómeque, Victor 67
Patriotic Union Party (*Unión
    Patriótica*; UP) 71, 103, 108,
    132, 133, 136, 184; paramilitary
    groups and 131–132, 133, 136,
    143; *see also* FARC
Pax Christi 74, 143
Peace Corps 3, 12
PEPES *see* paramilitary groups
Pérez, Gonzalo 125–126
Pérez, Henry 72, 73, 83, 125–126,
    137
Pérez, Manuel ("El Cura Pérez")
    15, 98
Pérez Alzate, Rodrigo ("Julián
    Bolívar") 146
Peru 36, 39; *Sendero Luminoso*
    (Shining Path) guerrillas 170
pescas milagrosas (miraculous fish-
    ing expeditions) 117, 118, 149,
    154; *see also* crime; kidnapping,
    extortionate
Pinochet, Augusto 37
Pizarro, Carlos 63, 64, 107–108,

133, 137, 138, 203n38, 203n39,
    210n50
Plan Colombia 4, 5, 119, 156,
    158, 165–173, 176, 182, 213n23;
    Campesino Soldiers (*Soldados
    Campesinos*) 170; child soldiers
    169; criticism of 172–173;
    funding 168–169, 170; homi-
    cide rates 170; human rights
    worker protection 167; judicial
    reform 169, 173; Justice Houses
    (*Casas de Justicia*) 169; para-
    military demobilization 169–
    170; Police, National 170;
    "Project Houston" (1998) 167;
    refugee resettlement 170; repa-
    rations and reconciliation 169;
    witness protection 169
Plan Colombia II 170, 173, 182
police: corruption 76; paramili-
    tary 135
Police, National 156, 162, 180,
    181; Anti-drug Jungle Unit 181,
    189; Search Force (*Bloque de
    Búsqueda*) 79, 81, 84–86; *see
    also* Dijín (*Dirección Central
    de Policía e Investigación* [Police
    Central Investigative Unit]);
    Plan Colombia
political parties 14–15, 71, 81;
    ANAPO (Alianza Nacional
    Popular) 14, 24; Communist
    Party of Colombia 93, 94, 98,
    102, 122, 124, 131, 143, 205n6
    (*see also* Communist Party of
    Colombia); Conservative Party
    14, 81, 93, 94, 95, 102, 122,
    186; *see also* National Front;
    Democratic Alliance M-19
    (*Alianza Democrática M-19*)
    108; Hope, Peace, and Liberty
    Party (*Esperanza, Paz y Liber-
    tad*) 110, 134, 140, 143; Liberal
    Party 14, 81, 93, 94, 122, 186
    (*see also* National Front);
    Marxist-Leninist Communist
    Party 97; MRL (*Movimiento
    Revolucionario Liberal* [Revolu-
    tionary Liberal Movement])
    14; National Restauration
    Movement (*Movimiento de
    Restauración Nacional*) 157;
    Patriotic Union Party *see* Patri-
    otic Union Party (*Unión
    Patriótica;* UP)
Porras, Evaristo 55
poverty *see* Colombia
Pretelt, Sabas 172
Prías Alape, Jacobo ("Charro
    Negro") 95
Pulido, Jorge Enrique 64–65

Quaaludes 47, 49, 51, 201*n*104

Ramírez, Coronado 128
Ramírez, Jaime 57–58, 65, 76, 180, 102*n*13
Ramírez, Marta Lucía 156
Ramírez Abadía, Juan Carlos ("Chupeta") 69, 203*n*54
Los Rastrojos (criminal gang) 181
Reagan, Ronald 32, 202*n*8; Contra rebels 202*n*32
refugees, internal *see* violence, displaced population
Rendón, Daniel ("Don Mario") 181–182
Rendón Herrera, Freddy ("El Alemán") 146
Restrepo, Luis Carlos 158, 159
Retat, Juan Manuel 30
Reyes, Rafael 166
Rincón, Ramón 98
Rivera, Guillermo 147
Roberts, Jon 49
Rodríguez, Aureliano 206*n*6
Rodríguez, Freddy 79
Rodríguez Gacha, José Gonzalo 51, 52, 53, 54, 58, 59, 60, 66–68, 71–73, 76, 77, 78, 79, 83, 136, 211*n*74
Rodríguez Orejuela, Gilberto 37, 49, 54, 61, 62, 63, 67–68, 87, 113
Rodríguez Orejuela, Miguel 49, 67–68, 87
Rojas, Clara 163, 164
Rojas, Fernando 99
Rojas Pinilla, Gustavo 14, 15, 24, 69, 93, 103
Roldán, Antonio 78
Rubio, Luis Alfredo 126
rural Colombia 174–177, 188, 191; premodern carácter 174

Saade, Nicolás 42
SAC (*Sociedad de Agricultores de Colombia* [Colombian Agricultural Society]) 123
Sáenz Vargas, Guillermo ("Alfonso Cano") 71, 114, 119, 164, 177, 191
Salazar, Álvaro 71
Salazar, Gustavo 202*n*27
Samper Pizano, Ernesto 32, 50, 87, 92, 113–114, 115, 116, 140, 141, 142, 144, 147, 154, 167, 199*n*29, 199*n*30, 205*n*132
Sandinistas *see* Nicaragua
Santacruz Londoño, Jorge 42–43, 48, 60–65
Santander, Francisco de Paula 166

Santofimio Botero, Alberto 50, 52, 53
Santos, Alejandro 157
Santos, Francisco 173
Santos, Juan Manuel 161, 162, 164, 165, 177, 180, 184, 186, 190, 191, 214*n*89, 215*n*18
Scarface (film) 185
Seal, Barry 49, 60, 109, 201*n*115
Semana (magazine) 154, 156, 163, 173
Serpa, Horacio 142
Serrano, Rozo José 144
Simón Bolívar Guerrilla Coordinating Group (CGSB) *see* guerrillas
Smith, William French 202*n*23
smuggling *see* contraband
Stansell, Keith 164
State of Siege (film) 45
States, market forces and 173
Suárez, Víctor ("El Mono Jojoy") 114, 117, 120, 150, 161, 177, 178, 188–189, 209*n*107
Supreme Court of Colombia 76, 77, 78, 183; intimidation of Justices 76–77
Swann, Zachary 36–37

Tamayo, Luis Fernando 42–43
Tambs, Lewis 58, 61
Tiro Fijo (Sureshot) *see* Marulanda Vélez, Manuel
Tobón, José 127
Toft, Joseph 86, 87, 113, 205*n*128
Torres, Jorge ("Pablo Catatumbo") 191
Torrijos, Omar 49
Tovar Pupo, Rodrigo ("Jorge 40") 142, 146, 151, 175
Traficante, Santos, Jr. 35, 50, 201*n*117
Tranquilandia 47, 48, 50, 51, 53, 56, 57–58, 71
Turbay, Diana 81
Turbay Ayala, Julio César 31, 48, 50, 80, 91, 99–100, 102, 125

Unión Patriótica Party (UP) *see* Patriotic Union Party
United Fruit Company 27, 28
United States 91; "the American disease" 19; Andean Regional Initiative 167; Bay of Pigs invasion 94; CENTAC 26 54; Centra Spike 79; CIA (Central Intelligence Agency) 31, 84 (*see also* CIA); coca-reduction programs 117–118 (*see also* Plan Colombia); cocaine 22, 32, 35; cocaine imports 38, 48, 86;

cocaine, retail price (kilo) 18, 61, 86; Colombia policy 24, 116, 167, 173 (*see also* Plan Colombia); Contra War 49, 61, 62, 77; crack epidemic 62; DEA *see* Drug Enforcement Administration; decertification of Colombia 114, 144, 149–150; Department of Justice 169, 183; Department of State 183; drug addicts (1976) 24; drug culture 5, 18–22, 35; Drug Enforcement Administration (DEA) 28–29, 39, 41, 51–52, 57–58, 61, 62–63, 84, 86, 138, 171, 180, 183; extradition warrants 180 (*see also* extradition); FBI (Federal Bureau of Investigation) 84; Harrison Narcotic Act (1914) 19; hippies 23; illegal drug imports 28–33, 35 (*see also* cocaine; marijuana; Quaaludes); marijuana 21–22, 23; Marijuana Tax Act (1937) 20; marijuana traffickers 27–28; Operation Intercept (1969) 23, 27; parents' movement against drugs 32; Plan Colombia *see* Plan Colombia; "prison-industrial complex" 19; Pure Food and Drug Act (1906) 19; racism 20, 204*n*98; *Reefer Madness* (1936 film) 20, 22; School of the Americas 12; Southern Command 96, 182; terrorist attack of September 11, 2001 168; terrorist organizations 158; traffickers 21, 24, 31, 36–37; *Up in Smoke* (1978 film) 22; USAID (United States Agency for International Development) 175; War on Drugs 4–5, 23, 29, 32, 77, 86–87
UP (*Unión Patriótica*) *see* Patriotic Union Party; political parties
Urabá War (1995–1997) *see* paramilitary groups
Urdinola, Iván 69–70, 87, 204*n*64
Uribe Vélez, Álvaro 3–4, 121, 142, 148, 151–152, 154–162, 165–166, 168–170, 171, 177, 180, 182, 183, 186, 189, 191; assassination attempts 160, 162; Democratic Security program 4, 6, 155, 156, 162, 168, 170, 171, 175–176, 177, 184, 187, 189; extradition of traffickers 180; Patriot Plan ("*Plan*

Patriota") 161, 168, 171, 176; popularity 165–166; town meetings (*concejos comunitarios*) 156

Valencia, Guillermo León 13, 123
Vallejo, Virginia 52
Varela, Wilber ("Jabón") 147, 181
Varela García, Oscar ("Capachivo") 180
Vargas, Willington ("Caraquemada") 175
Vásquez Castaño, Fabio 96
Vaughan, Federico 201*n*115
Velandia, José Juvenal ("Iván Ríos") 162–163
Velásquez, Jhon Jairo ("Popeye") 65, 203*n*39, 203*n*43
Veloza, Éver ("H.H.") 142, 143, 145, 146

Venezuela 162, 164, 177–179, 183, 190; FARC 178–179; illegal drugs 146, 148, 181, 190
Viáfara, Diego 138, 204*n*82
violence: cocaine wars *see* cocaine wars; decline 156, 157, 158, 166, 179; displaced citizens (*desplazados*) 117, 119, 142, 143, 144, 148, 170, 187, 191; illegal drugs and 1, 41, 180; levels 173; massacres *see* massacres; Medellín Massacre (1975) 17–18, 41; New Violence 65–75, 173, 174, 180, 186–187, 190; refugees *see* refugees; "social cleansing" 68–69, 70; *violentólogos* (violentologists) 7–8, 74–75, 187; *see also* iron triangle of violence; massacres
La Violencia 2–3, 6–7, 11, 13, 41,

54, 69, 93, 94, 96, 122, 175, 186; *pájaros* (birds) 69

Walters, John 172
War of the Thousand Days (1899–1902) 17, 94
Wood, William 165, 172
World Finance Corporation 45, 50

Yanini Díaz, Faruk 124

Zambrano, Jorge Eliécer ("Caliche") 191
Zedillo, Ernesto 205*n*132
Zuloaga, Félix 55, 57